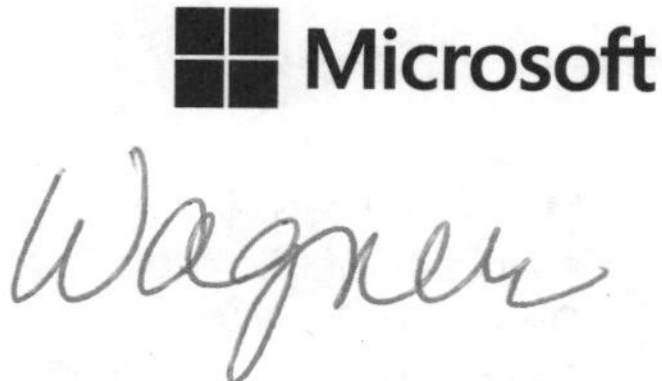

Exam Ref 70-687: Configuring Windows 8.1

Joli Ballew

PUBLISHED BY
Microsoft Press
A Division of Microsoft Corporation
One Microsoft Way
Redmond, Washington 98052-6399

Library of Congress Control Number: 2014931890
ISBN: 978-0-7356-8477-5

Printed and bound in the United States of America.

Second Printing: April 2014

Microsoft Press books are available through booksellers and distributors worldwide. If you need support related to this book, email Microsoft Press Book Support at mspinput@microsoft.com. Please tell us what you think of this book at http://www.microsoft.com/learning/booksurvey.

Acquisitions Editor: Anne Hamilton
Developmental Editor: Karen Szall
Editorial Production: nSight, Inc.
Technical Reviewer: Randall Galloway; Technical Review services provided by Content Master, a member of CM Group, Ltd.
Copyeditor: Teresa Horton
Indexer: Lucie Haskins
Cover: Twist Creative • Seattle

Contents at a glance

Contents

Introduction

The Configuring Windows 8.1 exam (70-687) is separated into seven sets of objectives. This book contains seven chapters that clearly detail what those objectives are and what you can expect to see on the exam. While most certification books focus on how to perform tasks as they relate to the exam objectives, this book covers the general, high-level knowledge you need to know to answer questions regarding why and when you'd actually perform those tasks.

We assume you've been working in a related industry for a while and have the general knowledge needed to support Windows 8.1; we assume you feel almost ready to take the exam. Thus, in this book you'll only see how-to steps and walkthroughs when we feel that it's something you might not have done before or might be confusing. For example, we include steps that show how to set up a virtual machine and install an operating system on it, as well as steps that walk you through configuring options for VPM Reconnect, but we won't offer steps for installing a device driver or configuring Windows Update. We'll also include things you might not think you need to study or even know; we'll offer exam tips that include command-line tools and parameters and PowerShell commands for performing tasks, and we'll offer links to resources on the internet we feel would benefit you on the job and on the exam.

This book covers every exam objective, but it does not cover every exam question. Only the Microsoft exam team has access to the exam questions themselves and Microsoft regularly adds new questions to the exam, making it impossible to cover specific questions. You should consider this book a supplement to your relevant real-world experience and other study materials. If you encounter a topic in this book that you do not feel completely comfortable with, use the links you'll find in the text to find more information and take the time to research and study the topic. Great information is available on MSDN, TechNet, and in blogs and forums.

Microsoft certifications

Microsoft certifications distinguish you by proving your command of a broad set of skills and experience with current Microsoft products and technologies. The exams and corresponding certifications are developed to validate your mastery of critical competencies as you design and develop, or implement and support, solutions with Microsoft products and technologies both on-premises and in the cloud. Certification brings a variety of benefits to the individual and to employers and organizations.

> ***MORE INFO*** **ALL MICROSOFT CERTIFICATIONS**
>
> **For information about Microsoft certifications, including a full list of available certifications, go to** ***http://www.microsoft.com/learning/en/us/certification/cert-default.aspx.***

Acknowledgments

I'd like to thank the people at Microsoft Press for having faith in my work once again, and for selecting me to write this book. I enjoy writing for the Microsoft team, specifically with Karen Szall, my acquisitions and project editor. She is positive, informative, and friendly, and is always around when I need her. (She's also very patient when I completely ruin a writing template or accidentally edit it!) I'd also like to thank my technical editor, Randall Galloway, for meticulously reading every word and correcting my missteps. Of course, the book would not flow as you would expect without a copy editor, and mine was incredible; thanks Teresa Horton.

Finally, I'd like to acknowledge my family, including Cosmo, Jennifer, my dad, Andrew, and even little Allie, for being patient while I work my odd hours and sometimes stay in my "writer's head" long after my work is complete for the day. I'd also like to call out my literary agents and representatives, including Stacey Barone, Katrina Bevin, and Renee Midrack at Studio B.

Errata & book support

We've made every effort to ensure the accuracy of this book and its companion content. Any errors that have been reported since this book was published are listed at:

http://aka.ms/ER687R2/errata

If you find an error that is not already listed, you can report it to us through the same page.

If you need additional support, email Microsoft Press Book Support at mspinput@microsoft.com.

Please note that product support for Microsoft software is not offered through the addresses above.

We want to hear from you

At Microsoft Press, your satisfaction is our top priority, and your feedback our most valuable asset. Please tell us what you think of this book at:

http://aka.ms/tellpress

The survey is short, and we read every one of your comments and ideas. Thanks in advance for your input!

Stay in touch

Let's keep the conversation going! We're on Twitter: *http://twitter.com/MicrosoftPress*.

Preparing for the exam

Microsoft certification exams are a great way to build your resume and let the world know about your level of expertise. Certification exams validate your on-the-job experience and product knowledge. Although there is no substitute for on-the-job experience, preparation through study and hands-on practice can help you prepare for the exam. We recommend that you augment your exam preparation plan by using a combination of available study materials and courses. For example, you might use the Exam Ref and another study guide for your "at home" preparation, and take a Microsoft Official Curriculum course for the classroom experience. Choose the combination that you think works best for you.

CHAPTER 1

Install and upgrade to Windows 8.1

Deploying a new operating system, whether it is to a single computer for a home user, a dozen computers for a small business, or 10,000 computers for a large enterprise (complete with myriad laptops, tablets, and other mobile devices), requires, in a nutshell, careful planning, researching, and testing.

First, you must decide which edition of Windows 8.1 will meet your clients' needs. That requires some research and a knowledge of what each edition offers. Next, you'll need to determine if there are existing hardware and software compatibility issues and decide what to do when compatibility poses a problem. You'll also have to choose a clean installation or an upgrade given the scenario, and you'll have to know what limitations exist for these options with regard to the currently installed operating system. Beyond that, you'll need a plan to migrate users' data, accounts, user profiles, Windows settings, and even applications before installing the new operating system.

IMPORTANT

Have you read page xvi?

It contains valuable information regarding the skills you need to pass the exam.

Once you've done all of this, you might also have to determine how you'll do it. You might perform the installation using an installation disk or installation files you've downloaded. There are other ways to deploy an operating system, though, especially if you have a lot of machines to update, which can include using the available large-scale assessment and deployment tools from Microsoft including the Application Compatibility Toolkit (ACT), the Windows Assessment and Deployment Toolkit (ADK), and the Microsoft Deployment Toolkit (MDT) 2013, among others. It all starts with evaluating existing hardware and software and assessing compatibility, though, so that's where we'll start.

Objectives in this chapter:

- Objective 1.1: Evaluate hardware readiness and compatibility
- Objective 1.2: Install Windows 8.1
- Objective 1.3: Migrate and configure user data

Objective 1.1: Evaluate hardware readiness and compatibility

Windows 8.1 is available in four editions. One, Windows RT, only runs on the ARM platform, but the other three can be installed on traditional 32-bit or 64-bit computing platforms. Beyond that, there are minimum requirements for installing each edition. There are various upgrade paths to consider, too, should you decide to go that route.

> **This objective covers how to:**
> - Choose the ideal Windows 8.1 edition
> - Perform readiness tests
> - Choose an installation option (clean or upgrade)

Choose the ideal Windows 8.1 edition

There are four Windows 8.1 editions, and each offers specific features. You can narrow your options for selecting an operating system by learning the basics about each:

- **Windows RT** This edition comes preinstalled on tablets and similar devices that run on ARM processors. You can't buy it as a stand-alone product. It won't run on anything other than ARM processors, so there is no need to consider it if you are looking for an operating system to install on a typical laptop or desktop PC. In addition, it can run apps from the Windows Store, but it cannot be used to install or run the traditional Windows x86/x64 applications you'd normally obtain from the Internet, network shares, CDs, or DVDs. Windows RT devices come with a special version of Microsoft Office for completing tasks that require it, but they do not come with Windows Media Player and have other limitations.
- **Windows 8.1** This edition is the popular retail edition of Windows. It is most often used by home users but might also work for some home office users. This edition comes preinstalled on the majority of PCs available from big-box stores, and you'll see it on most of the devices your end users bring to work (from home). You can buy this edition and install it on x86/x64 platforms. The main limitation of this edition in an enterprise is that it can't join a domain. Thus, if your client needs to join a domain, this isn't the edition you'll select. (It's easy to upgrade to Windows 8.1 Professional, though, should that be necessary.)
- **Windows 8.1 Professional (Windows 8.1 Pro)** This edition is used mostly by small to medium-sized businesses (with or without a domain) and by larger enterprises. It offers features not available in Windows 8.1 or Windows RT such as BitLocker (computers running Windows RT, Windows RT 8.1, or Windows 8.1 can be protected using Device Encryption, which is a customized version of BitLocker) and BitLocker to Go, the ability to host a Remote Desktop Connection, Client Hyper-V, and Virtual Hard Disk

(VHD) Boot. If your client needs any of these features and you don't have (and don't want) a volume licensing agreement to purchase Windows 8.1 Enterprise, this is the edition you'll choose.

> ***MORE INFO*** **BITLOCKER**
>
> **To learn more about BitLocker, refer to this TechNet article: *http://technet.microsoft.com/en-us/library/hh831507.aspx#BKMK_Overview*. There is quite a bit of information here you might see on the exam, such as the following: BitLocker does not support dynamic disks; the boot order must be set to start first from the hard disk, and not the USB or CD drives; and BitLocker supports multifactor authentication for operating system drives.**

- **Windows 8.1 Enterprise** This edition is only available through the Microsoft volume licensing program. Customers can purchase an Enterprise Agreement (EA), Select Agreement, or Open License. Customers have the ability to purchase Software Assurance (SA) with each license for Windows 8. Not all customers buy SA on Windows and therefore sometimes pay after each product release. If you are enrolled, you'll get all of the features in Windows 8.1 Professional and these features that are exclusive to Windows 8.1 Enterprise: Start screen control, Windows To Go Creator, AppLocker, BranchCache, DirectAccess, and Virtual Desktop Infrastructure (VDI) Enhancements.

Each Windows 8.1 edition has minimum and maximum system settings for CPU sockets and RAM, among other things. The hardware you use to install Windows 8.1 must meet these requirements.

Table 1-1 details minimum system requirements for Windows 8.1.

TABLE 1-1 Minimums for common resources

	32-bit (x86)	64-bit (x64)
Processor speed	1 gigahertz (GHz) or faster	1 GHz or faster
System memory (RAM)	1 GB	2 GB
Available hard disk space	16 GB	20 GB
Graphics adapter	DirectX 9 graphics adapter with WDDM driver	DirectX 9 graphics adapter with WDDM driver
Secure Boot	Unified Extensible Firmware Interface (UEFI)–based BIOS	UEFI-based BIOS

EXAM TIP

You might be asked why certain features won't work on a specific machine, and you'll be given the machine's specifications. One notable problem is that you can't snap two apps on the screen unless the screen resolution is at least 1024 x 768. It'll need to be 1600 x 1200 to snap three. It will have to be higher than this to snap four.

It's important to note, when talking about 32-bit and 64-bit operating systems, that you can't perform an in-place upgrade of a compatible and upgradable 32-bit operating system to a 64-bit operating system (in-place means you can opt to keep the user's personal files, applications, and Windows settings, or some combination of those). You'll have to perform a clean installation in these instances, and your hardware will have to support the 64-bit edition.

There are lots of other features to compare among these four Windows 8.1 editions. The best way to see every option is to visit *http://www.microsoft.com* and search for Compare Windows 8.1 Editions and then choose Windows 8.1 Enterprise | Compare Editions in the results. However, Table 1-2 shows the most notable differences among them, which will certainly be enough information to rule out editions that won't work for a client. (Don't worry if you aren't familiar with all of the features in the list; you'll learn about most, if not all of them, throughout this book.)

EXAM TIP

The questions on the exam won't ask you to recite what features are included with which editions of Windows 8.1. Instead you'll be asked to choose an edition based on a specific scenario. Cost might be a factor; the limitations of an installed CPU or RAM might be a factor, too. Incompatible proprietary software (perhaps 32-bit) or software applications that can't be updated might rule out a 64-bit edition (or even the upgrade itself). Make sure that you know what edition you'd need to select if, say, a question on the exam states that a client needs to join a domain, install and run desktop apps, or use Client Hyper-V.

Table 1-2 details the most notable differences among the four Windows 8.1 editions.

TABLE 1-2 Notable differences among Windows 8.1 editions

	Windows RT 8.1	Windows 8.1	Windows 8.1 Professional	Windows 8.1 Enterprise
Install and run desktop apps	No	Yes	Yes	Yes
Microsoft Office Home and Student 2013 RT included	Yes	No	No	No
Windows Media Player	No	Yes	Yes	Yes
Storage Spaces	No	Yes	Yes	Yes
VHD Boot	No	No	Yes	Yes
Assigned Access	Yes	No	Yes	Yes
Client Hyper-V	No	No	Yes	Yes
Domain Join	No	No	Yes	Yes
Group Policy	No	No	Yes	Yes
Side-loading LOB apps	Sold separately	No	Sold separately	Yes

	Windows RT 8.1	Windows 8.1	Windows 8.1 Professional	Windows 8.1 Enterprise
Smart Screen control	No	No	Yes	Yes
Windows To Go Creator	No	No	No	Yes
AppLocker	No	No	No	Yes
BitLocker and BitLocker To Go	No	No	Yes	Yes
BranchCache	No	No	No	Yes
DirectAccess	No	No	No	Yes
Remote Desktop Host	No	No	Yes	Yes
VDI Enhancements	No	No	No	Yes

There are a few other requirements not listed thus far; you'll need an Internet connection to access the Windows Store and to get online, and you'll need a compatible touch device to use touch features. Users will also need a Microsoft Account to use certain apps and the Windows Store.

> ***NOTE*** **STUDY FOR THE EXAM WITH THE IDEAL OPERATING SYSTEM**
>
> **Throughout this book I assume you are running Windows 8.1 Professional or Enterprise edition.**

Finally, all editions offer automatic app updates from the Windows Store, Internet Explorer 11, 3-D printing support, Biometric Enrollment, InstantGo, MiraCast Wireless Display Support, Mobile Hotspot and Wi-Fi Tethering, Wi-Fi Direct Wireless Printing Support, Device Enrollment, Exchange ActiveSync, Open MDM Support, Work Folders, Workplace Join, Device Encryption, Family Safety, Multifactor Authentication for Bring Your Own Device (BYOD) support, Remote Business Data Removal, Trusted Boot, Windows SmartScreen, Built-In Virtual Private Network (VPN) Clients, Remote Desktop Client, and others. Make sure you are familiar with the entire list of features before sitting for the exam.

Perform readiness tests

After you have decided which edition of Windows 8.1 you want to install on a particular workstation or in a specific scenario, you'll need to verify the computer meets the minimum requirements to support it. One way is to manually compare the requirements to the hardware that is installed on the workstation(s) in question.

> ***REAL WORLD*** **THE MINIMUM REQUIREMENTS AREN'T ENOUGH**
>
> **If you install Windows 8.1 on a computer that meets or barely exceeds the minimum requirements for RAM shown in Table 1-1, you can expect that the user will encounter problems while using the computer. In my experience, the computer can run so slowly**

that the user will become agitated and frustrated. If the computer freezes at the wrong moment, the user may well unplug the machine to restart it (or worse).

If you install Windows 8.1 on a computer with 16 GB, 20 GB, or even 40 GB of free hard disk space, in cases involving home and small business users who are not part of a domain, you're setting up yourself and your end user for trouble. Although you can perform an installation, you can expect that ordinary users will run out of disk space quickly (if that's where they save their data).

If you install Windows 8.1 on a computer that will be used primarily for gaming, you will need to have more than a DirectX 9 graphics adapter. Many new games require DirectX 10. You'll also need much more RAM and a much faster CPU for games to play properly and without any lag.

Beyond frustration, a full hard drive, and problems playing certain games, there are other instances when minimum requirements just won't do. Client Hyper-V requires a 64-bit system with Second Level Address Translation (SLAT) capabilities and additional 2 GB of RAM in Windows 8.1 Professional or Enterprise, for example. This isn't mentioned in the basic list of minimum requirements.

There are several ways to check a computer for hardware readiness; if you only have a handful of computers to evaluate, you can you do so using the System Information tool. You can manually compare what is listed there to the list of minimum requirements for the edition of Windows you want to install. This will become tedious quickly though, especially if you have more than a half-dozen or so workstations to assess. You can access the System Information window (see Figure 1-1) by typing **msinfo32.exe** on the Start screen.

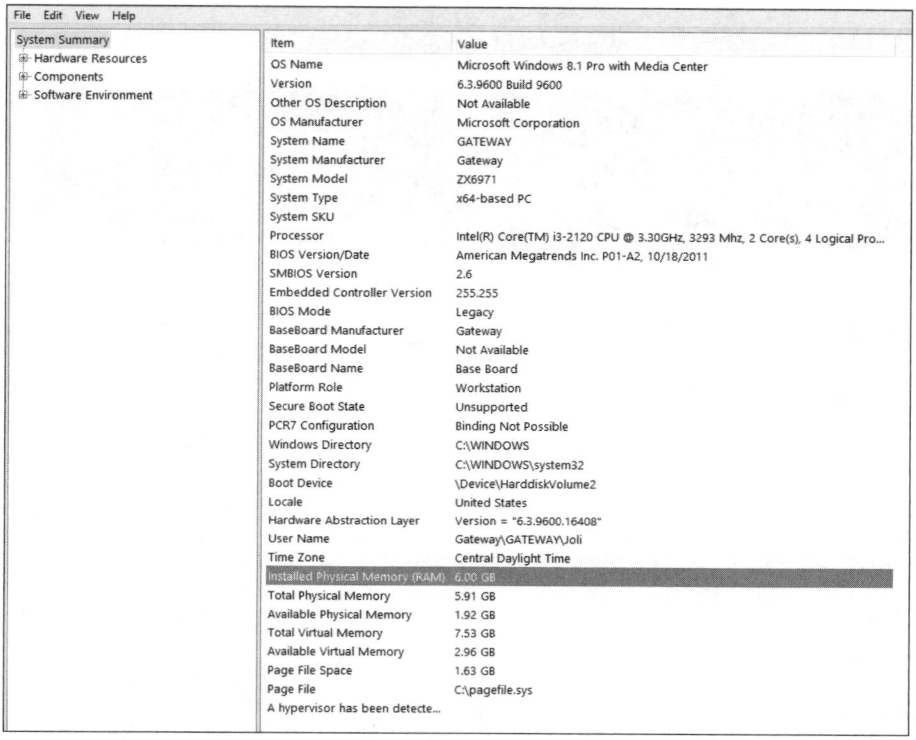

File Edit View Help

System Summary
- Hardware Resources
- Components
- Software Environment

Item	Value
OS Name	Microsoft Windows 8.1 Pro with Media Center
Version	6.3.9600 Build 9600
Other OS Description	Not Available
OS Manufacturer	Microsoft Corporation
System Name	GATEWAY
System Manufacturer	Gateway
System Model	ZX6971
System Type	x64-based PC
System SKU	
Processor	Intel(R) Core(TM) i3-2120 CPU @ 3.30GHz, 3293 Mhz, 2 Core(s), 4 Logical Pro...
BIOS Version/Date	American Megatrends Inc. P01-A2, 10/18/2011
SMBIOS Version	2.6
Embedded Controller Version	255.255
BIOS Mode	Legacy
BaseBoard Manufacturer	Gateway
BaseBoard Model	Not Available
BaseBoard Name	Base Board
Platform Role	Workstation
Secure Boot State	Unsupported
PCR7 Configuration	Binding Not Possible
Windows Directory	C:\WINDOWS
System Directory	C:\WINDOWS\system32
Boot Device	\Device\HarddiskVolume2
Locale	United States
Hardware Abstraction Layer	Version = "6.3.9600.16408"
User Name	Gateway\GATEWAY\Joli
Time Zone	Central Daylight Time
Installed Physical Memory (RAM)	6.00 GB
Total Physical Memory	5.91 GB
Available Physical Memory	1.92 GB
Total Virtual Memory	7.53 GB
Available Virtual Memory	2.96 GB
Page File Space	1.63 GB
Page File	C:\pagefile.sys
A hypervisor has been detecte...	

FIGURE 1-1 Using the System Information tool.

If you'd rather automate the task of assessing a computer, you can use the Windows Upgrade Assistant, which is much more user-friendly than manual evaluations. Again, though, this is a per-computer evaluation. You can access the Windows 8.1 Upgrade Assistant from *http://windows.microsoft.com/en-US/windows-8/upgrade-to-windows-8*. Click the link to Windows 8.1 Upgrade Assistant. That webpage is shown in Figure 1-2.

You should, in any circumstance, run the Windows 8.1 Upgrade Assistant at least on a user's single computer, on all computers if possible in a small business (because their configurations and software will likely vary from one computer to another), and on machines that are representative of what you want to upgrade in an enterprise. This can help you uncover problems you might not have thought of (or will need to test for later). For instance, the screen resolution of a small netbook might not be supported by Windows 8.1. This type of conflict will certainly cause problems. You might also discover that software you currently use will have to be updated to work with Windows 8.1 or that you need new device drivers for legacy printers and other hardware. Figure 1-3 shows a sample compatibility report.

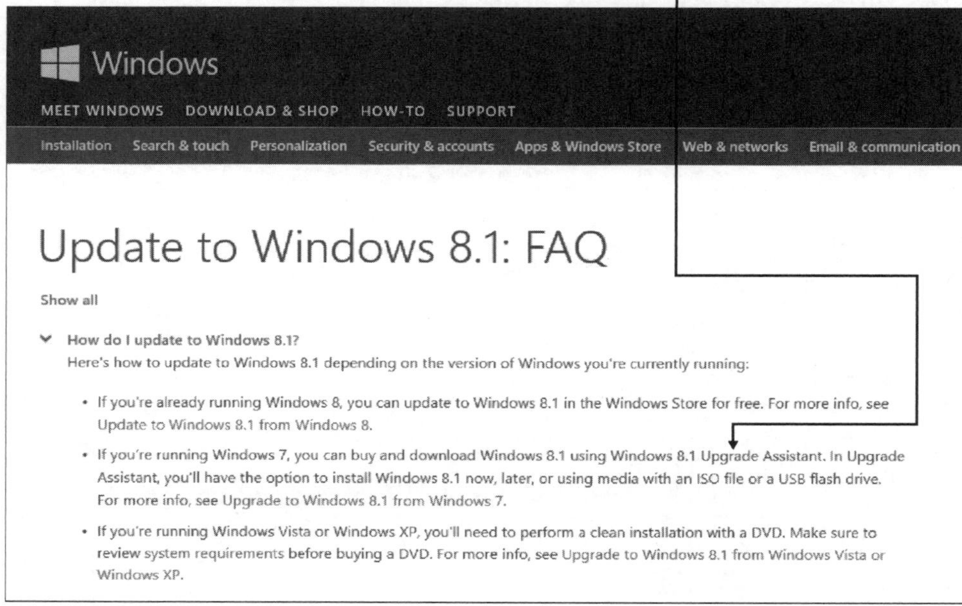

FIGURE 1-2 Locating the Windows 8.1 Upgrade Assistant.

FIGURE 1-3 Results of the Windows 8.1 Upgrade Assistant can help you determine compatibility.

NOTE **USE ENTERPRISE TOOLS TO EVALUATE READINESS IN A DOMAIN**

If you are assessing an enterprise group of computers that are part of a domain (hundreds or even thousands, perhaps), you'll want to use a program or application that is capable of comparing what is currently in inventory to what is required of the new operating system you've selected. Neither of the options offered thus far (manual comparison or Windows Upgrade Assistant) would work in an enterprise with a large number of computers. Additionally, you'll likely incorporate programs such as the Application Compatibility Toolkit (ACT) to help you determine the readiness of your software.

After you've determined what edition of Windows 8.1 to install and assessed the available hardware, you might have to perform some hardware upgrades. You might even have to replace older computers with new ones. Often though, you can repurpose the older computers and buy new ones for only those clients that require them to help minimize costs.

With the hardware evaluation complete, you'll need to take a few more steps. One of the most important is to verify that the software the client uses and depends on works properly with Windows 8.1. You'll have to set up a test machine (or multiple test machines) to determine this, and if the software doesn't work you can try it in Program Compatibility mode (see Figure 1-4). You open the Program Compatibility Troubleshooter from Control Panel and work through it to define the problem and try solutions. For the most part, the solution comes down to running the problematic application in the mode in which it was designed to run (perhaps Windows Vista or Windows XP). If problems persist or can't be resolved, you'll have to reassess the upgrade or try other options such as hosting the application on a network server or in the cloud. (A better option is to replace the outdated software with something that is compatible for the long term, but this isn't generally something that's easy to do.)

If Program Compatibility mode doesn't resolve compatibility problems, you still have options. You can use Microsoft Application Virtualization software (MS App-V), which allows applications to be streamed to any client from a virtual application server. It removes the need for traditional local installation of the applications, which resolves problems associated with incompatibility. On single workstations, Client Hyper-V might be more suitable. However, Client Hyper-V only runs on 64-bit PCs that are running the 64-bit version of Windows 8 Professional or Enterprise.

In the end, you might determine that you can't afford the upgrade, that proprietary company software has to be updated to something compatible before you can, that you'll need to stream the application or run it on a virtual machine, or that an upgrade is warranted and will be successful. If you decide that an upgrade is warranted, you'll have to choose to install the operating system as an upgrade or to install the operating system clean.

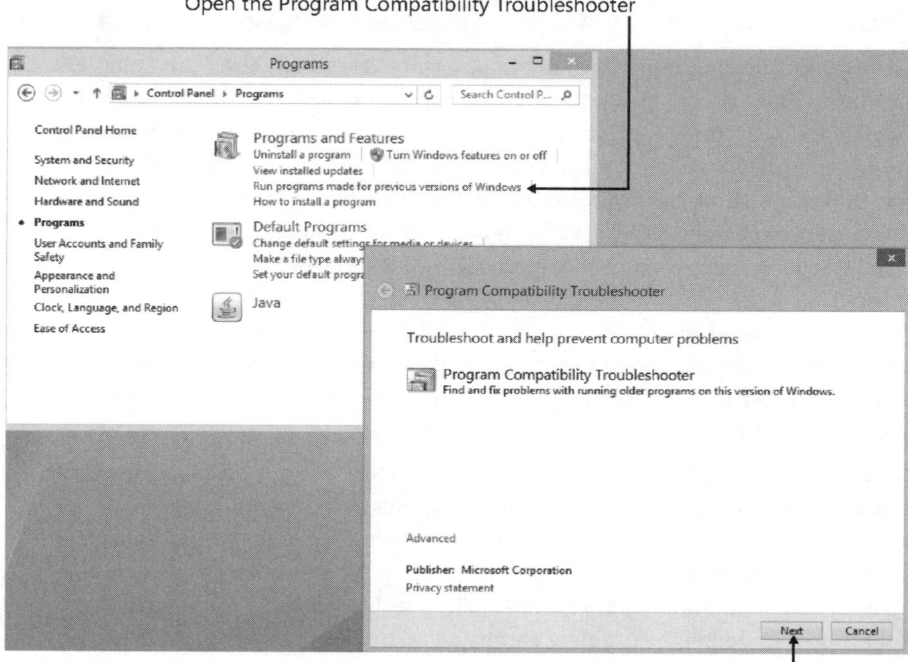

FIGURE 1-4 Locate and run the Program Compatibility Troubleshooter.

> ***NOTE*** **THERE'S MORE TO UPGRADING THAN INSTALLING THE OPERATING SYSTEM**
>
> **If you are updating all of the computers in a company from, say, Microsoft Windows XP to Windows 8.1, you'll have more to worry about than the cost of upgrading the hardware, finding compatible drivers for legacy peripherals, and upgrading software. You have to also consider the cost required to retrain users, make hardware and software purchases, and create a substantial help desk infrastructure, at least for a while, to get help to users immediately when they need it.**

Choose an installation option (clean or upgrade)

The question of whether to install an operating system clean or to upgrade what's already there, for a home or small business user at least, often comes down to how much data there is to move. It could also depend on whether the user has the product ID codes required to reinstall applications if a clean installation is performed, whether the computer is functioning normally and efficiently, and whether it is also free of malware and viruses. What operating system is being upgraded also matters; you can perform an in-place upgrade on a Windows 7 or Windows 8 computer, which retains the user's personal data, applications, and configuration settings, which a home user often desires.

EXAM TIP

In many, if not most instances, opting to perform a clean installation is a better solution to upgrading. If you see a test question that asks about this, carefully assess the information given. You might be better served by migrating the data off the machine, performing a clean installation, and then transferring the data back.

Often, upgrading a healthy Windows 7 computer is preferable for end users who aren't computer savvy because (except for the changes in the operating system itself) their settings, applications, printer configurations, network settings, desktop backgrounds, screensavers, and so forth come out of the installation unscathed. Users aren't bombarded with change when an in-place upgrade is performed, and you don't have to reinstall their applications, network, and so forth.

NOTE **UNDERSTAND SUPPORTED UPGRADE PATHS FROM WINDOWS 7**

Within Windows 7 editions, there are limitations as to which Windows 8.1 edition you can upgrade to. You can upgrade Windows 7 Starter, Windows 7 Home Basic, and Windows 7 Home Premium to Windows 8.1 or Windows 8.1 Professional. You can upgrade Windows 7 Professional and Windows 7 Ultimate to Windows 8.1 Professional. You can update Windows 7 Professional and Windows 7 Enterprise to Windows 8.1 Enterprise, too, provided there is a volume licensing agreement in place.

Upgrading isn't always an option for home users (or for that matter, any user). If a computer must be replaced because it is old or incompatible, or if the computer is plagued with impossible-to-remove malware, web browser toolbars, and unwanted search engines, the in-place upgrade can't be performed. In general, it's best to do a clean install. True in-place upgrades can't be performed on computers that run any compatible operating system before Windows 7 either. Table 1-3 outlines what is and isn't transferred when any kind of upgrade is performed.

TABLE 1-3 Upgrade paths for Windows 8.1

Upgrading from	What you can keep
Windows 8	Windows Store apps, desktop applications, personal files, Windows settings
Windows 7	Applications, personal files, Windows settings
Windows Vista SP 1	Personal files, Windows settings
Windows XP SP3	Personal files

NOTE UNDERSTAND UPGRADE PATHS FROM WINDOWS 8

Within Windows 8 editions, there are limitations as to which Windows 8.1 edition you can perform an in-place upgrade to. You can upgrade Windows 8 to Windows 8.1. You can upgrade Windows 8, Windows 8 Professional, and Windows 8 Professional with Media Center to Windows 8.1 Professional. You can upgrade from Windows 8 Professional, Windows 8 Professional with Media Center, Windows 8 Enterprise, and Windows 8.1 Professional to Windows 8.1 Enterprise provided there is a volume license in place.

In larger enterprises, the decision to upgrade or perform a clean installation depends on the factors listed thus far (and perhaps others, such as how much time and money it will cost to retrain thousands of employees, install updated hardware, update proprietary software, and so on), but more often than not a clean installation will be performed on computers in an enterprise. The reasons are many, but knowing exactly what is on each machine lets the enterprise reduce costs associated with training, support, and upgrades, which is always a major coup for network administrators. Also, network administrators can test Windows updates, app updates, and other software before it's installed, knowing that it is an appropriate test for all of the affected computers. A clean install also strips the computer of lingering problems or hidden malware.

In addition, in enterprises, most users store their data on network servers, and those same servers maintain user profiles including but not limited to configuration settings and logon credentials, which makes migrating data pretty straightforward (and safe). Data is stored on servers, too, so you don't have to worry too much about accidental data loss. Additionally, larger domains likely have the tools already in place to migrate user data, profiles, settings, and so on, and making use of those tools is a plus. Whatever the reason, when all of the computers are virtually identical, they are much easier to manage. There are lots of enterprise-compatible options to help you assess upgrade strategies, many of which are introduced later in this chapter.

Thought experiment

Select the best Windows 8 edition based on a client's needs

In this thought experiment, apply what you've learned about this objective. You can find answers to these questions in the "Answers" section at the end of this chapter.

You have been hired by a small company to serve on a planning committee to help choose the best option for upgrading its Windows Vista workstations to Windows 8.1. There are 25 workstations, and although they all run a 32-bit edition of Windows Vista, they were purchased over a period of three years and from different computer manufacturers. The company runs a proprietary database application to manage its inventory, which was specifically tailored to meet its needs and was created six years ago. Each workstation is part of the company's

Active Directory domain, and there is one Windows Server 2008 R2 server on the network. The company does not have a Microsoft volume licensing agreement.

All of the machines have at least a 1 GHz processor and 2 GB of RAM, and each has at least an 80 GB hard drive. The video cards support the minimum requirements for DirectX 9. All of the computers are located in a single large warehouse.

The committee would like to spend the least amount of money possible on the upgrade. It would prefer to also have the option to upgrade existing computers but wants to know the ramifications of doing so and could reconsider. Beyond that, the workstation users need to have access to Active Directory domain support and Storage Spaces, and a handful of users need Client Hyper-V.

Answer the following questions for your manager:

1. What edition of Windows 8.1 should you install, which platform option, and why? Explain why your choice of edition is the only applicable choice for the company.
2. Detail where you would start in the testing process to verify compatibility for these 25 computers.
3. Would you suggest a clean installation over an upgrade? Why or why not?

Objective summary

- There are four Windows 8.1 editions: Windows RT, Windows 8.1, Windows 8.1 Professional, and Windows 8.1 Enterprise.
- Each Windows 8.1 edition offers its own set of features. You choose the edition to install based on the features you need.
- There are upgrade paths from Windows XP, Windows Vista, Windows 7, and Windows 8, but you can only perform an in-place upgrade from Windows 7 and Windows 8 (to keep applications, personal files, and Windows settings intact). A clean installation is best in most instances, if feasible.
- In most instances, you can use Program Compatibility mode to force older, noncompatible programs to function in Windows 8.1. You can also opt for App-V or Client Hyper-V if necessary.

Objective review

Answer the following questions to test your knowledge of the information in this objective. You can find the answers to these questions and explanations of why each answer choice is correct or incorrect in the "Answers" section at the end of this chapter.

1. You need to perform an in-place upgrade for the computers in your small business. You have nine computers to update to Windows 8.1. These computers all run different editions of Windows, some with service packs and some without. Which of the following operating systems can be upgraded while retaining at least Windows settings and users' personal files? (Choose all that apply.)
   - **A.** Windows Vista
   - **B.** Windows XP SP3
   - **C.** Windows 7 Home Premium (with or without SP1)
   - **D.** Windows 8
2. You want to install Windows 8.1 Professional 64-bit onto a laptop with this hardware: 1 GHz processor, 1 GB of RAM, 16 GB solid state drive (SSD), and a monitor with a maximum screen resolution of 800 x 600. Which of these will you need to upgrade? (Choose all that apply.)
   - **A.** Hard disk
   - **B.** Processor
   - **C.** Monitor (or related hardware)
   - **D.** RAM
3. You need to select a Windows 8.1 edition to install for a client who needs the following: AppLocker, Boot from VHD, BranchCache, and Client Hyper-V. Which edition supports all of these?
   - **A.** Windows 8.1 RT
   - **B.** Windows 8.1
   - **C.** Windows 8.1 Professional
   - **D.** Windows 8.1 Enterprise
4. Your client wants to install Windows 8.1 Professional on all of the computers in his organization. He wants to perform an in-place upgrade to minimize the impact of the installation on his employees. Which of the following will not support this upgrade; in other words, which of these will require a clean installation? (Choose all that apply.)
   - **A.** Windows 7 Home Premium
   - **B.** Windows 7 Enterprise
   - **C.** Windows 7 Ultimate
   - **D.** Windows 7 Professional (Volume License)

Objective 1.2: Install Windows 8.1

There are lots of ways to install Windows 8.1 and lots of scenarios to consider. There are upgrades, including in-place upgrades from Windows 7 and Windows 8 and limited upgrades from earlier operating systems. Depending on the currently installed operating system, you will be able to keep some combination of user accounts, user profiles, personal files and folders, Windows settings, and applications, which you learned about in the previous section.

There is also the clean installation, in which you format the hard drive before you install the operating system. If you need a clean installation on a computer that contains user data you need to keep, you have to back up the data before you begin. You can opt to migrate user data off the machine, perform a clean installation, and transfer the data back. In a similar scenario, you can migrate data off an old computer and onto a new one. (Migration options are detailed in Objective 1.3.) These are traditional installations and migration options, but now there are more installation options to consider, including installing Windows 8.1 as Windows To Go and to VHD.

On an enterprise level, installations are automated and customized. It would be extremely time-consuming to go from machine to machine to perform the upgrades manually. Although you won't learn how to perform an automated installation or create a custom Windows 8.1 image here (that topic could fill more than a couple of chapters), you will gain a high-level understanding of it. You'll likely be tested on general knowledge related to automated installations.

This objective covers how to:

- Perform manual installations and upgrades
- Install additional Windows features
- Install as Windows to Go and to VHD
- Explore the custom Windows 8.1 installation

Perform manual installations and upgrades

Most installations that you perform manually go smoothly, whether they are clean installs or upgrades. A wizard walks you through the tasks necessary and lets you configure your own disks and partitions if you choose; the computer reboots when it needs to without interaction from you; and once the process is complete you are prompted to work through various setup tasks to personalize the computer with settings, account information, available networks, and even the color of the Start screen, among other things. No matter which option you choose (clean or upgrade), though, you should always back up the users' data before you start.

> ***MORE INFO*** **WINDOWS EASY TRANSFER**
>
> **Windows Easy Transfer (WET), outlined in Objective 1.3 in this chapter, is a tool that you can use to migrate user profile information, data, and settings off the computer before you reinstall it. You use WET again to put the data back on. You can also use WET to transfer data from an old computer to a new one. It's a popular tool for home users and small businesses because it is graphical and wizard-led. Consider using WET before you perform a clean installation. Similarly, the User State Migration Tool (USMT) is also discussed in Objective 1.3. This command-line migration tool is used by larger organizations.**

Perform a clean installation

A clean installation is the simplest way to install Windows 8.1 on a new computer or a computer or disk partition off of which you are willing to wipe all data (format). After you've backed up the users' data (if applicable), there are two ways to get started: You can supply a boot disk if the computer has no operating system on it, or you can boot the computer from the Windows 8.1 installation files if it does. During the installation you might opt to choose a custom installation option, in which you will choose on which partition to install Windows if multiple options exist or create and delete partitions as applicable.

> ***NOTE*** **ONE PARTITION AND A MULTIBOOT SYSTEM**
>
> **You can create a multiboot system on a computer that contains only one partition by using Disk Management to first shrink the partition and then create a new simple volume on it. Then, during the normal installation of Windows 8.1, choose this partition using the Custom Installation option.**

These are the steps for installing the operating system clean on a computer that already has one installed (and you'll see some of the related screens throughout this chapter). This is the simplest installation scenario (except for upgrading a Windows 8 computer to Windows 8.1).

1. Turn on the computer and insert the Windows 8.1 installation media into the DVD drive or USB port.
2. If prompted, opt to boot from the DVD or USB drive (or other applicable media). You'll have to restart the computer and press a specific key such as F12 or F2 to see this prompt if the computer doesn't offer it on its own. The key you'll choose is assigned by the manufacturer.
3. Choose your language, time zone, and keyboard or input method and click Next.
4. Click Install Now.
5. Select the I Accept The License Terms check box and click Next.
6. Choose Custom: Install Windows Only (Advanced).

7. From the list provided, select the partition on which to install Windows. Click Drive Options (Advanced) to add or delete existing partitions if desired and necessary.
8. Wait while the installation completes.
9. Work through the setup process to do the following:
   A. Agree to the license terms.
   B. Configure default settings.
   C. Sign in to your account.
   D. Choose a method to verify your account.
   E. Opt to use SkyDrive (or not). Note that the name SkyDrive is changing to OneDrive and at some point the exam will also make the terminology change.

> ***NOTE*** **CUSTOM INSTALLATIONS OFFER MORE OPTIONS**
>
> **When you choose to install Windows with a custom installation, you're presented with the "Where do you want to install Windows?" options. From there, you can either select an available partition or click Drive Options (Advanced) to delete, format, and create new partitions.**

Upgrade from Windows 7

To upgrade a computer running Windows 7 to a compatible, upgradable edition of Windows 8.1, perform the following steps (the steps you take might be slightly different from these depending on the edition you're installing). These are the steps for upgrading Windows 7 Ultimate to Windows 8.1 Enterprise.

1. Insert the Windows 8.1 installation disk into the DVD drive.
2. Click Run Setup.exe (Figure 1-5).

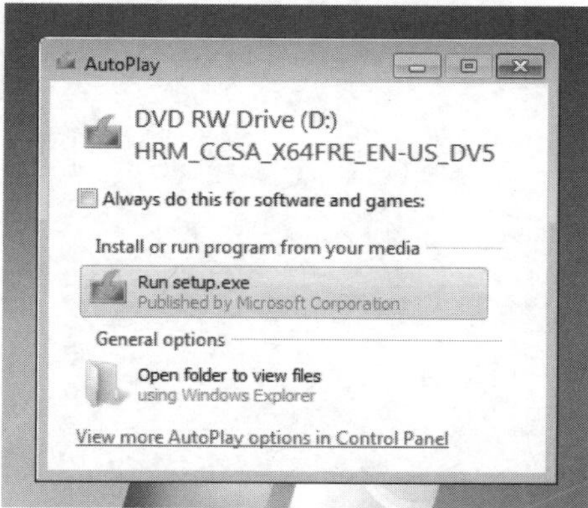

FIGURE 1-5 Run setup.exe to start the upgrade process.

3. Click Yes in the User Account Control box.
4. Select the Go Online And Install Updates (Recommended) button and click Next.
5. Select the I Accept The License Terms check box and click Accept.
6. Verify that the items to keep are correct and click Next.
7. Click Install.
8. After the installation completes, work through the setup process.

The setup process for Windows 8.1 requires you work through the same setup steps. You'll need to do the following:

- Agree to the license terms.
- Configure default settings.
- Sign in to your account.
- Choose a method to verify your account.
- Opt to use SkyDrive (or not).

When the installation and setup is complete, you'll see the Windows 8.1 Start screen, shown in Figure 1-6.

FIGURE 1-6 The Windows 8.1 Start screen.

Upgrade from Windows 8

To upgrade Windows 8 to Windows 8.1, you'll use the Windows Store, provided the user has a retail or OEM-activated version of Windows 8. If the computer was activated using Volume Licensing, the user won't be offered the update there.

> ***NOTE*** **UPGRADE OPTIONS FOR WINDOWS 8 TO WINDOWS 8.1**
>
> **Windows 8.1 upgrades are available in the Windows Store or on media. Note that when you upgrade to Windows 8.1 from the Windows Store, you cannot change editions. Upgrading to a different edition of Windows 8.1 is supported from media only. However, you can upgrade Windows 8.1 to Windows 8.1 Professional, as outlined later in this chapter.**

To install Windows 8.1 from the Windows Store, follow these steps:

1. On the Start screen, click Store.
2. Click the option to update Windows 8.1.
3. Click Download (see Figure 1-7).

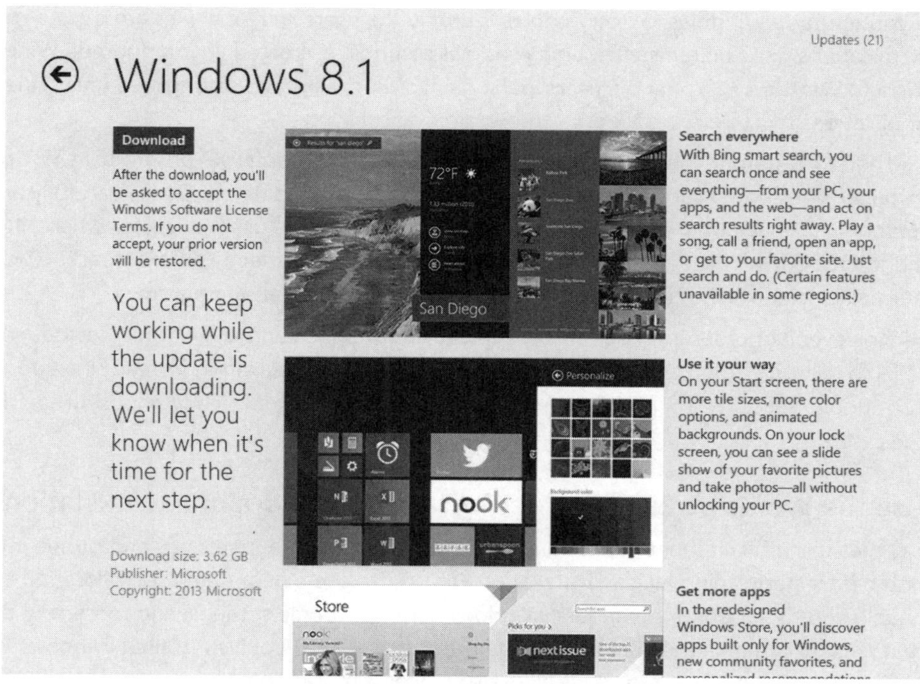

FIGURE 1-7 Download Windows 8.1 from the Windows Store.

4. Click Restart Now when prompted.
5. Follow the prompts to complete setup.

EXAM TIP

Sometimes you'll be asked to identify the path to a specific setting in Group Policy. Group Policy enables network administrators to assign specific permission to groups of users to secure resources, among other things. (You'll learn about Group Policy in various chapters in this book.) Here's one you might see: If you want to prevent users from seeing the option to update to Windows 8.1 from the Windows Store under any circumstances, you can set the Group Policy Turn Off The Offer To Upgrade To The Latest Version Of Windows located under Computer\Administrative Templates\Windows Components\Store. Make sure you're familiar with Group Policy and the most used settings before attempting the exam. For more information about this and other frequently asked questions regarding Windows 8.1, refer to the article at *http://technet.microsoft.com/en-us/windows/jj721676.aspx*.

Migrate from previous versions of Windows

You learned earlier that it is possible to upgrade Windows XP and Windows Vista machines to Windows 8.1. The steps for performing the installation are the same as outlined already in this objective. However, you also learned that not everything gets transferred during the upgrade. If you upgrade Windows XP to Windows 8.1, only the users' personal files are carried over. Applications must be reinstalled and Windows settings re-created. If you upgrade Windows Vista to Windows 8.1, only the users' personal files and Windows settings are maintained, and applications must be reinstalled.

Therefore, before you upgrade any machine that has Windows XP or Windows Vista installed, you should carefully and methodically back up the data on it. I say carefully and methodically because if a computer is that old, there could be user data everywhere, including the root drive, the Program Files folder, and other places that a common backup won't normally include. With that done, you can perform the installation upgrade.

However, upgrades aren't generally the better option. Clean installations provide more reliable results. Thus, if there's any way to perform a clean installation instead of an upgrade, you should opt for it. There are several migration options from which to choose when this is the case.

Use the Windows Easy Transfer Wizard on stand-alone workstations

Because it is difficult if not impossible to back up all of the users' settings and profile information before performing a clean installation, it's best to use a migration tool. Migration tools enable you to back up files, folders, Windows settings, profile settings, and more, and then that backup can be applied to repopulate the machine after you've installed Windows 8.1 on it. Knowing that migration options exist also makes it more likely that you and your clients will opt to perform a clean installation, too, which is always a better option when dealing with a machine that is older.

To learn about migration options, refer to Objective 1.3 in this chapter. For home users and businesses with a manageable number of computers to upgrade, consider the Windows Easy Transfer Wizard. For larger organizations, consider the User State Migration Tool.

Automate installations in enterprises

You can also automate installations. This is how enterprises install upgrades for hundreds or thousands of workstations. To automate an installation, you'll need to have a Windows 8.1 Volume Licensing Agreement with Microsoft. Then, to start, you'll need to create an installation image and choose a way to deploy that image. You might have multiple images, perhaps one image for all of the computers used by the Sales department, another for computers in the Inventory department, and so on. You need the Microsoft Deployment Toolkit (MDT), Windows Assessment and Deployment Kit (ADK), a file server to hold the installation files (as a share), and media that can be used to start the computers during deployment or a server configured with the Windows Deployment Services (WDS) role (and network cards on the PCs to upgrade that can boot to the installation image). If you have all of this in place, Microsoft recommends a Lite-Touch, High-Volume Deployment strategy if your enterprise has between 200 and 500 computers and recommends a Zero-Touch, High-Volume Deployment strategy if your enterprise has 500 or more machines.

Regarding images, an image is a custom installation file that can contain device drivers, applications, specific settings for the desktop background, and so on. There are thin images and thick images. A *thin image* has little or no customization, and most of the device drivers, applications, and updates are installed using another method on each client computer. A *thick image* includes applications, device drivers, and updates, among other things, and requires much more planning, network bandwidth, and other resources than a thin image. Microsoft recommends using thin images in most instances, because they can reduce installation time, maintenance time, storage requirements, and costs, among other things. MDT makes using thin images with the Lite-Touch, High-Volume Deployment strategy pretty straightforward for experienced network administrators. For more information visit *http://technet.microsoft.com/en-us/windows/dn282138.*

EXAM TIP

In previous editions of this exam and the related exam for Windows 7, automated installations were a big part of Objective 1. The objectives have changed quite a bit though, and we don't think that they'll be covered as heavily as before (if at all). However, you should understand the big picture with regard to automated installations, just in case.

Install additional Windows features

After installation is complete, you might need or want to install additional Windows features. There are two areas where you can do this. You can install Windows features from Control Panel (which is technically turning them on, not installing them), and you can install additional features by purchasing those features from Microsoft. You can also configure Windows 8.1 for additional languages.

Install additional features

One place to enable additional features is Control Panel. If you're new to Windows 8.1, you can right-click the Start button in the lower-left corner of the screen to get to it quickly. Once in Control Panel, in Category view, click Programs, and then select Turn Windows features on or off, as shown in Figure 1-8.

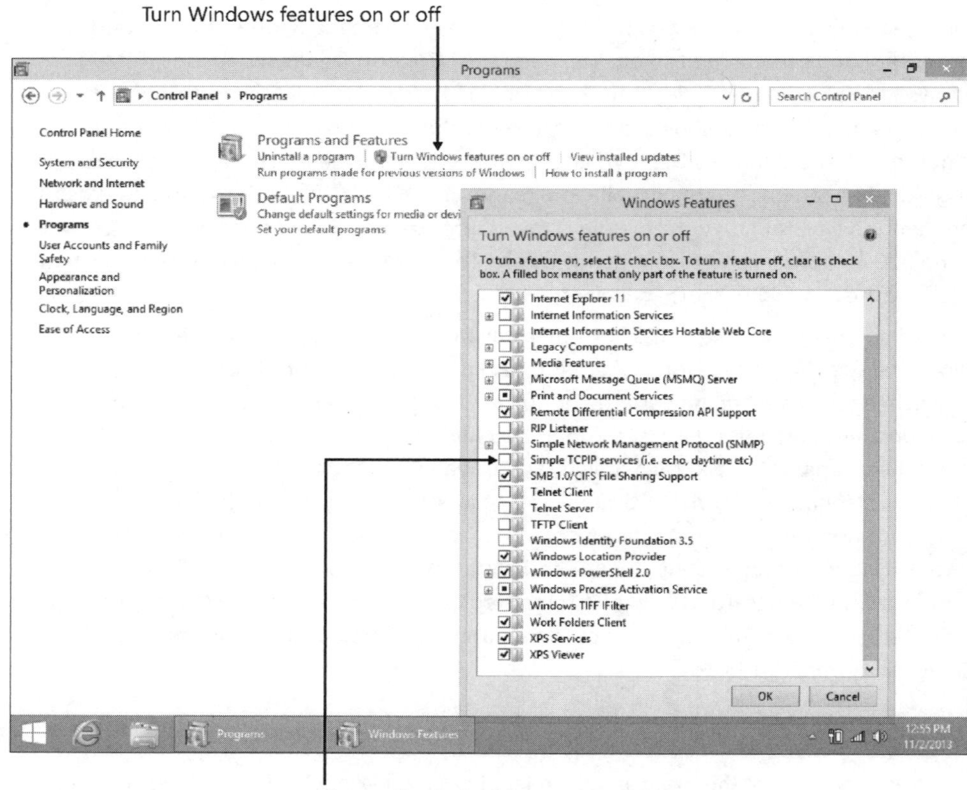

FIGURE 1-8 Turn Windows features on or off.

You can also add new features to Windows 8.1 that are not included with it. If you have Windows 8.1 installed, you can add the Windows 8.1 Pro Pack, which gives you access to all of the features in Windows 8.1 Pro and Media Center. If you have Windows 8.1 Pro already, you can just add Media Center. To get started, type **add features** on the Start screen and in the results click Add features To Windows 8.1 (see Figure 1-9). You can also navigate to *http://windows.microsoft.com/en-US/windows-8/feature-packs* using Internet Explorer.

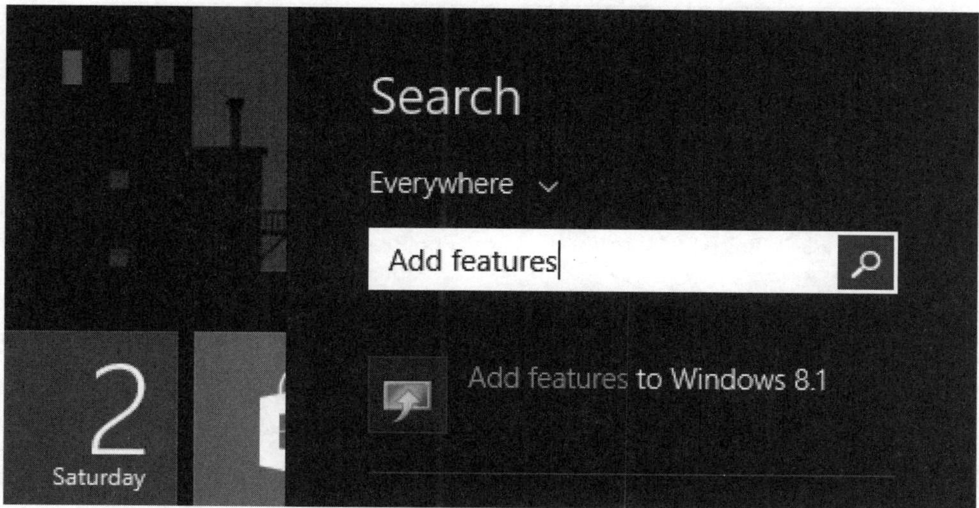

FIGURE 1-9 Add features to Windows 8.1.

After you click Yes to bypass the User Account Control box, you'll have the option to either buy a key online or type a product key you already own. Whichever you select, follow the prompts to purchase and install the new features. Once installation completes (the computer will restart during the installation), you'll see the new features.

Configure Windows for additional languages

Windows 8.1 includes support for additional languages. By adding a language, you can change the language you use to read and write in Windows, apps, and the web. Adding a language involves five steps, each outlined in its own section here.

ADD A LANGUAGE

To add a language (using the Windows 8.1 charms with which you should become familiar), follow these steps:

1. Position your cursor at the bottom or top right of the screen, click Settings, and then click Change PC Settings.
2. Click Time And Language, click Region And Language, and then click Add A Language.
3. Click the desired language from the list. If another list appears, click the desired option (see Figure 1-10).

FIGURE 1-10 Sometimes a language has several options.

DOWNLOAD AND INSTALL LANGUAGE PACKS

To see your preferred language used in Windows and apps, you might need to download the appropriate language pack. To download a language pack, follow these steps:

1. Continuing from the previous set of steps, click the language you want to use in the right pane.
2. Some languages such as English (United Kingdom) have Language Pack Available underneath them. If that is the case, click Options.
3. Click Download. (This might take some time.)

CHANGE YOUR WINDOWS DISPLAY LANGUAGE

To change your display language, follow these steps:

1. Continuing from the previous set of steps, return to the Time And Language, Region And Language section of PC Settings if applicable.
2. Click the language to set as the primary language.
3. Click Set As Primary. If the language can become your Windows display language, you'll see Will Be Display Language After Next Sign-In appear under the language.
4. Sign out and then sign back in to finish.

SWITCH BETWEEN KEYBOARDS

When you add a language, you can type in that language. Before you can do that, you must switch between keyboards or input methods. The easiest way is to press the Windows key + Spacebar. You can also switch by using the language abbreviation on the taskbar (see Figure 1-11). Note that the taskbar shows the time and date format the way it is displayed in the selected language.

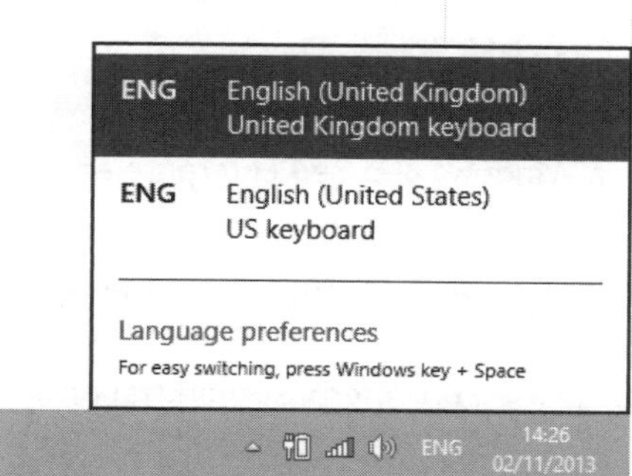

FIGURE 1-11 Switch languages by using the taskbar.

ADD A KEYBOARD LAYOUT FOR A LANGUAGE

Finally, you'll need to add a keyboard layout for your language and possibly make it your default keyboard. To add a keyboard layout for a language, follow these steps:

1. Open Control Panel and in Small Icons or Large Icons view, click Language.
2. Click Advanced Settings.
3. Under Override For Default Input Method, choose the keyboard layout you'd like to make your default keyboard and then click Save.

Install as Windows To Go and to VHD

There are two more ways to install Windows 8.1 to discuss here. You can install as Windows To Go and you can install Windows 8.1 onto a VHD. You'll need to be able to activate the operating system in either instance, so make sure you have the proper activation codes (or volume licensing) to do so before you start.

EXAM TIP

Sometimes you'll be asked to choose the correct syntax for performing a task at a command prompt. You might have never seen or heard of the command before—either in this text or in others you've read. There's really no way to prepare for such questions short of trying to memorize all of the syntax available, but this makes for an important tip all the same. Here's an example of something you might see: What command can you use to check the activation status of a computer? The answer is slmgr.vbs /dlv. The acronym

stands for (Windows) Server License Manager Script, and dlv stands for Display License information (Verbose). If you've never heard of a command, try figuring out what the letters in the command might stand for, and you might be able to make an educated guess.

Install as Windows To Go

You can give users a Windows To Go USB flash drive that holds a copy of Windows 8.1 Enterprise. They can use this USB drive to run Windows from a computer other than their own, provided the computer can be configured to boot to a USB drive.

There are a few things that are unique about Windows To Go:

- You can only create Windows To Go drives from a Windows 8–based Enterprise edition computer.
- The computer used to boot to the drive must meet Windows 7 certification requirements, but it doesn't have to be running Windows 7.
- The Windows To Go drive can hold the same image used on enterprise workstations and can be managed using the same methods.
- Windows To Go isn't a desktop replacement operating system; it is simply a short-term solution when the user can't be at his or her workstation.
- The host computer's internal hard disks aren't accessible to ensure data isn't accidentally or maliciously accessed. Likewise, Windows To Go won't be listed in File Explorer.
- Trusted Platform Model (TPM) can't be used with Windows To Go drives. TPM protects a specific computer from unauthorized access, and Windows To Go is used on more than one computer. When BitLocker is used, though, you can configure a system boot password.
- Hibernate and sleep aren't enabled by default, although they can be enabled through Group Policy.
- Neither Windows Recovery Environment (RE) nor resetting or refreshing is available. Problematic drives should be reimaged.
- For Windows To Go images that are running Windows 8.1, Windows Store apps can roam between multiple PCs on a Windows To Go drive.
- The USB drive you use must be Windows To Go certified.

To create a Windows To Go drive, you use the Windows To Go Creator Wizard. You will have to have access to a .wim file, which can be on a network share, a DVD, or a USB drive. A .wim file contains a disk image that can be mounted inside the Windows operating system. In simple terms, it's a type of installation file. These files allow a user to use the disk image on multiple computer platforms, including a Windows To Go drive.

To create a Windows To Go USB drive, follow these steps:

1. Sign into your Windows 8–based Enterprise computer using your Administrator account credentials.

2. Insert a Windows To Go certified USB drive.
3. Press Windows key + W to open Search Settings, type **Windows To Go,** and then press Enter.
4. If the User Account Control dialog box appears, click Yes.
5. On the Choose The Drive You Want To Use page, select the drive that represents the USB drive you inserted previously and then click Next.
6. On the Choose A Windows 8 Image page, click Add Search Location and locate the .wim file.
7. Click Select Folder and then click Next.
8. If desired, select the Use BitLocker With My Windows To Go Workspace check box and enter the required passwords and password hint.
9. Click Create. Note that any data on the drive will be erased.
10. Wait for the process to complete, which could take up to 30 minutes.

Install to VHD

A VHD contains the entire contents of a hard disk in a portable file that network administrators can use to transport entire virtual machines (VMs) from one host computer to another. A VHD functions exactly like a hard disk does in a physical machine. VHDs can also exist on a computer for the long term, without any intention of porting them. In this instance, a single computer, even with a single partition, can host multiple VHDs, all running different operating systems at the same time, giving network administrators a single computer for testing software on various operating systems easily. These types of VHDs are created on computers that have a parent operating system, meaning an operating system is installed on the computer that hosts the VHD. A *native-boot* VHD is a VHD that is created and runs without a parent operating system. Windows 8.1 supports native boot to these types of VHDs.

Often, VHDs are used to test applications and hardware under various circumstances, but there are lots of other reasons to use them. VHDs are quite useful in circumstances in which the operating system(s) needs to be reinstalled often, which is true of testing environments but also true of public kiosks, school computer labs, public libraries, and anywhere else a computer is open to guests or otherwise apt to be compromised. They're also useful in companies with a high turnover rate because computers can be repurposed easily. When you need to reinstall the VHD, you just copy your master VHD back over it and the VHD is as good as new. You can create a VHD by using DiskPart or the Disk Management Console.

In this set of steps, you'll install Windows 8.1 into a VHD by using the Disk Management Console. You can use an existing VHD if you have one, or you can create a new VHD here. Before you start, you need to locate your Windows 8.1 installation media. The computer on which you are going to install the VHD must also have the Windows ADK installed on it. You can download the ADK from *http://www.microsoft.com/en-us/download/details.aspx?id=39982*.

To create a VHD and install Windows 8.1 on it, follow these steps:

1. In File Explorer, right-click This PC and then click Manage.
2. In the left pane, click Disk Management.
3. Right-click Disk Management and click Create VHD. See Figure 1-12.

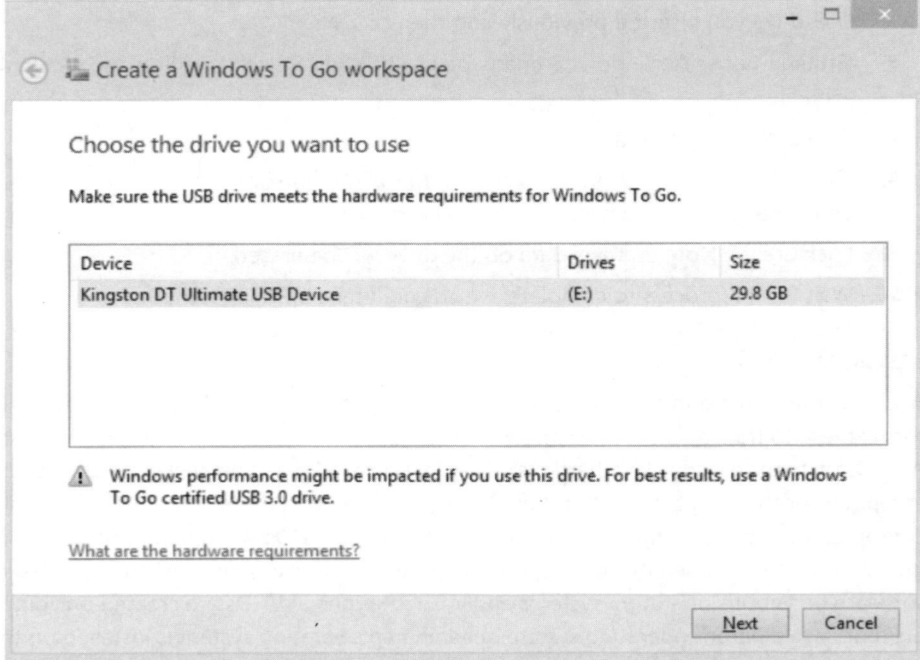

FIGURE 1-12 Create a new VHD.

4. In the Location box, type the location and name of the VHD you want to create.
5. In the Virtual Hard Disk Size box, choose GB to avoid calculation errors and type a number in the box. See Figure 1-13.

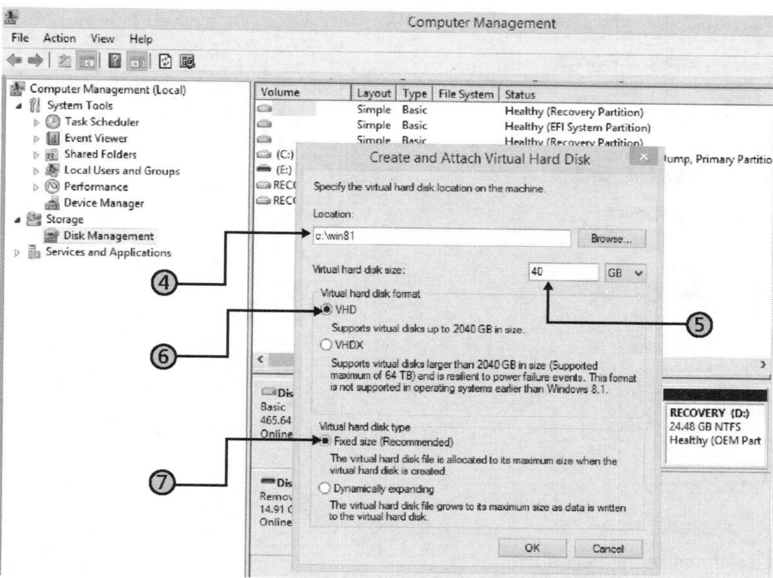

FIGURE 1-13 Configure the new VHD.

6. Under Virtual Hard Disk Format, choose VHD or VHDX after reading the information offered.
7. Choose Fixed Size (Recommended) or Dynamically Expanding.
8. Click OK.
9. Wait while the VHD is created.
10. Right-click the new disk and click Initialize Disk, as shown in Figure 1-14.

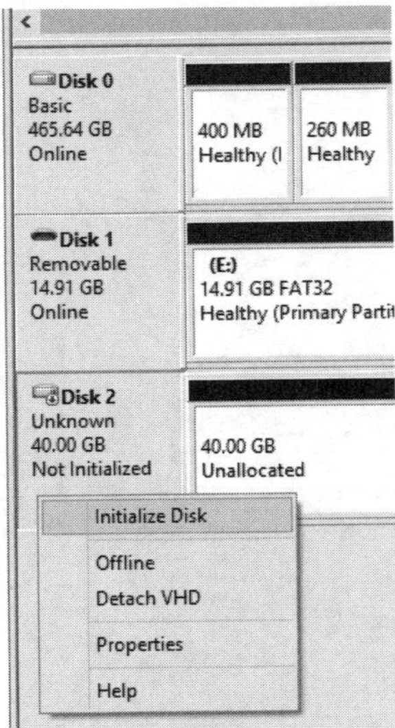

FIGURE 1-14 Initialize the new disk.

11. Choose MBR or GPT, noting that GPT is not recognized by all previous versions of Windows, and click OK.
12. Right-click the new disk near Unallocated, and click New Simple Volume, as shown in Figure 1-15.

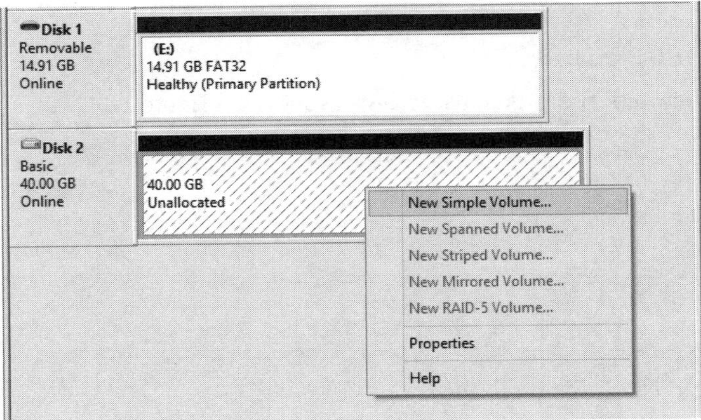

FIGURE 1-15 Create a new simple volume on the new disk.

13. Click Next four times to accept the defaults for the new volume and then click Finish.
14. Make a note of the drive letter assigned to the new disk (mine is F).
15. Locate Windows ADK on your computer. The best way is to open File Explorer and search for Windows ADK.

16. Right-click the shortcut to Deployment And Imaging Tools Environment and click Run As Administrator.

17. At the command prompt, type the following command, also shown in Figure 1-16, and press Enter.

```
Dism /apply-image /imagefile:<path to install.wim> /index:1 /ApplyDir:<drive
letter of VHD>
```

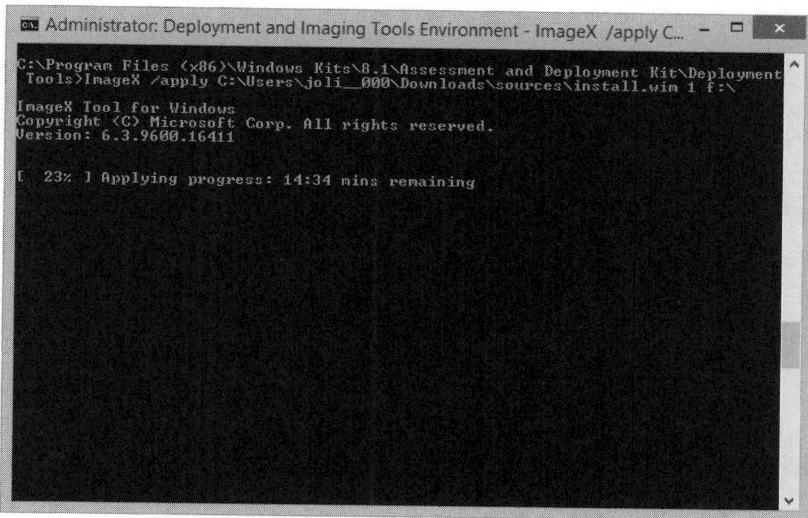

FIGURE 1-16 Apply the image to the new VHD.

18. Once the process completes, at the command prompt type **bcdboot F:\windows** to add the VHD to the boot menu (if desired).

19. At any time, you can right-click the VHD in Disk Management and click Detach VHD. (Click Attach VHD from Disk Management in the left pane when you need it again.)

You can now restart the computer and choose the VHD from the boot menu. You'll have to work through the setup process just as you would with any new installation, which includes inputting a product key, choosing the color of the Start screen, joining a network, and so on.

EXAM TIP

Make sure to familiarize yourself with the tools in the ADK. Deployment Imaging Servicing and Management (DISM) is a command line tool you can use to apply, capture, delete, export and perform other tasks with images. This new command line tool replaces ImageX, so if you see that command in an answer it's probably a red herring. Refer to the article here to learn more about DISM: *http://technet.microsoft.com/en-US/library/hh825258.aspx*. At the very least, read the Windows ADK Quickstart document.

Explore the custom Windows 8.1 installation

Network administrators often create their own custom installation files with Windows 8.1 so that the installation file contains device drivers, software, updates, custom wallpapers and screensavers, and other items required by the target computers. You can add these to minimize what must be done after installation completes. There are a lot of steps involved in creating a custom installation, and a high-level outline is provided here.

To create a custom installation, you'll need to download and install the Windows ADK. The ADK contains the tools you'll need to perform the required tasks. You'll also need a reference computer that you'll set up to represent a typical computer in your organization. You'll need a test computer to test the installation image you'll create from the reference computer, an empty USB drive or CD for creating a Windows PE disk, and an external storage device where you can create the share that contains the installation files.

With all of those things in place, you'll do the following:

1. Create a share on the network to hold the installation files and other files related to the deployment of Windows 8.1.
2. Create a reference computer that will serve as a template for the workstation configuration, complete with all of the software you want to install, language packs, settings, required device drivers, custom wallpapers, and anything else you want to include.
3. Prepare the reference computer for imaging by removing certain values unique to the reference computer. You'll use the following commands:
   - Sysprep /generalize to remove unique IDs. You might add other command-line options like /oobe (to give the installation an out-of-box experience).
   - Copype.cmd to create a Windows PE boot disk, with the proper command-line options like c:\winpe (to note the location of the required PE files).
   - Oscdimg.exe to package the Windows PE files into a sector-based image file, along with proper command-line options.
4. Capture an image of the reference computer, which results in an image file. Using this file, you can install as many workstations as desired and apply your image to all of them, creating uniformity. You'll use these commands:
   - DISM with command-line options including /capture-image to capture the image of the computer's hard disk.
   - Net use with command-line options including something like z: \\server\share to denote the location of the network share where the files are stored.
5. Create an answer file to partially automate the installation or an unattended answer file to completely automate the answers asked during installation. You'll use tools including Windows System Image Manager (SIM; available in Windows ADK) to select the image and create and apply the answer file.

6. Boot the target computers with either a Windows PE disk or a boot image that the computer can download from the server.
7. Apply the reference computer image to create your duplicate workstations. This will include copying and applying the desired image, among other things.

Thought experiment

Upgrading computers in a home office

In this thought experiment, apply what you've learned about this objective. You can find answers to these questions in the "Answers" section at the end of this chapter.

A home user maintains his office at home. His five computers include one that currently runs Windows 7, one that runs Windows Vista with SP1, one that runs Windows XP SP3, and two that run Windows 8. He likes Windows 8 and would like to update this computer to Windows 8.1, and for continuity he'd also like to update the other computers to Windows 8.1. He does not have a domain, isn't particularly computer savvy, and doesn't want to have to reconfigure any of the five computers he owns after they are upgraded to Windows 8.1. You've run hardware and software compatibility tests and decide it's possible to successfully upgrade all but Windows XP. The Windows XP machine has a long list of compatibility problems, including a full hard drive and an incompatible graphics adapter.

Answer the following questions regarding the upgrade process:

1. What computers will only require you back up the data and perform the update?
2. Will you use Windows Easy Transfer or the User State Migration Tool on the computer(s) that require migration? Why?
3. What should you do with the Windows XP machine?

Objective summary

- You can upgrade Windows XP, Windows Vista, and Windows 7 computers, but you won't get to keep everything in the case of Windows XP and Windows Vista.
- You can install additional features from Control Panel and from Microsoft. Windows Media Center and Windows 8.1 Pro Pack are options from the latter.
- You can change the language Windows uses in apps, windows, and other areas, and you can configure matching keyboards.
- You can install Windows 8.1 as Windows To Go and to a VHD.

Objective review

Answer the following questions to test your knowledge of the information in this objective. You can find the answers to these questions and explanations of why each answer choice is correct or incorrect in the "Answers" section at the end of this chapter.

1. What types of data and files can you keep if you opt to upgrade a Windows 7 machine to Windows 8.1? What types of data and files can you keep if you opt to upgrade a Windows XP machine to Windows 8.1?
   - **A.** Files, settings, applications; Files and settings
   - **B.** Files, settings, applications; Files
   - **C.** Files, applications; Nothing
   - **D.** Files, settings; Personal files
2. Which of the following are valid ways to perform a clean installation of Windows 8.1? (Choose all that apply.)
   - **A.** Booting to a Windows To Go USB drive
   - **B.** Running Install.exe from the installation DVD
   - **C.** Using an accessible and compatible image file
   - **D.** Running Setup.exe from a shared and accessible network folder
3. Which one of the following is true regarding Windows To Go? (Choose all that apply.)
   - **A.** Windows To Go drives can be created only from Windows 8.1 Enterprise.
   - **B.** While using Windows To Go, hibernate and sleep are enabled by default.
   - **C.** You can install Windows To Go on any USB drive that is 32 GB or larger.
   - **D.** Windows To Go blocks access to local drives by default.
4. Which of these tools can you use to create a new VHD? (Choose all that apply.)
   - **A.** Windows PE
   - **B.** DiskPart
   - **C.** Disk Management
   - **D.** SysPrep

Objective 1.3: Migrate and configure user data

Users have data you need to back up prior to performing any type of installation task. They have more than data, though; they have settings unique to their computers, including desktop wallpaper, application settings and preferences, configurations for when the computer should sleep, and even settings for how the taskbar looks or what items appear in the Notification area. If you are upgrading Windows 7 or Windows 8 computers, you can keep all of these settings along with users' personal files, but this kind of installation is only one of many scenarios. As you've learned already, there is no direct upgrade path from Windows XP or Windows Vista to Windows 8.1. Also, you can't effectively back up and restore all of these settings and data using ordinary backup tools. To update these operating systems successfully while also maintaining user data, you need to use a data migration tool.

In this section, you'll learn about two migration tools. The first is Windows Easy Transfer (WET), a tool best suited for migrating data for home users, small office users, and anywhere a limited number of workstations exist. The second is the User State Migration Tool (part of the MDT). This tool is best suited for experienced administrators who are migrating data in large enterprises. You'll also learn about folder redirection and the various types of user profiles, both of which are important to larger organizations. Following migration options, you'll learn how to change the location where files are stored by default and the various kinds of user profiles.

This objective covers how to:

- Migrate data with Windows Easy Transfer
- Explore the User State Migration Tool
- Configure folder redirection
- Configure profiles

IMPORTANT **BACK UP, BACK UP, BACK UP!**

Always back up data before any migration or installation. Things can and do go awry, and it's better to be safe than sorry.

Use Windows Easy Transfer

There are two scenarios to consider when a migration of data is required. The first is when the user wants to upgrade a single computer that is currently running Windows XP or Windows Vista to Windows 8.1. This type of migration is called wipe-and-load because that's what you do; you migrate the data off the hard drive and store it somewhere else, and then you format (wipe) the hard disk and install (load) the new operating system. With a wipe-and-load migration, you need somewhere to store the data temporarily, until you can transfer it back. This is generally a network drive or an external hard drive.

The other migration scenario is when the user obtains a new computer and wants to migrate data from the old computer to the new one. This is called a side-by-side migration because that's what you have; there is an old computer with data on it sitting next to (physically or virtually) the new one to which you'd like to transfer the data. You can connect these computers directly to transfer the data. Generally this involves connecting the two with a Windows Easy Transfer cable. However, you can also use this method to migrate files, settings, accounts, and so on over a network to another computer.

You can achieve migrations using the Windows Easy Transfer Wizard by either starting from the old computer or starting, if applicable, from the new one. If you have a new computer that already runs Windows 8.1, you can type **migwiz** at the Start screen to begin. You'll be prompted to go to the old computer and run WET from there though, so it doesn't really matter where you start. If you only have one computer, you have several options for starting Windows Easy Transfer:

- In Windows Vista, click Start, All Programs, Accessories, System Tools, and then click Windows Easy Transfer. Click Next to proceed.
- In Windows XP, locate the Getting Started folder and click Transfer Your Files.
- Alternatively, you can locate WET on your physical installation media here: E:\support\migwiz (assuming E is the letter of your DVD drive).

Whatever option you choose, once you've launched Windows Easy Transfer, you can begin the migration process. The wizard will walk you through the migration process. There are a lot of scenarios because there are various options regarding where to save the data, what to save, and whether you're starting from the old computer, starting from the new one, or upgrading a single computer. Instead of covering each scenario here, I'll list the general process you'll work through as you follow the wizard's prompts. Remember, you'll need to have an area where you can store the files you collect until you can transfer them or have a network in place for transferring them.

The Windows Easy Transfer Wizard will ask for the following information:

- How you will perform the transfer (direct link to another computer, external hard disk, or over a network).
- Whether this computer is the old one or the new one.
- If you are transferring files over a network, you'll need to write down the code given so that you can enter it on the host PC when prompted.
- What to transfer. You can accept the defaults or opt to customize what parts of the user account and files you'd like to transfer. If you opt for the defaults, you'll be transferring virtually everything related to the user.

IMPORTANT **TRANSFER ONLY WHAT YOU NEED**

The migration can take a lot of time if there's a lot of data to move. Instead of transferring everything, carefully select the files to transfer. You might not want to transfer downloaded movies, podcasts, audiobooks, or other large files you might not need.

Explore the User State Migration Tool

USMT is a scriptable command-line tool that you can use to migrate user data from a previous edition of Windows to Windows 8.1. By using USMT, you can copy the user data you select (and exclude any data that does not need to be migrated) and then transfer the data back to the computer once it's been installed clean with Windows 8.1. You can also transfer the data to a brand-new or newly installed Windows 8.1 computer. It's somewhat like using Windows Easy Transfer. However, although USMT has the same basic capabilities as WET, USMT is a command-line tool and WET is graphical. This isn't a disadvantage in a large organization, because administrators can use USMT to incorporate USMT tasks into scripts, which are better suited for domains and enterprises and automated deployments. (Scripts, task sequences, answer files, and so on are what help automate a deployment.) Two of the tools included with USMT are ScanState and LoadState, both command-line tools.

When you use USMT, you'll also use the Windows Preinstallation Environment (Windows PE). You'll need to know a little about Windows PE to understand how USMT works, so let's start there.

EXAM TIP

Windows PE and USMT are available in Windows ADK; you might be required to know this to select the proper solution given a scenario. Additionally, it's likely you'll see one question on the exam regarding ScanState and LoadState and their related parameters. To learn about the parameters available for these two commands, refer to the USMT Technical Reference sheet offered at *http://technet.microsoft.com/en-us/library/hh825256.aspx*.

EXPLORE WINDOWS PE

The boot process has changed over the years. When Windows ME was retired, so was MS-DOS. Windows 8, Windows 7, and Windows Vista no longer rely on MS-DOS for any part of the installation and boot process. To replace it, Windows uses Windows PE. Windows PE is a minimal operating system you can use to prepare a computer for a Windows installation, and it can start a computer that has no operating system (or has other problems). When deploying Windows 8.1, Windows PE can be used to partition and format hard drives, copy disk images to a computer, and initiate Windows Setup from a network share. You can create a Windows PE disk using the tools in the ADK. With regard to USMT, you use a customized Windows PE boot disk to boot the source computer (the computer that holds the files to migrate) and use the tools available on the disk to collect the data you want to migrate.

EXAM TIP

Windows PE can help you deploy custom Windows 8.1 images to computers. It can help you create disk partitions and format hard drives, too, but notably it helps initiate an installation from a network share. There is also something called the Windows Recovery Environment (Windows RE). Windows RE is built from Windows PE, which makes sense. Both assist in installations (and recovery).

Windows PE offers the following improvements and advantages over MS-DOS (as you read through this list, think about how important each of these entries is to automated and custom operating system deployments):

- Native 32-bit or 64-bit support (MS-DOS is a 16-bit operating system).

- Native 32-bit and 64-bit driver support, or the ability to use the same drivers as a full Windows 8 installation.
- Internal networking support.
- Internal NTFS support.
- Scripting language support for a subset of Win32 application programming interface (API), Windows Management Instrumentation (WMI), Windows Data Access Components (Windows DAC), HTML Applications (HTAs), and Windows Script Host. Administrators can create scripts that are much more robust than the MS-DOS batch files.
- Myriad boot options, including CDs, DVDs, USB devices such as flash drives, a temporary folder on a hard disk, RAM disk, network share, and Windows Deployment Services (WDS) server.
- Support for offline sessions and offline servicing of images.
- Inclusion of Hyper-V drivers (except display drivers), which enables Windows PE to run in a hypervisor. Support includes mass storage, mouse integration, and network adapters.

EXAM TIP

There are other tools besides Windows PE and USMT included with the ADK that you might have heard of but that won't be discussed here: the Application Compatibility Toolkit (ACT), various deployment tools including the DISM command-line tool, DISM PowerShell cmdlets, DISM API, Windows System Image Manager (Windows SIM), and OSCDIMG. The ADK also includes the Volume Activation Management Tool (VAMT), Windows Performance Toolkit (WPT), Windows Assessment Toolkit, and Windows Assessment Services. Make sure you are familiar with these tools. An overview is available at *http://msdn.microsoft.com/en-us/library/windows/hardware/hh825486.aspx*.

Windows PE has various restrictions, not limited to the following: Windows PE restarts after 72 hours so it can't be used as an operating system for the long term; it does support TCP/IP and NetBIOS over TCP/IP, but doesn't support other methods, like the Internetwork Packet Exchange/Sequenced Packet Exchange (IPX/SPX) network protocol; Windows PE doesn't support applications that are packaged through Windows Installer (.msi files); and it doesn't support cross-platform scenarios like installing a 64-bit Windows image on a 32-bit computer (among others).

MORE INFO **WINDOWS PE**

Visit *www.msdn.com* and type What is Windows PE? in the search box to locate related technical information.

EXPLORE USMT

USMT provides a highly customizable user-profile migration experience. As mentioned earlier, USMT includes two unique command-line tools: ScanState.exe and LoadState.exe. You use these tools to collect and restore user data from the host computer. Another command-line tool, UsmtUtils, can be used to verify that the data you collect isn't corrupt before you continue. USMT also includes a set of three customizable .xml files—MigApp.xml, MigDocs.xml, and MigUser.xml—that you can use to customize the migration. You create your own .xml files to support your migration needs. You'll use a Config.xml file to further customize the migration and to exclude specific files from migrations.

Here is a breakdown of the tools you'll use with USMT in the ADK:

- **ScanState.exe** Use this tool to state what data to migrate from the source computer (and to migrate it to a migration store). You can choose files, settings, and account information, among other things.
- **UsmtUtils** Use this tool to verify that the migration store data is not corrupt, to extract compressed files from the migration store, to delete hard link stores that cannot be deleted because of a sharing lock, and to determine cryptographic options for your migration.
- **LoadState.exe** Use this tool to import the data you exported with ScanState.exe to the destination computer.
- **MigUser.xml** Use this file to detail what user accounts to migrate.
- **MigDocs.xml** Use this file to detail the documents and files to migrate.
- **Custom.xml** Use this file to create a custom file to migrate additional files and data or modify the default migration behavior.
- **Config.xml** Use this file to exclude certain items from migration. You can create this file with the /genconfig option with the ScanState.exe command.

At a very high level, the process involved in migrations includes, among other things, deciding what to migrate. You might need to migrate account information, application settings, operating system settings, personal files and folders, and registry keys. You'll also have to determine where you'll store the data you collect from each computer (this is called the migration store). You'll also modify or create XML files to modify the migration behavior and exclude files you don't want transferred. You might also use MDT to incorporate migration tasks into an installation script called a task sequence; a task sequence can be used to perform the entire migration, installation, and restoration of data with little or no interaction from the user.

No matter what you decide during the planning stages, when you're ready to perform the migration you'll use the following commands along with the appropriate parameters to perform the migration (this is a high-level overview):

1. Install Windows ADK on a technician computer.
2. Modify the Config.xml file to include user-group membership.

3. If needed, create an optional Offline.xml file to include information on how to work with additional drives on the destination computer if those drives exist.
4. Copy the customized USMT files and tools to a USB flash drive (or network share).
5. Suspend BitLocker if applicable and boot the source computer using the Windows PE disk. Booting to a share is more complex but certainly possible.
6. Use the **ScanState** command on the source computer to collect files and settings and save them to a migration store.
7. Install Windows 8.1 and additional applications on the destination computer.
8. Copy the USMT files to the destination computer and then run the **LoadState** command to apply the saved files and settings to the new computer.

EXAM TIP

You'll be asked to verify specific ScanState and LoadState syntax for some command-line options. Often these are obscure, or at least seem to be. Review ScanState syntax at *http://technet.microsoft.com/en-us/library/hh825093.aspx* and LoadState syntax at *http://technet.microsoft.com/en-us/library/cc766226(v=WS.10).aspx.*

Configure folder location

In a domain, users do not generally store their files on their workstations. Instead, they store their files on file servers. This provides a great deal of security because files and folders can be backed up on a regular basis, access can be globally controlled and limited to only those who require it, and users can access the data when away from their workstations from virtually any computer. Also, a computer can be reimaged quickly because the users' data and profile information is stored off of their workstation; a full migration isn't needed. Additionally, if a user loses a laptop, data that is stored on the file server doesn't go missing with it; the data is safe on the central server. Often, this type of configuration is complimented with other technologies such as BitLocker, roaming user profiles, offline files, and even technologies related to accessing data from domain servers over the Internet using various forms of secure connections. In an enterprise, redirecting where data is saved involves connecting the workstation to an Active Directory Domain Services domain and creating a Group Policy object that specifies what folders to relocate and where that new location is.

On a Windows 8.1 workstation, you can configure something similar. You can change the save location to another folder on the same computer, another drive on the computer, a drive attached externally, or a share in a workgroup.

To configure folder location on a Windows 8.1 computer, follow these steps:

1. Open File Explorer and locate the folder to redirect to a new location.
2. Right-click the folder and click Properties.
3. Click the Location tab, shown in Figure 1-17.

4. Click Move.
5. In the Select A Destination dialog box, navigate to the folder to use.
6. Click Select Folder.
7. Note the new location in the Properties dialog box.
8. Click OK.

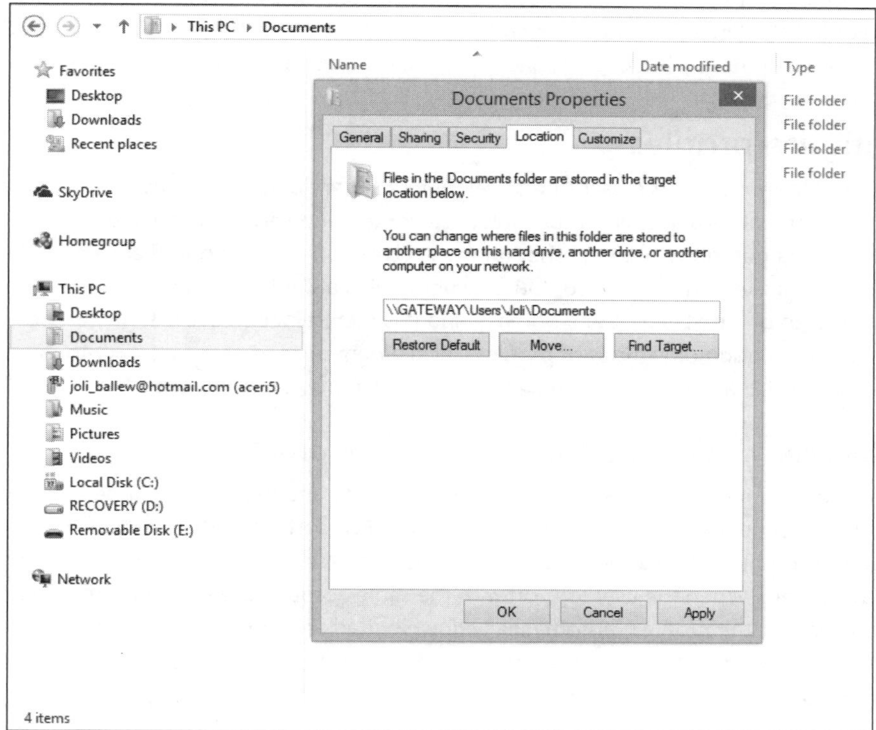

FIGURE 1-17 Configure a new location for saving data in default folders.

9. When prompted Do You Want To Move All Of The Files From The Old Location To The New Location? as shown in Figure 1-18, click Yes, No, or Cancel, as applicable.
10. Click OK again to close the Properties dialog box, if applicable.

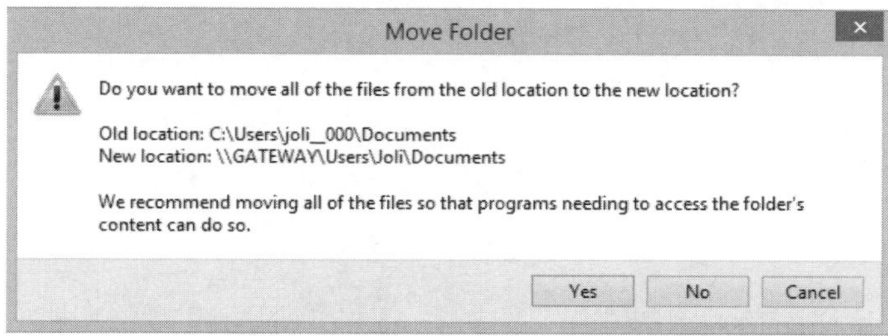

FIGURE 1-18 Indicate whether to copy existing files from the old location to the new one.

MORE INFO **REMOTELY ACCESSING DATA**

For more information on remotely accessing data from a file server, refer to Chapter 5, "Configure remote access and mobility." In that chapter, you'll find information regarding offline file policies, Work Folders, and other mobility options.

There are other methods to redirect and manage data for the mobile user: Sync Center, Work Folders, Offline Files, and Roaming User Profiles. Sync Center, Work Folders, and Offline file policies are outlined in Chapter 5. Roaming user profiles are detailed in the next section.

Configure profiles

A user profile consists of the user's personal folders, library data, user-specific registry settings, desktop backgrounds, Internet Explorer favorites, and various application settings and computer configurations, among other things. A user profile is configured automatically the first time a user logs on to a computer, whether it is a single computer, a computer in a workgroup, or one that is part of a domain, and it is then reloaded every time the user logs in. There are three traditional types of profiles: Local, Roaming, and Mandatory. With Windows 8 and Windows 8.1, a new kind of profile has emerged, though. Let's look at that first.

Explore and configure a Microsoft Account profile

Starting with Windows 8, users are encouraged to create and log on to their new Windows 8–based computers with a Microsoft Account. This Microsoft Account is really a new kind of limited user profile. When applied, part of the user's profile is stored in (synced to) the cloud and saved there. When the user logs on with the same account to that same computer or any other computer, the profile is automatically downloaded and applied, provided an Internet connection is available to obtain the latest saved profile. This means that a fair portion of the user's profile follows from computer to computer.

Some items that are synced to the cloud and included in the profile are the Start screen background color, screen tiles, and tile layout; lock screen and account pictures; desktop themes, taskbar settings, web browser favorites, open tabs, and history; language preferences; Ease of Access settings, and more. A Microsoft Account is required to use the Windows Store, SkyDrive, Calendar, and other Windows 8–based features as well. Figure 1-19 shows some of the settings that can be synced.

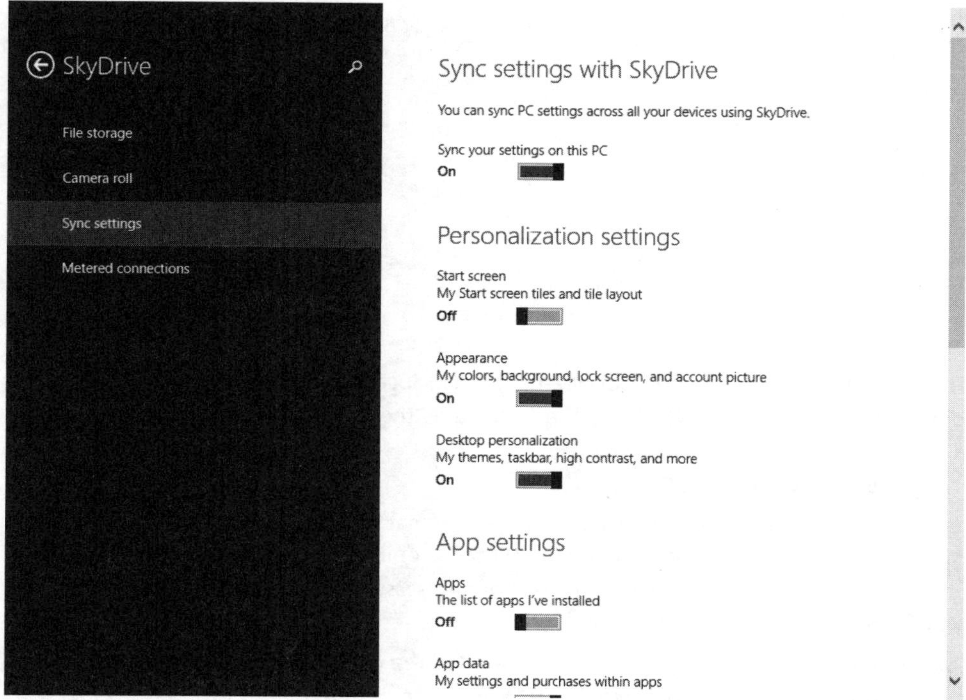

FIGURE 1-19 When using a Microsoft Account, parts of the user's profile are available no matter what computer he or she logs on to.

Your clients might not want to sync everything to the cloud. To change what is synced to the cloud with a Microsoft Account, follow these steps:

1. Open PC settings.
2. On the main PC settings screen, click SkyDrive.
3. Click Sync settings.
4. Move the sliders as applicable to configure what to sync.

Understand the local user profile

A local user profile is a profile that is applied to a single computer. The profile defines the user to the computer, including where folders are saved and what settings have been applied. If you have multiple users who access a single computer and they all have their own user accounts, each user has his or her own profile.

A typical user has these folders to hold data:

- AppData
- Contacts
- Desktop

- Downloads
- Favorites
- Links
- My Documents
- My Music
- My Pictures
- My Videos
- Saved Games
- Searches

There isn't much more to know about an end user's local profile. Changes will be saved automatically, and the profile will be applied each time the user logs on to the local machine.

Configure a roaming user profile

A roaming user profile is a copy of a local user profile that is stored on a network server. Thus, the profile is available no matter what computer the user logs on to in the workplace. If a user makes any changes to the profile during a computing session, the changes are saved to the network server when the user logs off.

Roaming user profiles aren't enabled by default. In the workplace, specifically in an Active Directory domain, administrators create a share for saving roaming user profiles and then the path to the profile is added to the user's Properties dialog box (see Figure 1-20).

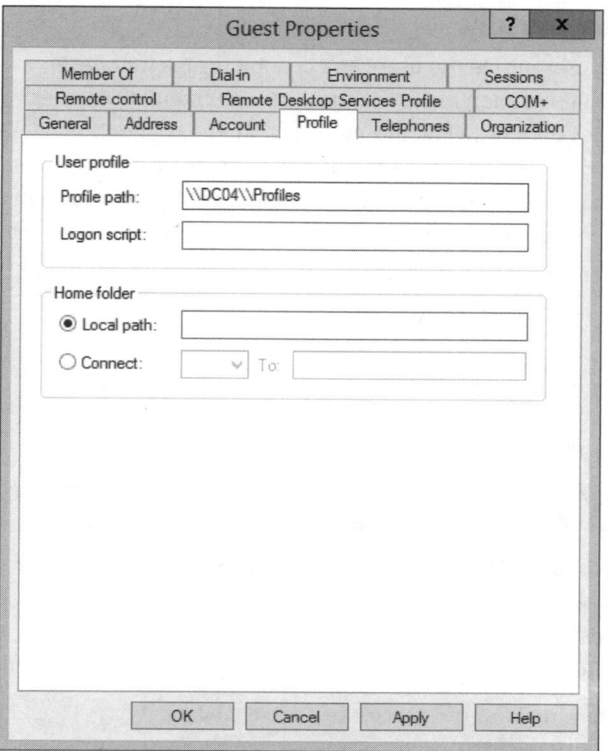

FIGURE 1-20 Configure the profile path of the roaming user profile on the user's Properties dialog box.

EXAM TIP

Because users must access and download their profile when they log on, make sure you save profiles to a file server that you back up frequently. Also, if the network bogs down in the morning when users log on, consider moving the share to a member server instead of a domain controller.

Here's how the roaming user profile is applied when the user logs on:

1. The first time a user logs on, the entire user profile is copied from the server to the local drive. This allows access to the profile should the server become unavailable.
2. The profile is applied, and any changes made to the profile during the computing session are saved to the local drive.
3. When the user logs off, the profile is copied back to the server and includes any changes the user made during the session.
4. At the next logon, only the parts of the profile that are changed are copied from the server to the local machine, which speeds up the logon process.

Understand the mandatory user profile

A mandatory user profile is a roaming user profile the user can't change for the long term. With a mandatory user profile, although users can make changes (such as changing the desktop background) and use those changes during their computing session, the changes won't be saved at logoff. The profile is read-only. The next time the user logs on, the original profile will be reapplied. A network administrator can create a single mandatory profile and apply it to multiple users. To create a mandatory user profile, you must locate the folder that contains the roaming user profile. Then, you must change the name of that profile from Ntuser.dat to Ntuser.man.

Thought experiment

Working with a BYOD scenario

In this thought experiment, apply what you've learned about this objective. You can find answers to these questions in the "Answers" section at the end of this chapter.

You are the network administrator of a 2012 Active Directory domain. All 20 client computers run Windows 8 Professional. One of your users purchased her own computer and brought it to work, and it too runs Windows 8 Professional. You approve the computer and join it to the domain. There are some issues, though.

1. **After logging on to the domain, the user can't access her personal data. What should you do?**
2. **You want the data the user would normally save to her Documents folder to instead be saved to a share on the network. What should you do?**
3. **The user wants her local user profile to follow her from computer to computer. What should you do?**

Objective review

Answer the following questions to test your knowledge of the information in this objective. You can find the answers to these questions and explanations of why each answer choice is correct or incorrect in the "Answers" section at the end of this chapter.

1. Three family members share a single computer. All of their documents are saved in a single Documents folder, as is the case with their pictures, videos, and music. All of their data is mixed together, and this is causing problems. You've determined that they are all using the same user profile. What should you do first to remedy this?
   - **A.** Configure a new folder location for each of the default folders.
   - **B.** Configure a roaming user profile for each user.

- **C.** Apply passwords to each user account.
- **D.** Create a user account for each user.

2. Which of the following must you address when you run the Windows Easy Transfer Wizard? (Choose all that apply.)
   - **A.** How you will perform the transfer (direct link to another computer, external hard disk, or over a network)
   - **B.** What types of task sequences you'd like to include
   - **C.** Whether this computer is the old one or the new one
   - **D.** What you want to transfer
   - **E.** Where the local user profiles are stored
3. What happens when a user who has been assigned a mandatory user profile makes changes to the desktop background and screensaver?
   - **A.** The changes are saved to the user profile when the user logs off because it is acceptable to change personalization options.
   - **B.** The user can't make these kinds of changes, so the question itself is invalid.
   - **C.** The changes are not saved to the user profile when the user logs off.
   - **D.** The Ntuser.man file is renamed Ntuser.dat.
4. Where do you configure folder location?
   - **A.** The Location tab of the default folder's Properties dialog box
   - **B.** The Sharing tab of the default folder's Properties dialog box
   - **C.** In PC Settings, SkyDrive, on the Sync Settings tab
   - **D.** From File Explorer, opt to map a network drive

Chapter summary

- There are four Windows 8.1 editions: Windows RT, Windows 8.1, Windows 8.1 Professional, and Windows 8.1 Enterprise. Each offers its own set of features.
- It is extremely important to know which features are unique to both Windows 8.1 Professional and Windows 8.1 Enterprise so that you can select the proper operating system for the corporate client.
- You can perform upgrades, but in-place upgrades to keep users' files, Windows settings, and applications can only be performed from Windows 7 and Windows 8.
- Various tools exist to help enterprises plan, test, and deploy Windows 8.1 including, but not limited to, Windows Application Deployment Toolkit (Windows ADK), Microsoft Deployment Toolkit (MDT), and Application Compatibility Toolkit (ACT).
- When applications aren't compatible with Windows 8.1, you can try to force compatibility by using Program Compatibility mode.

- You can automate installations in large enterprises with various tools including the Windows ADK. You'll use tools including Sysprep, DISM, ScanState, and LoadState, among others.
- Answer files can be used to answer questions asked during installation without user input.
- Windows To Go lets users take Windows with them on a USB flash drive.
- You can install Windows 8.1 on a VHD. Windows 8.1 supports booting to native VHDs.
- You can migrate user data with Windows Easy Transfer and the User State Migration Tool. The former is better for a small number of computers; the latter is better for larger organizations.
- You can change where data is saved by default using folder location.
- User profiles define users to a computer, and there are three user profiles: Local, Roaming, and Mandatory. The Microsoft Account provides a new type of limited user profile.

Answers

This section contains the solutions to the thought experiments and answers to the objective review questions in this chapter.

Objective 1.1: Thought experiment

1. You'd suggest Windows 8.1 Professional because it can be used to join a domain. Windows 8.1 cannot. Windows Enterprise is not an option because of the volume licensing requirement. Windows RT comes preinstalled on tablets and similar devices, not workstations, so you can't select that either. You'd choose 32-bit because you know all computers support it and because you can perform an upgrade from Windows Vista (even though you'd have to install Service Pack 1 and its applications). If you opted for 64-bit, you'd have a lot more testing to do and likely have hardware upgrading as well, which increases cost.
2. You would start by setting up test machines to represent all of the computers on the network. If there are five different computer manufacturers, you'd need at least five test machines. You would install Service Pack 1 for Windows Vista before performing the test upgrade. You'd need to test the database program too, and if the program proved problematic, you'd need to try to run it in Program Compatibility mode or host it on the server if it isn't already hosted there. Based on those tests, more planning might be required before you can roll out the upgrade.
3. Because there are computers from five different computer manufacturers, a clean installation is probably best. You could, at the very least, reduce problems that arise due to hidden malware, unwanted temporary files, and data fragments, and minimize the differences that carry over from desktop settings, personal files, unwanted files, and so forth. Generally, a clean installation is best no matter the circumstance, when feasible.

Objective 1.1: Review

1. **Correct answers:** C and D
   - **A. Incorrect:** Windows Vista SP1 can keep personal files and Windows settings during an upgrade. Windows Vista without SP1 can't be upgraded.
   - **B. Incorrect:** Windows XP SP3 can only keep personal files during an upgrade.
   - **C. Correct:** Windows 7 Home Premium can keep personal files, Windows settings, and applications.
   - **D. Correct:** Windows 8 can keep personal files, Windows settings, and applications.
2. **Correct answers:** A, C, and D
   - **A. Correct:** The hard disk must have at least 20 GB of free disk space. It only has 16 GB.

   - **B. Incorrect:** The processor is compatible at 1 GHz.
   - **C. Correct:** The screen resolution must be at least 1024 x 768. Something will need to be upgraded to make it compatible, which might or might not be possible.
   - **D. Correct:** To install a 64-bit operating system requires at least 2 GB of RAM.
3. **Correct answer:** D
   - **A. Incorrect:** The only edition of Windows 8.1 that supports all of these features is Windows 8.1 Enterprise.
   - **B. Incorrect:** The only edition of Windows 8.1 that supports all of these features is Windows 8.1 Enterprise.
   - **C. Incorrect:** The only edition of Windows 8.1 that supports all of these features is Windows 8.1 Enterprise.
   - **D. Correct:** The only edition of Windows 8.1 that supports all of these features is Windows 8.1 Enterprise.
4. **Correct answers:** B and D
   - **A. Incorrect:** Windows 7 Home Premium can be upgraded to Windows 8.1 Professional.
   - **B. Correct:** Windows 7 Enterprise cannot be upgraded to Windows 8.1 Professional. (It can be upgraded to Windows 8.1 Enterprise, though.)
   - **C. Incorrect:** Windows 7 Ultimate can be upgraded to Windows 8.1 Professional.
   - **D. Correct:** Windows 7 Professional (Volume License) cannot be upgraded to Windows 8.1 Professional.

Objective 1.2: Thought experiment

1. Windows 7 and Windows 8.
2. Because there are only five computers, it's best to use WET. USMT is intended for administrators who need to perform large-scale automated deployments, which this scenario is not.
3. It would be unwise to try to upgrade the hard drive and the graphics adapter in a computer that is as old as this one apparently is. Your best option is to copy the data from the computer and save it where it is needed. This could be on other computers, on an external hard drive, or on CDs and DVDs. You can still use the Windows XP machine, at least until it is no longer functional.

Objective 1.2: Review

1. **Correct answer:** B
   - **A. Incorrect:** Windows XP cannot be upgraded while keeping files and settings, just files.

- **B. Correct:** Windows 7 can be upgraded to Windows 8.1 while keeping files, settings, and applications. When upgrading from Windows XP to Windows 8.1, only personal files can be saved.
- **C. Incorrect:** Windows 7 can be upgraded to Windows 8.1 while keeping files, settings, and applications. When upgrading from Windows XP to Windows 8.1, only personal files can be saved.
- **D. Incorrect:** Windows 7 can be upgraded to Windows 8.1 while keeping files, settings, and applications. When upgrading from Windows XP to Windows 8.1, only personal files can be saved.

2. **Correct answers:** C and D
   - **A. Incorrect:** You cannot perform an installation on Windows 8.1 from a Windows To Go drive. Windows To Go is Windows on a USB drive and is portable.
   - **B. Incorrect:** The proper file name is Setup.exe, not Install.exe.
   - **C. Correct:** This is a valid way to install Windows 8.1.
   - **D. Correct:** This is a valid way to install Windows 8.1.
3. **Correct answers:** A and D
   - **A. Correct:** Windows To Go drives can only be created using Windows 8 or Windows 8.1 Enterprise.
   - **B. Incorrect:** Hibernate and sleep are disabled by default when using Windows To Go.
   - **C. Incorrect:** The USB drive must be compatible with Windows To Go.
   - **D. Correct:** For security reasons, Windows To Go blocks access to local drives by default.
4. **Correct answers:** B and C
   - **A. Incorrect:** Windows PE is used to boot a computer using a minimized operating system, often for the purpose of installing or repairing one.
   - **B. Correct:** DiskPart is a valid command-line tool for creating VHDs.
   - **C. Correct:** Disk Management is a valid graphical tool for creating VHDs.
   - **D. Incorrect:** SysPrep is a tool used before capturing an image of a reference computer to strip away personalized information such as the activation ID.

Objective 1.3: Thought experiment

1. Use WET to transfer the user's local profile to her domain profile.
2. Configure folder location.
3. Configure a roaming user profile.

Objective 1.3: Review

1. **Correct answer:** D
   - **A. Incorrect:** Choosing a different location for the default folders to save to will only change where they are saved. You can't configure three different places for one folder.
   - **B. Incorrect:** Roaming user profiles are used in domains. This would not solve the problem.
   - **C. Incorrect:** If you were to create accounts for each user, you could then apply passwords to protect those accounts.
   - **D. Correct:** You need to create an account for each user. The first time each user logs on, a user profile will be created. Then, each user will have his or her own secure place to save personal files, and the files won't be mixed together. (You'll have to move the existing files to the proper folders, too.)
2. **Correct answers:** A, C, and D
   - **A. Correct:** You must state how you will store and transfer the data prior to the migration.
   - **B. Incorrect:** Task sequences are part of the USMT and do not apply here.
   - **C. Correct:** Because you can start from either the old computer or the new one, this is a valid question that must be answered.
   - **D. Correct:** You must state what you want to transfer.
   - **E. Incorrect:** User profiles are automatically included and do not need to be manually called out.
3. **Correct answer:** C
   - **A. Incorrect:** Mandatory user profiles don't allow any changes to the profile to be saved.
   - **B. Incorrect:** The user can make changes during the session, but they won't be saved to the mandatory user profile.
   - **C. Correct:** This is the correct behavior.
   - **D. Incorrect:** This does not happen. These two terms refer to how to make a roaming user profile mandatory, but it doesn't work both ways.
4. **Correct answer:** A
   - **A. Correct:** The is the proper tab and dialog box.
   - **B. Incorrect:** Location is configured from the folder's Properties dialog box on the Location tab.
   - **C. Incorrect:** Location is configured from the folder's Properties dialog box on the Location tab.
   - **D. Incorrect:** Location is configured from the folder's Properties dialog box on the Location tab.

CHAPTER 2

Configure hardware and applications

It is fitting that what follows Objective 1, Install and upgrade to Windows 8.1, is Objective 2, Configure hardware and applications. That's most likely what you'll do immediately after an installation of Windows 8.1, no matter how large or small the deployment.

In this chapter, you'll learn the various methods you can use to install and manage devices and their device drivers and control access to them. You'll also learn how to manage users' access to the Windows Store. While doing these things, you'll explore a bit of Group Policy, including new options and settings created specifically for Windows 8 and Windows 8.1. You'll discover ways to manage, control, and secure Internet Explorer 11, too, again incorporating Group Policy. Finally, you'll learn how to configure Hyper-V (technically Client Hyper-V), which enables you to run multiple virtual machines on one computer.

Objectives in this chapter:

- Objective 2.1: Configure devices and device drivers
- Objective 2.2: Install and configure desktop apps and Windows Store apps
- Objective 2.3: Control access to local hardware and applications
- Objective 2.4: Configure Internet Explorer 11 and Internet Explorer for the desktop
- Objective 2.5: Configure Hyper-V

Objective 2.1: Configure devices and device drivers

Device drivers and computer hardware go hand in hand. Each requires the other to function properly. A long time ago, most devices came with their own device driver disk for installing the appropriate driver, but now driver installation is generally automatic. In most instances, the necessary device driver is available in the Windows 8.1 Driver Store (on the computer itself) or from Windows Update (on the Internet), and the driver obtained there works fine. Occasionally though, problems arise. This happens when a compatible Windows 8.1 device driver isn't available, when the installed driver doesn't function properly, or when the driver isn't approved by the Microsoft Windows Hardware Certification Program (and is thus unsigned).

This objective covers how to:

- Install and manage drivers with Device Manager
- Configure devices
- Use Sigverif.exe to manage unsigned drivers
- Use Pnputil.exe to manage the Driver Store
- Create a driver update policy

Install and manage drivers with Device Manager

You use Device Manager to view, install, uninstall, disable, and otherwise manage hardware devices. You can access Device Manager from a number of places, including by right-clicking the Start button and clicking Device Manager from the resulting list. You can also find it in the Computer Management Console, under the System Tools node. By default, the list is organized by the various types of devices as shown in Figure 2-1, but there are other viewing and sorting options.

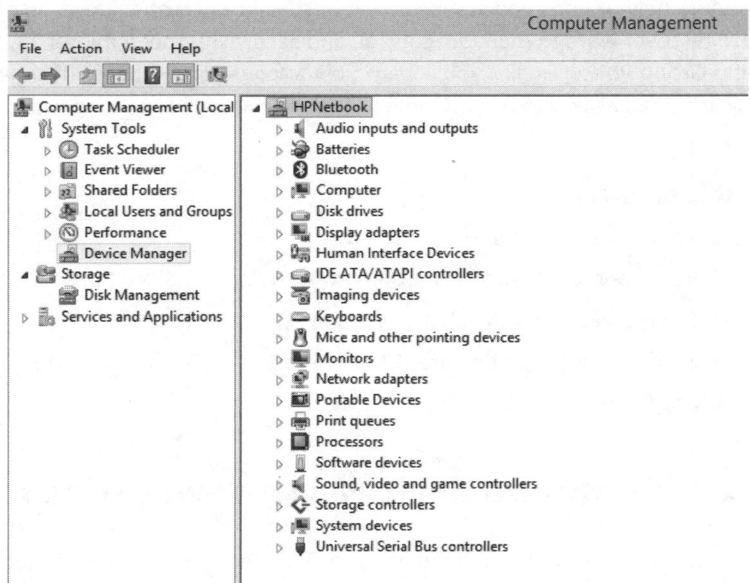

FIGURE 2-1 Device Manager is available from the Computer Management Console.

You can expand any node in Device Manager to view the installed device(s) that relate to the selected device family. In Figure 2-2, you can see that the Monitors entry only has one item listed, whereas Network Adapters has several. You can right-click any entry and select Properties to view information about its driver, among other things. You might see only four tabs for a simple device like a Plug-and-Play monitor (General, Driver, Details, and Events), or you might see more than that for more complicated devices like network adapters, also shown in Figure 2-2.

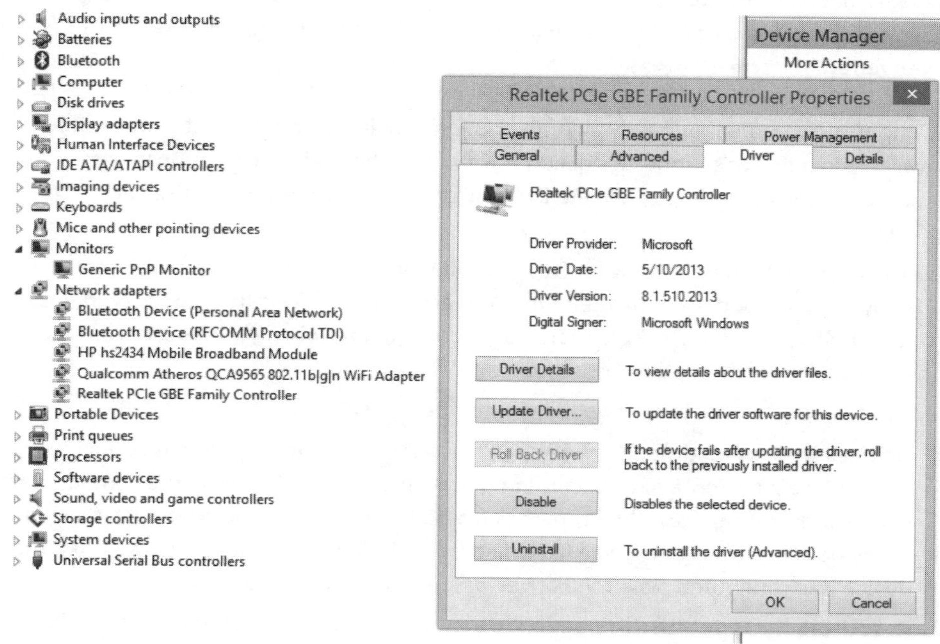

FIGURE 2-2 Expand any node, right-click the desired device, and click Properties to access its Properties dialog box.

Additionally, Device Manager offers four menus you can use to work with any of the installed devices:

- **File** Your profile holds files that store information about the changes you've made to the console. You can delete these files from Options in this menu.
- **Action** This menu enables you to access several commands, including Update Driver Software, Disable, Uninstall, Scan For Hardware Changes, Add Legacy Hardware, Properties, and Help.
- **View** This menu enables you to change how you view devices in Device Manager. You can opt to view devices by type or connection or to view resources by type or connection. You can also opt to show hidden devices and customize the console.
- **Help** This menu offers access to help topics from various places including the TechCenter website.

EXAM TIP

If you are presented a scenario in which you've made changes to a device driver in Device Manager, added hardware, updated a driver, or performed a related task but don't see the changes, you should click Action, Scan For Hardware Changes. You can also press the F5 key to refresh the screen.

It's important to note that nearly all of the options available from the Action menu are also available in a device's Properties dialog box or from the options that appear when you right-click an entry. For example, Update Driver, Disable, and Uninstall are available on the Driver tab.

You can change the default view for Device Manager when you need to access other options beyond a list of devices by their type. You access these views from the View menu. One option is Show Hidden Devices. There might come a time when you need to view hidden devices to troubleshoot something obscure.

Beyond this you can opt to change the view in these other ways:

- **Devices By Connection** This view can be useful when viewing what is connected to a virtual machine, organized according to how the various devices in the computer are connected. You can view the Properties dialog box of these devices by right-clicking (or by double-clicking). You can likely find helpful information here, such as when the device was configured, when the driver was installed and started, and so on.
- **Resources By Type** Use this option to view resources organized by how they are connected to other types of system resources: Direct Memory Access (DMA), Input/Output (IO), Interrupt Request (IRQ), and Memory. Only experienced system administrators should make changes here because a misstep can render the system inoperable. Consider searching for conflicts found by Device Manager before you do anything here.
- **Resources By Connection** This view is useful when you want to view the device hardware resources by DMA, IO, IRQ, and Memory for the purpose of troubleshooting and repairing problems. Consider searching for conflicts found by Device Manager before you do anything here.

If you need to troubleshoot hardware because you believe there is a conflict of some sort among resources, it's best to see if Device Manager knows of any by following these steps:

1. In Device Manager, select the view desired, either Resources By Type or Resources By Connection.
2. Double-click the suspected device.
3. Click the Resources tab.
4. Check for entries in the Conflicting Device List. See Figure 2-3.
5. Click OK to close.

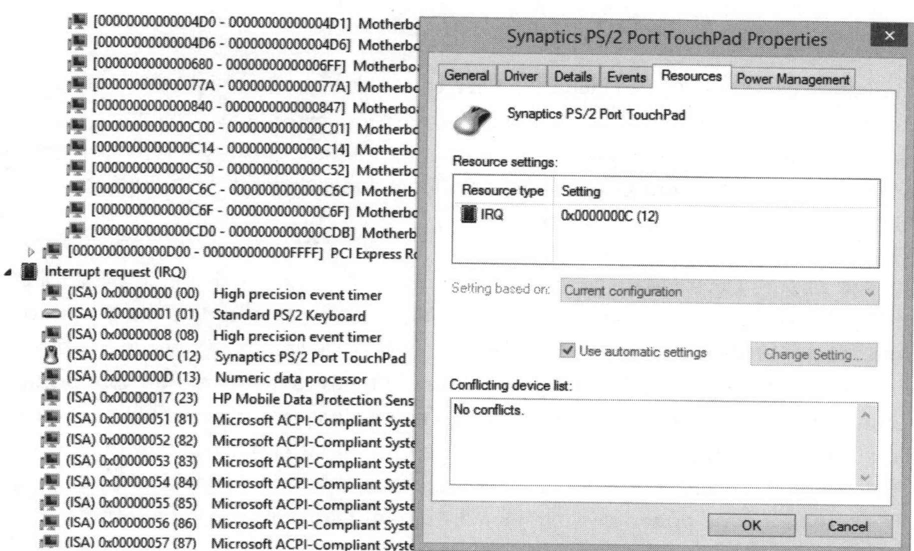

FIGURE 2-3 Let Device Manager determine conflicts.

Although there is a lot more to learn about drivers, including managing unsigned drivers, disabling driver signing at boot up, managing the drivers in the Driver Store, and even configuring Group Polices that define what types of drivers can be installed and by whom, we don't have enough space here to go into great detail. However, there's enough here to get you started, and we suggest you continue your studies using the resources on TechNet and other trusted places on the Internet.

EXAM TIP

As is the case with other software installations, you can't use a 32-bit driver for a 64-bit resource. You can't use a 64-bit driver to communicate with a 32-bit resource either.

Install and uninstall

There are several ways to install drivers when they aren't installed automatically or offered by Windows Update. One is by responding to a prompt from the Action Center. Although this is an end-user solution to a driver problem and not necessarily a network administrator solution, it's still an option, especially when working with a home user. Action Center can discover problems and search for solutions automatically, and when a solution is found, it offers it up.

Another option for installing a driver is to download it from the manufacturer's website and then double-click an executable file that contains the driver. You have to do this manually; there's no automated task in place to do it for you.

EXAM TIP

Updated drivers won't be downloaded over metered connections. You might see a question on the exam that asks something based on this scenario. Expect that sometimes a simple answer such as "The user is on a metered connection" can be asked through a large, complex scenario, perhaps one or two paragraphs long, that includes lots of information that isn't necessary for finding the solution.

Finally, you can use Device Manager. Because a driver will likely already be installed for a device, even if it doesn't work properly, much of the time you'll opt to update the driver. To get started, locate the device in Device Manager (try View > Devices by Type) and double-click the device. On the Driver tab, click Update Driver. In the Update Driver Software dialog box, choose how to locate the driver. If it's one you've downloaded and saved to your computer, click Browse My Computer For Driver Software. Otherwise, click Search Automatically For Updated Driver Software, which will automatically look for a driver in all of the usual places. The latter is a good option if you think a driver is available from Windows Update.

Once you've located the driver, you can install it. If this goes well, the driver will be updated. However, sometimes Windows responds to your request with a message that states that the best driver is already installed (or a driver can't be found), resulting in an unexpected complication. If Windows deems that the best driver is already installed, or if you want to install your own anyway, from the Properties dialog box in Device Manager, opt to uninstall the driver and make sure to select the Delete The Driver Software For The Device check box shown in Figure 2-4 (otherwise, Windows will keep reinstalling it).

IMPORTANT **MANUALLY UNINSTALL A PROBLEMATIC DEVICE DRIVER**

Sometimes, even when you tell Windows to delete the software for a device, that software will continue to reinstall itself when you opt to scan for new hardware in Device Manager. When this happens you'll have to delete the driver manually using the Pnputil.exe command-line tool, detailed later in this section, with the –f and –d switches.

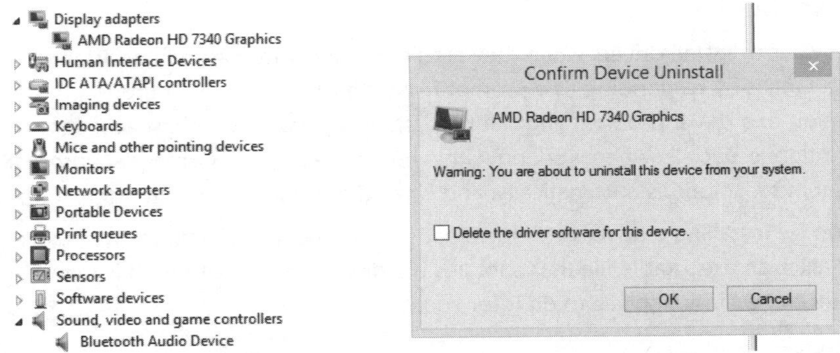

FIGURE 2-4 If necessary, delete the existing driver files to prevent Windows from attempting to update the driver again.

REAL WORLD **INSTALL LEGACY HARDWARE**

In many organizations, legacy hardware still plays a very important role in getting the job done. It might be a legacy printer, an infrared device, or even a modem. This hardware might not be detected automatically. There's an option in Device Manager that can help you install these kinds of devices. To do so, insert any installation media you have for the device and then follow these steps:

1. **Open Device Manager. On the Action tab, click Add Legacy Hardware.**
2. **Click Next on the Welcome page and then select one of these options:**
   - **Search For And Install The Hardware Automatically (Recommended)**
   - **Install The Hardware That I Manually Select From A List**
3. **Follow the resulting prompts. This might involve selecting a port for a printer, selecting the device from a list, or making other choices.**

Once installed, you can manage the device in Device Manager.

Disable and rollback

You use similar methods to disable and troubleshoot drivers as you do to update them. Disable is an option on the Driver tab of the device's Properties dialog box. When you disable a device, you turn it off. This is different from uninstalling a device. When the device is turned off, Windows can't use it and won't try to reactivate it. In contrast, if you uninstall a device such as a graphics or audio driver, Windows will reinstall the device on reboot in most instances. You might want to disable a device to determine if that specific device is causing a system conflict or problem. Additionally, you can disable devices that don't work properly or that you don't need to free up system resources.

There are instances when installing a new driver over an older driver causes more problems than it resolves. In these cases you can roll back the driver. The Roll Back Driver button is available only after you've installed a second driver, though; otherwise it is dimmed.

EXAM TIP

It's important to understand that the device driver rollback feature can only roll back to the previously installed driver. Thus, if you have driver A installed, then install driver B, and then install driver C, so when you roll back driver C it only rolls back to driver B (not to the original driver A).

Configure devices

With the proper driver installed you can now configure the installed devices. As is true with virtually any task in Windows 8.1, there are multiple ways to do this. There are two I'd like to introduce here: Devices and Printers and Device Stage. Although both are consumer and end-user tools, they can be of some use to network administrators.

Use Devices and Printers

Devices and Printers, available from Control Panel or by searching for it from the Start screen, offers a place to view connected devices including printers, mice, media devices, fax machines, and more. You can immediately discern if a device has a known problem because it will have an exclamation point over the top of it. You can right-click any device listed to configure device preferences, create a shortcut, troubleshoot the device, and view the device's properties.

Depending on what you click on the shortcut menu, you can configure all kinds of settings and preferences for the selected device. For instance, if you click Printer Properties for any installed printer, you can access more than just whether you want to print on both sides of the page or print a test page. You can also configure the following (among other things):

- **Sharing** Use this option to choose whether to share the printer and render print jobs on client computers. You can also opt to provide additional drivers to other workstations that need it.
- **Ports** Use this option to add, delete, and configure the port to which the printer is connected. You can also enable printer pooling and bidirectional support here.
- **Security** Use this option to choose the groups or users that are allowed or denied access to the printer.

This is a quick way to access device properties and configure those devices, but Devices and Printers really shines in its ability to easily add wireless printers and other wireless devices (even Bluetooth devices). You can't do that in Device Manager. Once those devices are found, the Internet Protocol (IP) or Media Access Control (MAC) address (or a unique identifier) is displayed as applicable. Of course, you can find network devices, including network printers, from here too.

To add a device using the Devices And Printers window, follow these steps:

1. Open Devices And Printers using any method.
2. Click Add A Device.
3. Click the desired device in the list and click Next. See Figure 2-5.

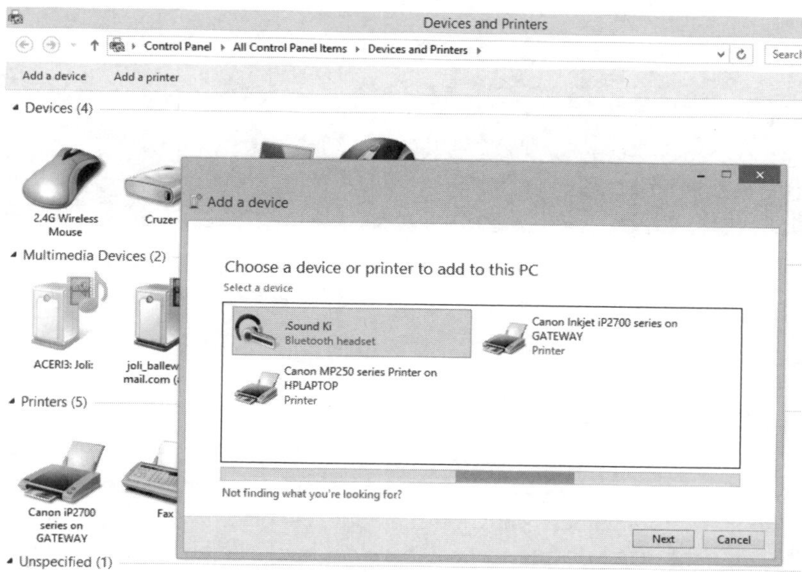

FIGURE 2-5 Use the Devices And Printers window to add wired, network, and wireless devices.

4. Wait while the driver installs and setup completes. The new device will appear in the Devices And Printers window.
5. In the Devices And Printers window, right-click the new device to access configuration options. You can click Properties to see the device's unique identifier and other data.

EXAM TIP

Don't let yourself miss the easiest questions on the exam! You might be asked where to install a wireless printer on a workgroup workstation "with the least amount of administrative effort," so make sure you understand the capabilities of the Devices And Printers window.

Use Device Stage

Sometimes you can double-click a device in the Devices And Printers window to access it in Device Stage. It has been my experience that Device Stage opens less and less frequently for installed devices, though. Double-clicking a printer often opens the print queue, not Device Stage. Double-clicking a Bluetooth headset opens its Properties dialog box. Only rarely does Device Stage open for a device, but for the sake of covering it, Figure 2-6 shows Device Stage for a wireless mouse. You can see that there are options to download software, find solutions, and even register your mouse. This feature appears to be fading out, though.

FIGURE 2-6 Device Stage offers another method to access device properties.

Device drivers have the potential to damage a computer if they are laced with hidden malware by dishonest programmers. Thus, a technology is in place to test, approve, and then sign drivers to verify they are safe to install and have not been altered since the testing and approval process has been completed. Once approved, the drivers are digitally signed with a digital signature by an approved authority (often a trusted organization or publisher). This signature is created using a cryptographic algorithm and is appended to the device driver. This verifies that the driver is authentic and secure when you get it, because the algorithm is verified.

Unsigned drivers can be the cause of various computer problems, especially those that are difficult to diagnose. You can check if any unsigned drivers are installed on any computer by using the command-line tool Sigverif.exe. To perform this check, follow these steps:

1. Right-click the Start button and click Command Prompt (Admin).
2. At the command prompt, type **sigverif.exe** and press Enter.
3. Click Start to run File Signature Verification and then view the results. See Figure 2-7.
4. Click Close (not shown).

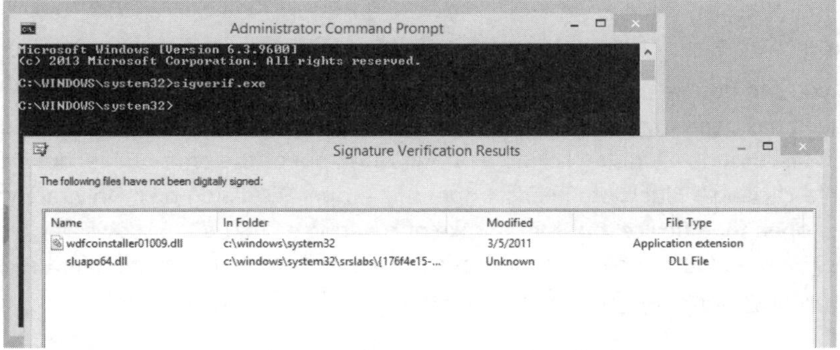

FIGURE 2-7 Use the command Sigverif.exe to see if there are any unsigned drivers on a computer.

If you find unsigned drivers, you might be able to look at the path of those drivers to see where they are saved and perhaps what device they are installed with or refer to. This might help you uncover which device is causing difficult-to-diagnose system problems.

> ***MORE INFO*** **LEARN MORE ABOUT DIGITAL SIGNATURES**
>
> **For more information about digital signatures and signed drivers, refer to the MSDN article at *http://msdn.microsoft.com/en-us/library/windows/hardware/ff543743(v=vs.85).aspx.***

So, just how do unsigned drivers get on a system? For the most part, they either are installed by the computer manufacturer or installed by the end user. If Windows suspects a driver has been tampered with or knows the driver is unsigned, the user will receive a prompt and, in many cases, have the option to install it anyway.

Here are the three messages offered for unsigned drivers:

- **Windows Can't Verify The Publisher Of This Driver** Either there is no digital signature or the signature has not been verified by a trusted authority (an organization or publisher that has been authorized to sign). If you must install the driver, make sure it is from the manufacturer of the device and that you download it from the manufacturer's website.
- **This Driver Has Been Altered** The driver has been verified by a trusted authority but has been altered since then. The protected checksum (a value stored with the device dependent on the content) is not what it is expected to be. It might have been altered on purpose to include malware, or it might have been altered by the manufacturer. If you must install the driver, make sure it is from the manufacturer of the device and that you download it from the manufacturer's website.
- **Windows Cannot Install This Driver** Windows 8.1 64-bit operating systems will not install a device driver that has been altered since it was verified or one that has not been verified at all. It is possible to bypass these digital signature requirements, but you must reboot the computer in Advanced mode.

If there is no way around the inability to install an unsigned driver, you can disable digital signing, reboot the computer, and install it anyway using PC Settings, on the Update And Recovery tab, under Recovery options. As shown in Figure 2-8, under Advanced Startup, click Restart Now.

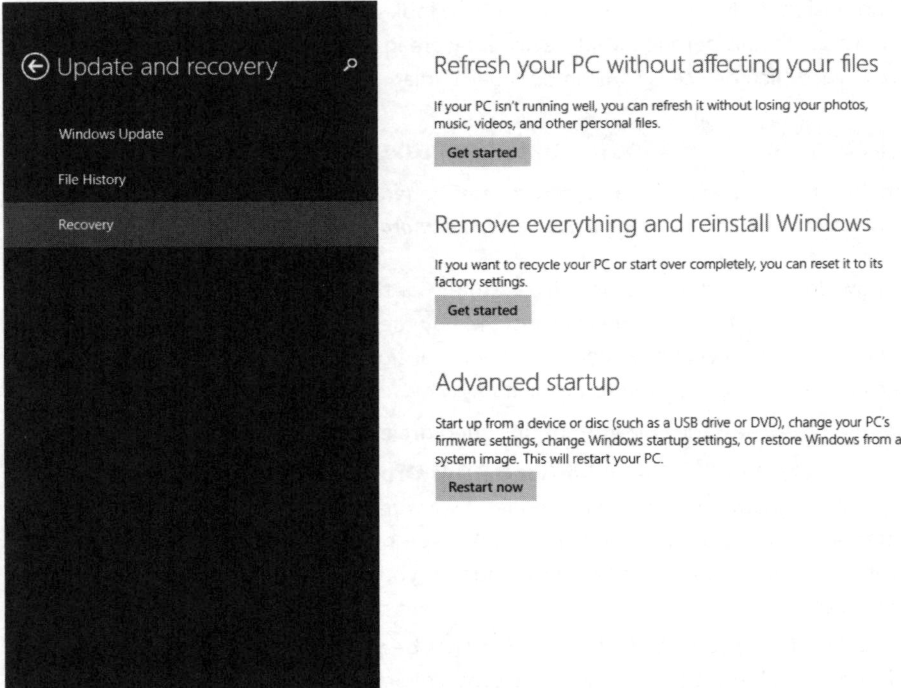

FIGURE 2-8 To disable driver signing you must restart the computer in Advanced mode.

After you click Restart Now on the screen shown in Figure 2-8, follow these steps:

1. Click Troubleshoot.
2. Click Advanced Options.
3. Click Startup Settings.
4. Click Restart.
5. After the computer restarts into the boot menu, press 7 on the keyboard. (The computer restarts.)

You can now install unsigned drivers as necessary. When complete, restart the machine normally.

EXAM TIP

Windows 8.1 64-bit operating systems block the installation of unsigned drivers by default. This might be the answer required for a much larger question, perhaps a scenario about device driver installation, in a domain, with no changes to Group Policy, and so on.

Use Pnputil.exe to manage the Driver Store

Windows 8.1 contains a Driver Store to hold device drivers that have been tested and approved by Microsoft and thus digitally signed. The Driver Store can be updated via Windows Update and other means. When you connect a device, this is where Windows looks for a driver first. If it doesn't find one, it searches Windows Update. This method works in most circumstances, but sometimes Windows installs a driver it deems best and there's no way to uninstall it, update it, or successfully delete the driver files by using Device Manager or other methods.

If you know this is the case for a specific device, you can install a driver manually before connecting the device. To do this you use the Pnputil.exe command at an elevated command prompt. You can also use the command to manage the Driver Store, including adding, deleting, and listing driver packages. A driver package consists of all of the data needed to install the driver, including but not limited to the following:

- **Driver files** Generally this is a dynamic link library (DLL) with the .sys file extension.
- **Installation files** These files have the file extension .inf and contain the installation files.
- **Driver Catalog file** Included with the installation files, this contains the information related to the driver's digital signature. This is a .cat file.
- **Additional files** These could be icons, device property pages, and even items related to an installation wizard.

The syntax for the Pnputil.exe command is to type **pnputil.exe –a <path to the driver>\<drivername>.inf.** The following are some parameters to consider:

- -a to specify the path to the driver's .inf file
- -d to delete a specific .inf file
- -f to force the deletion of a specific .inf file

If you are interested in seeing the DriverStore folder, navigate to C:\Windows\System32\DriverStore\FileRepository.

> ***IMPORTANT*** **CHOICES FOR UPDATING NEW DRIVERS**
>
> **There are two schools of thought regarding updating drivers. You either want the latest and the greatest or you want to leave well enough alone (if it ain't broke, don't fix it). However, in the real world, you don't always get to decide what you want to do with regard to a driver. Sometimes, a driver is installed as part of a Windows Update, and you might not know you've opted to install it. If this happens, you'll have to roll back the driver by using Device Manager and then open Windows Update, locate the offending update, and uninstall it. Then, you should hide the update so it doesn't get reinstalled the next time around. The general steps are as follows (after you've rolled back the driver in Device Manager):**

1. Open Windows Update.
2. Click View Update History.
3. Click Installed Updates.
4. Select the update and click Uninstall. Click Uninstall to verify and then click Close when prompted.
5. Return to Windows Update (click the Back arrow twice) and locate the update you just uninstalled.
6. Deselect the update.
7. Right-click the update and select Hide Update (see Figure 2-9).

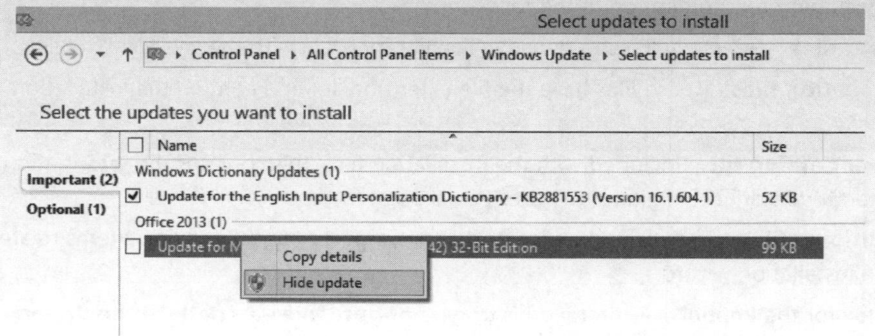

FIGURE 2-9 Hide updates you don't want to install.

Create a driver update policy

When working with a lot of users and computers, it is unsafe to leave users in charge of installing their own driver updates. You, as a network administrator, need to control what happens with driver updates by creating a driver policy. You might institute a driver policy that doesn't allow anyone to install any device drivers until something stops working. Your driver policy might be the exact opposite of this, with your reasoning being that because drivers often address problems, offer new features, and even improve device performance, all updates (once tested) should be installed. Generally though, it isn't this cut and dried. You'll test and install some updates and you won't worry with others.

Whatever you decide, you should set up a test lab, even it if is small, to try device drivers before you deploy them. In addition, just to be on the safe side, you should opt to install drivers only after a couple of weeks have passed since their availability so that any problems can be resolved by the manufacturer, if any exist. You should institute a rule regarding unsigned drivers or drivers that offer prompts during installation, too.

You can also apply Group Policy to manage what users can do with regard to driver installation. Here you'll experience one item you can change: By default, only members of the Administrators group are allowed to install new device drivers on the system. If you enable this in Group Policy, then members of the Users group can install new drivers for device setup classes that you specify. If you disable it (or do not configure it), only members of the Administrators group can install new device drivers on the system. There are other settings to explore beyond what you find in the Driver Installation node you see here, as you'll see in the next set of steps.

To sample how group policies can be applied to control driver installation on a local machine, follow these steps:

1. Open the Local Group Policy Editor. You can type **gpedit.msc** at the Start screen and click the first entry for gpedit in the results list if you are unfamiliar with this feature.
2. Expand the following nodes: Computer Configuration, Administrative Templates, System, and Driver Installation.
3. Double-click Allow Non-Administrators To Install Drivers For These Device Setup Classes, shown in Figure 2-10.

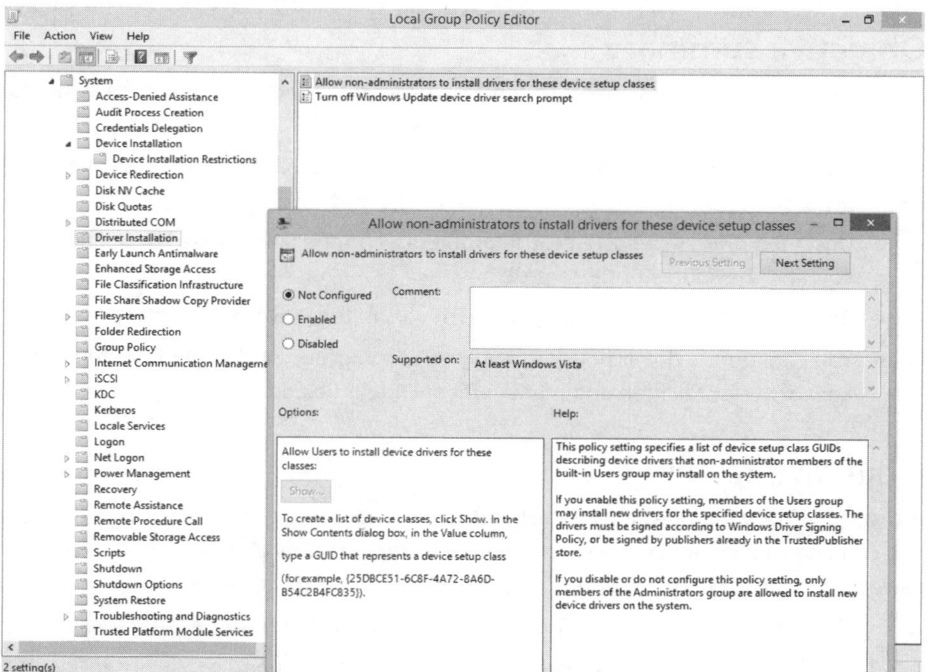

FIGURE 2-10 Explore group policies that relate to driver and device installation.

You can use this group policy and setting to restrict or enable access both on local machines and in domains.

Thought experiment

Working with drivers in a test lab

In this thought experiment, apply what you've learned about this objective. You can find answers to these questions in the "Answers" section at the end of this chapter.

You are the network administrator of a large organization that is part of an Active Directory domain. You do extensive testing of hardware and software before you deploy any device drivers to the computers in the organization. Answer the following questions regarding the test lab:

1. **What should you configure so that your test lab employees can install unsigned drivers on their 64-bit test machines?**
2. **How do you access those configuration options?**
3. **What command-line tool can be used in the lab to manage the Driver Store? What command-line parameters enable you to permanently delete a specific driver from the Driver Store?**

Objective summary

- Devices need device drivers to function properly. Device drivers can be signed or unsigned, 32-bit or 64-bit.
- Device Manager enables you to easily install, update, disable (devices), and roll back drivers.
- Unsigned drivers can often cause problems, and the Sigverif.exe command can help you find the source of those problems.
- Pnputil.exe can help you manage the drivers in the Driver Store on the local machine.
- You configure a driver policy to apply to a workgroup or domain to determine exactly how driver installation and management should be addressed.

Objective review

Answer the following questions to test your knowledge of the information in this objective. You can find the answers to these questions and explanations of why each answer choice is correct or incorrect in the "Answers" section at the end of this chapter.

1. What does it mean when a driver is digitally signed? (Choose all that apply.)
   - **A.** The manufacturer has extensively tested the driver and can verify with authority that it is safe to install.
   - **B.** The driver has undergone testing by Microsoft, has been approved as safe to install, and is unaltered.

C. The driver is a 32-bit driver.

D. The driver has not been altered since it was signed by a qualified authority.

2. How are drivers automatically installed when a device is first connected? (Choose all that apply.)

   A. Windows installs a driver it finds from Windows Update.

   B. Windows installs a driver if it's found in the Driver Store.

   C. Windows downloads a driver from the manufacturer's website and runs the downloaded executable file.

   D. Device Manager installs the driver from the Driver Store.

3. Your computer runs a 64-bit edition of Windows 8.1, and you have a camera whose manufacturer has only supplied a 32-bit driver disk. Windows does not install the driver automatically the first time you connect it. What can you do? (Choose all that apply.)

   A. Visit the manufacturer's website and hope a 64-bit driver exists. If it does, download and install it manually.

   B. Restart the computer in Advanced mode and disable driver signing. When the computer reboots, manually install the driver by using Device Manager.

   C. Use Device Manager to browse to the driver and initiate the installation yourself.

   D. Wait for the manufacturer to create a compatible device driver and for Microsoft to test it. Watch the Action Center and Windows Update notifications carefully to know when this is available.

4. You are trying to diagnose a performance problem on a client machine. After talking to the user about what has changed lately, if anything, you find out that he recently purchased and installed a new scanner and installed the drivers for it. He recalls some sort of prompt that contained a warning, but he can't remember what it said. What do you try first?

   A. In Device Manager, locate the resources the scanner uses and see if there is a conflict. If you find a conflict, reassign the conflicting resources so the scanner can run properly.

   B. Restart the computer in Advanced mode and disable driver signing. This will allow the problematic driver to run without restrictions.

   C. Run Sigverif.exe at an elevated command prompt.

   D. In Device Manager, locate the scanner and roll back the driver.

5. Where can you easily install a wireless printer for a client that is part of a workgroup?

   A. In Device Manager.

   B. You won't have to; Windows will detect the printer and install it automatically.

   C. In Device Stage.

   D. In the Devices And Printers window.

Objective 2.2: Install and configure desktop apps and Windows Store apps

In this objective you learn how to install and configure desktop applications and Windows Store apps. For most end users, installation involves running an installation program for a desktop app or acquiring an app from the Windows Store. You can download and install desktop applications from the Internet, too, and even from network shares. Installation hasn't changed much, except for the process of getting applications from the Windows Store. However, sometimes you need to install an application from a command prompt, and you'll learn how to do that here using the MSIExec command. Beyond that, you'll learn how to configure default programs and file associations when multiple apps exist for performing a task or viewing data and how to manage your users' access to the Windows Store.

This objective covers how to:

- Configure default program settings and file associations
- Install and repair applications
- Manage access to the Windows Store
- Configure default program settings and file associations

When a user performs certain tasks, such as opening an email attachment (a picture, PDF file, video file, spreadsheet, and so on), inserting a DVD, or even clicking a hyperlink in a document or email message, something specific happens. A program opens, a window opens, a web browser opens, and so on. The user can have multiple apps available that can open a single data type. As an example, clicking a link in an email message causes a web browser to open, but that web browser might be the Internet Explorer 11 app, Internet Explorer on the desktop, or even a third-party app like Google Chrome or Mozilla Firefox. In some instances, what happens is not what the user wants or expects. Beyond that, it might not be what you, as a network administrator, want either.

One way to configure which app opens when a user clicks a specific type of data is to configure default programs. To get started, open the Default Programs window from Control Panel. This is most easily accessed when Control Panel is configured to show large or small icons. See Figure 2-11.

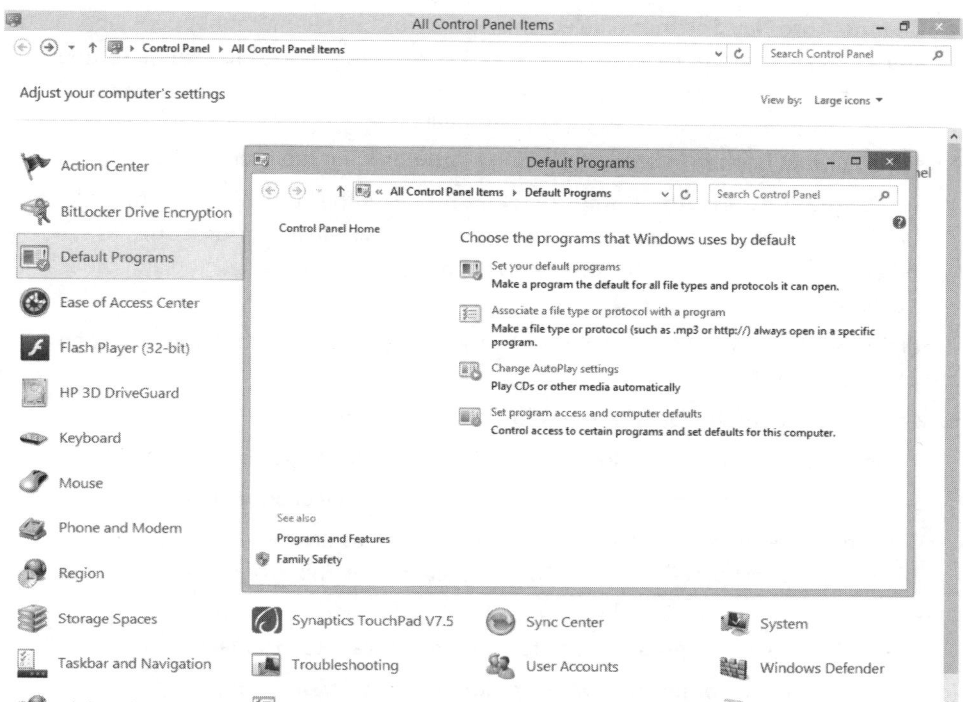

FIGURE 2-11 Open the Default Programs window to access the option to set your default programs.

EXAM TIP

Some applications will name themselves as the default program without asking the user for permission or at least hide the prompt asking for permission in an obscure place the user might not notice while performing the installation. It might also happen when you open the program for the first time. You'll have to open the Default Programs window to change the default back to what you want.

As you can see in Figure 2-11, there are four options:

- **Set Your Default Programs** Select this option to make a program the default for all file types and protocols it can open. This is one of the quickest ways to configure a default program and its file associations.
- **Associate A File Type Or Protocol With A Program** Use this option to select a single, specific file type or protocol, such as .bmp, to open with a specific program, such as Microsoft Paint. In this example, this won't cause all picture files to open in the designated program, just one type of picture file (.bmp). This can be helpful when you want to call out one file type that has other, similar file types you do not want to reassociate.

- **Change AutoPlay Settings** Select this option to configure what happens when CDs and DVDs are inserted into the disk drive. This is where you'll go to change settings users have put in place when they selected the option in a prompt to "always" do something specific when a certain type of media is inserted. This also lets you set what should always happen instead of offering a prompt to let the user decide.
- **Set Program Access And Computer Defaults** Use this setting to control access to specific programs that relate to specific activities the user will perform, such as sending email, and to specify what programs are available from the desktop and other locations.

To configure any of these four options, you click what you want to configure and then construct the settings for it.

To set a default program, follow these steps:

1. In the Default Programs window, click Set Your Default Programs.
2. Select the program to configure as a default. You can select apps and desktop apps.
3. Click Set This Program As The Default to configure it as the default for all compatible file types and click OK or click Choose Defaults For This Program and continue to step 4.
4. Clear the check boxes for any file types you do not want to include and click Save.

To associate a file type or protocol with a program, follow these steps:

1. In the Default Programs window, click Associate A File Type Or Protocol With A Program.
2. Select the file type or protocol in the left pane.
3. Click Change Program.
4. Select the desired program from the list or click More Options if you don't see what you're looking for.

To change AutoPlay settings, follow these steps:

1. In the Default Programs window, click Change AutoPlay Settings.
2. Use the drop-down lists to set the defaults for each media type.
3. Click Save.

To set program access and computer defaults, follow these steps:

1. In the Default Programs window, click Set Program Access And Computer Defaults.
2. Select one of the following:
   - Microsoft Windows, to configure all Microsoft Windows apps to be set as the default. If you've already set a program such as Microsoft Outlook as a default, that will not be changed. Click OK.
   - Non-Microsoft Windows, to remove access to all Microsoft apps including Internet Explorer, any Microsoft-based email program, Windows Media Center, Windows Media Player, and so on. Click OK.

- Custom, to select exactly what you'd like to use for the five items shown in Figure 2-12. Click OK.

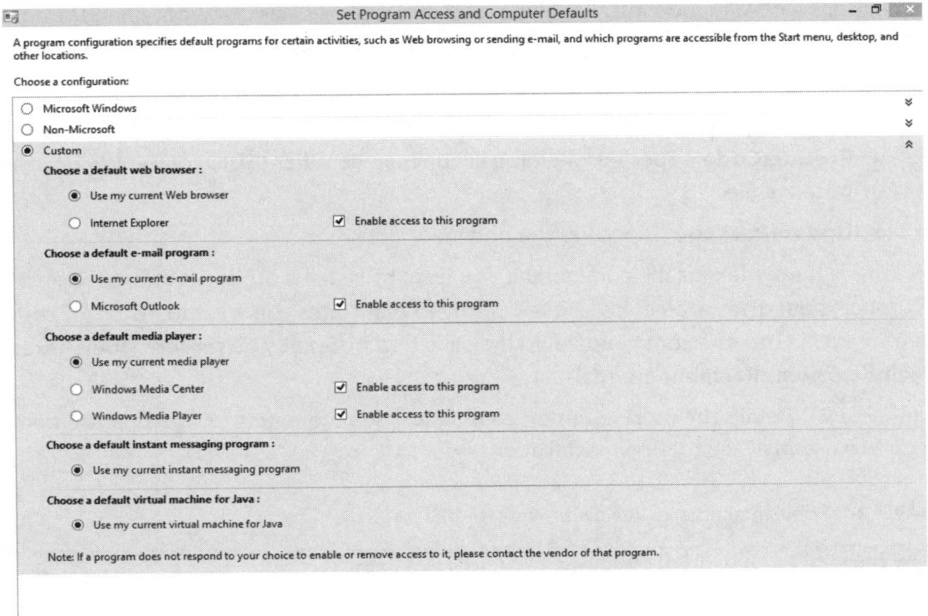

FIGURE 2-12 Configure program access and computer defaults.

Install and repair applications

There are several ways to install and repair applications. You are probably aware of the traditional options: You can insert the application CD or DVD and choose the repair option, uninstall an application from Control Panel and then reinstall it by using other methods, or even select the program in Control Panel and click Repair. Here you'll learn about two lesser-known options: using Windows Installer files (MSIExec) and the Application Compatibility Toolkit (ACT).

> ***MORE INFO*** **TRY REPAIRING USING THE TRADITIONAL OPTIONS FIRST**
>
> **As a first line of defense, especially on a workstation, you should try the more familiar options when an application needs to be reinstalled or repaired. Some of the options with which you might already be familiar include running the Program Compatibility Troubleshooter available from Windows 8.1; uninstalling, reinstalling, and automatically updating Windows Store apps from PC Settings; and even uninstalling desktop applications using Control Panel when a program simply won't work.**

MSIExec

MSIExec provides a way for network administrators to install, modify, and perform other operations with Windows Installer files at a command line. This involves typing the command **MSIExec** along with the appropriate command-line options. Before starting, you need to understand a few terms:

- **Package** Specifies the name (and location) of the Windows Installer package file.
- **ProductCode** Specifies the globally unique identifier (GUID) of the Windows Installer package file.
- **UpdatePackage** Specifies the update to apply.

This is the syntax for the command if you want to install a product: msiexec /i {Package | ProductCode}. The parameter /i is the command that states you want to install (or configure) a package. In use, the command could look like this: **msiexec /i \\servername\sharename \windowsinstallerfilename.msi**.

Table 2-1 details the most common command-line parameters for MSIExec. Remember, you can use MSIExec to repair installations, too.

TABLE 2-1 Popular command-line parameters for MSIExec

Parameter	Additional commands	What it does
/a		Applies the administrative installation option.
/f	Below are the additional commands you can use with /f and may be used as so: msiexec /fpecms Example .msi	Enables the use of various repair parameters and is used as so: msiexec /f [p][o][e][d][c][a][u][m][s][v]{Package | ProductCode}
	P	Reinstalls only if file is missing.
	O	Reinstalls if file is missing or if an older version is installed.
	E	Reinstalls if file is missing or an equal or older version is installed.
	D	Reinstalls if file is missing or a different version is installed.
	C	Reinstalls if file is missing or the stored checksum does not match the calculated value.
	A	Forces all files to be reinstalled.
	U	Rewrites all required user-specific registry entries.
	m	Rewrites all required computer-specific registry entries.
	s	Overwrites all existing shortcuts.
	v	Runs from source and recaches the local package.
/x		Uninstalls a product.

Parameter	Additional commands	What it does
/j	Below are commands you can use with /j and may be used as so: msiexec /j [{u | m}] Package	Advertises a product.
	U	Advertises a product to the current user.
	M	Advertises a product to all users of the computer.
/p		Applies an update.

EXAM TIP

It's highly likely that you'll be asked to verify the proper syntax for an MSIExec command or to choose which command and parameters should be used. Make sure to learn all of the command-line options and parameters offered in Table 2-1.

Explore the Application Compatibility Toolkit

The Application Compatibility Toolkit (ACT) helps you determine whether the applications, devices, and computers in your organization are compatible with Windows 8.1. You can use it to obtain compatibility information from Microsoft and software vendors (and if desired, to share what you learn). In a large organization you can use ACT to do the following:

- Take an inventory of applications, devices, and computers so you know exactly what you want to test.
- Test the compatibility of the applications in your organization.
- Manage the data you create during testing.
- Analyze available compatibility information.
- Prioritize the solutions and fix compatibility issues.

EXAM TIP

ACT only tests desktop applications because apps from the Windows Store are already known to be compatible with Windows 8.1.

If you recall from Chapter 1, "Install and Upgrade to Windows 8.1," the Application Deployment Toolkit, which is a free download from Microsoft, contains ACT. ACT enables you to discover what applications are incompatible with Windows 8.1 and create "shims" to fix those problems. ACT can also help you create additional solutions, such as when applications try to write to protected areas of the operating system when they don't need to (or shouldn't).

To prepare ACT you must do the following (at a high level):

- Create and configure an ACT database (which requires you to have and use Microsoft SQL Server or Microsoft SQL Server Express. The path to this is %SystemDrive%\ProgramData\Applications Compatibility Toolkit\CreateDB.sql.
- Configure the proper permissions at the share level and folder level that are required by the ACT LOG Processing Service.
- Work through the five tasks in the previous bulleted list using ACT and the database you created.
- Run the Application Compatibility Manager and work through the setup wizard.

It's likely that you won't be tested on how to set up, configure, and use ACT and work with SQL Services databases; these are tasks required of experienced domain network administrators. However, you might see questions related to the steps involved in using the Application Compatibility Manager to perform the inventory, collect data, and analyze what you collect. To learn more about Application Compatibility, refer to *http://technet.microsoft.com/en-us/windows/aa905066.*

EXAM TIP

You can verify the compatibility of your application, device, and computer with a new version of the Windows operating system by using ACT; test your applications for issues related to User Account Control (UAC) by using the Standard User Analyzer (SUA) tool; and test your web applications and websites for compatibility with new releases and security updates to Windows Internet Explorer by using the Internet Explorer Compatibility Test Tool.

Manage access to the Windows Store

By default, all users can access the Windows Store. You might want to change this behavior. There are two ways to modify access. You can configure it so users can't access the Windows Store at all, or you can limit their use by allowing them to acquire only specific apps.

Disable access using Group Policy Editor

To disable access completely, you'll use the Group Policy Editor. To restrict access to only some of the Windows Store content, you'll use AppLocker. We look at these two features in detail next. Before that, though, there is one more Windows Store setting you need to know about, and that is how to disable app updates from the Windows Store (they are installed automatically in Windows 8.1).

To disable updates on a single client computer, follow these steps:

1. From the Start screen, click the Store app.
2. Press Windows key+I to open the Settings charm.

3. Click App Updates.
4. Move the slider under Automatically Update My Apps from Yes to No (see Figure 2-13).

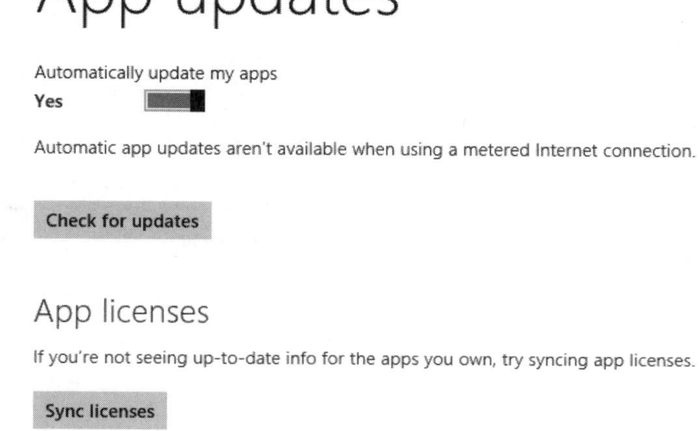

FIGURE 2-13 Disable app updates using the Store's Settings.

If you need to manage a group of computers in a workgroup or domain, you'll need to apply group policies. The location of the Group Policy setting is the same whether you use the Local Group Policy or the related Group Policy Management Console (GPMC) on your domain server. The path to the Local Group Policy setting (in Gpedit.msc) is Computer Configuration, Administrative Templates, Windows Components, Store. If you enable the setting Turn Off Automatic Download Of Updates On Win8 Machines, updates will be disabled.

Disable access using group policies

You can't disable access to the Windows Store from the Settings charm like you can disable app updates. To disable access you must use the applicable Group Policy editor. You might want to do this if your employees are downloading and installing games, among other things. You might need to disable access to meet a company's security needs. Whatever the case, to disable access to the Windows Store using the Local Group Policy Editor, follow these steps:

1. At the Start screen, type **gpedit.msc** and click it in the results. (You could also use the Run box on the desktop.)
2. In the Group Policy Editor, expand the following nodes: Computer, User Configuration, Administrative Templates, Windows Components, Store.
3. Double-click Turn Off The Store Application.
4. Select Enabled, as shown in Figure 2-14.
5. Click OK.

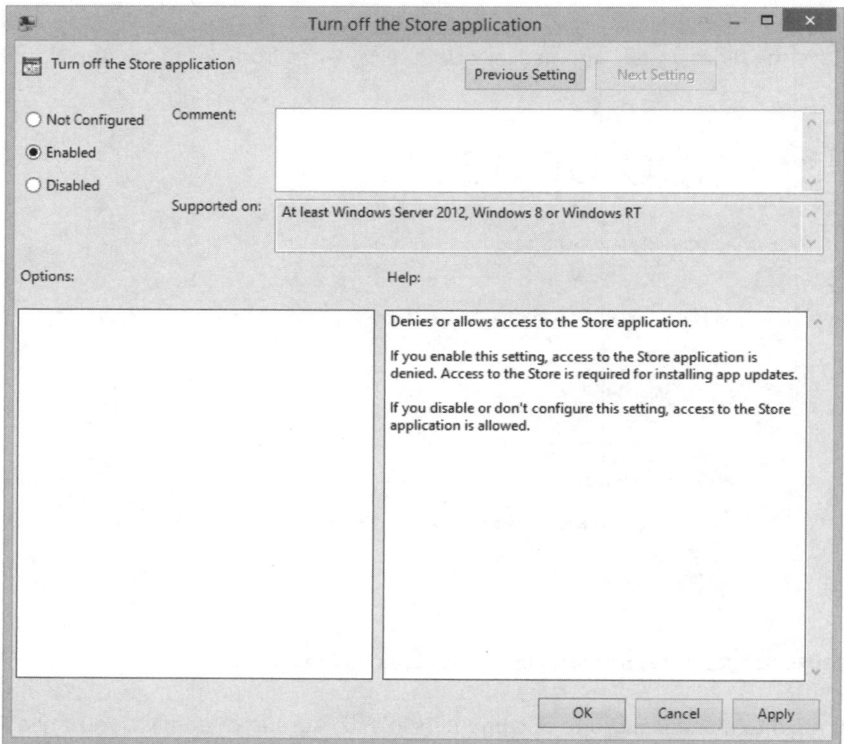

FIGURE 2-14 Turn off the Store application in the appropriate Group Policy editor.

EXAM TIP

There will be questions on the exam that ask how to open all manner of features by using various text-based shortcuts. For instance, instead of searching for the Local Group Policy Editor on the Start screen of a workstation computer, you might be expected to know you can also use Windows key+R, and in the Run box that opens, type **gpedit.msc**. So, as you work through this book and perform any task, know that there are likely other ways to do it.

Here are a few examples you can type in the Run box or on the Start screen to open a few of the popular Administrative and Computer Management tools: File Signature Verification Tool = sigverif; Group Policy Editor = gpedit.msc; Local Security Settings = secpol.msc; System Configuration Utility = msconfig; Task Manager = taskmgr; Computer Management = compmgmt.msc; Event Viewer = eventvwr.msc; Performance Monitor = perfmon.msc; Disk Management = diskmgmt.msc. To find more, perform a web search for "List Run command for Windows 8".

EXAM TIP

Users get apps from the Windows Store, but that's not the only place they can be acquired. In an enterprise environment, network administrators often use a technique called sideloading (which must be enabled in Group Policy) to install apps they create onto the organization's computers. Although sideloading is no longer listed as an objective for this exam, it's possible a question or two might slip through. Look for commands like import-module.appx and others that end in the .appx file format. Remember, too, that this is a Windows PowerShell command.

Thought experiment

Disallow access to specific programs

In this thought experiment, apply what you've learned about this objective. You can find answers to these questions in the "Answers" section at the end of this chapter.

You are a network administrator for a small company that runs Windows 7 on six machines and Windows 8 on four more. There are eight employees. The network is not part of an Active Directory domain. You have found that the general staff is watching DVDs while at work. You want to disable access to both Windows Media Center and Windows Media Player on the computers the staff members use, while leaving them available on the bosses' computers. You already have restrictions in place to prevent staff members from installing their own media applications. Apply what you've learned in this objective to disable access to these default programs. Note that you do not want to limit what web browser the staff uses or make other forced changes to the existing application configuration.

1. Is it possible to put these limitations in place?
2. If so, what window do you open in Control Panel to make these changes, and what option in that window gives you access to options to make these programs inaccessible on the computers the staff uses?
3. What type of configuration would you choose when making these changes (Microsoft Windows, Non-Microsoft, or Custom)?

Objective summary

- Configure default settings and file associations to configure how specific file types should open.
- Disable access to specific apps from the Set Program Access And Computer Defaults window.
- Limit or disable access to the Windows Store by using Group Policy.

- Use MSIExec at a command line to install and repair applications.
- Explore the Application Compatibility Toolkit (ACT) and know it can be used to inventory the enterprise, test applications for compatibility, and help decide how to shim incompatible applications, among other things.

Objective review

Answer the following questions to test your knowledge of the information in this objective. You can find the answers to these questions and explanations of why each answer choice is correct or incorrect in the "Answers" section at the end of this chapter.

1. Which of the following commands can be used to repair an installation that is missing a file and also to overwrite all existing shortcuts?
   - **A.** msiexec /fps {Package | ProductCode}
   - **B.** msiexec /i {Package | ProductCode}
   - **C.** msiexec /fa {Package | ProductCode}
   - **D.** msiexec /x {Package | ProductCode}
2. How do you keep the Store app from installing app updates automatically on a single workstation?
   - **A.** Use Local Security Policy to configure the setting.
   - **B.** Access the feature to disable this from Control Panel, Default Programs windows, under Set Your Default Programs.
   - **C.** At an elevated command prompt, type **msiexec –f –d WindowsStore**.
   - **D.** Open the Store app, open the Settings charm, and click App Updates to access the setting.
3. Where can users get Start screen apps? (Choose all that apply.)
   - **A.** From the Windows Store
   - **B.** Through a process called sideloading
   - **C.** By installing them on the machine using the command line msiexec –i –a *<path to app>*
   - **D.** From the ACT
4. A user complains that every time she inserts a USB drive, nothing happens. She wants to automatically open the drive in File Explorer. Which tool in Default Programs do you use to resolve this problem?
   - **A.** Set Program Access And Computer Defaults
   - **B.** Associate A File Type Or Protocol With A Program
   - **C.** Set Your Default Programs
   - **D.** Change AutoPlay Settings

Objective 2.3: Control access to local hardware and applications

As a network administrator, you need to control access to various applications and hardware (such as removable devices). You also need to be able to control the installation of devices, create rules specific to your organization, and understand which of the available tools are available for what operating system editions. There are four tools you'll learn about that can help you achieve this, each outlined in this section.

This objective covers how to:

- Configure application restrictions using AppLocker
- Configure application restrictions using Software Restriction Policies
- Manage installation of and access to removable devices
- Configure Assigned Access

NOTE **CONFIGURE STORE APPS**

To configure apps you get from the Store, open the app and then access the charms. Click Settings to see what options are available.

Configure application restrictions using AppLocker

It's difficult, if not impossible, to prevent users from accessing specific apps without using the tools designed for that purpose. AppLocker (also known as application control policies) can help in this regard. By using it, you can control what applications and files users can run by creating specific rules with the restrictions you want to apply.

IMPORTANT **WHEN YOU CAN APPLY APPLOCKER RULES**

AppLocker rules can only be applied to computers running Windows 7, Windows 8, Windows Server 2008 R2, and Windows Server 2012. If you need to create rules for other operating systems, you'll have to use an older technology, Software Restriction Policies, detailed in the next section.

On a high level, AppLocker, available inside the Group Policy Editor, is organized into four areas called rule collections, where you can create rules for the various types of applications in your workgroup or enterprise. You can see the four entries in the left pane in Figure 2-15. No rules exist by default. The four areas of rule collections (or containers) are executable files (.exe, .com), scripts (.ps2, .bat, .js, .cmd, .vbs), Windows Installer files (.msi, .mst, .msp), and packaged apps (.appx). AppLocker uses these rules to determine which applications users can run. The path is Computer Configuration, Windows Settings, Security Settings, Application Control Policies, AppLocker.

After you've decided which container to use for your rule (your choices are Executable Rules, Windows Installer Rules, Script Rules, or Packaged App Rules), you need to decide what kind of rule to create. There are three choices:

- **Publisher rules** Use this selection to create rules for applications that are digitally signed by a software publisher. This type of rule uses the digital certificate (publisher name and product name) and properties of the file (file name and file version). You can create the rule to apply to entire product suites.
- **Path rules** Use this selection to create rules that are based on the file or folder's installation path to specific application(s).
- **File hash rules** Use this selection to create rules based on the unique file hash that Windows cryptographically computes for each file. If a publisher updates a file, you must create a new rule, because the file is unique and will change with an update.

If you plan to use AppLocker, understand that once enabled and in use, AppLocker blocks all executable files, installer packages, and scripts unless otherwise noted. You therefore must create default rules that enable users to access the files needed to run their system first. After that, you can begin configuring what you do and do not want them to use.

MORE INFO **APPLOCKER FILE TYPES YOU CAN MANAGE**

In Windows Server 2008 R2 and Windows 7, you can manage four types of files: executable (.exe), Windows Installer (.msi and .msp), script (.bat, .cmd, .js, .ps1, and .vbs), and DLL (.dll and .ocx). Each of these file types is managed in its own rule collection. In Windows Server 2012 and Windows 8, you can also manage .mst and .appx files.

One way to apply AppLocker is to create a rule to deny access to a specific app that appears on the Start screen. You might want to do this on a machine if you find the users are playing games, using Skype, and so on. On a high level you'll need to open the applicable Group Policy Editor, create a Packaged App Rule, opt to automatically generate rules for everyone, and then locate an entry such as Microsoft.BingTravel. Using the wizard, opt to deny the app. You'll also need to enable and start the Application Identity Service on the local machine to which you want to apply the restriction. This is necessary because you could create a set of rules that doesn't allow access to files Windows needs to run.

EXAM TIP

If a question is posed that asks why a new group policy was not applied to a user's computer, the answer might be that the user needs to reboot her computer. You can tell the user to do that or you can configure a forced reboot in Group Policy with settings for how many minutes to let pass.

Configure application restrictions using Software Restriction Policies

In scenarios in which AppLocker won't work, you'll have to create your rules using Software Restriction Policies. This feature has been around a long time, so it is backward-compatible with Windows XP and Windows Vista and can also be used for Windows 7 and Windows 8 computers if you only want to use one feature to manage all the computers in your organization. Because the feature is older, it isn't as efficient as AppLocker, though. It can't generate rules automatically, for one thing, which means you must configure rules manually and one at a time.

As with AppLocker, you can create rules based on specific conditions:

- **Certificate rules** Use this choice to create rules for applications that are digitally signed by a software publisher. This type of rule uses the digital certificate (publisher name and product name) and properties of the file (file name and file version).
- **Hash rules** Use this option to create rules based on the unique file hash that Windows cryptographically computes for each file. If a publisher updates a file, you must create a new rule, because the file is unique and will change with an update.
- **Network zone rules** Use this choice to create rules for Windows Installer (.msi) packages that come from the Internet through Internet Explorer. You can configure rules based on the security zone the website is from.
- **Path rules** Use this option to create rules that are based on the file or folder's installation path to specific application(s).

To create a Software Restriction Policy you use Group Policy Editor. Navigate to a Group Policy object and then to Computer Configuration, Windows Settings, Security Settings, Software Restriction Policies. Right-click Software Restriction Policies and click New Software Restriction Policies. You can now create rules of your own.

Click Additional Rules to get started. Right-click inside the Additional Rules pane and click the desired option for creating a new rule. You'll have to configure your rule manually, without a wizard, by inputting the required components. See Figure 2-15.

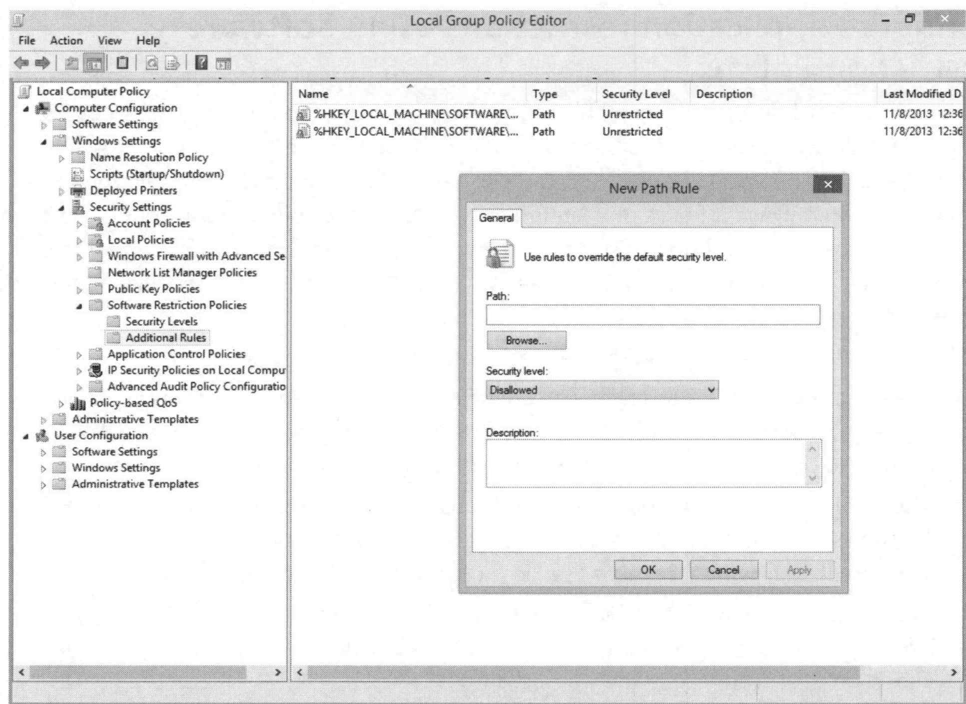

FIGURE 2-15 Create rules manually using Software Restriction Policies.

When you configure rules, there are three settings:

- Disallowed, to prevent the configured installation from running.
- Basic User, to allow all applications that do not require administrative approval to run. If they do require approval, they must match a configured rule.
- Unrestricted, to allow an application that matches the rule to run.

Manage installation of and access to removable devices

It's common for users to carry USB flash drives with them everywhere they go. I have a USB key on my keychain (really, it is shaped like a key!). Having access to a portable drive makes it easy for users to take data with them without having to carry a laptop, connect to a network or domain, transfer data to a tablet or phone, or access a cloud drive. Unfortunately, this is also a common way for viruses to spread and for sensitive data to be taken off premises (and potentially lost or stolen). In an even worse scenario, a malicious user could access another's computer and copy data without anyone knowing, should the ability arise due to a workstation left unattended or unlocked. Beyond USB drives, users can also copy data to CDs and DVDs and even memory cards.

Deciding who can use these kinds of drives to transfer data is a difficult task. Some employees will need this ability. Some won't. You'll have to take careful inventory and decide which employees fit into these two groups and then configure your group polices accordingly. Whatever you decide, the option to configure settings for removable storage access, whether on a local machine or on a domain server, is available in the Group Policy Editor.

To access removable access policies, follow these steps:

1. Open the Group Policy Editor (gpedit.msc).
2. Navigate to Computer Configuration, Administrative Templates, System, Removable Storage Access. Note the options. See Figure 2-16.

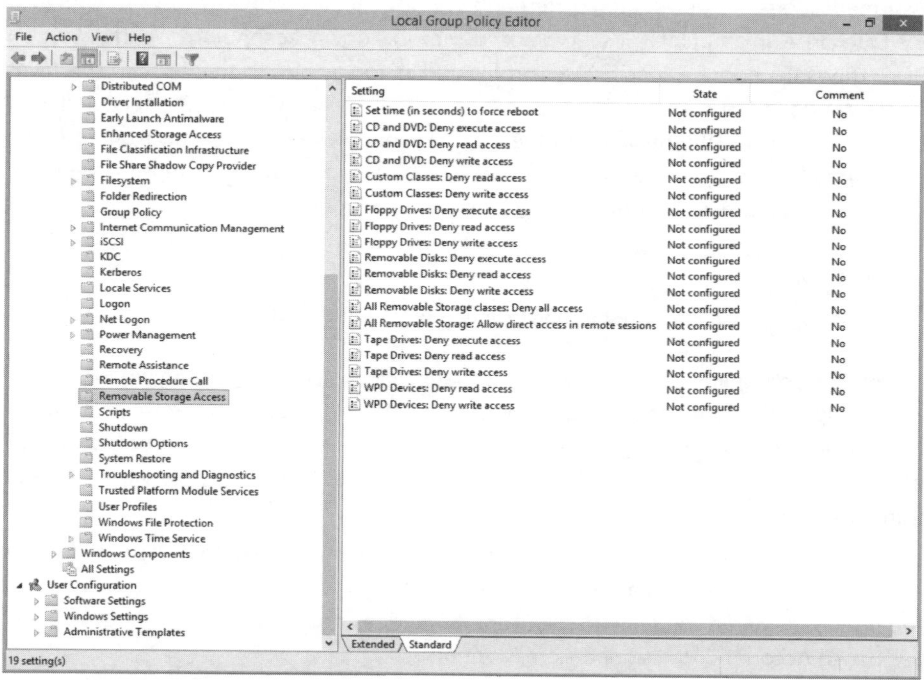

FIGURE 2-16 Locate Removable Storage Access.

3. Alternatively, to configure this for an individual user, navigate to User Configuration, Administrative Templates, System, Removable Storage Access.
4. Double-click the setting to configure. To enable the setting, click Enabled.
5. Click OK.

EXAM TIP

What can a remotely logged-in user access with regard to removable media? Read from USB and DVD only.

Take some time now to open the screen shown in Figure 2-16 and double-click each entry to see what it offers. You need to be able to name the policies and know what they do if you enable them. For instance, the setting All Removable Storage Classes: Deny All Access enables you to block access to all classes of removable storage devices, and this policy takes precedence over all of the policy settings for individual classes. Similarly, CD And DVD: Deny Read/Write/Execute Access, if enabled, denies users all access to the CD or DVD drivers in the computer or gives users only the access you specifically allow or deny.

Configure Assigned Access

Assigned Access is a new feature offered in Windows 8.1 RT, Windows 8.1 Pro, and Windows 8.1 Enterprise. In a nutshell, it's a type of "device lockdown" technology. With it, you can use PC Settings to choose a specific user profile and assign an app to that profile. This gives a single Windows Store application experience on the device by opening a specified app at boot up and after authentication of the user. You can prevent other apps from opening and configure filters to keep the logged-in user from changing system settings or even using specific keys on the keyboard.

EXAM TIP

Assigned Access is restricted to one user and one Windows Store app.

You can configure Assigned Access in situations in which the user only needs to access one thing. Perhaps it's a reading app used by elementary school students. Perhaps it's a tablet that's available at a makeup counter in a department store. It could even be a specialty device offered by a manufacturer to only do one thing, such as manage a fantasy football team using a single app designed for just that.

To use Assigned Access you need to configure at least one standard user account. You can do this in many ways, the easiest being using PC Settings. Click Accounts and work through the process required to create the account if one does not exist. Once created, you see the Set Up An Account For Assigned Access option.

Then you do the following (see Figure 2-17):

1. Choose the account to use.
2. Choose an app.
3. Restart your computer.
4. Log on with the user account.

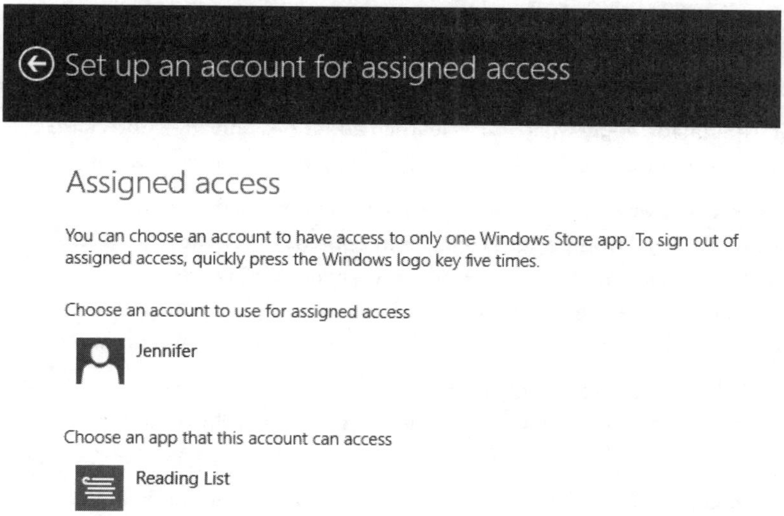

Set up an account for assigned access

Assigned access

You can choose an account to have access to only one Windows Store app. To sign out of assigned access, quickly press the Windows logo key five times.

Choose an account to use for assigned access

Jennifer

Choose an app that this account can access

Reading List

FIGURE 2-17 Set up Assigned Access.

When you reboot the computer, the standard user account will be the only option available and the app you've configured as the single available app will be available, too.

> ***IMPORTANT*** **HOW TO STOP USING ASSIGNED ACCESS**
>
> **If you want to stop using your Assigned Access account but still want it to be available on your PC, quickly press the Windows key five times. This will restart your PC and allow you to sign in with a different account. To turn off Assigned Access, log on as Administrator and in PC Settings, Accounts, Other Accounts, click Set Up For Assigned Access. Choose the standard account and click Don't Use Assigned Access.**

To really personalize Assigned Access for large-scale deployments, you'll need to use Windows Embedded and Lockdown features. When you do, you can employ remote scripting and management, customization of gestures, limitations on the use of keyboard, and restrictions configured for system notifications, among other things. There's a seemingly unlimited number of combinations that can be assigned to different users on a device, allowing for different levels of restriction. For more information about Windows Embedded technologies, refer to this article on MSDN: *http://blogs.msdn.com/b/windows-embedded/archive/2013/10/16/windows-embedded-8-1-assigned-access-and-windows-embedded-lockdown.aspx.*

Thought experiment

Creating application restrictions

In this thought experiment, apply what you've learned about this objective. You can find answers to these questions in the "Answers" section at the end of this chapter.

You are required to create application restrictions for a group of users in an Active Directory domain. The users' workstations run various editions of Windows Vista, Windows 7, and Windows 8.1. However, there are only a handful of Windows Vista machines, and you're likely to upgrade those soon. You would like to create automatic rules where possible to restrict what kinds of programs these users can run.

1. Which Group Policy option would you have to use to create restrictions for the Windows Vista workstations? Can you create rules automatically using this method?
2. Which Group Policy option would you use to create restrictions for the Windows 7 and Windows 8 computers? Can you create rules automatically using this method?
3. If you needed to restrict access to only applications offered as .msi files on the Windows 7 and Windows 8 computers, what type of rule would you create; specifically, what container would you create the rule in?

Objective summary

- You use AppLocker to create rules that can restrict what applications employees can access and use. The available containers for rules are Executable Rules, Windows Installer Rules, Script Rules, and Packaged App Rules. These can be generated automatically and applied to newer Windows operating systems.
- You can use Software Restriction Policies to restrict applications on legacy Windows Vista and Windows XP computers, but you can also apply them to Windows 7 and Windows 8 computers. There are Certificate, Hash, Network Zone, and Path rules.
- You will likely need to manage the installation of and access to removable devices such as CDs, DVDs, and USB flash drives. You can configure this in Group Policy on the local machine or domain controller.
- You can use Assigned Access to lock down a machine for one user and one Windows Store app to create a specific user experience.

Objective review

Answer the following questions to test your knowledge of the information in this objective. You can find the answers to these questions and explanations of why each answer choice is correct or incorrect in the "Answers" section at the end of this chapter.

1. What type of rule in Software Restriction Policies and AppLocker would you create if you needed to restrict access to an application based on its digital fingerprint, even if the name or location of the file changes?
   - **A.** Certificate rule
   - **B.** Path rule
   - **C.** Script rule
   - **D.** Hash or File Hash rule
2. Which of the following removable storage access policies would you configure to keep all selected users from writing to DVDs without placing limitations on other removable media?
   - **A.** CD and DVD: Deny read/write/execute access
   - **B.** CD and DVD: Deny write access
   - **C.** Removable Disks: Deny read/write/execute access
   - **D.** All of the above
3. What technology can you use to create a unique experience for a single user account and to limit that user to only one Windows Store app?
   - **A.** AppLocker
   - **B.** Assigned Access
   - **C.** Software Restriction Policies
   - **D.** Executable rules
4. You have set up Assigned Access for a standard user. When you boot the machine, you are not given the option of logging on to your own account. The only thing that happens is that the app you've configured opens in the standard user account you assigned. What can you do to get back into your own account?
   - **A.** Open PC Settings, navigate to Accounts, Other Accounts, select the standard user account, and click Disable Assigned Access. Input your administrator account and password when prompted.
   - **B.** Reboot the computer and press F12 to access the boot options. Opt to disable Assigned Access.
   - **C.** Press the Windows key five times and let the computer reboot.
   - **D.** Open PC Settings, open Accounts, and click Disable Assigned Access. Press the Windows key four times to reboot.

Objective 2.4: Configure Internet Explorer 11 and Internet Explorer for the desktop

Windows 8 and Windows 8.1 have two options for Internet Explorer (IE) 11. There is an app on the Start screen and Internet Explorer on the desktop. The former is like other apps, streamlined with charms you can use to configure settings and preferences, among other things. The latter is the traditional IE 11 app with which you're already familiar, complete with menus you can opt to show and access to all of the IE settings, including privacy and security. The app you find on the Start screen uses the entire screen and does not contain menu bars or commands, is optimized for touch, and is popular with tablet and laptop users. IE 11 on the desktop is generally used when that app doesn't provide what the end user needs or when the user prefers that traditional look and feel of IE. The two are the same application, but they have different interfaces. Thus, changes you make in one are applied to the other.

In this section you won't learn how to use these apps. You won't learn much about the end-user settings you find in the various menus and toolbars in IE on the desktop either. You won't learn about what's available in the app's charms. You'll need to explore those features and be familiar with them, but I'll use the pages here to discuss the objectives on the exam; namely, how to use Compatibility View, configure security and privacy, and configure the Download Manager.

This objective covers how to:

- Configure Compatibility View and explore Group Policy settings
- Configure security and privacy settings
- Manage add-ons, toolbars, extensions, search providers, and more
- Configure Download Manager

Configure Compatibility View and explore Group Policy settings

The technology used to create websites is ever-changing, like everything else that has anything to do with computing. The transitions that have occurred over the years have left some websites (and website managers) behind the times. Older websites, whether they are Internet or intranet, that are still configured with the older technologies often don't display well when opened and viewed in newer web browsers like IE 11. Thus, IE 11 offers Compatibility View. When enabled, the browser displays the selected page in Compatibility View mode and the webpage can be viewed properly.

An end user can quickly enable Compatibility View mode for a webpage by clicking the Compatibility View icon in the IE 11 address bar on the desktop. This button will be available to the end user if the site is on Microsoft's list of websites that aren't compatible. Users can also manually add websites to their own personal lists. Figure 2-18 shows what the Compatibility View icon looks like and the Compatibility View Settings dialog box. To add a website manually, type the name of the website in the Add This Website text box and click Add and then click Close.

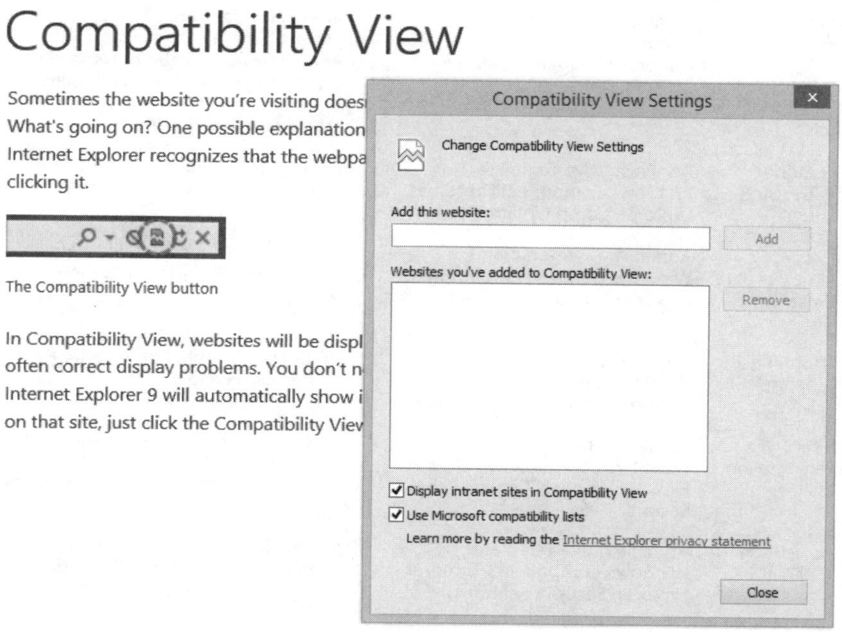

FIGURE 2-18 Use Compatibility View.

In larger organizations, you will probably want to control what happens with Compatibility View using Group Policies. You can find the options for Compatibility View in the Group Policy Management Editor from Computer Configuration, Policies, Administrative Templates, Windows Components, Internet Explorer, Compatibility View. Make sure you are familiar with all of these options.

Table 2-2 outlines the available Group Policy settings for IE 11.

TABLE 2-2 Available Group Policy settings for IE 11

Activity	Location	Setting the policy object
Turn on Compatibility View for all intranet zones	Administrative Templates, Windows Components, Internet Explorer, Compatibility View	Double-click Turn On Internet Explorer Standards Mode For Local Intranet and then click Disabled.
Turn on Compatibility View for all websites by using Group Policy	Administrative Templates, Windows Components, Internet Explorer, Compatibility View	Double-click Use Policy List Of Internet Explorer 7 Sites and then click Enabled. Users will be able to add or remove sites manually to their local Compatibility View list, but they won't be able to remove the sites you specifically added.
Turn on Quirks mode for all websites by using Group Policy	Administrative Templates, Windows Components, Internet Explorer, Compatibility View	Double-click Use Policy List Of Quirks Mode Sites and then click Enabled.
Ensure your users are using the most up-to-date version of Microsoft's compatibility list	Administrative Templates, Windows Components, Internet Explorer, Compatibility View	Double-click Include Updated Web Site Lists From Microsoft and then click Enabled.
Restrict users from making security zone configuration changes	Administrative Templates, Windows Components, Internet Explorer, Internet Control Panel	Double-click Disable The Security Page and then click Enabled.
Control which security zone settings are applied to specific websites	Administrative Templates, Windows Components, Internet Explorer, Internet Control Panel, Security Page	Double-click Site To Zone Assignment List, click Enabled, and then enter your list of websites and their applicable security zones.
Turn off Data Execution Prevention (DEP)	Administrative Templates, Windows Components, Internet Explorer, Security Features	Double-click Turn Off Data Execution Prevention and then click Enabled.

Configure security and privacy settings

IE 11 also offers various security and privacy options. You can access the same feature as any end user can by using the Tools button and clicking Internet Explorer Options. There are two tabs to explore: Security and Privacy. These two tabs offer options related to security settings for the four zones (Internet, Local intranet, Trusted sites, Restricted sites) and how you want to protect your privacy (such as never allowing websites to require your physical location, using the Pop-Up Blocker, and so on).

The other tabs offer a few security and privacy options, too. For example, the General tab offers the ability to delete your browsing history each time you exit IE 11. The Content tab lets you manage AutoComplete settings and how you'd like to use certificates for encrypted connections and identifications. You'll need to explore each of these tabs to see what's available and to make sure you know how to make changes. Understand that the changes you make here also affect the IE app on the Start screen. You can open the Internet Options dialog box by clicking the Tools button and then clicking Internet Options. For the most part though, you'll control IE through Group Policy.

EXAM TIP

You might be asked how older websites can configure their webpages to always show in Compatibility mode. They do this by adding this tag into their HTML files: <meta http-equiv="X-UA-Compatible" content="IE=EmulateIE7"/.

There are lots of new IE 11 Group Policy settings you need to be familiar with. Make sure you understand what happens when you enable, disable, or do not configure various policies. Figure 2-19 shows some of the options in Group Policy that are available to configure in the Local Group Policy Editor. Note these options specifically: Turn Off InPrivate Filter and Turn Off InPrivate Browsing.

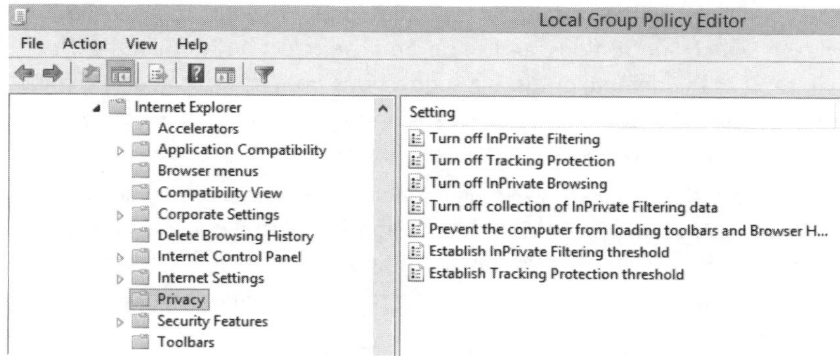

FIGURE 2-19 Configure Local Group Policy settings for Internet Explorer 11.

There are other areas of Group Policy to explore beyond the Privacy node. For example, if you click Internet Explorer in the left pane, in the right you'll see options that include Security Zones: Do Not Allow Users To Change Policies and Disable Automatic Install Of Internet Explorer Components.

EXAM TIP

We don't think you'll be tested too heavily on Group Policy settings for IE 11, but you should familiarize yourself with the newly added entries. Some of these directly relate to security and privacy settings. This list is available on TechNet at *http://technet.microsoft.com/library/dn321453.aspx*.

EXAM TIP

You might be asked about InPrivate Browsing on the exam. InPrivate Browsing prevents the browser from collecting any data during the session, including cookies, tracking, browsing history, passwords, and user names. Like other features, you can control InPrivate behavior through Group Policy.

Manage add-ons, toolbars, extensions, search providers, and more

There's another area of IE 11 on the desktop to explore, and that is the Manage Add-Ons dialog box, shown in Figure 2-20. From there you can view information about the following and how each is configured on the local computer:

- **Toolbars And Extensions** Click this choice to see what toolbars have been added to IE 11 and disable them if desired. These are sometimes from Microsoft Corporation, as you can see in Figure 2-20, and other times they are from third parties. This is where some malware appears, too. Click any entry to see options to enable or disable it.
- **Search Providers** Use this option to see what search providers are in use on the local computer. You'll see Bing, but you might also see additional providers such as eBay, Ask.com, Amazon Search Suggestions, and so on. You can select any item in the list and remove it, set it as the default, or disable suggestions from it. You can also change the order of the list. Select and then right-click any entry to see additional options that do not appear in the dialog box itself.
- **Accelerators** Choose this option to view the accelerators configured for the local machine. You'll probably see Map with Bing Maps, Translate with Bing, and perhaps others. These features help users perform tasks in a single click (such as getting directions to a place by using Bing Maps). Click any entry to disable, remove, or set it as the default.
- **Tracking Protection** Use this option to get a Tracking Protections List online and use it to help enhance your privacy by preventing websites from automatically sending data they collect about your visits to websites and content providers. Those providers use the information to tailor advertisements based on what you do online. You have to right-click Your Personalized List and click Enable to get started. Once you've selected a list you can configure settings for it that include the ability to block all content or choose the content to block or allow.

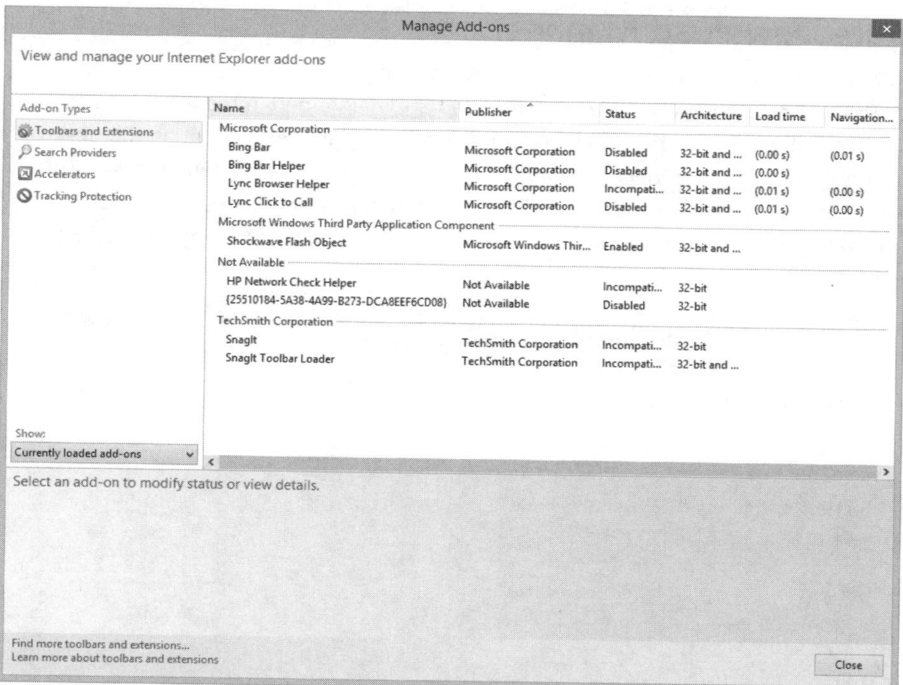

FIGURE 2-20 The Manage Add-Ons dialog box lets you enable and disable features that have been added by the user.

EXAM TIP

Objective 2, which is what this entire chapter covers, is only about 10 to 15 percent of the exam. That means that if your test contains 50 questions, only five to eight questions will come from the material in this chapter. If one of those questions is about Tracking Protection, InPrivate Browsing, or the available Security levels in the Internet Options dialog box, it sure would be a shame to miss it! Spend some time getting to know all of the features of IE before you take the exam.

MORE INFO **REVIEW ALL OPTIONS AVAILABLE IN IE 11**

On the Tools menu in the IE 11 desktop app, point to Safety and review the options there. You can delete your browsing history and report unsafe websites, among other things. Make sure you understand what each entry does, including the SmartScreen filter.

Configure Download Manager

Download Manager is a feature in IE 11 that keeps track of your downloads and download processes. The names of the files you've downloaded are maintained in the list, which makes these easily accessible at any time. You can open Download Manager from IE on the desktop from the Tools menu; just click View Downloads. Once it's open, note the Options link. This is where you configure options for Download Manager, specifically where to store downloads by default and whether to be notified when a download completes. Figure 2-21 shows Download Manager.

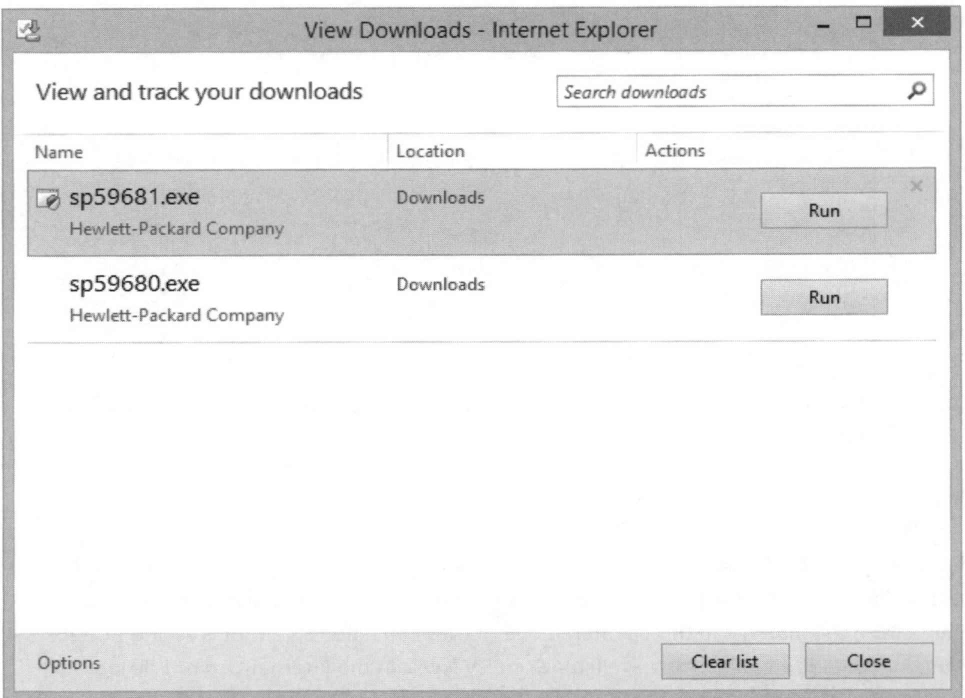

FIGURE 2-21 Download Manager keeps track of the files you download from the Internet.

You can also right-click any entry in the list to delete the download, copy the download link, go to the download webpage, open the containing folder, report that the file is unsafe, and rerun the security checks that were run after the file finished downloading. You can manage Download Manager in Group Policy.

Thought experiment

Manage a company's intranet website's display issues

In this thought experiment, apply what you've learned about this objective. You can find answers to these questions in the "Answers" section at the end of this chapter.

You are the network administrator for a large organization that uses Active Directory Domain Services. There are two domain controllers, several file servers, and about 100 client computers. The company has its own intranet website that was created eight years ago. You've recently updated the workstations from Windows Vista to Windows 8.1, and users are complaining that the company's intranet website doesn't display properly.

1. What feature do you need to configure on the workstations so that users can view the intranet website properly?
2. How do you apply this change to the 100 workstations on the network?
3. Where do you find the setting you want to change? What is the name of that setting?

Objective summary

- Use Compatibility View mode to make older websites that do not yet meet new standards display properly.
- Use Group Policy to configure Internet Explorer (IE) 11 for an entire organization or group easily.
- Configure security and privacy settings from the Internet Options dialog box. There are many options to explore.
- Manage add-ons, toolbars, extensions, search providers, and more with the Manage Add-Ons dialog box.
- Use Download Manager to keep track of and manage the files you download from the Internet.

Objective review

Answer the following questions to test your knowledge of the information in this objective. You can find the answers to these questions and explanations of why each answer choice is correct or incorrect in the "Answers" section at the end of this chapter.

1. You want to ensure your users are using the most up-to-date version of the Microsoft compatibility list. Where in Group Policy do you configure this?
   - **A.** Administrative Templates, Windows Components, Internet Explorer, Compatibility View
   - **B.** Administrative Templates, Windows Components, Internet Explorer, Internet Control Panel
   - **C.** Administrative Templates, Windows Components, Internet Explorer, Control Panel
   - **D.** Administrative Templates, Windows Components, Internet Explorer, Security Features

2. On which tab in the Internet Options dialog box can you configure the security level for the Internet zone?
   - **A.** General
   - **B.** Security
   - **C.** Content
   - **D.** Programs
   - **E.** Advanced
3. How can you delete your personal browsing history? (Choose all that apply.)
   - **A.** From the Internet Options dialog box on the General tab
   - **B.** From the Internet Options dialog box on the Content tab
   - **C.** From the Tools button
   - **D.** From the Tools button from the Safety option
4. Which of the following is a new Group Policy entry for Internet Explorer?
   - **A.** Turn off Data Execution Prevention (DEP)
   - **B.** Restrict users from making security zone configuration changes
   - **C.** Turn off the flip ahead with page prediction feature
   - **D.** Turn on Compatibility View for all intranet zones
5. You downloaded a file using Internet Explorer (IE) 11. Two days later you decide you are ready to install the program included in the download. You can't remember where you saved it. What can you do?
   - **A.** From the Tools button in IE 11, click Manage Add-Ons. Double-click the downloaded file to begin the installation.
   - **B.** From the Tools button in IE 11, click View Downloads. Then, right-click the downloaded file and click Open Containing Folder.
   - **C.** Because you did not use the file right away, IE 11 deleted the file. You'll have to download it again.
   - **D.** From the Internet Options dialog box, on the Programs tab, in the Internet Programs area, click Set Programs.

Objective 2.5: Configure Hyper-V

With Windows 8 Professional and Windows 8 Enterprise, you can create virtual machines that are housed inside a single operating system on a single computer. These virtual machines can run their own operating systems, and you can separate and secure them with virtual switches. A Hypervisor keeps these child operating systems separate from the parent operating system. This enables network administrators to combine multiple machines into one, which saves money, power consumption, resources, and space, among other things. In Windows 8.1, this technology is called Client Hyper-V and is a free component.

To use Client Hyper-V, you'll need the following:

- Windows 8.1 Professional or Enterprise, 64-bit
- Second Level Address Translation (SLAT) processor
- 2 GB of RAM (in addition to the 2 GB for the operating system)
- BIOS-level Hardware Virtualization support

This objective covers how to:

- Create and configure a virtual machine
- Create and manage checkpoints
- Create and configure virtual switches
- Create and configure virtual disks
- Move a virtual machine

Create and configure a virtual machine

If you have a computer that is compatible, you can create and configure a virtual machine. However, you must first install Client Hyper-V. You do this in Control Panel, under Programs. Click Turn Windows Features On Or Off, locate Hyper-V, and select all related entries. See Figure 2-22. Once enabled, click OK and restart the computer.

IMPORTANT **BIOS MUST SUPPORT VIRTUALIZATION**

You might have to enter the BIOS to enable virtualization support.

EXAM TIP

You can enable Hyper-V in Windows PowerShell: Enable-WindowsOptionalFeature –FeatureName Microsoft-Hyper-V –All.

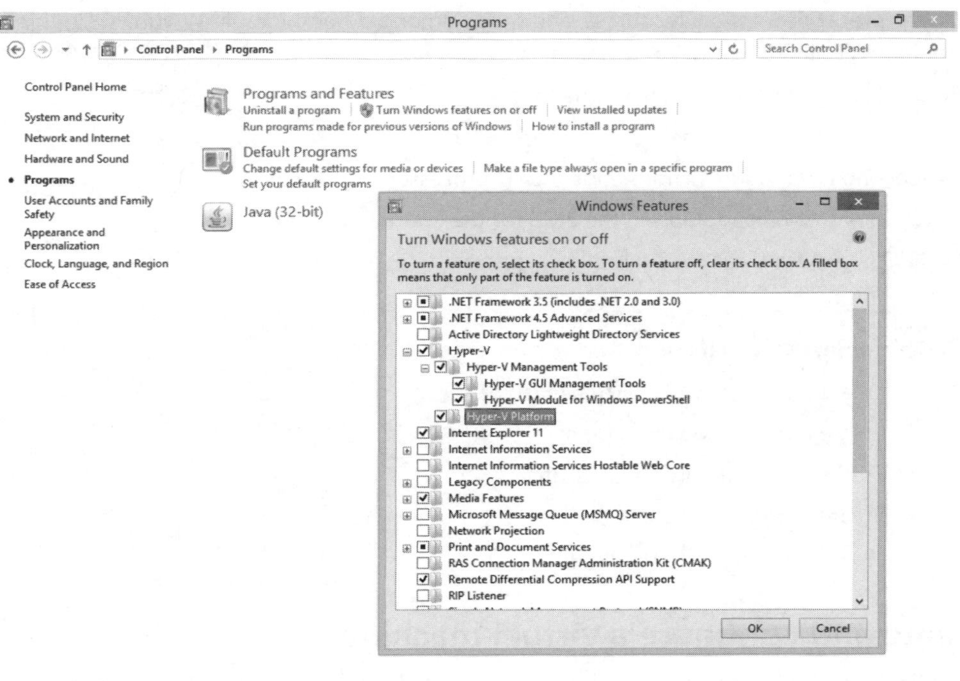

FIGURE 2-22 Install Hyper-V and its components.

> ***NOTE*** **SOMETIMES HYPER-V ISN'T AVAILABLE IN THE WINDOWS FEATURES DIALOG BOX**
>
> **If you don't see any entries for Hyper-V in the Windows Features dialog box, the computer is either running Windows 8.1 (not Professional or Enterprise) or is 32-bit. If you see everything, but Hyper-V Platform is unavailable and everything else is okay, then the computer's processor isn't SLAT.**

Create a virtual machine

You use the Hyper-V Manager (Figure 2-23) to create a virtual machine. You can open this manager from the Start screen by typing **Hyper-V Manager** and clicking it in the results. By default, no virtual machines exist. The Hyper-V Manager window is separated into five panes:

- Hyper-V Hosts, which enables a local and remote connection to Hyper-V host computers.
- Virtual Machines, which lists the virtual machines on the selected Hyper-V host.
- Actions, which enables you to configure host networking and settings.

- Checkpoints, which enables you to access saved checkpoints (or snapshots) of the selected virtual machine. (A checkpoint is like a picture of a virtual machine; it is a point-in-time image of the current settings and configurations.)
- Details, which enables you to view available tabs to configure functionality options.

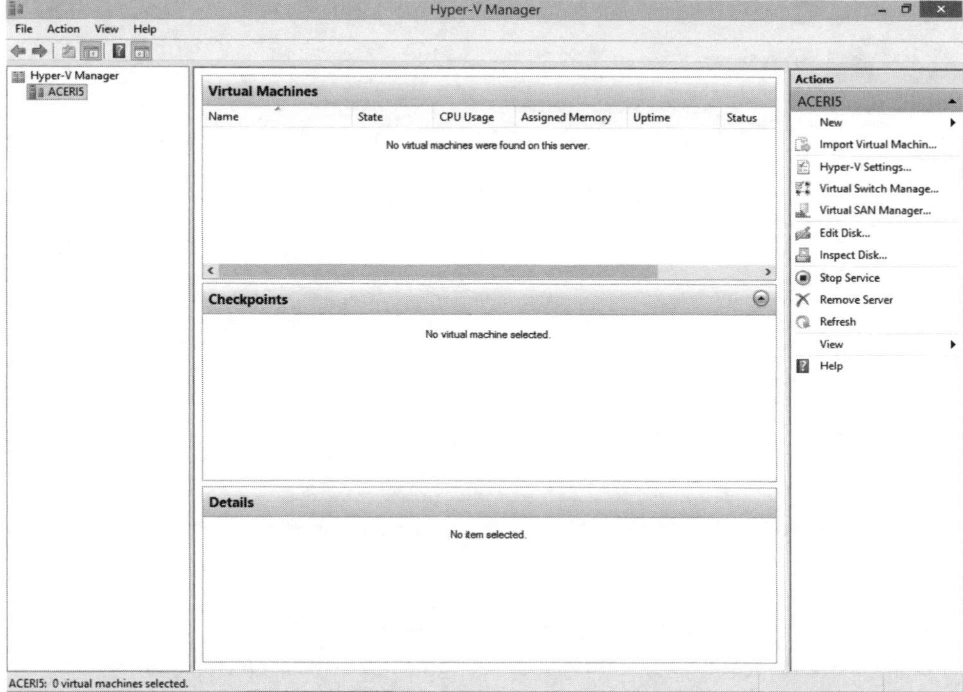

FIGURE 2-23 Use the Hyper-V Manager to create and configure a virtual machine.

To create a virtual machine, follow these steps:

1. Log on with Administrator credentials, open the Hyper-V Manager, and from the Action menu, click New>Virtual Machine.
2. Click Next to start the creation process.
3. Specify the name and location of the new virtual machine. It's best, for now, to keep the default location, so click Next. See Figure 2-24.

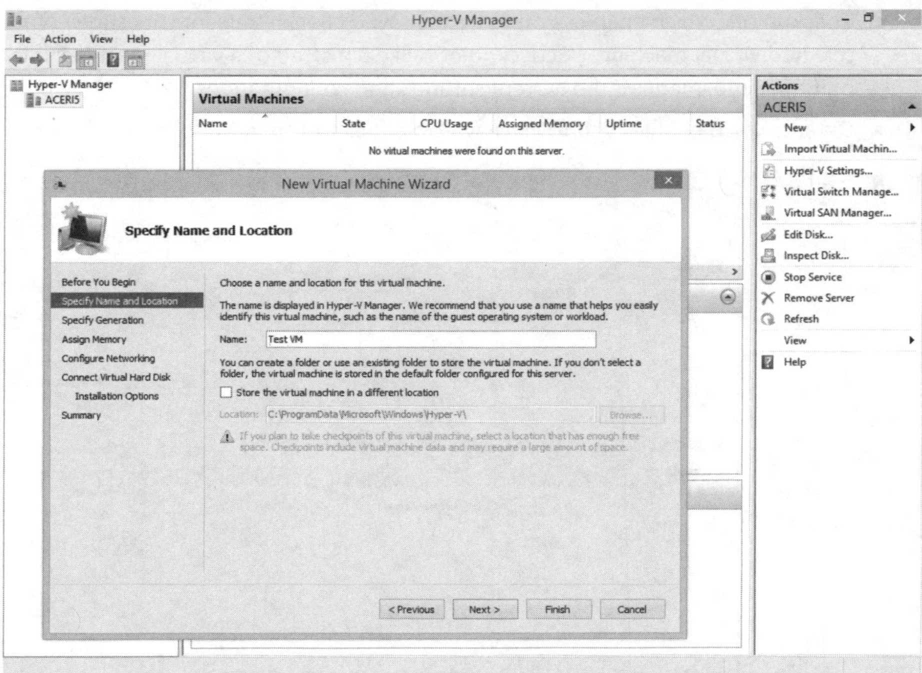

FIGURE 2-24 Work through the wizard to create a virtual machine. Name it in this window.

> ***IMPORTANT*** **MAKING CHANGES TO THE VIRTUAL MACHINE**
>
> **You cannot change the generation type applied to a virtual machine after you've created it.**

4. Choose the Generation option that best suits your needs and click Next:
   - Generation 1 supports the same virtual hardware that the previous version of Hyper-V did. You can use it on operating systems including Windows Server 2008 and Windows 7, among others.
   - Generation 2 supports Secure Boot, SCSI boot, and PXE boot using a standard network adapter. Guest operating systems must run at least Windows Server 2012 or 64-bit versions of Windows 8 or Windows 8.1.
5. Enter the amount of startup memory required and choose whether to use dynamic memory for this machine. Click Next.
6. On the Configure Networking page, click Next. You'll only see options here if you've previously created Network Switch settings.
7. Verify that the Create A Virtual Hard Disk option is selected and that the settings are correct. Click Next. See Figure 2-25.

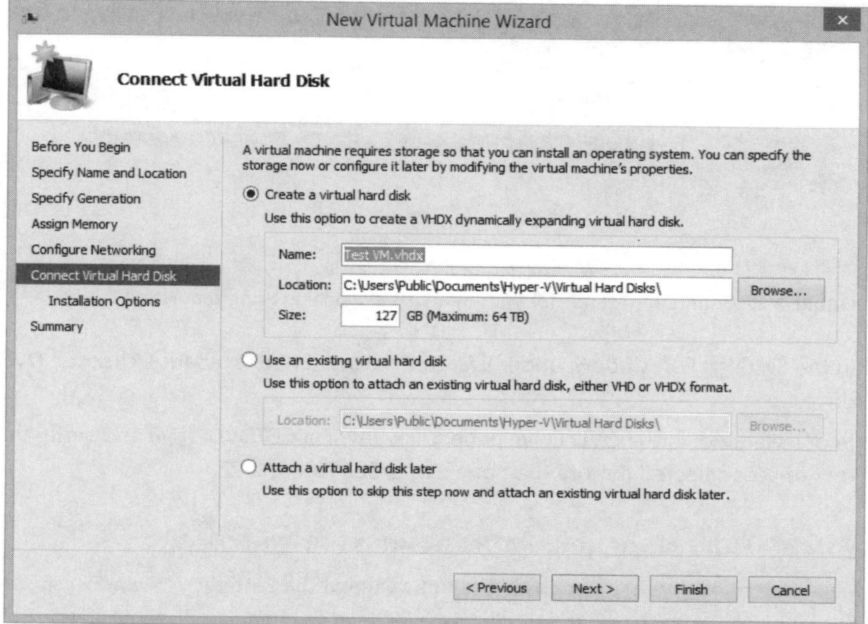

FIGURE 2-25 Verify the settings you've configured.

8. For our example here, leave Install An Operating System Later selected and click Next. (You could opt to install an operating system now, though.)
9. Click Finish (note the new virtual machine in the bottom pane of the Hyper-V Manager).
10. Leave the Hyper-V Manager open.

Configure a virtual machine

Once you've created the virtual machine, you can configure it; until then, it isn't really useful. This involves installing an operating system and configuring the hardware settings to suit your current needs. Before you start, locate an operating system disc or disc image. In this example, we'll insert a Windows 8 disc into the DVD drive.

To configure a virtual machine, follow these steps:

1. In the Hyper-V Manager, in the top-middle Virtual Machines pane, click the virtual machine to configure. See Figure 2-26.
2. Click Action and click Settings.

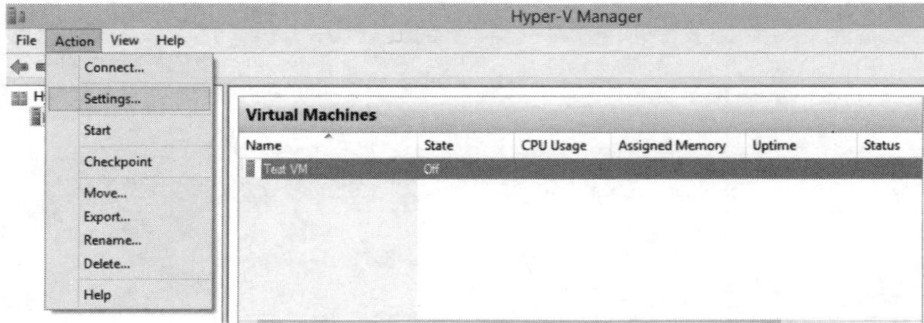

FIGURE 2-26 Configure settings for your new virtual machine using the Action tab.

3. In the Settings For window, under IDE Controller 1 (in our scenario), click the DVD drive.
4. In our scenario, in the DVD Drive pane, click Physical CD/DVD drive and verify the correct drive is selected if more than one exists. See Figure 2-27.

> ***NOTE*** **EXPLORE ALL OPTIONS IN THE SETTINGS FOR WINDOW**
>
> **Make sure to explore the options in the right pane of the Settings For window shown in Figure 2-27. Click each one to see what's available. It's generally self-explanatory: BIOS, Memory, Processor, and so on.**

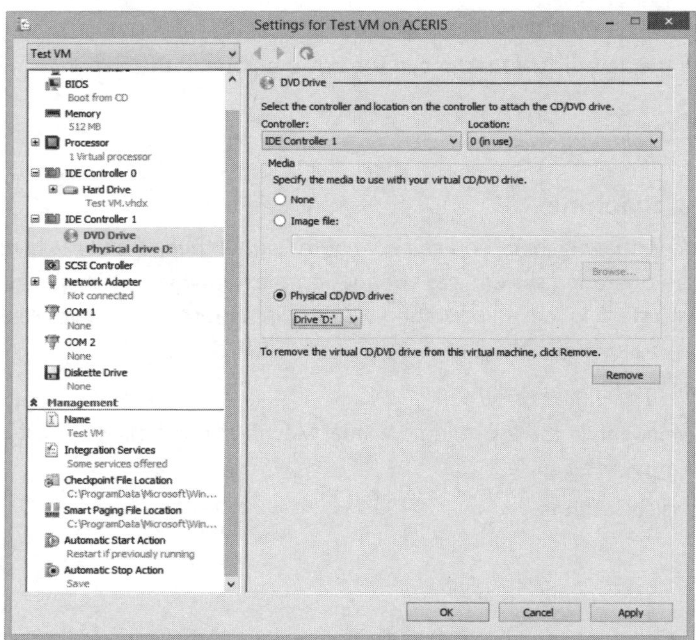

FIGURE 2-27 Choose the option that represents where the operating system disk or image exists.

5. In the Virtual Machines pane, click the newly created VM again.
6. Right-click the VM you selected and then click Start.
7. Right-click the VM again and click Connect.
8. If setup doesn't start, inside the virtual machine's window, click Action, and click Ctrl+Alt+Del. This will restart the virtual machine and allow the installation process to start. You can see the Action menu in Figure 2-28, as well as the first screen of the Windows 8 installation process.

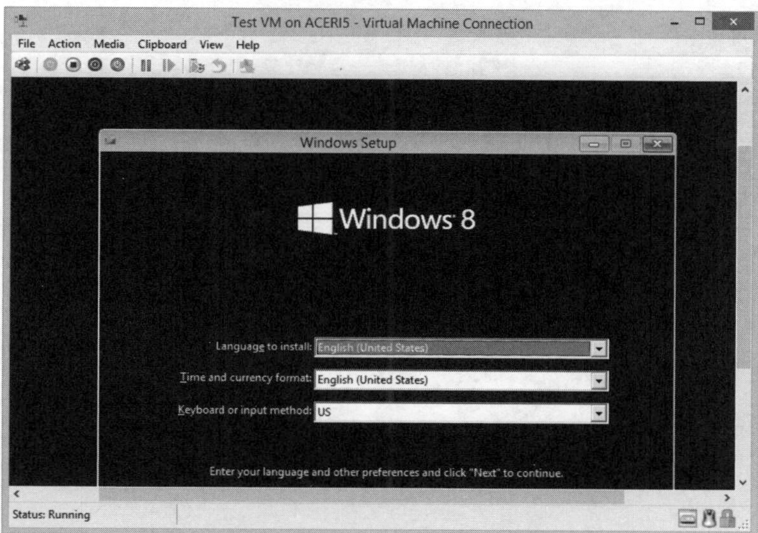

FIGURE 2-28 Configure the new VM by installing an operating system.

IMPORTANT **A VIRTUAL MACHINE NEEDS A PRODUCT ID**

If you're installing a new client on a Windows 8.1 Professional machine, you'll need a valid product ID.

Once installation completes, you can work with the new VM just as you'd work with any operating system. Figure 2-29 shows an example of what a running, installed, VM looks like.

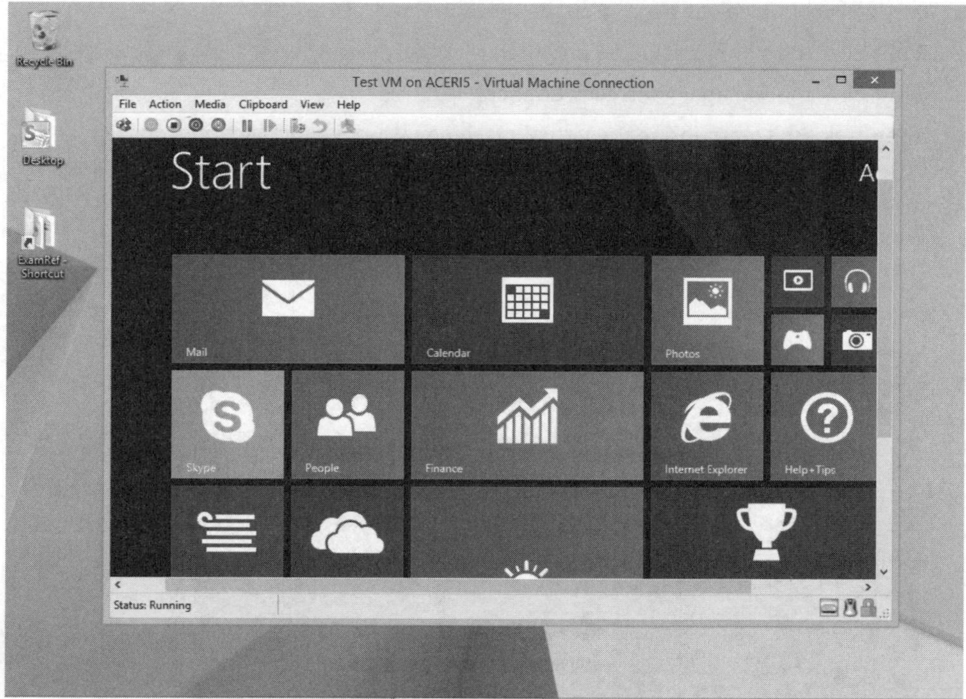

FIGURE 2-29 A VM running on a Windows 8.1 computer.

Install integration services

Hyper-V includes a software package called Integration Services to improve integration between the physical computer and the VM. For the most part, you should install Integration Services after you install the desired operating system. After the installation of these services completes, all integration services will be enabled.

EXAM TIP

Integration Services can only be installed using the Hyper-V Manager. It can't be automated or performed with Windows PowerShell.

To install Integration Services onto the new VM, follow these steps:

1. In Hyper-V Manager, right-click the virtual machine and click Connect.
2. On the Action menu of Virtual Machine Connection, click Insert Integration Services Setup Disk. (If you don't see the menu, put the VM window in Restore mode.)
3. Click the notification that appears in the right corner of the VM window and then click Install HyperV Integration Services.
4. Click Yes in the User Account Control box.

5. If you see a prompt that says This Computer Is Already Running The Current Version Of Integration Services, click OK. Otherwise, work through the installation process.

Client Hyper-V is often the perfect tool for testing software on different platforms and with varying hardware and deployment scenarios. It has some limitations, though, and many enhancements. Review all of the information you find here to verify you are familiar with all of these features and limitations: *http://technet.microsoft.com/en-us/library/hh857623.aspx*.

Create and manage checkpoints

If you were familiar with Client Hyper-V before you started using it in Windows 8.1, you probably know the term *snapshot*. This has been replaced with a newer term, *checkpoint*. You manually create a checkpoint to save the state of a virtual machine. This saves all of the hard disk's contents, including application data files, settings, configurations, and so on. When you're sure you don't need the checkpoint anymore, you can delete it (these files can be quite large). Additionally, checkpoints are portable.

To create a checkpoint, follow these steps:

1. In the Hyper-V Manager, click the new VM you just created and configured.
2. As applicable, click Action and click Start; then click Action and click Connect.
3. Right-click the VM and click Checkpoint. See Figure 2-30.

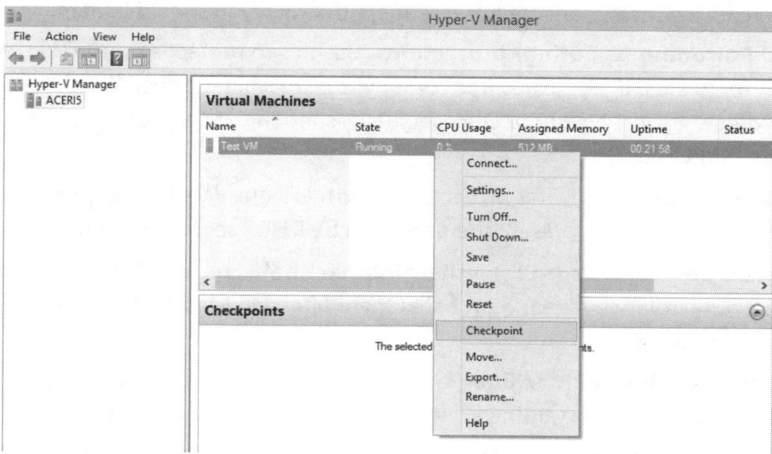

FIGURE 2-30 Create a checkpoint.

4. In the Checkpoints pane, right-click the new checkpoint and click Rename.
5. Name the checkpoint appropriately (Day1AfterInstall, for instance).

To test a checkpoint, follow these steps:

1. Inside the virtual machine, make a change. Perhaps change the desktop background.
2. In Hyper-V Manager, in the Virtual Machines pane, right-click the VM and click Revert.

3. Click Revert again to verify.
4. Return to the running VM and note that the change has been undone.

> ***NOTE* DIFFERENCING DISKS**
>
> **A differencing disk is a virtual hard disk (VHD) you create to quarantine changes you've made to a VHD or the guest operating system. You store these changes in a separate file. The differencing disk is associated with another VHD (that already exists) and can be any kind of virtual disk. You choose the disk when you create the differencing disk. This VHD is called the parent disk, and the differencing disk is the child disk.**

Create and configure virtual switches

Client Hyper-V provides a Layer 2 network switch, which is software based. This is what enables the VMs you create to connect to networks. You can use the switch to connect to a physical, external network or to virtual networks you've already configured in other Hyper-V hosts. The switch also provides security for the VM because it is positioned between the host's physical network interface card (NIC) and the VM's virtual NIC. Additionally, the Hyper-V Virtual Switch has policies already in place for various isolation, security, and service levels and protects against malicious VMs and external ones. The switch is already installed.

Before you create a switch, there are a few terms with which you should be familiar:

- **ARP/ND Poisoning (spoofing) protection** Use this to protect against malicious VMs that try to steal IP addresses from other virtual machines. When IPv6 is involved, it also protects against Neighbor Discovery (ND) spoofing. It uses Address Resolution Protocol (ARP) to do this.
- **DHCP Guard Protection** This protects against malicious VMs that employ man-in-the-middle attacks that represent themselves to be DHCP servers when they are not.
- **Port Access Control Lists (ACLs)** These lists filter traffic so that you can set up virtual network isolation scenarios. It bases these filters on MAC addresses and IP addresses and ranges.
- **Trunk mode to a Virtual Machine** Use this to set up a VM as a virtual appliance so that it can be used to direct traffic from other virtual area local networks to that VM.
- **Network traffic monitoring** This reviews traffic that traverses the network switch.
- **Isolated (private) VLAN** This segregates traffic on multiple virtual area local networks to better create isolated networks.

You can create three types of virtual switches:

- **External**, to let the VM connect to a physical NIC on the computer to communicate with the external network, perhaps for the purpose of connecting to the Internet. If desired, it can also be configured to connect to the host computer. The physical NIC can only connect to one network in this scenario.

- **Internal**, to let the VM communicate with other VMs and with the host computer.
- **Private**, to let the VM communicate with other VMs but not with the host computer.

EXAM TIP

It's highly likely you'll see something about the three types of virtual switches on the exam: External, Internal, and Private. Additionally, you should know that nearly anything you want to do in the Hyper-V Manager requires you to log on with an Administrator account.

To create and configure a virtual switch, follow these steps:

1. In the Hyper-V Manager, click Action and click Virtual Switch Manager.
2. In the Virtual Switch Manager For window, select the type of switch to create. (We click External here.)
3. Click Create Virtual Switch. See Figure 2-31.

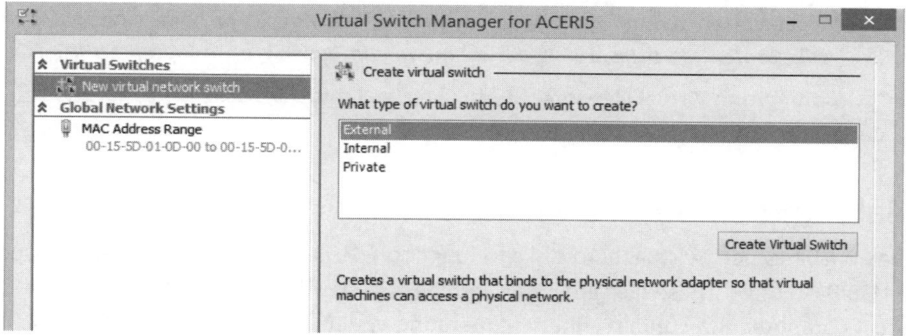

FIGURE 2-31 Create a virtual switch.

4. From the drop-down list under What Do You Want To Connect This Virtual Switch To, select the external network to use, if applicable. For now, make sure to select an Ethernet-based solution. You can also enable virtual LAN identification if the network switch is going to be used with a specific VLAN.
5. Click OK.
6. If prompted, click Yes to apply the changes.

After you have created the switch, you can test it. If you created an external switch, for instance, you can test connectivity to the Internet easily. You can also open the Virtual Switch Manager from the Action pane on the right side of the Hyper-V console and rename the new switch or make notes regarding it.

IMPORTANT **REGARDING DEVICE DRIVERS**

If you had to install a device driver for the host machine's network adapter, you might have to install that same driver on the VM.

In the set of steps that precedes this paragraph, you were instructed to select an Ethernet-based solution when selecting the network to which to connect. That's because the virtual switch in Hyper-V is a Layer 2 switch, and data can only be sent and received through a physical network adapter. A wireless adapter won't work. So, if you want to use a wireless connection, you need to configure a workaround. However, employing the workaround is a fairly complicated task, so if Ethernet is an option, use it.

> ***MORE INFO*** **HYPER-V AND THE WIRELESS CONNECTION WORKAROUND**
>
> **There is a long, detailed explanation for why you can't select a wireless adapter and have it connect to external networks when creating a switch. Additionally, there are specific steps you'll have to take to create a workaround if you do need the capability. To learn more about why this happens and how to work around it, refer to the following articles:**
>
> - **Bringing Hyper-V to "Windows 8" at *http://blogs.msdn.com/b/b8/archive/2011/09/07/bringing-hyper-v-to-windows-8.aspx***
> - **Hyper-V: How to Run Hyper-V on a Laptop at *http://social.technet.microsoft.com/wiki/contents/articles/185.hyper-v-how-to-run-hyper-v-on-a-laptop-en-us.aspx***
> - **Configuring Virtual Networks at *http://technet.microsoft.com/en-us/library/cc816585(v=WS.10).aspx***

Create and configure virtual disks

Virtual machines need virtual hard disks to function. VHDs are files that you can transport on a USB flash drive. These files are in the format of either VHD or VHDX. VHDs reside on the host computer and contain either an operating system or data that is used by the VMs. You can boot to a VHD if the host is running Windows 7 or Windows 8. You learned quite a bit about VHDs in Chapter 1, specifically how to install Windows 8.1 onto a VHD. You also learned quite a bit about VHD technology. If you haven't read that part of Chapter 1, read it now and return here when you're done.

There are two main differences between the two types of VHD formats:

- **VHD** can be as large as 2048 GB (about 2 TB), and the technology has been around a long time. It was even used in the older Virtual PC and the last version of Hyper-V. You use this format when you know you'll be running the VHD on older operating systems, specifically anything before Windows Server 2012 and Windows 8.
- **VHDX** can be much larger, up to 64 TB. It is not compatible with versions of Hyper-V or operating systems created before Windows Server 2012 or Windows 8. You use this format when you know you'll be using the VHD on compatible machines.

If you can use the VHDX format, you will have access to the larger file size and these features not available in the older VHD format:

- Protection against data corruption when there is a power failure (because updates are logged effectively).

- Improved performance on large sector disks.
- Larger block sizes for dynamic and differencing disks to enhance performance.
- Custom metadata that can be used to record information about the file such as operating system version, among other things.
- The use of "trim" technology to reduce file size and access and use free disk space. (Trim requires disks to be directly attached to the VM, and hardware must be compatible.)

To create a VHD from the Hyper-V Manager, in the Action pane, click New, and then click Hard Disk. Work through the wizard and select the file type format to use (VHD, VHDX), the size (Fixed, Dynamically expanding, Differencing), and name and location, and then opt how to configure the disk. If you want to apply the VM you created in this section, in the Name box you'll need to type the name of the VM to use. When prompted, create a new blank VHD. You can now attach the hard disk to a VM, export it, import it, inspect it, and so on.

Move a virtual machine

The easiest way to move a VM is to shut it down, export it to the new disk, and then import it to the desired location. You might need to export a VM from your production environment, open it somewhere else (perhaps on your desktop with Client Hyper-V), perform any required troubleshooting, and then export it back into the production environment.

To move a virtual machine, follow these steps:

1. In Hyper-V Manager, right-click the VM to move and click Shut Down. Click Shut Down again to verify.
2. Wait until the state of the VM shows Off. Then right-click the VM and click Export.
3. Specify where to save the file or click Browse to choose a location. If you receive an error, save to a different location or create a subfolder.
4. Click Export.
5. If desired, open the folder that contains the exported VM and note the subfolders: Snapshots, Virtual Hard Disks, and Virtual Machines.

When you import the VM, you work through a similar wizard that prompts you to browse to the VM, select the VM, and so on. Once you've done that, you are prompted to select an import type. The three options are described here:

- **Register The Virtual Machine In-Place (Use The Existing Unique ID For The VM)** If you only need to start using the VM where it is currently stored and you do not want to move it or copy it, choose this option.
- **Restore The Virtual Machine (Use The Existing Unique ID For The VM)** If your VM files are stored on a file share, a removable drive, a network drive, and so on, and you want to move it, choose this option.

- **Copy The Virtual Machine (Create A New Unique ID For The VM)** If you have a folder of VM files that you want to import multiple times (perhaps you are using them as a template for new VMs), choose this option and copy the files.

To import a VM, follow these steps:

1. To import the VM to another location, open Hyper-V on the target computer.
2. In the Actions pane, click Import Virtual Machine.
3. Click Next on the Import Virtual Machine Wizard.
4. Click Browse to locate the top-level folder associated with the export process. Click Next.
5. Select the VM to import (see Figure 2-32). Click Next.

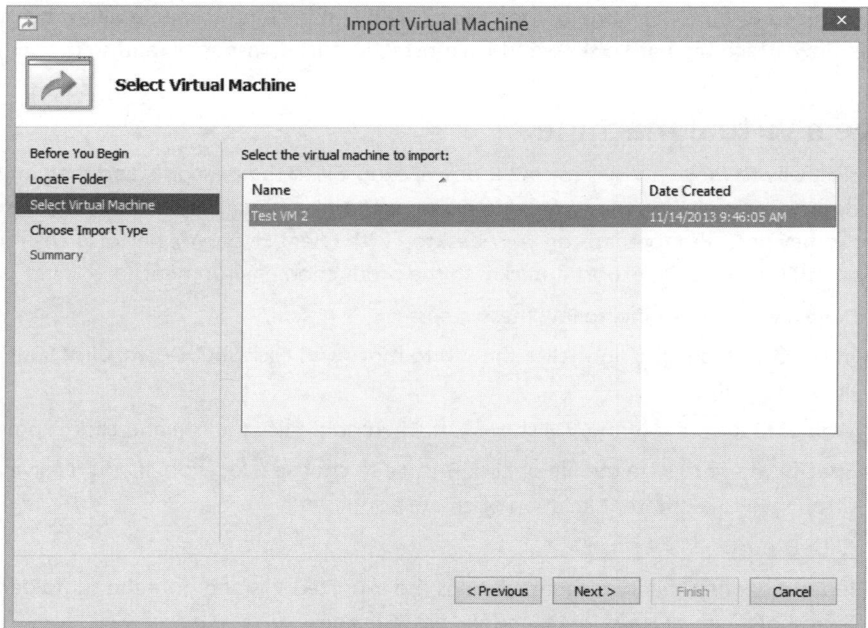

FIGURE 2-32 Select the VM to import.

6. Read the options available to you and choose how to register the VM. (Here we restore the VM and use the existing unique ID.) Click Next.
7. Accept the default store folder for the VM files and click Next. If you receive an error, create a new folder inside the default store to hold the files.
8. Accept the default store folder for the VHDs and click Next. If you receive an error, create a new folder inside the default store to hold the VHD.
9. Click Finish.

Thought experiment

Create the most effective VM for a situation

In this thought experiment, apply what you've learned about this objective. You can find answers to these questions in the "Answers" section at the end of this chapter.

You need to create a VM using a Windows 8.1 computer as the host that you can move from computer to computer on a USB drive. You'll be using the VM on the newest operating systems only: Windows Server 2012 and Windows 8. The VM needs to support Secure Boot and PXE boot. Answer the following questions:

1. **When you create the VM, which Generation option should you choose?**
2. **Will you need a valid product ID for the operating system you will install on the VM?**
3. **You want the VM to be able to communicate with other VMs on the host computer but not with any host computer directly. What type of virtual switch should you configure?**
4. **When you configure your VHD, what file format should you use?**
5. **To export the VM stored on the USB drive, which export option should you choose?**

Objective summary

- To use Client Hyper-V the host computer must:
  - Have Windows 8 or Windows 8.1 Professional or Enterprise 64-bit installed.
  - Have a compatible Second Level Address Translation (SLAT) processor.
  - Have an additional 2 GB of RAM and BIOS-level Hardware Virtualization support.
- You create VMs to use a single computer to house multiple operating systems to test various hardware and software scenarios and to save money, resources, space, power consumption, and more.
- Checkpoints let you take snapshots of the configuration of a VM. You can restore to a saved checkpoint at any time.
- Virtual switches can be used to separate and secure multiple VMs.
- Virtual disks let you port VMs and are saved as either VHM or VHDX file formats. VHDX is the newer format and is compatible only with Windows Server 2012 and Windows 8 and Windows 8.1.

Objective review

Answer the following questions to test your knowledge of the information in this objective. You can find the answers to these questions and explanations of why each answer choice is correct or incorrect in the "Answers" section at the end of this chapter.

1. You are trying to install Hyper-V on a computer running Windows 8.1 Professional, from Control Panel, using the Turn Windows Features On Or Off option. However, Hyper-V Platform is unavailable and can't be enabled. What is the reason for this?
   - **A.** The computer's processor doesn't support SLAT.
   - **B.** The computer is running Windows 8.1, not Windows 8.1 Professional.
   - **C.** The computer is running a 32-bit operating system.
   - **D.** You can't install the Hyper-V Platform from here; you have to run the Windows PowerShell command: Enable-WindowsOptionalFeature –FeatureName Microsoft-Hyper-V –All.
2. In what pane of Hyper-V Manager do you configure host networking and settings, import virtual machines, and create new virtual machines?
   - **A.** Hyper-V Hosts
   - **B.** Checkpoints
   - **C.** Details
   - **D.** Actions
3. You are creating a VM and need it to be backward-compatible with operating systems prior to Windows Server 2012 and Windows 8. Which of the following describes the type of VM you need to create?
   - **A.** Generation 1 with Integration Services
   - **B.** Generation 1
   - **C.** Generation 2
   - **D.** Generation 2 with Integration Services
4. Which of the following is *not* a type of virtual switch?
   - **A.** Internal
   - **B.** External
   - **C.** Public
   - **D.** Private
5. What are some advantages of using the VHDX format for your VHD files (instead of the VHD format)? (Choose all that apply.)
   - **A.** Protection against data corruption when there is a power failure (because updates are logged effectively)
   - **B.** Improved performance on large sector disks

C. Larger block sizes for dynamic and differencing disks to enhance performance

D. The ability to create differencing disks

Chapter summary

- You can configure devices and device drivers in a number of ways, including but not limited to using Device Manager, the Devices And Printers window, Device Stage, and command-line tools like Sigverif.exe and Pnputil.exe.
- To manage what applications open and how the computer responds to DVDs, USB drives, and so on, you can configure preferences by using the Default Programs window.
- MSIExec provides a way for network administrators to install, modify, and perform other operations with Windows Installer files at a command line. The Application Compatibility Toolkit (ACT) helps you determine whether the applications, devices, and computers in your organization are compatible with Windows 8.1.
- You can control access to the Windows Store, applications, removable hardware, and more by using Group Policies.
- AppLocker, Software Restriction Policies, and Assigned Access can help you further control users' access to software and hardware.
- You can use the options in Internet Explorer (IE) 11 to control user access, secure and protect, and manage downloads, and you can use Group Policy to manage groups of users.
- Hyper-V is a virtualization technology you can use to run multiple operating systems in their own space on a single host computer. This saves money, time, resources, power consumption, and much more.

Answers

This section contains the solutions to the thought experiments and answers to the objective review questions in this chapter.

Objective 2.1: Thought experiment

1. You need to configure the computers to bypass digital signature requirements.
2. Open PC Settings, Update And Recovery, and the Recovery tab. Under Advanced Startup, click Restart Now. During the reboot:
   - **A.** Click Troubleshoot.
   - **B.** Click Advanced Options.
   - **C.** Click Startup Settings. Click Restart.
   - **D.** Press 7 on the keyboard. (The computer restarts.)
3. Use the command-line tool Pnputil.exe with –d and –f.

Objective 2.1: Review

1. **Correct answers:** B and D
   - **A. Incorrect.** A manufacturer's extensive testing does not mean the driver is certified. It must be certified by an independent and authorized organization or publisher.
   - **B. Correct.** The driver has undergone testing by Microsoft and its Windows Quality Hardware lab.
   - **C. Incorrect.** Being a 32-bit driver does not make it a signed driver.
   - **D. Correct.** Signing proves that the driver has not been altered.
2. **Correct answers**: A and B
   - **A. Correct.** When you connect a hardware device, Windows looks first to the Driver Store on the local machine and then to Windows Update.
   - **B. Correct.** When you connect a hardware device, Windows looks first to the Driver Store on the local machine and then to Windows Update.
   - **C. Incorrect.** Windows can't do this. Windows can only get drivers from the Driver Store and Windows Update.
   - **D. Incorrect.** Although you might be able to click Update Driver from Device Manager to have it located in the Driver Store, it doesn't do this when hardware is first connected.
3. **Correct answers:** A and D
   - **A. Correct.** To install a device on a machine that runs a 64-bit operating system you must use a 64-bit driver. You'll have to hope you can find one.

B. **Incorrect.** If you disable driver signing, you would be able to install an unsigned driver, but not one designed for another platform (32-bit on a 64-bit machine).

C. **Incorrect.** You can't install a 32-bit driver on a 64-bit machine, even with Device Manager.

D. **Correct.** You can wait, and Action Center and Windows Update will get the updates once the driver is signed.

4. **Correct answer:** C

   A. **Incorrect.** It's highly unlikely that Device Manager could be used to resolve this problem, and besides, it's pretty risky.

   B. **Incorrect.** This enables you to install unsigned drivers and has nothing to do with those already installed.

   C. **Correct.** It is likely that the user installed an unsigned driver. Sigverif.exe will help you determine if this is the problem.

   D. **Incorrect.** If you could find the driver in Device Manager you would not find a previous driver to roll it back to.

5. **Correct answer:** D

   A. **Incorrect.** You can't use Device Manager to install wireless devices.

   B. **Incorrect.** Wireless devices aren't Plug and Play and won't be installed automatically.

   C. **Incorrect.** Device Stage offers a place to view information about an installed device, purchase supplies for it, get help, and so on.

   D. **Correct.** Devices And Printers enables you to easily connect to wireless devices.

Objective 2.2: Thought experiment

1. Yes.
2. Use the Default Programs window. From there, you select Set Program Access And Computer Defaults.
3. You can't choose Microsoft Windows because that would configure all Microsoft programs as the default. Selecting Non-Microsoft would disallow access to all Microsoft programs. Custom is what you'd choose to configure settings only for the default media player.

Objective 2.2: Review

1. **Correct answer:** A

   A. **Correct.** This is the proper syntax.

   B. **Incorrect.** /i installs; it does not repair. /f must be used to denote that repair options follow.

C. **Incorrect.** /a forces all files to be reinstalled, not just the missing file.

D. **Incorrect.** /x uninstalls a package.

2. **Correct answer:** D

   A. **Incorrect.** There is no entry in the Local Security Policy console to configure this.

   B. **Incorrect.** The option is not available here.

   C. **Incorrect.** This command is used to install and repair applications at a command line and can't be used to disable app updates.

   D. **Correct.** This is the proper place to configure the setting.

3. **Correct answers:** A and B

   A. **Correct.** You can get apps for the Start screen at the Windows Store.

   B. **Correct.** You can get apps from a network through sideloading.

   C. **Incorrect.** MSIExec can't be used to install apps, only desktop applications.

   D. **Incorrect.** ACT can't be used to install apps; it is used to test compatibility.

4. **Correct answer:** D

   A. **Incorrect.** This makes a program the default for all compatible file types.

   B. **Incorrect.** This is used to make a file type or protocol always open in a specific program.

   C. **Incorrect.** This enables you to control access to certain programs on the computer.

   D. **Correct.** You can configure this setting in the AutoPlay options.

Objective 2.3: Thought experiment

1. Software Restriction Polices can be applied to workstations running Windows Vista (and the others listed), but you can't automate those rules.
2. Use AppLocker, and yes, you can create rules automatically.
3. You'd use the Windows Installer Rules container. You must create a rule for Windows Installer files in that window.

Objective 2.3 Review

1. **Correct answer:** D

   A. **Incorrect.** This is based on the assigned certificate, not the digital fingerprint.

   B. **Incorrect.** This rule is used to specify a specific path to a file.

   C. **Incorrect.** This type of rule is applied to script files like .bat, .vbs, and .cmd files.

   D. **Correct.** This is the proper type of rule to create.

2. **Correct answer:** A
   A. **Correct.** This is the setting that enables you to configure these settings either together or separately.
   B. **Incorrect.** This is not a valid setting.
   C. **Incorrect.** This configures read, write, or execute access (or a combination of these) but applies the settings to all removable disks in the computer, not just DVDs.
   D. **Incorrect**. All of the above is not correct because B and C are incorrect.
3. **Correct answer:** B
   A. **Incorrect.** AppLocker is used to test applications for compatibility, create reports, and fashion solutions.
   B. **Correct.** Assigned Access provides this functionality.
   C. **Incorrect.** Software Restriction Policies limit how users can access all software on the machine and can't limit that access to only one app that boots when the computer starts up.
   D. **Incorrect.** This is a type of AppLocker rule and won't limit the device to only one app for one user.
4. **Correct answer:** C
   A. **Incorrect.** Before you can do this, you must first log off and log back on as an Administrator.
   B. **Incorrect.** The proper key combination is to press the Windows key five times. In many instances, F12 at boot will offer boot options. However, boot options won't help you here.
   C. **Correct.** This is the proper way to resolve this issue.
   D. **Incorrect.** This is not how to resolve this issue.

Objective 2.4: Thought experiment

1. Compatibility View mode
2. You would not opt to go from desktop to desktop and configure each machine separately; you also would not want to configure Local Group Policies on each. Instead, you should use Group Policy.
3. You'd configure this in the Group Policy Management Editor here: Computer Configuration, Administrative Templates, Windows Components, Internet Explorer, Compatibility View. The name is Turn On Compatibility View For All Intranet Zones.

Objective 2.4: Review

1. **Correct answer:** A
   - **A. Correct.** Administrative Templates, Windows Components, Internet Explorer, Compatibility View is the proper path.
   - **B. Incorrect.** Administrative Templates, Windows Components, Internet Explorer, Compatibility View is the proper path.
   - **C. Incorrect**. Administrative Templates, Windows Components, Internet Explorer, Compatibility View is the proper path.
   - **D. Incorrect.** Administrative Templates, Windows Components, Internet Explorer, Compatibility View is the proper path.
2. **Correct answer:** B
   - **A. Incorrect.** The General tab offers a place to configure home pages and how IE 11 starts, includes the ability to delete your browsing history, and more.
   - **B. Correct.** You configure security levels on the Security tab.
   - **C. Incorrect.** The Content tab offers a place to set up Family Safety, manage certificates, and configure AutoComplete settings, among other things.
   - **D. Incorrect.** The Programs tab lets you configure add-ons, set programs, set file associations, and more.
   - **E. Incorrect.** The Advanced tab lets you configure advanced settings but does not offer a place to configure security for a specific zone.
3. **Correct answers:** A and D
   - **A. Correct.** This is a valid option for deleting your browsing history.
   - **B. Incorrect.** This is not a valid option for deleting your browsing history. The Content tab offers options regarding Family Safety, Certificates, AutoComplete, and Feeds and Web Slices.
   - **C. Incorrect.** This is not a valid option for deleting your browsing history. The Tools button offers many options, but not one for deleting your browsing history. Tools include but are not limited to managing add-ons, configuring the pop-up blocker, and showing specific Explorer bars.
   - **D. Correct.** This is a valid option for deleting your browsing history.
4. **Correct answer:** C
   - **A. Incorrect.** This is a valid feature, but it was an option in Group Policy in previous operating system editions.
   - **B. Incorrect.** This is a valid feature, but it was an option in Group Policy in previous operating system editions.

C. **Correct.** Flip ahead is a new feature in Windows 8 and is thus a new entry in Group Policy.

D. **Incorrect.** This is a valid feature, but it was an option in Group Policy in previous operating system editions.

5. **Correct answer:** B

   A. **Incorrect.** Add-ons are things like toolbars, extensions, and search providers; they are not downloaded files.

   B. **Correct.** This is the proper way to locate the downloaded file.

   C. **Incorrect.** No downloaded file will be automatically deleted if you don't use it.

   D. **Incorrect.** The Set Programs option is used to select default programs for various file types and protocols.

Objective 2.5: Thought experiment

1. Generation 2, because it supports the listed requirements and Generation 1 doesn't.
2. Yes. All installations of an operating system, even those installed on virtual drives, require a product ID.
3. Private. You want the VM to be able to communicate with other VMs on the host computer but not with any host computer directly. The other options, External and Internal, do not meet these criteria.
4. VHDX. Although you won't likely need the feature that enables the disk to be up to 64 TB, you do use this format when you know you'll be using the VHD on Windows Server 2012 and Windows 8 only.
5. Restore The Virtual Machine (Use The Existing Unique ID For The VM). If your VM files are stored on a file share, a removable drive, a network drive, and so on, and you want to move it, choose this option.

Objective 2.5: Review

1. **Correct answer:** A

   A. **Correct.** If everything else is available except for Hyper-V Platform, the processor is not compatible.

   B. **Incorrect.** If the computer were running Windows 8.1, no Hyper-V options would appear.

   C. **Incorrect.** If the computer were running a 32-bit operating system, no Hyper-V options would be available.

   D. **Incorrect.** You can enable Hyper-V this way, but if the Hyper-V Platform can't be enabled from Control Panel it can't be enabled this way either.

2. **Correct answer:** D
   A. **Incorrect.** The Hyper-V Hosts pane lists the virtual machines available on the hosts.
   B. **Incorrect.** The Checkpoints pane shows a list of saved checkpoints for the selected VM.
   C. **Incorrect.** The Details pane shows information about the selected VM.
   D. **Correct.** The Actions pane offers a list of tasks you can perform.
3. **Correct answer:** B
   A. **Incorrect.** Generation 1 does support earlier operating systems, but uninstalling Integration Services is not required.
   B. **Correct.** Generation 1 supports the desired operating systems.
   C. **Incorrect.** Generation 2 does not support older operating systems.
   D. **Incorrect.** Generation 2 with Integration Services does not support older operating systems.
4. **Correct answer:** C
   A. **Incorrect.** Internal is a valid option for a virtual switch.
   B. **Incorrect.** External is a valid option for a virtual switch.
   C. **Correct**. Public is not a valid option for a virtual switch.
   D. **Incorrect.** Private is a valid option for a virtual switch.
5. **Correct answers:** A, B, and C
   A. **Correct.** Protection against data corruption when there is a power failure (because updates are logged effectively) is a valid feature.
   B. **Correct.** Improved performance on large sector disks is a valid feature.
   C. **Correct.** Larger block sizes for dynamic and differencing disks to enhance performance is a valid feature.
   D. **Incorrect.** You can create differencing disks with both file types.

CHAPTER 3

Configure network connectivity

In almost all instances and scenarios, using a computer to complete tasks involves connecting to a network of some sort, even if it's just to access the Internet or back up your work someplace other than your own PC. In many cases, it's a local area network in a small business, and the resources are configured as a workgroup. In homes, networked computers are often configured as homegroups. The purpose of both of these types of networks is frequently to share an Internet connection and files, folders, printers, and other resources. In both cases and in nearly all scenarios, the users control their own data and manage resources locally.

In other scenarios, a network is the foundation for an enterprise, complete with Active Directory domain controllers that authenticate users centrally and secure network resources. These larger networks can contain additional servers that manage storage, email, faxes, printers, and so on as well. It's important for all of the resources to be managed as a whole to keep everything secure and available, among other things.

No matter what kind of network you're dealing with though, the underlying skills in which you must be proficient are mostly the same. You need to be able to configure IP and network settings and you need to know how to configure and maintain the security of the network. Sometimes, you also need to configure ways to manage the workstations in your network remotely.

Objectives in this chapter:

- Objective 3.1: Configure IP settings
- Objective 3.2: Configure networking settings
- Objective 3.3: Configure and maintain network security
- Objective 3.4: Configure remote management

Objective 3.1: Configure IP settings

Networks are groups of computers and other resources. Networks can be public, private, or domains, and security settings are applied to your Windows 8.1 computer when you connect. Once connected, each resource that is connected to the network (computer, network printer, server, or other host) must acquire (or have previously been assigned) an exclusive address that will define it on that network. These addresses are unique, and you can't have two hosts on the same network with the same address. This makes addressing a very important part of configuring networks.

Unique addresses are also required of hosts that connect directly to the Internet such as servers in Internet service providers (ISPs), entities with their own domain name such as *http://www.microsoft.com*, and so on. Individual computers that are positioned (virtually) behind routers, modems, or networks that share an Internet connection for the purpose of giving those computers access don't connect directly and thus don't have this requirement. In these cases, other technologies are used for addressing, like Network Address Translation (NAT).

Because computers communicate and are defined by a numerical address and not a name, and because requiring users to type the address to access hosts would be cumbersome if not impossible, there is a technology in place that enables users to type a computer name instead of an address to get to a website. This is called resolving an address and is handled by Domain Name System (DNS). You'll learn about all of these things in this objective, as well as how to resolve connectivity issues when they arise.

This objective covers how to:

- Connect to a network
- Configure network locations
- Configure name resolution
- Resolve connectivity issues

Configure IP settings

Every computer (host) on a network (even the Internet) must have a unique Internet Protocol (IP) address. This address, when it's configured as an IPv4 address, is a 32-bit number that is styled as four sets of octets. An example is 192.168.4.20. The IP address (combined with the proper subnet, something like 255.255.255.0) defines the network and the host. Because every resource on a network must have a defined address, you need to know how to configure those addresses. There are two ways to get an address to a resource: You can define it manually or it can be assigned by a Dynamic Host Configuration Protocol (DHCP) server. When an address can't be assigned this way, Windows will assign its own IP address using a technology called Automatic Private IP Addressing (APIPA).

EXAM TIP

Make sure to review the IP address ranges for Class A, B, and C and have an idea of how many networks and hosts each offers. Know their default subnet masks, too. Beyond that, know the private addresses available for local networks (192.x.x.x, 172.x.x.x, and 10.x.x.x for Class C, B, and A, respectively).

Explore the Local Area Network Connections Properties dialog box

Figure 3-1 shows the Local Area Network Connections Properties dialog box for a Wi-Fi adapter, where you can configure networking. On the Networking tab you can access the available networking options, including TCP/IPv4, selected here.

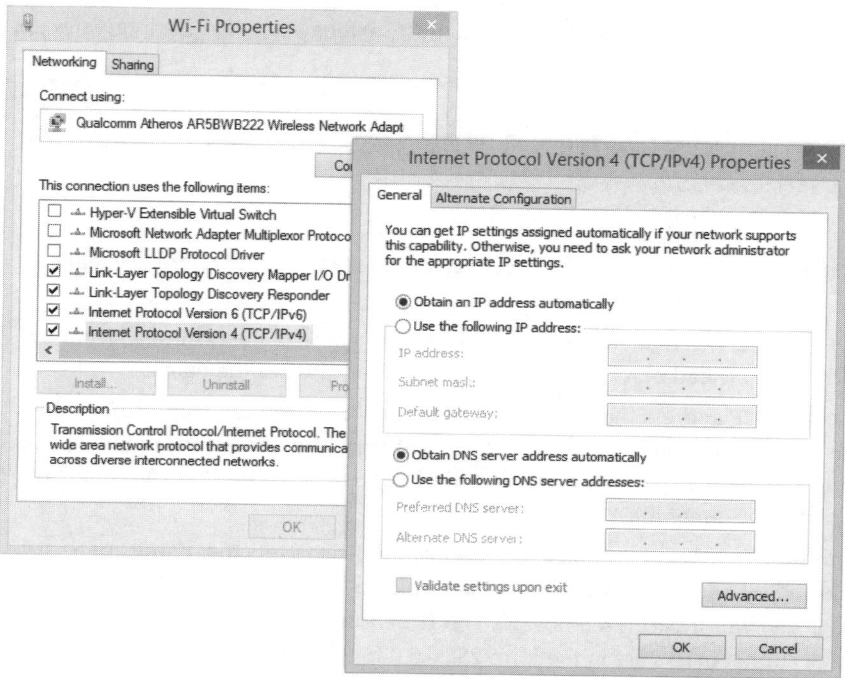

FIGURE 3-1 You can configure networking using the the Local Area Network Connections Properties dialog box.

EXAM TIP

You might be asked how to configure IPv4 or IPv6 addresses from the command line. The command to do this is Netsh. Make sure you understand the options associated with this command. You might be asked to select the proper command to apply a static address for a host, among other things. That command would look like this: "netsh interface ipv4 set address "Ethernet" static 192.168.5.12 255.255.255.0 192.168.1.10". If you want the address to come from a DHCP server, the command would look more like this: "netsh interface ipv4 set address name="Ethernet" source=dhcp".

Explore the options available from the dialog boxes shown in Figure 3-1 as time allows. Make sure you understand the terms listed here before continuing:

- **APIPA** This is a link-local (IP) address that is assigned by Windows when no other addressing mechanism can be found. This enables the host to function on the local network segment. Routers do not forward packets from these kinds of addresses.

- **Default Gateway** This hardware or software device lets hosts connect to other networks. Often that network is the Internet, but it could also be another network segment in an enterprise domain.
- **DHCP** DHCP is a networking protocol that dynamically configures IP addresses for hosts on a network. A DHCP server assigns these addresses. These IP addresses are generally granted for a specified interval and must be renewed when the interval is up.

> ***MORE INFO*** **DHCP**
>
> **To learn more about DHCP, refer to this article:** ***http://technet.microsoft.com/en-us/library/cc726865(v=WS.10).aspx.***

- **DHCP Scope** A DHCP scope is a consecutive range of possible IP addresses that can be offered to hosts on a subnet (part of a network).
- **DNS** DNS is a service that enables users to type the name of the host to which they want to connect instead of its IP address. A DNS server resolves the name.
- **IPv4** This is an IP address that consists of 32 bits, notated by four 8-bit octets. It has two parts: the network ID and the host ID. The network ID describes the network, and the host ID defines the specific device on it. IPv4 addresses can be Unicast, Broadcast, or Multicast. See Subnet mask, next.
- **Subnet mask** This 32-bit number, notated by four 8-bit octets that consist of a set of 1s followed by a set of 0s, is used to define which part of the IPv4 address is the network ID and which part is the host ID. The 1s denote the network; the 0s the host. The default subnet masks are in the form 255.0.0.0 for Class A addresses, 255.255.0.0 for Class B addresses, and 255.255.255.0 for Class C addresses. Translated to binary, 255.0.0.0 looks like this: 11111111 00000000 00000000 00000000.
- **IPv6** The available IPv4 address combinations are dwindling, thus the need for a better option. IPv6 is that option. Instead of a 32-bit space, it's a 128-bit space with 16-bit boundaries. This allows for many more addresses. An IPv6 address can look like this: 21DA:D3:0:2F3B:2AA:FF:FE28:9C5A.

EXAM TIP

You install network support (Client For Microsoft Networks, QoS Scheduler, File And Printer Sharing For Microsoft Networks, TCP/IPv4, TCP/IPv6, and others) from the Local Area Network Connections Properties dialog box. Know what is installed by default and how to install others.

Connect to a network

The first time you connect to a local network, you are prompted to choose from one of these options:

- **No, Don't Turn On Sharing Or Connect To Devices** This option is intended for public networks and hot spots (libraries, coffee shops). The user's computer can't be seen or accessed by others, and the user can't see other computers also accessing the network.
- **Yes, Turn On Sharing And Connect To Devices** This option is intended for private, trusted networks (home, work) and homegroups. Computers sit behind a trusted router and do not connect to the Internet directly.

These two options do not appear when you connect to an Active Directory Domain Services domain. However, when they do appear and when you choose an option, settings are configured automatically for network discovery, file and printer sharing, the state of the firewall, apps that can accept incoming connections, and so on. (Computers configured as Private or Domain have network discovery enabled; Public networks do not.)

If, for whatever reason, you are not prompted to connect to a known network, you can connect manually. To connect to a network manually, follow these steps:

1. Press the Windows key+I to open the Settings charm.
2. Click the Network icon.
3. Select the network from the list and click Connect.
4. If prompted, type the password or passcode to join the network.

If you need to connect to a network that's hidden and not broadcasting its Service Set Identifier (SSID), follow these steps:

1. Open the Network And Sharing Center.
2. Click Set Up A New Connection Or Network.
3. Click Manually Connect To A Wireless Network. Click Next.
4. Input the network name (SSID), the security type, the encryption type, and the security key as applicable and enable other options as desired (see Figure 3-2).
5. Click Next. The connection should be enabled.

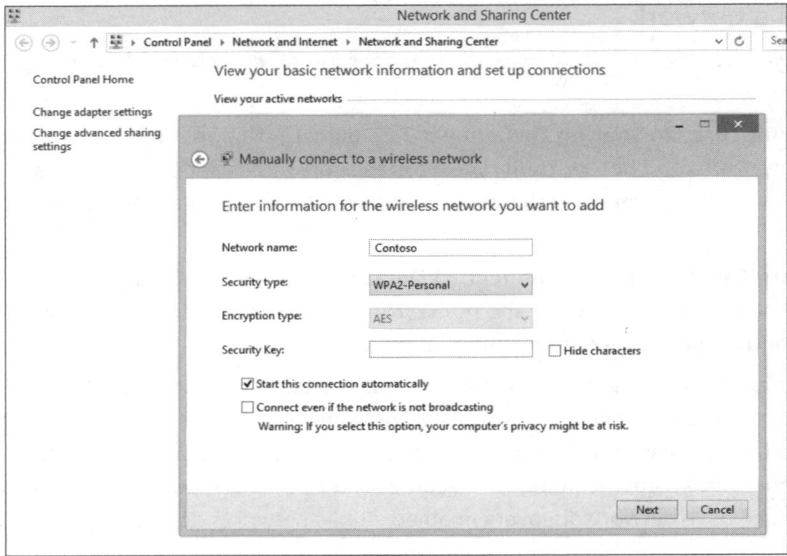

FIGURE 3-2 Connect to a network manually.

> ***MORE INFO*** **CONNECT TO A WORKPLACE**
>
> **One of the options in the Network And Sharing Wizard that walks you through connecting to a hidden network is Connect To A Workplace. You'd choose this option to set up a virtual private network (VPN). VPNs are covered in Chapter 5, "Configure remote access and mobility."**

Configure network locations

When you connect to a local area network and opt to share or not share on it, Windows automatically configures the settings for the network location. If you've joined a homegroup on the network, settings are also applied for you. Windows will always err on the side of caution when it can't determine the location type though, and occasionally you'll find that the location is configured incorrectly.

To make changes to the network location, if that location is a homegroup, you can run the Homegroup Troubleshooter. This might never happen in a homegroup, but it's worth noting that the Homegroup Troubleshooter is an option. If the location is a local network in a workgroup, you make changes in the PC Settings as follows:

1. Open PC Settings.
2. Click Network.
3. From the Connections pane, click the network to change.
4. Set Find Devices And Content to Off. See Figure 3-3.

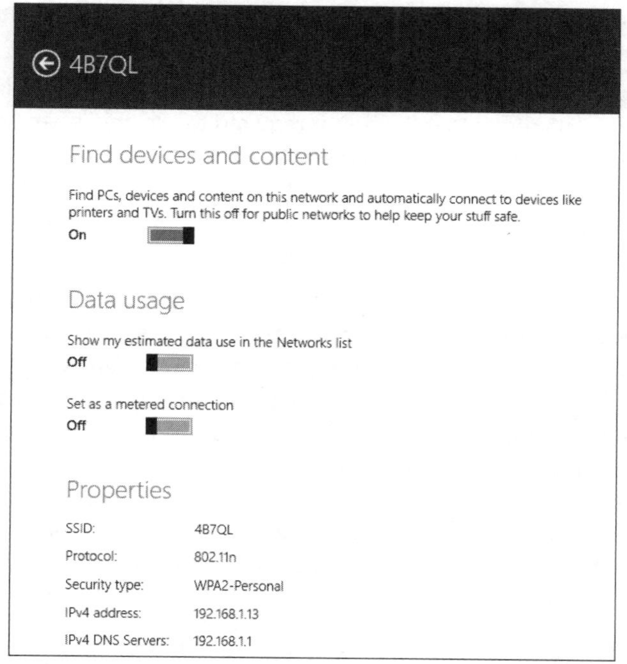

FIGURE 3-3 Make changes to network location in PC Settings, from Network.

> ***NOTE*** **ADVANCED SHARING**
>
> **You can configure advanced sharing from the Network And Sharing Center by clicking Change Advanced Sharing Settings. From there you can change settings for the various profiles available, including Private, Guest Or Public, and All Network. Settings include network discovery, file and print sharing, and various settings for public folder sharing, media streaming, encryption for file sharing, and password-protected sharing.**

Configure name resolution

Computers are represented by their unique IP address, and you can communicate with them using that address if you like. One way to communicate with an IP address is to do so at a command line. For instance, you can type something like **ping 192.168.4.5** to troubleshoot connectivity to another host on a local area network segment. Communicating this way is cumbersome, at least in real life. (Ping is defined in the next section, "Resolve connectivity issues.")

DNS enables users to type names instead of numbers, and the process is called name resolution. DNS servers store information about the names and addresses of Internet computers, and the lists they maintain are distributed among thousands of DNS servers available on the Internet, which are placed all over the world. The name resolution request is forwarded to one of these servers, and if the name can't be resolved it's passed to another and another, until it is.

You can configure a host to use a specific DNS server in the connection's Properties dialog box. On a domain with a unique DNS server that the host is required to use, this is necessary. It might also be necessary in a VPN or in a virtual machine.

Resolve connectivity issues

When a host can't reach a network, that host has connectivity issues. The issue might be isolated to only that device; perhaps the computer's Ethernet cable has come unplugged or the computer's wireless features have been disabled. Maybe there is an IP address conflict on the network and the user's IP address needs to be released and renewed. Often, using the troubleshooting tools in the Network And Sharing Center can uncover the problem and offer a solution. If the issue isn't isolated, though, you have larger problems. A network server, gateway, or other necessary resource might be down, a network segment or physical backbone might be damaged, or there could be an issue that is caused by the ISP, cloud services, or other technologies that are out of your control. In this section you'll learn three ways to troubleshoot a connectivity problem. You can use the Network And Sharing Center, the Action Center, or command-line tools.

> ***NOTE* VIEWING CONNECTION STATUS**
>
> **To view the status of any connection, open the Network And Sharing Center, then click Change Adapter Settings. Double-click the icon that represents the connected network and click Details. In the dialog box that appears, you can view the physical address, DHCP information, and IP addresses. You can even see the IP address of the DNS server, default gateway, and DHCP server, along with when the DHCP lease was obtained and when it must be renewed.**

NETWORK AND SHARING CENTER

The Network And Sharing Center enables you to view the status of your active networks. If there's a problem, you can click Troubleshoot Problems to see if the Network And Sharing Center can resolve it. Sometimes it can, by releasing and renewing the IP address, resetting adapter settings, or uncovering a simple problem such as a disconnected Ethernet cable (which you can then reconnect).

If a problem exists but can't be resolved automatically, you can choose from a list of troubleshooting options that include solving problems connecting to websites, accessing shared folders, finding computers or files in a homegroup, finding and fixing problems with wireless adapters, and troubleshooting incoming connections. Figure 3-4 shows this. When you select any option and start the troubleshooter, it generally finds the problem and performs the repair or prompts you to authorize the repair. It might also require you to do something first, like insert an Ethernet cable into the Ethernet port on the computer.

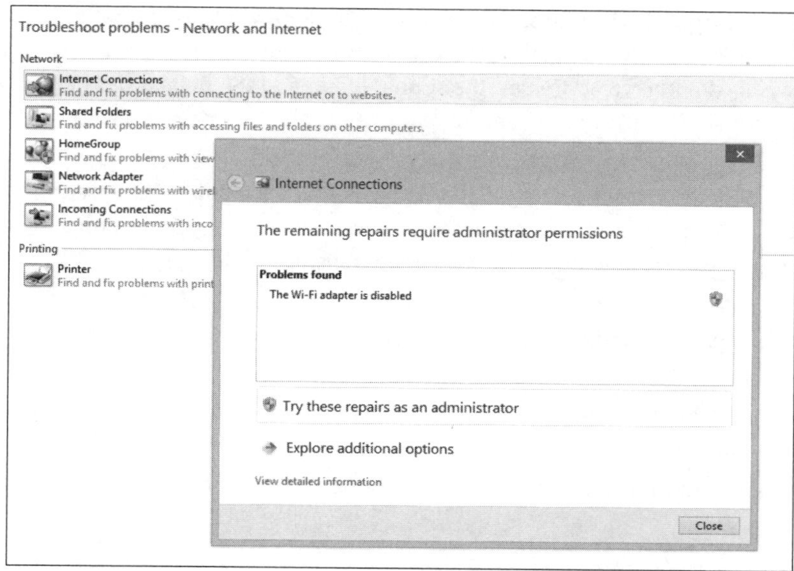

FIGURE 3-4 Use the Network And Sharing Center to troubleshoot a connectivity problem.

ACTION CENTER TROUBLESHOOTING TOOLS

If the Network And Sharing Center can't help you determine or resolve the problem, you can check the Action Center. Again you'll see a troubleshooting option. Here you can troubleshoot problems related to the network and to other things like hardware and sound or system and security. However, you might find something more valuable. Perhaps the network interface card's driver needs to be updated. Action Center will alert you to this in most instances. You can also review problems with the network firewall, virus protection, Internet security settings, network access protection, and the user's Microsoft Account, among other things. Sometimes you can resolve odd connectivity problems here.

COMMAND-LINE TOOLS

When the Network And Sharing Center and the Action Center can't help resolve a connectivity problem, it's likely a more complex issue. Perhaps a domain's (or network segment's) gateway is offline. Perhaps a router failed. Perhaps the DNS server isn't available or has been incorrectly configured on the host. Perhaps the unique, corporate, IP address of the computer has been changed to an APIPA address because of a currently unresolved network issue. When these kinds of problems exist, you can use command-line tools to resolve them.

Here are some of the tools you can use:

- **Ping** This tool verifies IP-level connectivity to another TCP/IP computer. To do this, it sends Internet Control Message Protocol (ICMP) Echo Request messages to the recipient. The receipt of these messages is displayed, along with round-trip times, if the connection is successful. Ping is the primary command used to troubleshoot connectivity, reachability, and name resolution.

- **Ipconfig and Ipconfig /all** This displays all current TCP/IP network configuration values. It can also refresh DHCP and DNS settings. Used without the /all parameter, Ipconfig displays IPv4 and IPv6 addresses, the subnet mask, and the default gateway for all adapters installed on the host. Common parameters are /release, /renew, and /flushdns.
- **Tracert** This tool determines the path taken to a destination and shows information about each hop a packet takes to get to where it's going. A *hop* is a pass through a router. You can use this information to see where the transmission fails.
- **Netstat** This displays a list of active TCP connections and the ports on which the computer is listening. It also displays Ethernet statistics, the IP routing table, and IPv4 and IPv6 statistics.
- **Netsh** This enables you to make changes to the network configuration of the current computer at the command line.
- **Nslookup** This tool displays information that you can use to diagnose problems with DNS.

EXAM TIP

You should review as many command-line tools as time allows. You will see these on the exam, and they might include more obscure tools such as Icacls, Attrib, Cipher, Fsutil, Auditpol, and others, along with associated parameters. (You might also see commands associated with deployment outlined in Chapter 2, "Configure hardware and applications," including DISM, DiskPart, Fdisk, BCDboot, and more.) Visit this page on TechNet to see a list of common command-line tools and their uses: *http://technet.microsoft.com/en-us/library/cc754340.aspx#BKMK_a*.

Thought experiment

Troubleshooting network connections

In this thought experiment, apply what you've learned about this objective. You can find answers to these questions in the "Answers" section at the end of this chapter.

You are troubleshooting connectivity problems on a new laptop that has been added to a local, small business network that already includes eight other computers. Three of these eight are laptops that have always connected without issues. The new laptop can connect when plugged in directly to the router with an Ethernet cable, but it cannot connect wirelessly.

Answer the following questions related to how you would troubleshoot this issue:

1. What do you suspect is causing this problem?

2. **Do you think that the troubleshooter in the Network And Sharing Center can resolve this problem?**
3. **If the Internet Connection troubleshooter uncovers the issue but can't resolve it, where would you turn next and why?**

Objective summary

- When you connect to a local network, you choose the network type and security settings are automatically configured. You are not prompted when you join a domain.
- After you connect to a network, your computer is given a unique IP address on that network segment. Every host connected to a network must have an IP address.
- Name resolution, handled by DNS, lets users type friendly names like *http://www.microsoft.com* instead of its IP address.
- When connectivity problems ensue, you can troubleshoot the issue by using the Network And Sharing Center, Action Center, and various command-line tools.

Objective review

Answer the following questions to test your knowledge of the information in this objective. You can find the answers to these questions and explanations of why each answer choice is correct or incorrect in the "Answers" section at the end of this chapter.

1. What is the purpose of DNS?
   - **A.** To automatically assign IP addresses to hosts on a local network or network segment
   - **B.** To transmit IPv6 traffic over an IPv4 network
   - **C.** To resolve host names into IP addresses
   - **D.** To assign an APIPA address when an IP address isn't available from a DHCP server
2. How can you apply a static IP address to a host on a network, such as a computer or network printer? (Choose all that apply.)
   - **A.** From the host adapter's Properties dialog box
   - **B.** In the Action Center, in the Security options
   - **C.** By using the Netsh command at a command prompt
   - **D.** From the Advanced Sharing Settings in the Network And Sharing Center
3. You need to access information for a specific network adapter, including the physical address, DHCP configuration, IPv4 and IPv6 addresses, applicable subnet mask, and the addresses configured for the DNS Server, DHCP server, default gateway, and when the DHCP lease must be renewed. Which command-line tool would you use?

A. Ipconfig

B. Ipconfig /all

C. Ping

D. Tracert

4. How do you change a configured network location in Windows 8.1?

    A. From the host adapter's Properties dialog box.

    B. In the Action Center, in the Maintenance options.

    C. From the Settings charm, right-click the network, click Forget This Network, then reconnect.

    D. From PC Settings, Network.

Objective 3.2: Configure networking settings

There are various networking settings you can configure. You can connect to wireless and broadband networks and manage the list of wireless networks to which you've connected previously. You can configure location-aware printing to enable users to print to the desired local printer automatically. You can configure network adapters, too, to reconfigure default settings and tweak performance.

> **This objective covers how to:**
>
> - Connect to a wireless network
> - Manage preferred wireless networks
> - Configure location-aware printing
> - Configure network adapters

Connect to a wireless network

When a wireless network is available, you will likely be prompted to join it. This is especially true of mobile devices, although the prompt might not appear until you try to connect to the Internet. When you opt to connect, the process is often as simple as typing the password, if applicable. You learned in the previous section that you can connect to a network using the Set Up A New Connection Or Network option as well, by working through the wizard provided. When you connect this way, you are prompted to type the network name (SSID) and password and select the applicable security settings. There is another way not yet discussed, and that's the simplest option of all: connecting to a network from the Settings charm.

To connect to a network from the Settings charm, follow these steps:

1. Press the Windows key+I to open the Settings charm and click the Network icon. See Figure 3-5. (You can also click the Network icon in the taskbar's system tray on the desktop.)

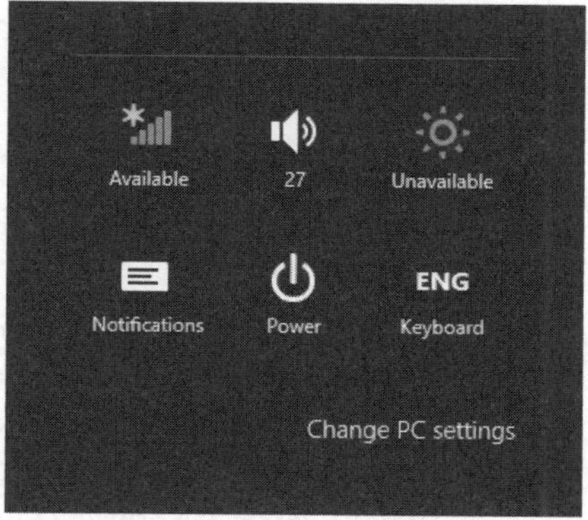

FIGURE 3-5 Click the Network icon to see the available networks.

2. Click the desired network. You can see and connect to available VPN and broadband connections here, too.
3. If desired, click Connect Automatically.
4. Click Connect. (You might be prompted to apply sharing options.)
5. If prompted:
   - **A.** Type the password and click Next.
   - **B.** Click Yes or No as applicable and click OK. See Figure 3-6.

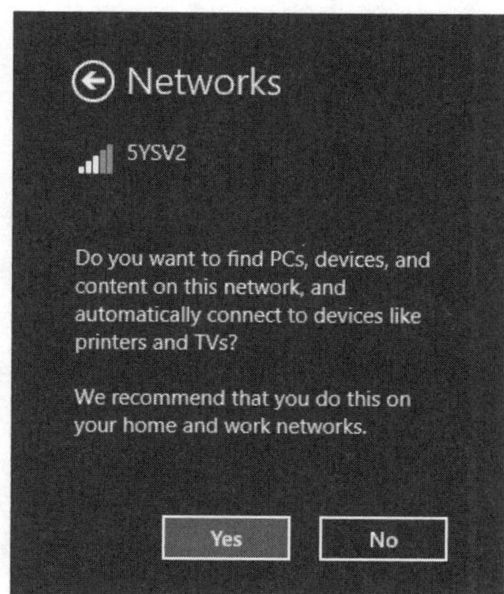

FIGURE 3-6 In some instances you might be prompted to choose some options before you actually connect.

EXAM TIP

You used to be able to right-click a network connection from the Settings charm and the list of networks you find there and forget a network. This enabled you to start fresh with network settings for that network the next time you connect. You can't do that anymore. If you want to forget a network, refer to the directions in the next section, "Manage preferred wireless networks."

Manage preferred wireless networks

Windows 8.1 keeps track of all of the networks to which you connect and prioritizes them automatically. When you have more than one connection option, Windows 8.1 determines which type it will connect to in this order: Ethernet, Wi-Fi, and then mobile broadband. To be clear, when all of these exist, it selects Ethernet. Otherwise, it selects Wi-Fi. If both become unavailable, then it connects with broadband (and will do so automatically if you've configured it to). With regard to the wireless networks to which you've connected in the past, when more than one of those is available at a given time, Windows 8.1 connects to the last one you used.

If you're connected to a network automatically but want to choose another, click it from the list of networks. You can access this list by clicking the Network icon in the taskbar's system tray on the desktop or by clicking the Network icon from the Settings charm. See Figure 3-7.

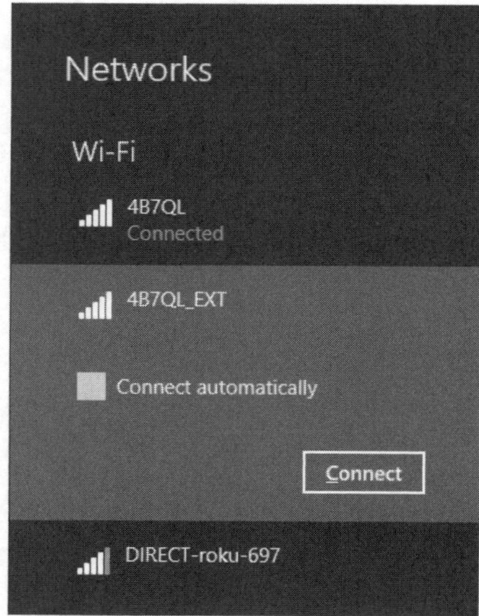

FIGURE 3-7 Switch networks from the Network list.

When you want to manage your list of wireless networks, you no longer have the option of using the Wireless Profile Manager you might have used in Windows 7, and there's no longer an option to right-click a network and opt to forget it from the Networks list shown in Figure 3-7, as you could in Windows 8. Now you must use the Netsh command to remove network profiles.

> ***NOTE*** **FORGETTING A CONNECTION**
>
> **You can forget a network from the Network list in one, specific instance. Try to connect to a network to which you have connected before, and when the connection fails, opt to forget that connection.**

To use the Netsh command to forget a network, at a command prompt, follow these steps:

1. Type **netsh wlan show profiles**. Note the profile to forget. See Figure 3-8.

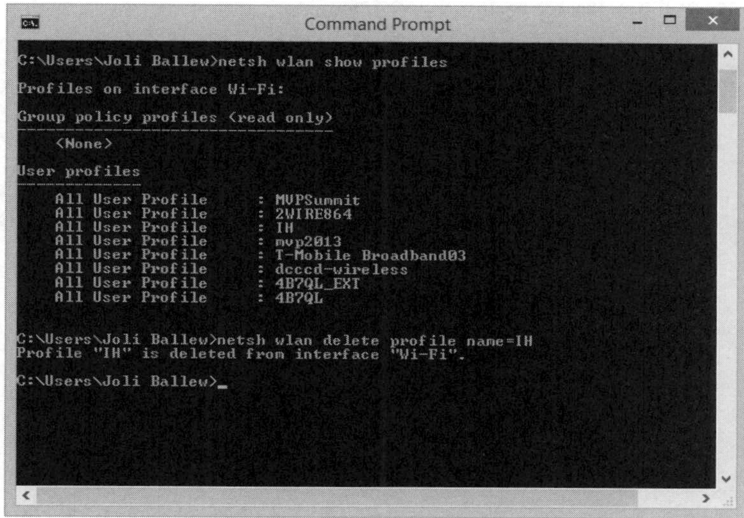

FIGURE 3-8 Use the Netsh command to find and forget a wireless profile.

2. Type **netsh wlan delete profile name=*<profile name>***. (Replace *<profile name>* with the name of the profile.) See Figure 3-8.
3. Press Enter.

Configure location-aware printing

Users are becoming more and more mobile, which means that they'll likely need to access printers from various locations. Those printers can be available on any kind of network, including a network at home, at the office, or even at a company kiosk. Having to choose a printer every time they connect to a new network can annoy users, thus the need for location-aware printing. With location-aware printing, a default printer can be set for each location from which the user prints. This also keeps the user from accidentally printing to the wrong printer, which poses a security issue if the printed data is confidential.

EXAM TIP

Location-aware printing uses the Network Location Awareness service and the Network List service to determine the network location. The former collects and maintains network configuration information, and the latter identifies the network to which the computer is connected. If this feature doesn't work, be aware that you need to check to make sure these services are running.

To configure location-aware printing, follow these steps:

1. Open the Devices And Printers window.
2. On the menu bar, click Manage Default Printers. (You won't see this option on a desktop computer or if a default printer is not installed.)
3. Select Change My Default Printer When I Change Networks.
4. In the Select Network drop-down list, choose a network to configure as shown in Figure 3-9.

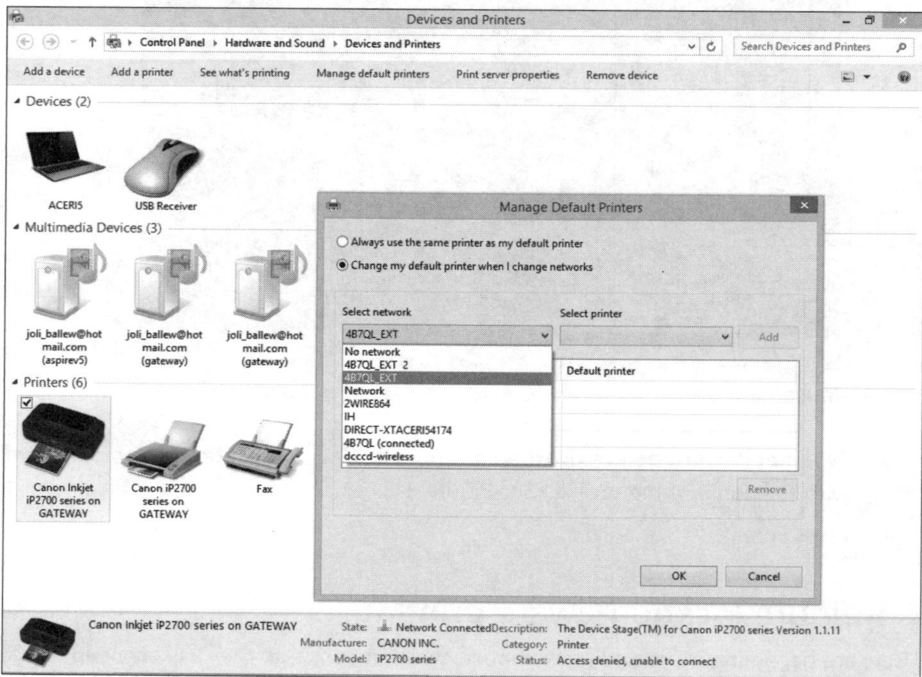

FIGURE 3-9 Open Devices And Printers, select a printer, and click Manage Default Printers to configure location-aware printing.

5. From the Select Printer drop-down list, select the printer to use.

6. Click Add.
7. To remove an entry, select it in the list of items you've added and click Remove.

Configure network adapters

A network adapter is a NIC. Depending on the type, it can transmit data via Ethernet, Wi-Fi, or both. You access the available adapters from the Network And Sharing Center by clicking Change Adapter Settings in the task pane on the left. From there it's easy to tell which network adapter is being used. Figure 3-10 shows that the Wi-Fi adapter is connected. You can right-click an entry to access the options available for it.

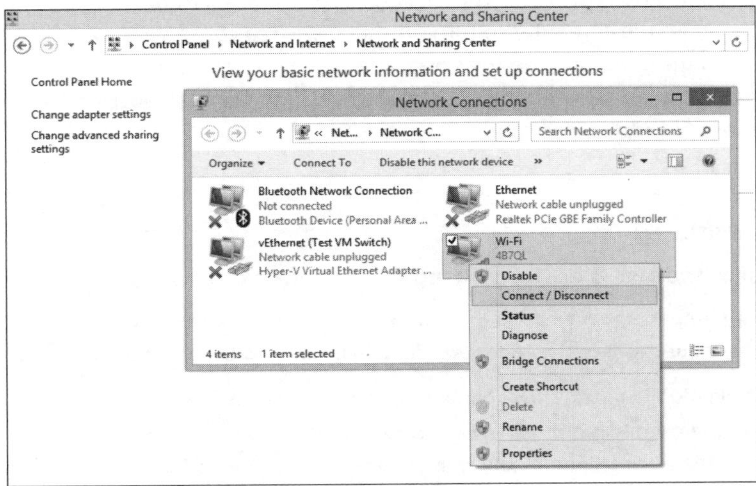

FIGURE 3-10 The Network Connections window shows the available adapters.

When you right-click an adapter in the Network Connections window, you can do any of the following:

- Enable or disable the adapter. (This can help you solve connection problems or keep wireless adapters from searching for networks when you don't need them to.)
- Connect to or disconnect from the associated network.
- See the status of the adapter or connection. (You can use this to view the number of bytes sent and received, to diagnose connection problems, to view signal quality and speed, and to view the SSID, among other things.)
- Diagnose problems with the adapter or connection. (You can use this to run an automated tool that can assist in diagnosing connection problems.)
- Bridge two or more connections. (You must select two connections that are LAN or High Speed Internet connections that are not being used by Internet Connection Sharing. A network bridge is a network device that connects to multiple network segments.)

- Create a shortcut to the adapter for easier access.
- Delete the entry, if the option is available.
- Rename the adapter.
- View the adapter's properties. (You'll see the familiar Properties dialog box you learned about earlier in this chapter. From there you can see the type of connection the adapter uses and install or uninstall protocols, Hyper-V Extensible Virtual Switch, Microsoft LLDP Protocol Driver, and more. When you select an option, you can view additional properties.)

Explore the options available from the adapters on a computer to which you have access. Make sure to click Configure in any Wi-Fi Properties dialog box to view the advanced options. You can, for instance, configure the computer to turn off that device to conserve power or to allow the device to wake up the computer (on the Power Management tab). You can also view events (Events tab), see adapter and driver details (Details, Driver, and General tabs), and view advanced configuration options (Advanced tab).

Thought experiment

Select the best Windows 8 edition based on a client's needs

In this thought experiment, apply what you've learned about this objective. You can find answers to these questions in the "Answers" section at the end of this chapter.

You support multiple mobile users. They connect to a dozen wireless networks a month and print to the printers on those networks regularly. Users complain that they have to choose their printers manually when a part of those networks and that sometimes they choose the wrong ones. Not only is this annoying, but because they print sensitive documents it's also a security issue for your company.

Beyond that, users have connected to wireless networks they'd rather have their laptops forget. The list of networks is quite long and they want you to remove entries for networks they'll never use again (or networks that offered poor connectivity, such as one they have connected to in the past at a hotel or conference center). In the case of networks with poor connections, they'd rather default to broadband.

Regarding this scenario, answer the following questions:

1. **What feature do you enable on the users' Windows 8.1 laptops to enable the network connection to define the printer to which the users will print by default, and what two services does this feature rely on?**
2. **When a user is in a hotel where she's stayed before, and that user has also connected to the hotel's free Wi-Fi, what must you do to forget that network so that the user can default to broadband when she stays there next time?**

Objective summary

- There are several ways to connect to a wireless network including using Control Panel, the Network icon in the desktop's taskbar, and the network icon from the Settings charm.
- There is a default priority for networks to which the user has previously connected: Ethernet, Wi-Fi, and mobile broadband. When there are two or more wireless connections available, Windows defaults to the last one used. You can manage networks by using the Netsh command.
- Location-aware printing lets users configure a default printer for each network they connect to.
- Each network adapter has options available for configuration. You can access these by right-clicking the network adapter in Network Connections and selecting an option from the shortcut menu.

Objective review

Answer the following questions to test your knowledge of the information in this objective. You can find the answers to these questions and explanations of why each answer choice is correct or incorrect in the "Answers" section at the end of this chapter.

1. A user has these connections available: an Ethernet connection, three Wi-Fi connections, and a broadband connection. Which will Windows 8.1 default to?
   A. Ethernet.
   B. The last wireless connection the user connected to.
   C. Broadband.
   D. The user will be prompted.
2. You need to configure the advanced properties of a wireless adapter; specifically, you need to make changes to the AdHoc 11n and Receive Buffer options. Where do you do this? (Choose two; each represents half of the answer.)
   A. Right-click the adapter in the Network Connections window and click Properties. Click Configure.
   B. Right-click the Wi-Fi adapter in the Network Connections window and click Properties. Click Install.
   C. Right-click the Wi-Fi adapter in the Network Connections window and click Status. Click Wireless Properties.
   D. Apply the changes from the Wi-Fi adapter's Properties dialog box on the Advanced tab.
3. You need to use the Netsh command to forget a network. Which of the following is true regarding the Netsh command? (Choose all that apply.)
   A. It must be typed in an elevated Windows PowerShell session.

B. It must be typed at a command prompt.

C. It must be typed at a command prompt with elevated privileges.

D. You must use the parameter wlan delete profile=<*profile name*>.

E. You must use the parameter wlan remove profile=<*profile name*>.

4. A client needs to connect to a wireless network that isn't broadcasting its SSID. How can you connect?

A. Use the command netsh wlan add profile=<*profile name*> to connect to the network.

B. In the Network And Sharing Center, use the Set Up A New Connection Or Network option.

C. From the Settings charm, click the Network icon. Then, click the network to add.

D. Open the Network And Sharing Center and click Troubleshoot Problems. Click Network Adapters. Resolve the problem with the network adapter and then connect when prompted.

Objective 3.3: Configure and maintain network security

There are a lot of ways to secure a stand-alone computer, but most of the options on which you'll be tested in this objective are in the firewall settings. There are other places to secure a computer, of course, including but not limited to applying group policies, enabling Windows Defender or some other anti-malware software, selecting the appropriate network type when connecting, and even requiring complex passwords. Here, though, we'll concentrate on what will be tested, as detailed next.

This objective covers how to:

- Configure Network Discovery
- Configure Windows Firewall
- Configure Windows Firewall with Advanced Security
- Configure connection security rules (IPsec)
- Create authenticated exceptions

Configure Network Discovery

By default, Network Discovery is enabled for private and domain networks and disabled for public ones. Network Discovery enables a computer to locate other computers on a network and allows computers on the network to see it as well. This is fine when the network is trusted, but it isn't a good idea when the network is not. By having these settings and others already configured for the various network types, along with the applicable settings for ports and protocols, the network administrator does not have to configure every aspect of a connection manually. There is one caveat. Even if Network Discovery is disabled, a Windows 8.1 computer can still access network resources if the user knows the names and locations of those resources (because they can't be discovered by browsing).

It is possible to make changes to how Network Discovery is configured. You do this from the Network And Sharing Center by following this procedure:

1. Open the Network And Sharing Center.
2. In the left pane, click Change Advanced Sharing Settings.
3. Click the down arrow, if applicable, beside the network type for which to change the settings: Private or Guest Or Public.
4. Make the desired change for Network Discovery settings. Note the other options. See Figure 3-11.
5. Click Save Changes, not shown.

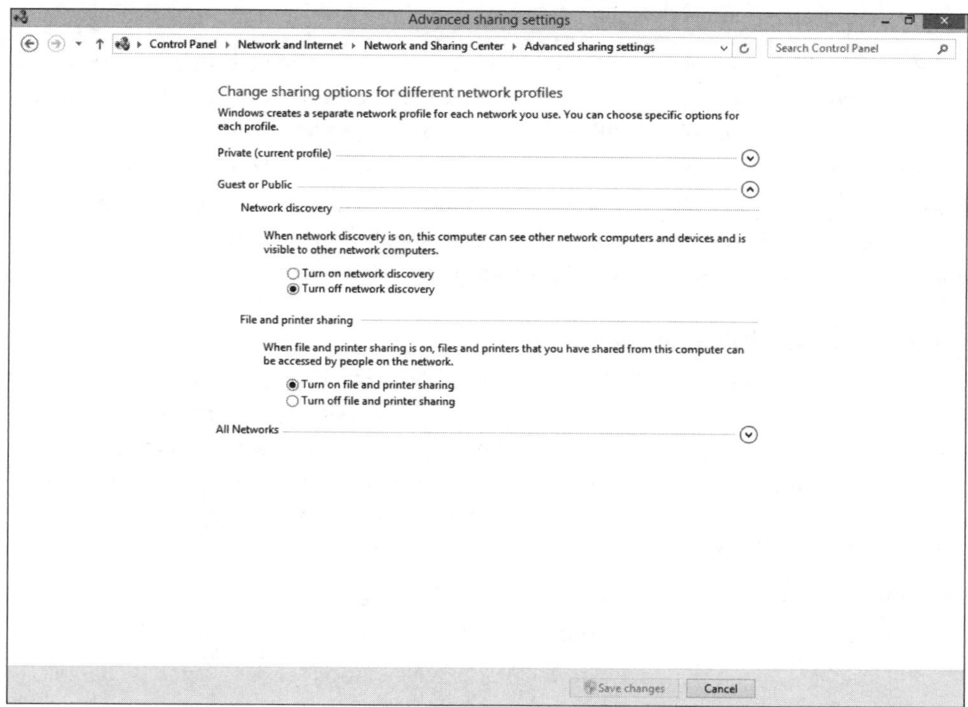

FIGURE 3-11 Enable and disable Network Discovery for a network type from the Network And Sharing Center.

Configure Windows Firewall

Windows Firewall is a software solution that comes with Windows 8.1 that creates a virtual barrier between a computer and the network to which it is connected for the purpose of protecting the computer from unwanted incoming traffic (data) and protecting the network from unwanted outgoing traffic (data). The firewall allows specific types of data to enter and exit the computer and blocks others, and settings are configured by default (but they can be changed). This type of protection is called filtering. The filters are generally based on IP addresses, ports, and protocols.

- **IP Address** IP addresses are assigned to every computer and network resource connected directly to the network. The firewall can block or allow traffic based on an IP address of a resource (or a scope of addresses).
- **Port** Port numbers identify the application that is running on the computer. For example, port 21 is associated with the File Transfer Protocol (FTP), port 25 is associated with Simple Mail Transfer Protocol (SMTP), port 53 is associated with DNS, port 80 is associated with Hypertext Transfer Protocol (HTTP), and port 443 is associated with HTTPS (HTTP Secure).
- **Protocol** Protocols are used to define the type of packet being sent or received. Common protocols are TCP, Telnet, FTP, HTTP, Post Office Protocol 3 (POP3), Internet Message Access Protocol (IMAP), HTTPS, and User Datagram Protocol (UDP). (You should be familiar with the most common protocols before taking the exam.)

Although there are plenty of rules already configured for the firewall, you can create your own inbound and outbound rules based on ports, protocols, programs, and more to configure the firewall to suit your exact needs. You'll learn how later in this chapter.

Monitor the Windows Firewall

You can monitor the state of the Windows Firewall in Control Panel. It's easy to tell from here if the firewall is on or off, what incoming connections are blocked by default, what is the active network, and how you are currently notified when the firewall takes action. It's all available in the main window. To make basic changes to the state of the firewall, in the left pane click Turn Windows Firewall On Or Off. From there you can change settings for both private and public networks. There are two options for each:

- Turn On Windows Firewall (this is selected by default)
  - Block All Incoming Connections, Including Those In The List Of Allowed Apps
  - Notify Me When Windows Firewall Blocks A New App (This is selected by default.)
- Turn Off Windows Firewall (not recommended)

What you'll be most interested in as a network administrator, though, at least from this window, are the options available in the left pane. Specifically, you'll use the Allow An App Or Feature Through Windows Firewall and Advanced Settings options. You'll learn about the Advanced Settings in the next section, but here we discuss allowing an app through the firewall that is blocked by default.

Allow an app through the Windows Firewall

Some data generated with and by specific apps is already allowed to pass through the Windows Firewall. You can see which apps are allowed by clicking Allow Apps To Communicate Through Windows Firewall in the left pane of the Windows Firewall window in Control Panel. As you scroll through the list, you'll see many apps you recognize, including Bing Food & Drink, Games, Maps, Music, Windows Media Player, and so on. See Figure 3-12. (Once you click Change Settings and give administrator approval, the Change Settings option will appear unavailable and the options in this list will be editable, as you see here.) You will also notice that some apps are not enabled by default, including Windows Media Player Network Sharing Service (Internet), Windows Remote Management, Remote Shutdown, Connect To A Network Projector, and so on.

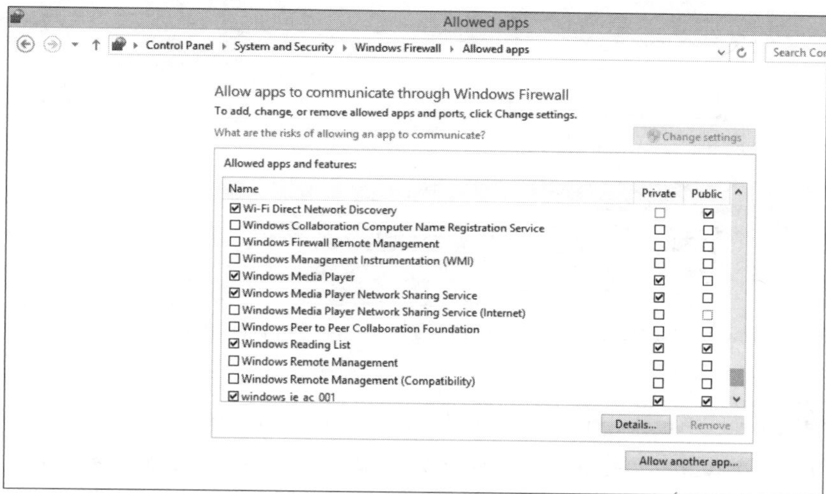

FIGURE 3-12 By default, some apps are already allowed through Windows Firewall.

To allow an app through the firewall or stop one from getting through, select the check box under the appropriate network profile for which it should be configured. As shown in Figure 3-12, there are two options for each: Private and Public. If you don't see the app you want to allow or block, click Allow Another App. You can then select the desired app from the Add An App dialog box.

Configure Windows Firewall with Advanced Security

Although you can configure a few options in the main Windows Firewall window, the real power lies with Windows Firewall with Advanced Security, shown in Figure 3-13. You can open this window in various ways, one of which is to click Advanced Settings in the Windows Firewall window shown in Figure 3-13.

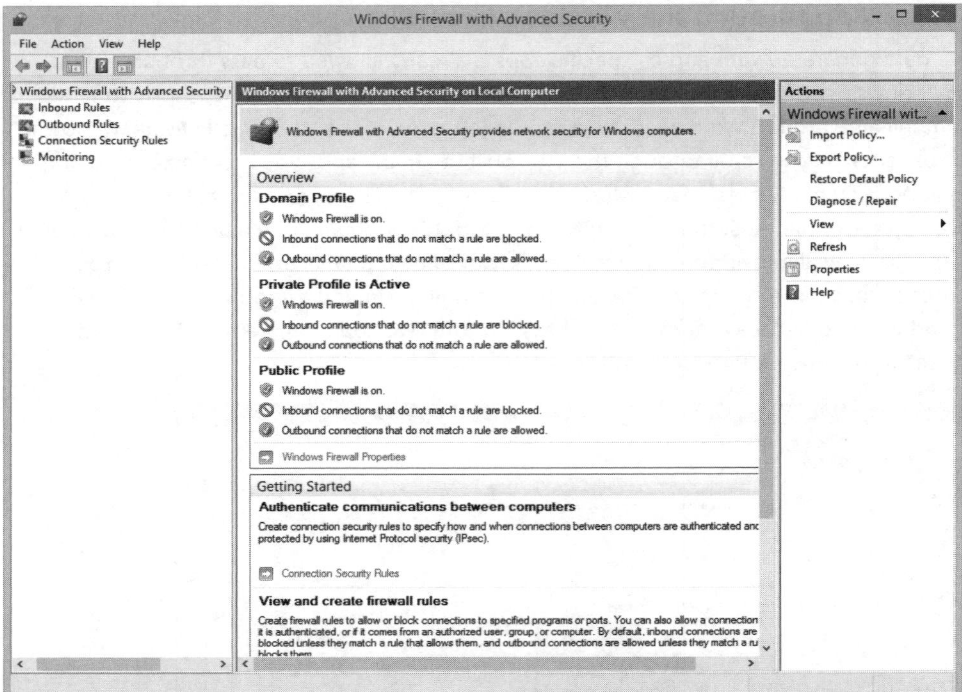

FIGURE 3-13 Windows Firewall with Advanced Security offers many more options than Windows Firewall.

Once opened, there are several options and terms with which you need to be familiar.

- In the left pane (note that the items in the middle and right panes change based on what you've selected here):
  - **Inbound Rules** Lists all configured inbound rules and enables you to double-click any item in the list and reconfigure it as desired. Some app rules are predefined and can't be modified much, although they can be disabled. Explore the other tabs as time allows. You can also right-click Inbound Rules in the left pane and create your own custom rule. Rule types include Program, Port, Predefined, and Custom, and they are detailed later in this section.
  - **Outbound Rules** Offers the same options as Inbound Rules, but these apply to outgoing data. You can also right-click Outbound Rules in the left pane and create your own custom rule. Rule types include Program, Port, Predefined, and Custom, and they are detailed later in this section.
  - **Connection Security Rules** Connection security rules you create manually appear here. Connection security rules establish how computers must authenticate before any data can be sent. IP Security (IPsec) standards define how data is secured while it is in transit over a TCP/IP network, and you can require a connection use

this type of authentication before computers can send data, if desired. You'll learn more about connection security rules in the next section.

- **Monitoring** Offers information about the active firewall status, state, general settings, and more for both the private and public profile types.

- In the right pane (what you see depends on what you've selected in the left pane):
  - **Import/Export/Restore/Diagnose/Repair Policies** Enables you to manage the settings you've configured for your firewall. Polices use the .wfw extension.
  - **New Rules** Enables you to start the applicable Rule Wizard to create a new rule. You can also do this from the Action menu.
  - **Filter By** Enables you to filter rules by Domain Profile, Private Profile, or Public Profile. You can also filter by state: Enabled or Disabled. Use this to narrow the rules listed to only those you want to view.
  - **View** Enables you to customize how and what you view in the middle pane of the Windows Firewall with Advanced Security window.

When you opt to create your own inbound or outbound rule, you can choose from four rule types. A wizard walks you through the process, and the process changes depending on the type of rule you want to create. The four types of rules are as follows:

- **Program** A program rule sets firewall behavior for a specific program you choose or for all programs that match the rule properties you set. You can't control apps, but you can configure traditional programs whose file format ends in .exe. You can't change items distributed through AppLocker either. Once you've selected the program for which to create the rule, you can allow the connection, allow the connection but only if the connection is secure and has been authenticated using IPsec, or block the connection. You can also choose the profiles to which the rule will be applied (domain, private, public) and name the rule. See Figure 3-14.
- **Port** A port rule sets firewall behavior for TCP and UDP port types and specifies which ports are allowed or blocked. You can apply the rule to all ports or only ports you specify. As with other rules, you can allow the connection, allow the connection but only if the connection is secured with IPsec, or block the connection. You can also choose the profiles to which the rule will be applied (domain, private, public) and name the rule.

MORE INFO **CONNECTIVITY AND SECURITY**

When you create inbound and outbound rules, and when you opt to allow the connection only if the connection is secured by authenticating the connection with IPsec, the connection will be secured using the settings in the IPsec properties and applicable rules in the Connection Security Rules node. The next section covers how to create connection security rules.

- **Predefined** A predefined rule sets firewall behavior for a program or service that you select from a list of rules that are already defined by Windows.
- **Custom** A custom rule is one you create from scratch, defining every aspect of the rule. Use this if the first three rule types don't offer the kind of rule you need.

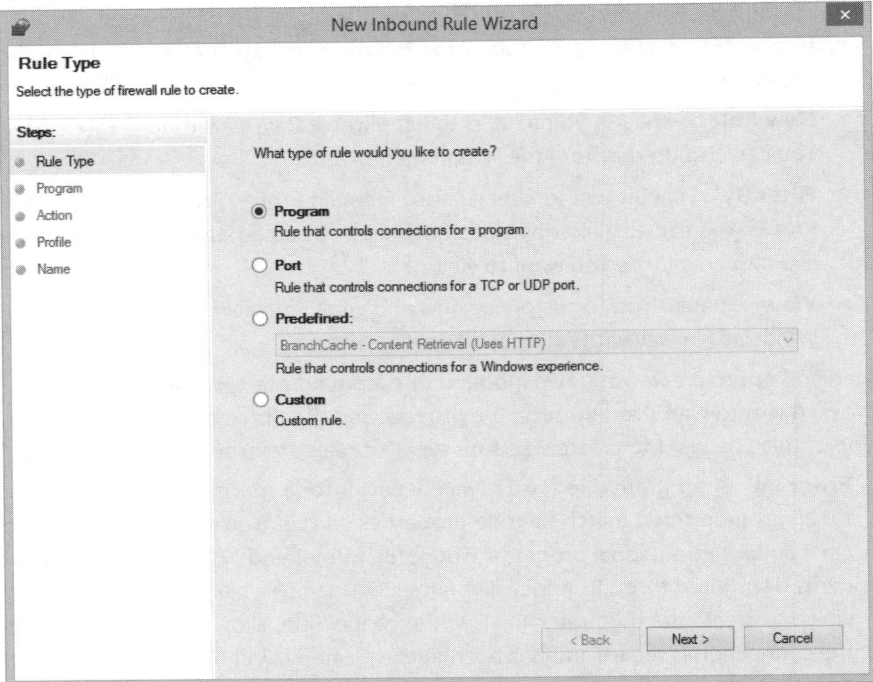

FIGURE 3-14 The New Inbound Rule Wizard walks you through the creation process.

EXAM TIP

When you are working inside the Windows Firewall With Advanced Security window and subsequent dialog boxes, you have access to and can configure rules for every profile, even if they aren't active. This includes Private, Public, and Domain profiles.

EXAM TIP

We're not sure if you'll be asked questions regarding how to create a rule. Thus, you should spend a few minutes working through the wizard a few times, selecting different rule types each time to become familiar with the process.

There are other areas to explore. With Windows Firewall With Advanced Security selected in the left pane and using the Overview section of the middle pane, click Windows Firewall Properties to see the dialog box shown in Figure 3-15. From there you can make changes to the firewall and the profiles, even if you aren't connected to the type of network you want to configure.

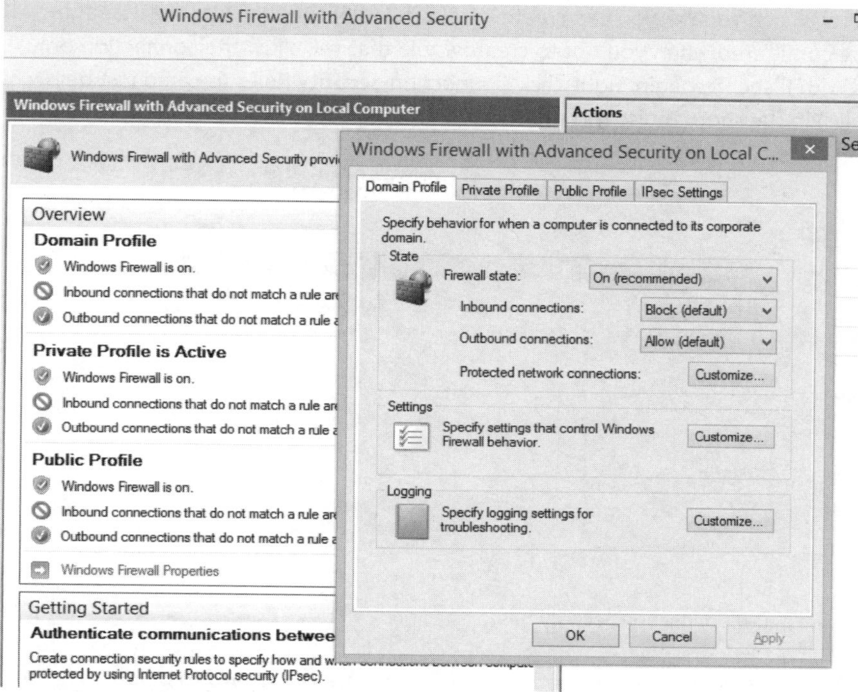

FIGURE 3-15 Use the Windows Firewall With Advanced Security dialog box to configure settings for specific profiles.

In Figure 3-15, the Domain Profile tab is selected. If you want to, you can configure the firewall to be turned off when connected to a domain network. Additionally, you can strengthen the settings for the Public profile and customize settings for the Private profile. Finally, you can customize IPsec defaults, exemptions, and tunnel authorization on the IPsec Settings tab. Make sure to explore all areas of this dialog box and research any terms you are not familiar with.

EXAM TIP

When Windows 8.1 is coupled with Windows Server 2012, new firewall features are available, including the following:

- **Internet Key Exchange version 2 (IKEv2) for IPsec transport mode**
- **Windows Store app network isolation**
- **Windows PowerShell cmdlets for Windows Firewall**

Configure connection security rules (IPsec)

You can create your own connection security rules in the Windows Firewall With Advanced Security window. When you do, you can create inbound and outbound rules that use the settings you've configured when you opt to create a rule that will allow the connection only if it is secured with IPsec. To begin, right-click Connection Security Rules (located just below Outbound Rules) in the shortcut list and click New Rule. See Figure 3-16.

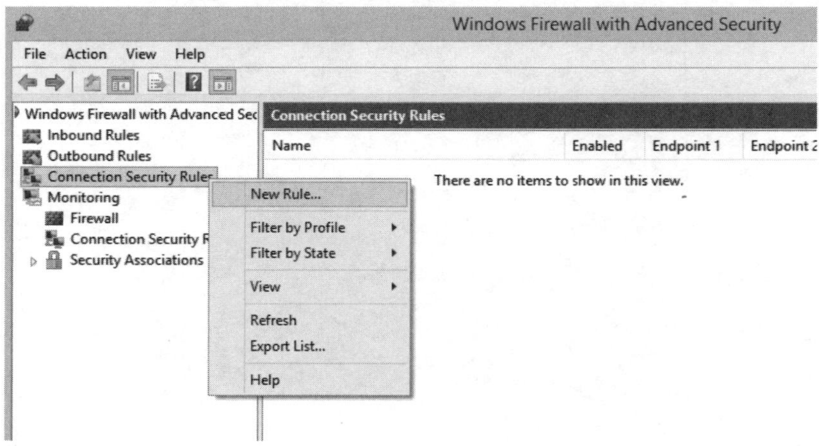

FIGURE 3-16 Create a new Connection Security rule.

There are several steps involved in creating a rule, and there is a wizard to guide you. The wizard pages that appear depend on the choices you make on the prior page. For instance, if on the first page where you choose a rule type, you choose Isolation, there are four additional steps to work through: Set the requirements, choose the authentication method, choose the profiles to which to apply the rule, and name the rule. However, if you choose to create an authentication exemption rule, you'll be prompted to add the remote computers for which you want to configure authentication requirements before you can continue.

> ***MORE INFO*** **THE PRIMARY BENEFIT OF USING IPSEC**
>
> **IPsec is used to securely transmit data between computers. The primary benefit of securing information using IPsec is that all programs and services using IP for data transport can be protected.**

Because there are numerous combinations of rule types and options, we can't possibly go through every scenario. However, you should be familiar with the options and the rule types.

- **Isolation** Use this rule type to create a rule restricting connections based on credentials, such as domain membership, computer status or health, or compliance with policies, among other things. You can opt to request authentication for inbound and outbound connections, to require authentication for inbound and request for outbound, or to require authentication for all connections. Following that, you select the type of authentication to use. You can choose from the defaults already configured or use the appropriate Kerberos or advanced authentication method.

- **Authentication Exemption** Use this rule type to create a rule to state what connection types can be excluded from authentication. You can apply the rule to a single IP address, a subnet, an IP address range, or from a predefined set of computers (such as DHCP or DNS servers, to name a few). With that done, you can choose the profiles to which to apply the rule (domain, private, public) and name the rule.
- **Server-To-Server** Use this rule type to create a rule that applies to named IP addresses or to all IP addresses to request authentication for inbound and outbound connections, to require authentication for inbound and request for outbound, or to require authentication for all connections. You also choose the authentication method, which might be a certificate from a certificate authority or a health certificate issued from Network Access Protection. You can do this to protect specific computers (servers) from interacting with each other.
- **Tunnel** Use this rule type to create a rule that authenticates connections between two computers by using tunnel mode in IPsec, perhaps between two computers such as client-to-gateway or gateway-to-client. You can opt to exempt IPsec-protected connections and choose the authentication requirements, too.
- **Custom** Use this rule type to create a custom rule if the previous options don't offer what you need.

EXAM TIP

Connection Security rules specify how and when authentication occurs, but they do not allow those connections. To allow a connection, you must create an inbound or outbound rule. During the inbound or outbound rule creation, you choose the required conditions for the connection, including requiring that the connections have been authenticated by using IPsec. When you do, connections will be secured using the settings in the IPsec properties and rules in the Connection Security Rule node.

Create authenticated exceptions

When you configure a rule to allow traffic only when the connection between the communicating computers is secured using IPsec, you are creating an authenticated exception. You configure this option from the application Action page of the Rule Wizard when creating an inbound or outbound rule. When you choose the Allow The Connection If It Is Secure option on the Action page, you are configuring the rule to allow the connection using the settings in IPsec properties and rules in the Connection Security Rule node.

To create an inbound rule that applies to a single TCP port (Telnet, port 23) and create an authenticated exception for it, follow these steps:

1. In Windows Firewall with Advanced Security, select and then right-click Inbound Rules.
2. Click New Rule.
3. For the rule type, click Port and then click Next.
4. On the Protocol And Ports page, leave TCP selected and in the Specific Local Ports box, type **23**. Click Next.
5. For the action to take, select Allow The Connection If It Is Secure and click Next.
6. To configure authorized users or authorized exceptions, select the applicable check box, click Add, and use the Select Users Or Groups dialog box to add the applicable entries.
7. Repeat step 6 for authorized computers and exceptions. Click Next.
8. Choose the profiles to which the rules should apply. Click Next. Name the rule. Click Finish.

IMPORTANT **WHAT WILL BE ON THE EXAM**

This book covers the objectives presented in the list of objectives for the exam. However, the Microsoft certification page for this exam clearly states, "Please note that the questions may test on, but will not be limited to, the topics described in the bulleted text." This means that you'll see questions on items that aren't addressed here, and we can't even guess at what those might be. However, to provide an example, you might see questions that ask you about the different types of Wi-Fi authentication, including Temporal Key Integrity Protocol (TKIP), Advanced Encryption System (AES), and the various Wi-Fi Protected Access (WPA) options. Likewise, you might be faced with questions that require you to know a specific file extension, such as .wfw, which is the file type used when you export a Windows Firewall policy. You might be expected to know a little about Branch Cache or Direct Access, too.

Because there is no way for us to address all of these things in a single book, it is vital you study and prepare for aspects other than what's offered here. To find out where to access additional resources, visit *http://www.microsoft.com/learning/en-us/exam-70-687.aspx* and under Skills Measured, click Show All. For each objective there is a list of additional preparation resources. Review that list and become familiar with the options presented.

Thought experiment

Configure Media Player sharing over the Internet

In this thought experiment, apply what you've learned about this objective. You can find answers to these questions in the "Answers" section at the end of this chapter.

A client has a large library of media that contains thousands of music files. He wants to share that media in such a way as to be able to access it over the Internet from another computer he owns and keeps at his office. He's enabled the appropriate options in Media Player on both computers. However, he can't get sharing to work.

1. What do you need to do regarding the firewall so that this client can allow Media Player to share music files over the Internet?
2. Will you perform the required task in Windows Firewall or Windows Firewall with Advanced Security?
3. Will you need to be logged on as an Administrator to do this?

Objective summary

- In Windows Firewall you can view the settings for private and public networks and make basic changes to the settings there. You can also disable the firewall there.
- You can make changes to how Network Discovery is configured for the available public and private profiles using the Advanced Sharing Settings in the Network And Sharing Center.
- In Windows Firewall, apps are either allowed through the firewall or not. You can create exceptions to configure specific apps to be able to get through the firewall.
- Windows Firewall with Advanced Security offers many more options for administrators, including configuring their own inbound, outbound, and connection security rules; configuring authenticated exceptions; and making changes to existing firewall settings.

Objective review

Answer the following questions to test your knowledge of the information in this objective. You can find the answers to these questions and explanations of why each answer choice is correct or incorrect in the "Answers" section at the end of this chapter.

1. When you create an inbound or outbound rule in Windows Firewall with Advanced Security and you choose the Allow The Connection If It Is Secure option on the Action page of the New Rule Wizard, what type of authentication requirements must be met before data can be transferred to and from the connecting computers?
    - **A.** Connections must be authenticated with IPsec and use null encapsulation.
    - **B.** Connections can be protected by IPsec, but they don't have to be.

C. Connections must require privacy and must be encrypted.
D. Connections will be secured using the settings in IPsec properties and rules in the Connection Security Rule node.

2. When you create a Connection Security rule in Windows Firewall with Advanced Security, what can you use an isolation rule for? (Choose all that apply.)
   A. You can restrict connections based on domain membership.
   B. You can restrict connections based on the health status of the computer.
   C. You can require a tunnel be created.
   D. You can use the rule to isolate a subnet based on a scope of IP addresses.
3. Where do you disable Network Discovery for the Private network profile?
   A. In the Network And Sharing Center, from Adapter Settings
   B. In Windows Firewall, from Advanced Settings
   C. In the Network And Sharing Center, from Advanced Properties
   D. In Windows Firewall with Advanced Security, from the Windows Firewall Properties dialog box
4. Where can you view a list of active firewall rules?
   A. In the Network And Sharing Center, from Adapter Settings
   B. In Windows Firewall, from Advanced Settings
   C. In the Network And Sharing Center, from Advanced Properties
   D. In Windows Firewall with Advanced Security, from the Monitoring option

Objective 3.4: Configure remote management

With remote management tools and technologies, a network administrator can access a computer on the network, take control of it, and perform tasks on it, without having to be physically in front of the computer. This saves both time and money by reducing the number of trips required to service problematic computers. Users can also remotely access their own computers for the purpose of working at them while not physically sitting in front of them.

This objective covers how to:

- Configure and use Remote Assistance and Remote Desktop
- Make modifications remotely using an MMC
- Explore Remote Management Tools and configure settings
- Make modifications remotely using Windows PowerShell

Configure and use Remote Assistance and Remote Desktop

There are two technologies both you and end users can employ to remotely access and manage a computer. Remote Assistance is one of those, and it enables a technician to take control of a computer to troubleshoot and perform maintenance tasks without having to physically travel to the problematic machine. This enables the technician to resolve problems without leaving his home or office. The end user must be there to authorize this, and the user can end the session at any time. This technology is generally used only to troubleshoot remote computers and is not used for telecommuting or accessing files or folders.

Remote Desktop is another remote option. Remote Desktop enables users to connect to their office computer from home for the purpose of telecommuting and accessing files and folders remotely. Once the connection is made, the remote computer is locked so that no one else can access it. The user can do anything that would be possible while sitting in front of the computer (short of pressing physical buttons or picking up print jobs), including running desktop programs and accessing files and folders. In another scenario, network administrators use this technology to service file servers, print servers, domain controllers, and so on without having to physically travel to the machine.

Remote Access and Remote Desktop are built-in, user-friendly tools. However, there are a few settings to take note of before sitting for the exam. You need to know how to enable or disable these features on an end user's computer; you need to understand what options are available when configuring a remote desktop session; and you need to know how to configure and hold a remote assistance session.

Enable or disable remote features

By default, Remote Assistance connections are enabled for a Windows 8.1 computer and Remote Desktop connections are disabled. You can change both in the System Properties dialog box, shown in Figure 3-17. You can open this dialog box in many ways. One is to type **System** on the Start screen and click System in the results. In the System dialog box, click Advanced System Settings or Remote Settings in the left pane. The options you want to configure are on the Remote tab. (If you plan to access this computer via Remote Desktop, enable the option now.)

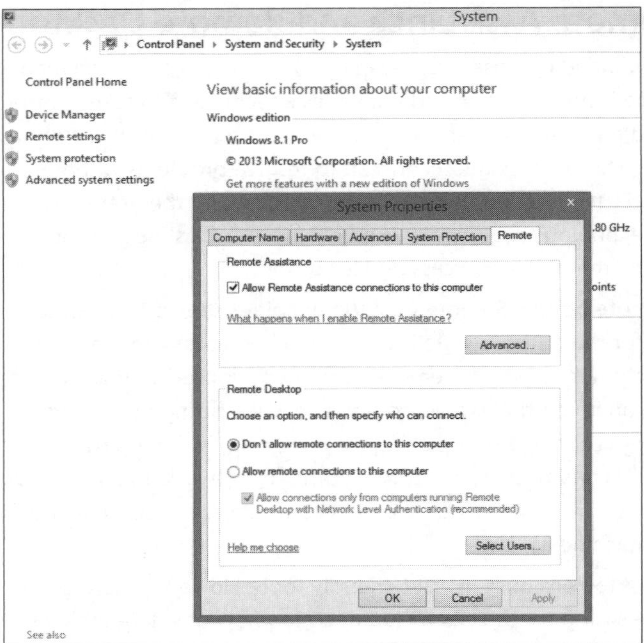

FIGURE 3-17 Use the System Properties dialog box to allow or disallow Remote Assistance and Remote Desktop sessions.

EXAM TIP

You can't access a computer remotely using Remote Desktop if the computer is in sleep or hibernation mode. Thus, if asked about why a Remote Desktop session can't be enabled, even though the technology has worked before, consider this as an answer option. (You might also want to make changes to the Power Options in Control Panel to overcome this issue.)

Explore Remote Desktop options

You and your end users can access the Remote Desktop Connection dialog box by typing **Remote** on the Start screen and clicking Remote Desktop Connection in the results. When the dialog box opens, click Show Options to access all of the options shown in Figure 3-18.

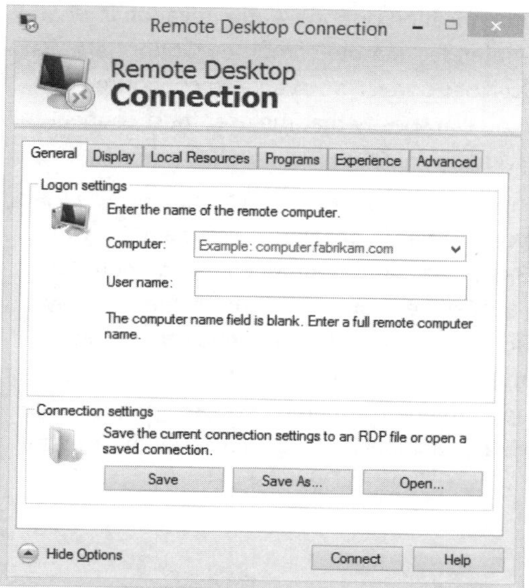

FIGURE 3-18 The Remote Desktop Connection dialog box offers several options.

The available tabs offer the options you need to configure your Remote Desktop connection:

- **General** Use the settings on this tab to specify the computer name and, optionally, the user name and to save connection settings.
- **Display** Use the settings on this tab to choose the size of the remote desktop, which is set to Large by default. You can also choose the color depth. If your user is connecting over a free and fast network, these default settings are fine. However, for users who access their desktop over metered mobile broadband, you should opt for more bandwidth-friendly settings.
- **Local Resources** Use this tab to configure settings for audio (perhaps to disable audio altogether), whether access to printers and the Clipboard should be enabled, and when to enable Windows key combinations, among other things.
- **Programs** Use this tab to name a program that should start when the connection is made.
- **Experience** Use the settings on this tab to configure how the network should be configured to optimize performance. By default, Windows automatically detects the settings, but in the case of metered connections, you might want to change this to a specific setting such as low-speed broadband. When you manually configure this setting, you can configure what options you want to allow, including but not limited to the desktop background and menu and window animation. By default, Reconnect If The Connection Is Dropped is enabled, but it can be changed if desired.

- **Advanced** Use this tab to configure authentication options. Authentication is what verifies that the user is connecting to the intended remote computer. Options are Warn Me, Connect And Don't Warn Me, and Do Not Connect. You can also configure the Connect From Anywhere setting, where you can specify that the user must connect to a dedicated remote desktop gateway server.

With the desired configuration set, you can now use the General tab to connect. You need to know the name of the computer to which to connect, though, and in a domain this can be a bit complicated. As you can see in Figure 3-18, that computer name looks something like this: computername.domainname.com. On a local area connection, the name is simply the computer name. Whatever the case, you also need to have the credentials to log on. In the case of Remote Desktop, that's the user name and password. Take note, though, that the user name will have to be something like \\computername\username. You can't just type the user name and get connected. To disconnect while in an active session, just click the X in the upper-right corner.

Configure and use Remote Assistance

To use Remote Assistance, the user must be at the problematic computer. A Remote Assistance session must be initiated by that user, and the user must approve the connection before it can be made. The key word to search for from the Start screen to initiate a Remote Assistance session is "invite," not "Remote Assistance" as you might guess. The user needs to access the Invite Someone To Connect To Your PC And Help You, Or Offer To Help Someone Else option from the Start screen in the results. The user can also search for "Invite" or "Remote Assistance" in Control Panel. However the user gets there, the user must click Invite Someone You Trust To Help You in the Windows Remote Assistance dialog box shown in Figure 3-19.

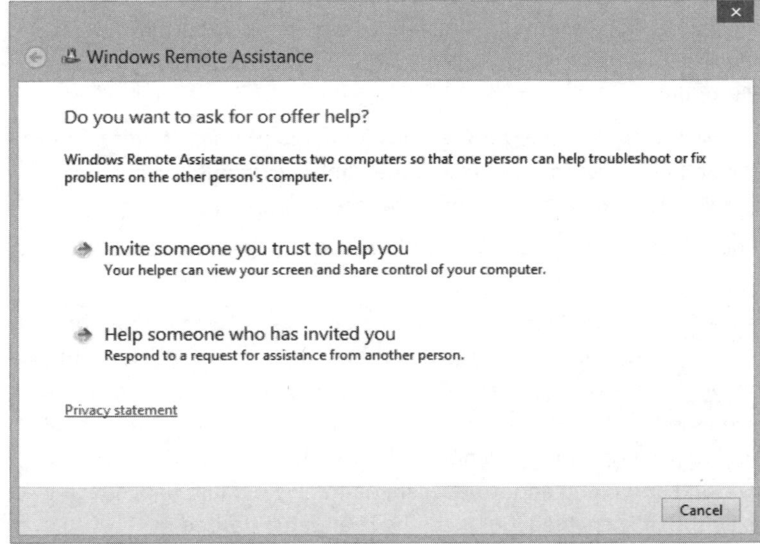

FIGURE 3-19 The user must initiate a Remote Assistance session.

The user then has three options: Save This Invitation As A File (the user saves the file and gets that file using her method of choice to the help and support team); Use Email To Send An Invitation (the user sends the invitation using an email client on the machine but cannot send it using any form of web-based email); and Use Easy Connect (the easiest option if it is enabled by the help and support team). Because one of the objectives on the exam is to configure Remote Assistance (which we've done) including Easy Connect (which we haven't done), we'll look at the Easy Connect option here. However, you also should understand how the other two options work.

When the user opts for Easy Connect, an Easy Connect password appears. The user only needs to relay that password to the help and support team. This can be done by phone, fax, email, or even text. The support technician can then send a connection request, which the user then accepts. Both of these items are shown in Figure 3-20. Once the connection is made, the "Expert" can ask to control the computer to resolve the problem, train the user, or perform other tasks.

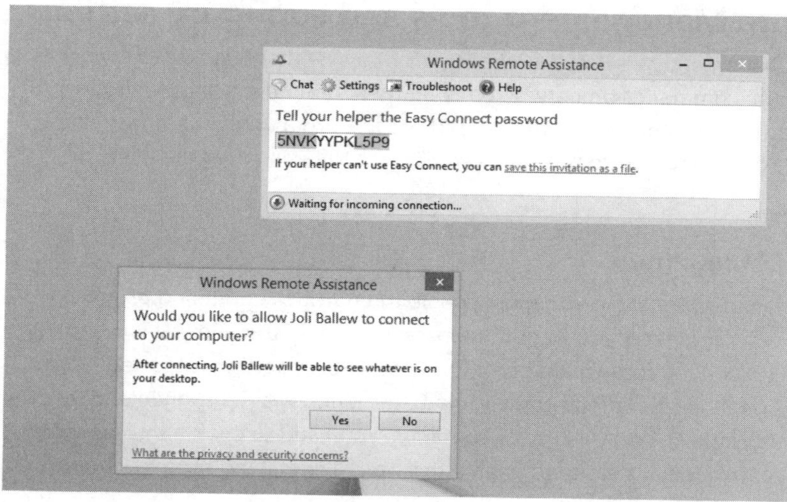

FIGURE 3-20 Use Easy Connect to get help quickly and easily using Remote Desktop.

Make modifications remotely using an MMC

Although the Microsoft Management Consoles (MMCs) available in Windows 8.1 are all configured to manage local resources by default, you use them to make modifications on remote machines using Computer Management or built-in MMCs.

To see how to connect to another computer to manage it, open Computer Management; in the left pane, right-click Computer Management (Local); and click Connect To Another Computer. In the dialog box that appears, verify that Another Computer is selected, type the name of the computer to which to connect, and click OK. Wait while the connection is made. If you are prompted to enable something to pass through the firewall in Windows Firewall with Advanced Policy or enable a policy setting in Group Policy, do so. Then, click the desired item to manage in the left pane and make configuration changes as desired in the right pane. See Figure 3-21.

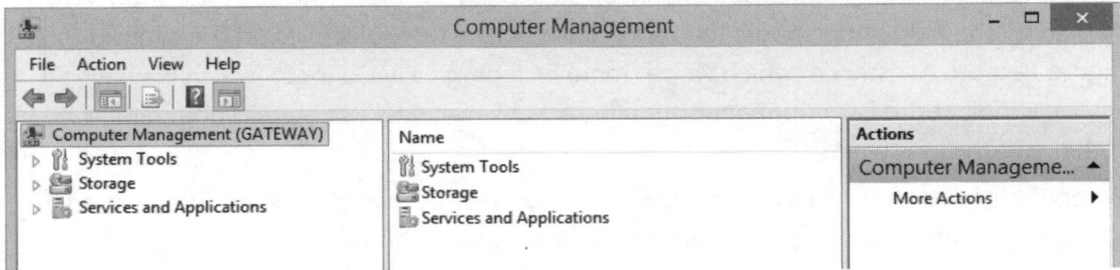

FIGURE 3-21 Use Computer Management to connect to and manage another computer on your network.

Explore Remote Management tools and configure settings

Windows Remote Management (WinRM) is a Windows 8.1 service that enables a network administrator to execute commands on networked computers remotely, using Windows PowerShell and Windows Remote Shell (WinRS.exe). There are Group Policy settings related to the WinRM Service and Windows Remote Shell you'll want to familiarize yourself with as well.

Enable Remote Management

To use the Remote Management tools, you must enable them from a command prompt or use Group Policy on each computer you want to manage (including the one you'll use to manage and the ones that need to be managed). The Group Policy setting is located here: Computer Configuration, Policies, Administrative Templates, Windows Components, Windows Remote Management (WinRM), WinRM Service container. You need to enable this for each Group Policy object to manage. It's easier to enable this from a command prompt, though.

To enable Remote Management, follow these steps:

1. Open an elevated command prompt.
2. Type **winrm quickconfig** and press Enter.
3. When prompted to make these changes, type **y** and press Enter again.
4. When prompted again, type **y** and press Enter. See Figure 3-22.
5. Close the command prompt window.

EXAM TIP

If you get a question about why the WinRM command won't work, it might be because the network type is set to Public. The network type must be Private or Domain.

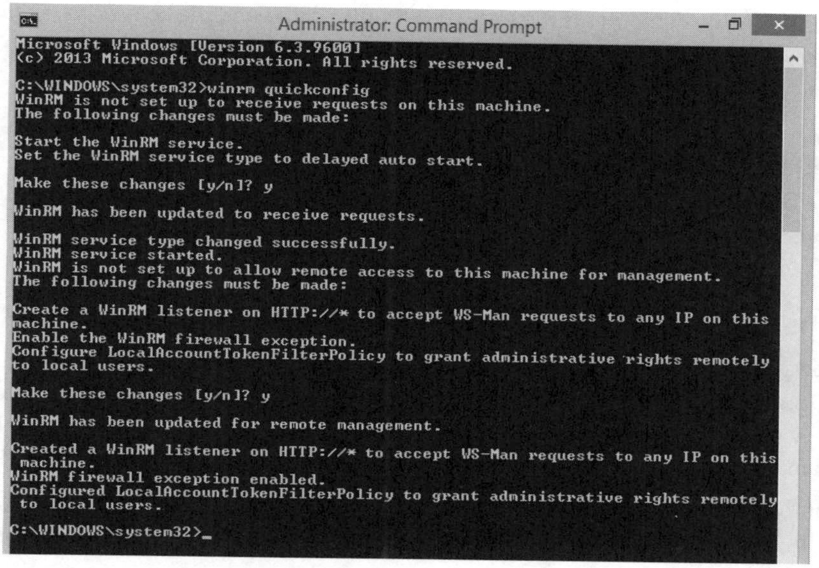

```
Administrator: Command Prompt
Microsoft Windows [Version 6.3.9600]
(c) 2013 Microsoft Corporation. All rights reserved.

C:\WINDOWS\system32>winrm quickconfig
WinRM is not set up to receive requests on this machine.
The following changes must be made:

Start the WinRM service.
Set the WinRM service type to delayed auto start.

Make these changes [y/n]? y

WinRM has been updated to receive requests.

WinRM service type changed successfully.
WinRM service started.
WinRM is not set up to allow remote access to this machine for management.
The following changes must be made:

Create a WinRM listener on HTTP://* to accept WS-Man requests to any IP on this
machine.
Enable the WinRM firewall exception.
Configure LocalAccountTokenFilterPolicy to grant administrative rights remotely
to local users.

Make these changes [y/n]? y

WinRM has been updated for remote management.

Created a WinRM listener on HTTP://* to accept WS-Man requests to any IP on this
 machine.
WinRM firewall exception enabled.
Configured LocalAccountTokenFilterPolicy to grant administrative rights remotely
 to local users.

C:\WINDOWS\system32>_
```

FIGURE 3-22 Enable Remote Management.

Execute commands from a command prompt

With WinRM enabled, WinRS is used at an elevated command prompt (or a Windows PowerShell session) using the WinRS command. Here are some of the applicable parameters:

- **–r:computer** Use this parameter to specify the computer on which to perform commands. You can use a NetBIOS name or a fully qualified domain name (FQDN).
- **[-u:user]** Use this parameter to specify the account you'll use to perform the command on the remote computer. This needs to be an account on the remote computer.
- **[-p:password]** Use this parameter to specify the password associated with the user account name. (You'll be prompted if you don't enter it here.)
- **Command** Use this parameter to specify the commands to use along with any additional associated parameters.
- More succinctly: **winrs [/<*parameter*>[:<*value*>]] <*command*>**.

There are other options beyond typing the computer, user, and password while using WinRS, although these are the most common. To see additional commands and syntax, refer to this page: *http://technet.microsoft.com/en-us/library/hh875630.aspx.*

Make modifications remotely using Windows PowerShell

You can use Windows PowerShell v3 to remotely manage another computer, using an elevated Windows PowerShell session. If you enabled WinRM at a command prompt as instructed earlier, Windows PowerShell is ready to receive commands. To execute a Windows PowerShell command on a remote computer, you use the following syntax: icm computer {*command*}, where the computer is the remote computer name and the command is the Windows PowerShell command you want to use. ICM is short for Invoke-Command. To see more about the syntax in a Windows PowerShell session, type **Winrs /? and icm -?**.

> ***MORE INFO*** **ICM SYNTAX**
>
> **For more information about ICM syntax, refer to this page on Technet: *http://technet.microsoft.com/en-us/library/hh849719.aspx*.**

Access the applicable Group Policy settings

The Windows Remote Shell Group Policy settings are located here on a domain server: Computer Configuration, Policies, Administrative Templates, Windows Components, Windows Remote Shell container. You'll need to configure any desired settings for each Group Policy object you manage. You can use these settings to change the default behavior of WinRS.

Some of the settings you might want to review include Allow Remote Shell Access, Specify Idle Timeout, and Specify Shell Timeout. These are available in the R2 update for Windows Server 2012.

The WinRM Service Group Policy settings are located here on a domain server: Computer Configuration, Policies, Administrative Templates, Windows Components, Windows Remote Management (WinRM), WinRM Service.

Some of the settings you might want to review include Allow Remote Server Management Through WinRM, Allow Basic Authentication, Allow Unencrypted Traffic, and Turn On Compatibility HTTP Listener. These are located in the R2 update for Windows Server 2012.

Thought experiment

Choose the applicable remote management tool

In this thought experiment, apply what you've learned about this objective. You can find answers to these questions in the "Answers" section at the end of this chapter.

You have a client who needs help with several items, including configuring her Windows 8.1 computer to boot directly to the desktop, installing a network printer, and setting her favorite pages as home pages in Internet Explorer on the desktop. You are in your office across the company complex, about a quarter of a mile away. You don't want to walk over there.

Answer the following questions regarding this scenario:

1. **Should you use Remote Assistance, Remote Desktop, or Remote Management Tools?**
2. **Does the user need to be at her computer to receive your help?**
3. **What must the user do before you can help her?**

Objective summary

- Remote Assistance can be used to troubleshoot problematic computers without having to physically access them. The user must be present, send an invitation, and accept your help when you offer it.
- Remote Desktop is a technology that enables end users to access their desktop when they are away from it. This can be configured so that a user can work from home or on the road when circumstances require it.
- It is possible to remotely manage a computer from a command line and in a Windows PowerShell session. Remote Management must be enabled on each computer first.

Objective review

Answer the following questions to test your knowledge of the information in this objective. You can find the answers to these questions and explanations of why each answer choice is correct or incorrect in the "Answers" section at the end of this chapter.

1. You've created an MMC and added three snap-ins. Each snap-in is exactly like the others, except they are each configured to manage a different networked computer. Only one works. What would you suspect is the problem? (Choose all that apply.)
   - **A.** You can only use one instance of a snap-in per MMC.
   - **B.** Windows Firewall is blocking access on the other two client computers.
   - **C.** Remote Management isn't enabled on the client computer.
   - **D.** You don't have appropriate credentials on the two computers that aren't allowing access.
2. What command is used to start the Windows Remote Management service from a command prompt?
   - **A.** Winrs quickconfig
   - **B.** Winrm [computername] quickconfig
   - **C.** Winrm quickconfig
   - **D.** Winrs startconfig
3. You are trying to connect to your office computer using Remote Desktop. You are at home. You can't connect. What could be the problem? (Choose all that apply.)
   - **A.** You need to allow Remote Desktop connections on your office computer.
   - **B.** The remote computer is asleep or hibernating.
   - **C.** You typed the computer name or password incorrectly.
   - **D.** You failed to configure the options in the Remote Desktop Connection window, specifically the options located on the Experience tab.

4. How can you use the WinRS command to remotely manage a computer? (Choose all that apply.)
   - **A.** You can't. You have to use the WinRM command.
   - **B.** By using the Group Policy Management Editor.
   - **C.** From an elevated command prompt.
   - **D.** In an elevated Windows PowerShell session.

Chapter summary

- A computer must have a unique IP address to communicate on a network; those addresses can be static, be assigned by DHCP, or come from Windows from APIPA.
- Location-aware printing enables you to configure what printer users should print to based on the network to which they are currently connected.
- You can make changes to IP addresses and name DNS servers, among other things, in a network adapter's Properties dialog box.
- Various network management tools are available, including command-line tools like Netsh, graphical tools like the Network And Sharing Center, and troubleshooting command-line tools like Ping and Tracert.
- Windows Firewall and Windows Firewall with Advanced Security let you control all aspects of the firewall. You can allow apps through the firewall and create your own inbound, outbound, and connection security rules, too.
- Several remote management tools are available, including Remote Assistance, Remote Desktop, and Remote Management Tools.

Answers

This section contains the solutions to the thought experiments and answers to the objective review questions in this chapter.

Objective 3.1: Thought experiment

1. There is probably something wrong with the wireless adapter. Maybe it isn't enabled or needs an updated driver to work.
2. Probably. The Network And Sharing Center Internet Connection troubleshooter can discover that the Wi-Fi adapter is disabled, although it might not know why. If the adapter is functional, it can enable it with administrator approval.
3. You can try the Action Center to see if a new driver is available for the Wi-Fi adapter. If not, you can try to locate one using Device Manager. You can also refer to the manufacturer's website to find out how to enable the Wi-Fi adapter, if that is the problem.

Objective 3.1: Review

1. **Correct Answer**: C
   - A. **Incorrect**. This is handled by a DHCP server.
   - B. **Incorrect**. There are technologies to handle this, including various tunneling options, but it is not the job of DNS.
   - C. **Correct**. DNS is responsible for this.
   - D. **Incorrect**. APIPA is performed by Windows to assign an IP address when one isn't available.
2. **Correct Answers**: A and C
   - A. **Correct**. You can assign a static IP address from the adapter's Properties dialog box.
   - B. **Incorrect**. You cannot assign an IP address here, although you can review the settings configured for the Network Firewall, Internet Security Settings, and so on.
   - C. **Correct**. Netsh can be used to assign IP addresses to hosts.
   - D. **Incorrect**. You cannot assign IP addresses in the Network And Sharing Center.
3. **Correct Answer**: B
   - A. **Incorrect**. This will display some, but not all, of the required information.
   - B. **Correct**. This will display the required information.
   - C. **Incorrect**. Ping is used to test connectivity between one host and another.
   - D. **Incorrect**. Tracert is used to determine the path a packet takes to get to its destination.

4. **Correct Answer**: D
   - A. **Incorrect**. You cannot change the network location here, but you can change many other settings, including assigning a static IP address.
   - B. **Incorrect**. This is not the proper place to change the network location. This is where you check for solutions to problems you've encountered.
   - C. **Incorrect**. This was how you changed the network location in Windows 8, but is no longer available in Windows 8.1.
   - D. **Correct**. This is the proper way to change the network location in Windows 8.1.

Objective 3.2: Thought experiment

1. Location-aware printing. This feature enables default printers to be configured based on the network the user is connected to. Location-aware printing uses the Network Location Awareness service and the Network List service to determine the network location.
2. Use the Netsh command to show the list of wireless profiles and then use this command to forget specific networks: Type **netsh wlan delete profile name=<*profile name*>**.

Objective 3.2: Review

1. **Correct Answer**: A
   - A. **Correct**. Windows always chooses Ethernet if it's available over other networking options.
   - B. **Incorrect**. If there were only three wireless connections but no Ethernet, this would be correct, but Windows defaults to Ethernet when it is available.
   - C. **Incorrect**. Broadband is used as a last resort. Ethernet and Wi-Fi are chosen before broadband.
   - D. **Incorrect**. The user will not be prompted to connect to an Ethernet network, and Ethernet is what Windows will use.
2. **Correct Answers**: A and D
   - A. **Correct**. This is the first step to making the required configuration changes.
   - B. **Incorrect**. You do not need to install anything to make the required changes.
   - C. **Incorrect**. This is not the proper option for making the required changes.
   - D. **Correct**. This is the second step to making the required configuration changes.
3. **Correct Answers**: B and D
   - A. **Incorrect**. Netsh is not a Windows PowerShell command.
   - B. **Correct**. Netsh is a command-line command.

   C. **Incorrect**. You do not need elevated privileges to use Netsh.
   D. **Correct**. This is the proper syntax.

4. **Correct Answer**: B
   A. **Incorrect**. Add is not a valid Netsh parameter.
   B. **Correct**. This is where you set up a new network.
   C. **Incorrect**. The network name will not appear in this list if it is not broadcasting its SSID.
   D. **Incorrect**. Using a troubleshooting tool won't help you connect to a network that is not broadcasting its SSID.

Objective 3.3: Thought experiment

1. You need to create an exception for the Media Player Network Sharing Server (Internet) in Windows Firewall.
2. You can perform this task in Windows Firewall. You will create an app exception.
3. Yes. You must be able to input Administrator credentials or be logged on as an Administrator to enable Change Settings in Windows Firewall.

Objective 3.3: Review

1. **Correct Answer**: D
   A. **Incorrect**. Although IPsec plays a role, null encapsulation is an option if you choose Custom after selecting the Allow The Connection If It Is Secure option. However, it is not required.
   B. **Incorrect**. This is the setting for Allow Connection, not Allow The Connection If It Is Secure.
   C. **Incorrect**. This is an option if you choose Custom after selecting the Allow The Connection If It Is Secure option. Privacy and encryption are not required in this scenario.
   D. **Correct**. This is called an authenticated exception.

2. **Correct Answers**: A and B
   A. **Correct**. This is true; you can restrict connections based on domain membership.
   B. **Correct**. This is true; you can restrict connections based on the health of the computer.
   C. **Incorrect**. If this were true, you'd be creating a Tunnel rule.
   D. **Incorrect**. You can name IP scopes of addresses in rules, such as server-to-server, but not with an isolation rule.

3. **Correct Answer**: C
   - A. **Incorrect**. You make these changes in the Network And Sharing Center, from Advanced Properties.
   - B. **Incorrect**. You make these changes in the Network And Sharing Center, from Advanced Properties.
   - C. **Correct**. Yes, this is where you make these changes.
   - D. **Incorrect**. You make these changes in the Network And Sharing Center, from Advanced Properties.
4. **Correct Answer**: D
   - A. **Incorrect**. The rules are listed in Windows Firewall with Advanced Security.
   - B. **Incorrect**. The rules are listed in Windows Firewall with Advanced Security.
   - C. **Incorrect**. The rules are listed in Windows Firewall with Advanced Security.
   - D. **Correct**. Yes, this is where you can view a list of active firewall rules.

Objective 3.4: Thought experiment

1. Remote Assistance is the best tool to use here.
2. Yes, the user needs to be present so that she can accept your help when you offer it.
3. She must relay an invitation to you. She must also accept your help when you offer it.

Objective 3.4: Review

1. **Correct Answers**: B and D
   - A. **Incorrect**. You can have multiple instances of the same snap-in in a single console.
   - B. **Correct**. It is most likely a firewall issue.
   - C. **Incorrect**. Windows Remote Management (WinRM) does not have to be enabled for this technology to work.
   - D. **Correct**. You must have the proper credentials to gain access to remote data.
2. **Correct Answer**: C
   - A. **Incorrect**. WinRM is used for Remote Management, not WinRS.
   - B. **Incorrect**. You don't type the computer name when enabling WinRM.
   - C. **Correct**. This is the correct syntax.
   - D. **Incorrect**. Startconfig is not a valid parameter.
3. **Correct Answers**: A, B, and C
   - A. **Correct**. This could be the problem because the option to accept Remote Desktop connections must be enabled.
   - B. **Correct**. The computer must be awake.

- **C. Correct**. This is a common mistake. You can't connect if you don't type the proper credentials.
- **D. Incorrect**. The settings here are configured with default settings. You don't have to change them.

4. **Correct Answers**: C and D

- **A. Incorrect**. WinRM is used to enable Remote Management. WinRS is used to send commands.
- **B. Incorrect**. Although you can enable Remote Management in the Group Policy Management Editor, you can't send commands from there.
- **C. Correct**. You can use WinRS at a command line.
- **D. Correct**. You can use WinRS in a Windows PowerShell session.

CHAPTER 4

Configure access to resources

Users need access to resources, including but not limited to files, folders, network shares, and printers. Your job, at times at least, is to let those users access what they need, and nothing more. That's how you keep resources secure and data in the right hands. This objective covers all aspects of this, from configuring shared resources to configuring file and folder (and printer) access, and on to configuring authentication and authorization for both workgroups and domains.

Objectives in this chapter:

- Objective 4.1: Configure shared resources
- Objective 4.2: Configure file and folder access
- Objective 4.3: Configure authentication and authorization

Objective 4.1: Configure shared resources

There are multiple objectives in this lesson, and they all relate to how to share and manage resources on local networks. Here you'll learn about homegroups, folder permissions, libraries, shared printers, and even SkyDrive. Regarding sharing, there are three ways to share discussed here: homegroup sharing, folder sharing, and public folder sharing. Folder sharing can be used in domain networks, too, although the way you handle it is a little different from simply sharing a few folders on a small, local network and letting users manage them as they like. (In an Active Directory Domain Services domain, network administrators manage authentication, authorization, and all aspects of sharing from the various servers they manage on the network.) SkyDrive can also be considered a sharing tool, although users might only use it to share data with themselves to have access to their files from anywhere.

This objective covers how to:

- Configure HomeGroup settings
- Configure shared folder permissions
- Configure file libraries
- Configure shared printers
- Set up and configure SkyDrive

NOTE

The name SkyDrive is changing to OneDrive and at some point the exam will also make the terminology change.

Configure HomeGroup settings

A homegroup lets home users easily share documents, printers, and media with others on their private, local network. This is the simplest kind of sharing, but it is limited in what permissions and restrictions can be placed on the data shared. By default, all users who join a homegroup (and there can be only one homegroup per network) have read-only access to what's already shared. Users can reconfigure this, though, allowing both read and write access if desired.

When opting for a homegroup, users can do the following:

- Create or join a homegroup from the prompt offered by Windows, provided the network is configured as Private.
- Create or join a homegroup from the Network And Sharing Center, provided the computers that want to join are Windows 7- or Windows 8-based.
- Work through the applicable homegroup wizard to create or join a homegroup. Windows will generate a random password other users will need to join.
- Share files from their original locations and from their default libraries.
- Grant read-only or read/write access to the data they've shared.
- Limit access to only those network users who also have an account and password on their computer.
- Configure the same permissions for all network users or set different permissions for individual users.

EXAM TIP

There are reasons why a homegroup can't be created or enabled, and one is that IPv6 isn't enabled on a particular computer on the network.

Although we could spend a few pages walking you through how to create and join a homegroup, because it's done with a wizard, that isn't really necessary. However, you should create a homegroup on your own local network to see how it's done and let other computers join it so that you are familiar with the process. Note that users might already be joined to a homegroup, as Windows detects existing homegroups automatically during setup. Figure 4-1 shows a computer that is connected to a private network and has joined a homegroup.

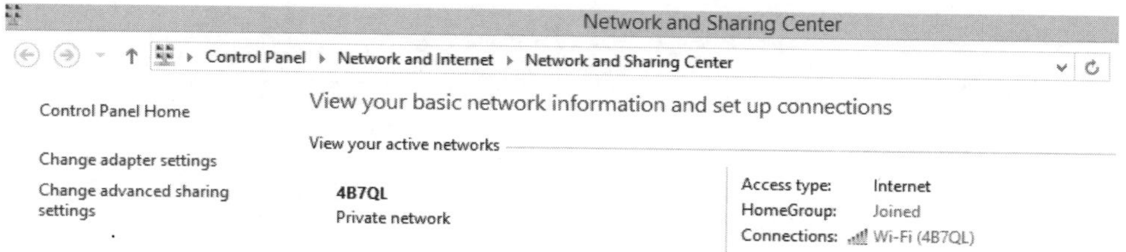

FIGURE 4-1 Create, join, or view homegroup status from the Network And Sharing Center.

Once a homegroup is configured, users can share data with the homegroup from File Explorer on the Share tab (among other places). Note the Stop Sharing option for the selected folder, shown in Figure 4-2, and the option to allow the entire homegroup to view or view and edit the selected data. You can see here that a specific user, BallewWin8@hotmail.com, also has an option.

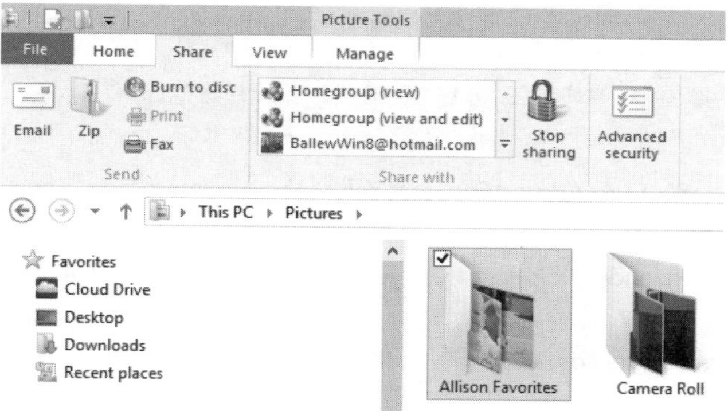

FIGURE 4-2 In File Explorer, use the Share tab to choose how to share selected data with homegroup participants.

If you don't want to share the data with everyone in the homegroup, you can opt to share it with only specific people. You can also set different permissions for the people you choose. This is a very simple way to share data, and it will work on small home networks but not too many other places. To do this, follow these steps:

1. Open File Explorer and select any folder.
2. Right-click the folder and from the shortcut menu, point to Share With, and then click Specific People.
3. In the File Sharing window, click Homegroup and click Remove. See Figure 4-3.

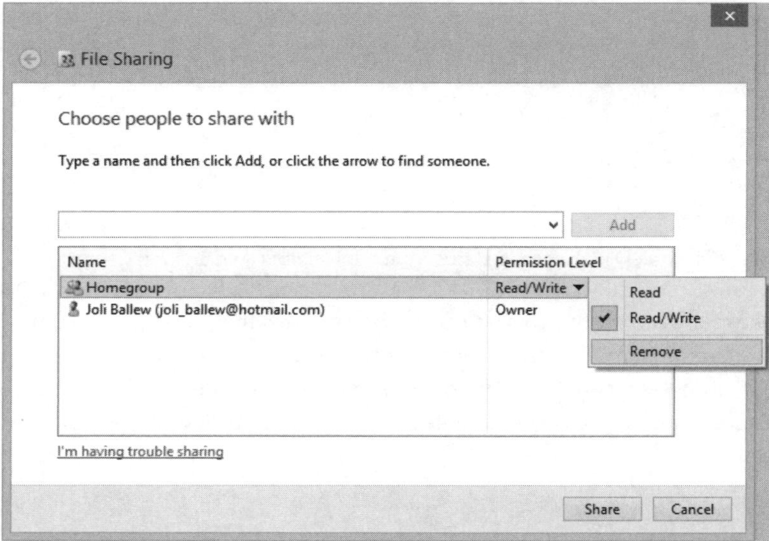

FIGURE 4-3 Remove Homegroup from the sharing list to set up sharing with only specific people.

4. Click the down arrow to the left of the Add option, and select the person to add. Then click Add to complete the task.
5. With that done, click the arrow beside the person you just added and choose Read or Read/Write.
6. Repeat to add other network users, as desired.

Configure shared folder permissions

There are two folder sharing options to discuss here: Public folder sharing and what we refer to as *Any* folder sharing. Any folder sharing is the more complex of the two and offers more options than Public folder sharing. You can also share from a command line, from a Microsoft Management Console (MMC), and using Windows PowerShell.

Public folder sharing

As you might guess, Public folder sharing involves the Public folders. There are several, including Public Documents, Public Music, Public Pictures, and Public Videos, and you can create your own. To use this kind of sharing you have to move the data to share to the applicable Public folder. (You could copy it, but this complicates document versioning and also creates duplicates on the computer.) The upside is that this is a very easy way to make data accessible to users who need it, at least after you've moved the data to share. The downside is that you have very little control of the level of sharing to configure.

Everyone with a user account and password on your computer can access the Public folder if Public folder sharing is enabled in this manner. You can make changes to Public Sharing from the Network And Sharing Center, Change Advanced Sharing Settings, and the All Networks option. There are two options:

- Turn On Sharing So Anyone With Network Access Can Read And Write Files In The Public Folders or Turn Off Public Folder Sharing (people logged on to this computer can still access these folders).
- Turn On Password Protected Sharing or Turn Off Password Protected Sharing. The former configures it so that users must have a user account and password on the computer to access shared files, printers, and the Public folders. The latter lets other people have access who do not have an account and password. You can also turn on file and printer sharing for the Private or Public profiles, if desired.

> ***MORE INFO*** **SHARE PERMISSIONS**
>
> **Understand that in these sections we are talking about Share permissions. There are three: Read, Change, and Full Control. However, there are also New Technology File System (NTFS) permissions you can configure, which you'll learn about in Objective 4.2. If both Share and NTFS permissions are applied to a share for a specific user, the least restrictive is calculated for both and then the two results are compared. The final permission applied to the share is the more restrictive of the two. However, Deny always overrides Allow.**

Any folder sharing

Any folder sharing has a lot more options than the other types you've seen so far. Any folder sharing lets users do the following:

- Share files from any location in addition to their original location
- Set different permissions for individual users
- Protect data in domain networks
- Protect data in local networks that require more security than the homegroup or public folder option can offer

To get started you must first choose or create a folder to share. Then, you can right-click the folder, click Properties, and click the Sharing tab to display the Properties dialog box shown in Figure 4-4. It's important to note that if you click Share in the Properties dialog box, you are given the same sharing options you saw earlier for homegroups (Figure 4-3). That's not where the power in Any folder sharing lies. Instead, click Advanced Sharing to access the Advanced Sharing dialog box, also shown in Figure 4-4.

> ***MORE INFO*** **SHARE CHARACTERISTICS**
>
> **Share permissions have the following characteristics:**
>
> - **They apply only to users who gain access to the resource over the network. They do not apply to users who log on locally. To protect a resource in these cases, you must use NTFS to set permissions.**

- **They are the only way to secure network resources on FAT and FAT32 volumes, because NTFS permissions are not available on those volumes.**
- **They specify the maximum number of users who are allowed to access the shared resource or folder over the network.**
- **When both Share and NTFS permissions are applied, the cumulative permission for both sets is compared and the more restrictive permission is applied.**

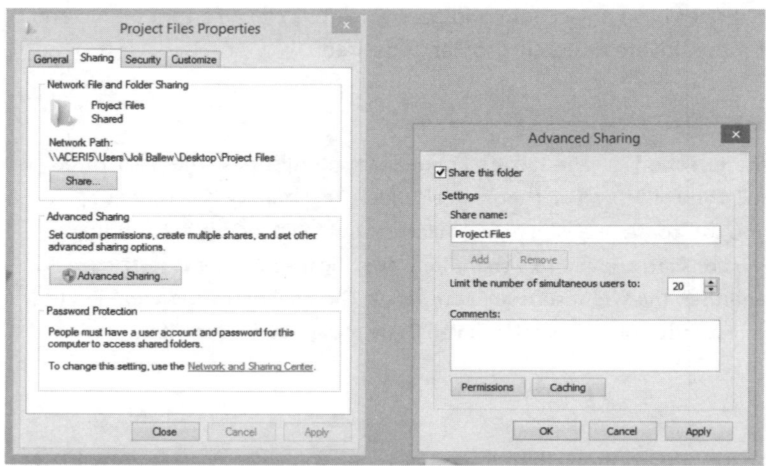

FIGURE 4-4 With Any folder sharing you're in complete control of what is shared and with whom.

Now you have several options. First, select the Share This Folder check box, which defaults to 20 simultaneous users. Next, click Permissions. Now you have access to the advanced sharing options shown in Figure 4-5. What you'll likely want to do here is remove Everyone from the list (I've done this in Figure 4-5 already) and then add specific users or groups whom you want to have access (I've done that, too). The default permission is Read, but you can add Change or Full Control for the selected user or group. You could also opt to deny access, although this is not the generally accepted way to limit access to a share.

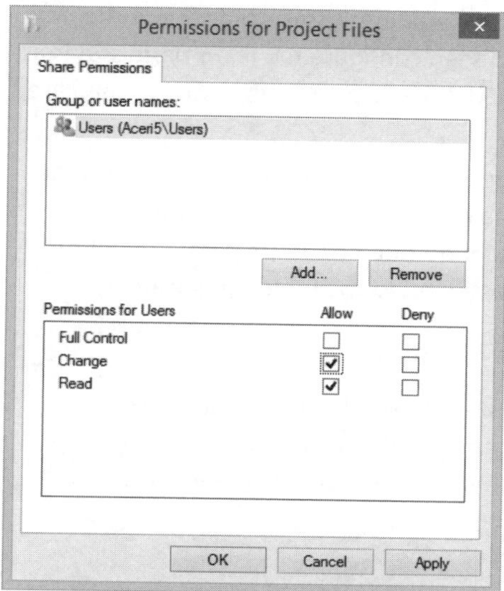

FIGURE 4-5 Remove the Everyone group and then add specific users or groups and apply permissions for them.

EXAM TIP

No matter what share permissions are applied to a group or a user and no matter what combination of permissions one has, Deny always means deny. You might see a long question on an exam that gives lots of information about a user, what groups he is in, and so on, and there might be one lone Deny permission for a share he also has permission to access. If he's denied access, that's that. He's denied access.

Table 4-1 shows the Share permissions and their limitations.

TABLE 4-1 Share permissions and their limitations

Share Permission	Limitations
Read	Display folder names; display file names, data, and attributes; execute program files; access other folders inside the shared folder
Change	Perform all read actions; create and add files to folders; change and append data to files; change file attributes; delete folders and files
Full Control	Perform all change permissions; change file permissions; take ownership of files

Here are a few more things to know about share permissions:

- Share permissions are completely separate from NTFS permissions.
- Share permissions are the simplest permissions you can configure.

- On networks that employ NTFS, most of the time administrators simply grant the Share permission Full Control to Everyone and then configure the NTFS permissions as desired. When both Share and NTFS are applied, the more restrictive wins; in this case, that is the NTFS permission.
- NTFS permissions on a subfolder inherit the permissions assigned to the parent folder. Share permissions do not combine in the same way. Succinctly, Share permissions applied to a folder that sits inside another folder do not inherit the parent folder's permissions. They use the permissions explicitly assigned to the folder in question.

Other ways to share

You don't have to use the available end-user tools to create and manage sharing. You can share at a command line by using the Shared Folders snap-in inside an MMC and by using Windows PowerShell. Although you might not opt to use these tools for sharing, it's likely you'll see questions about them on the exam.

SHARE FROM A COMMAND LINE

You can share folders at a command prompt. The command you use is net share, often in the form of net share [ShareName] to display information about a share and net share [ShareName=Drive:Path] to specify the path of the directory to be shared. You can also add these parameters:

- **/users: number** This parameter sets the maximum number of users who can simultaneously access the shared resource.
- **/unlimited** This parameter sets an unlimited number of users who can simultaneously access the shared resource.
- **/remark: " text "** This parameter adds a descriptive comment about the resource. Enclose the text in quotation marks.
- **/cache:automatic** This parameter enables offline client caching with automatic reintegration.
- **/cache:manual** This parameter enables offline client caching with manual reintegration.
- **/cache:no** This parameter advises the client that offline caching is inappropriate.
- **/delete** This parameter stops sharing the shared resource.
- **net help command** This parameter displays Help for the specified command.

EXAM TIP

To create a share that is invisible to users who browse the network, add a dollar sign ($) to the share name (CTest$, DShare$, and so on).

SHARE USING AN MMC

To share using an MMC, add the Shared Folders snap-in. Click the Shares node in the left pane, right-click in the middle, and click New Share, as shown in Figure 4-6, to start the Create A Shared Folder Wizard. You can also view sessions and open files using the console.

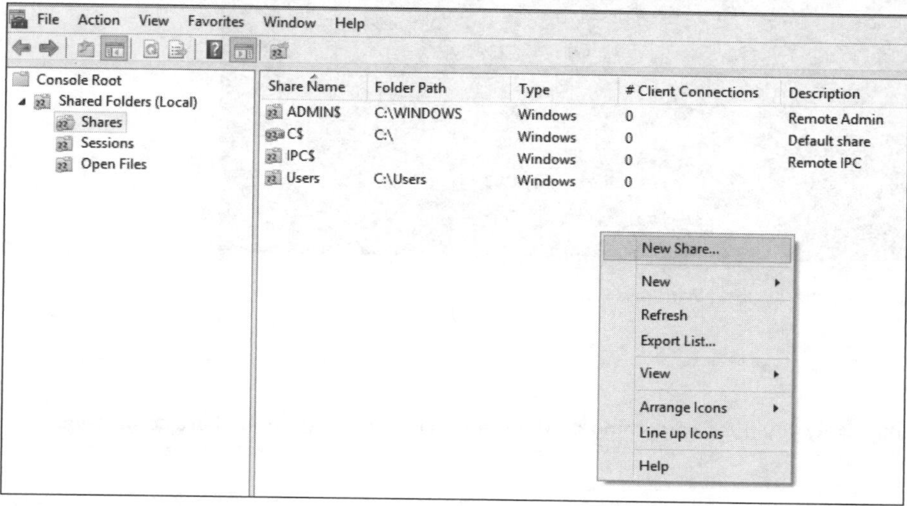

FIGURE 4-6 Use an MMC to create and manage a share.

SHARE USING WINDOWS POWERSHELL

You can use Windows PowerShell to create and manage shares. One command you'll likely use is New-SmbShare followed by the share name and path to the folder to share. (SMB stands for Server Message Block.) There are additional commands for managing shares using Windows PowerShell:

- **Get-SmbShare** Use this command to list the shares that already exist on the computer. See Figure 4-7.
- **Set-SmbShare** Use this command to modify a share.
- **Remove-SmbShare** Use this command to remove a share.
- **Grant-SmbShareAccess** Use this command to set permissions for a share.

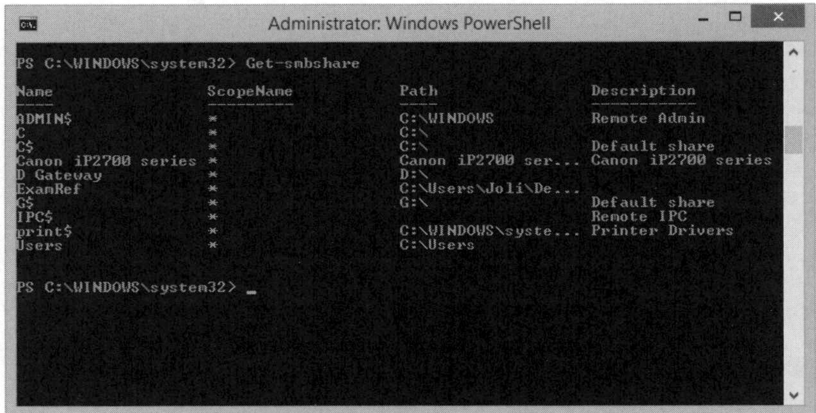

FIGURE 4-7 View shares using Windows PowerShell.

EXAM TIP

It's highly likely you'll see something on the exam that involves the SmbShare commands.

Configure file libraries

Windows 8.1 comes with its own library structure that includes libraries for Desktop, Documents, Downloads, Music, Pictures, and Videos. Anything you save to the related folder is available in the library with the same name. This means if you save a file to the Documents folder, you'll have access to it in the Documents library. The library doesn't actually hold the files though; it only keeps a record of where the files are stored. By default, libraries only offer access to data in the related personal folder. Libraries do not offer access to the related Public folders or any others, although you can add them if you like. (Note that libraries offered access to the Public folders in Windows 7.) There isn't that much more to know about libraries except how to create your own libraries and add folders to existing ones.

NOTE **SHOW LIBRARIES IN FILE EXPLORER**

To show or hide the Libraries option in the Navigation pane of File Explorer, click the View tab in any applicable window, click Navigation Pane, and in the resulting list, click Show Libraries.

To create your own library, follow these steps:

1. Open File Explorer, and on the View tab, click Navigation Pane. Click Show Libraries.
2. Right-click inside the Libraries pane, click New, and then click Library. See Figure 4-8.

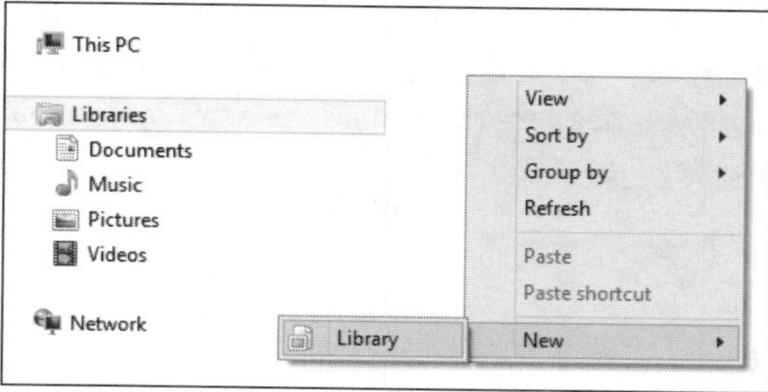

FIGURE 4-8 Create a new library.

3. Name the library and press Enter.
4. Double-click the new library and then click Include A Folder.
5. Double-click the folder to add.
6. To add more folders, click the Manage tab.
7. Click Manage Library.
8. Click Add and navigate to the folder to add.
9. Select the folder and click Include Folder.
10. Repeat as desired and click OK.

To add a location to an existing library, in File Explorer, double-click the library to which you'd like to add a folder and then click the Manage tab. From there, click Manage Library and add folders as desired.

Configure shared printers

If you've created a homegroup, your printers are already shared. Both the printer and the computer to which it's connected must be turned on and ready for a request, but the sharing is done automatically. When a homegroup isn't used, you have to share the printers manually. You might also have to enable file and print sharing in some instances, including if you're sharing printers on a public network.

In a workgroup or domain setting, sharing is basically the same. You locate the printer and access the option to share it. You can share the printer with a mix of computers on your network, including x86-based and x64-based PCs. You only need to make sure the applicable drivers are available, and for the most part they are. You'll likely need administrator approval to install drivers, though, so you need to keep that in mind if you think drivers are going to be an issue.

Add a printer and configure sharing

You can add a printer in Windows 8.1 from the Devices And Printers window, available in Control Panel. There, click Add A Printer and choose it from the list. If the printer you want isn't listed, you can add it manually, which is likely what you'll have to do if you have an old printer connected to an LPT port or if you need to add a printer using its TCP/IP address or host name. You can connect a wireless printer from this window, but you can also use the manual option to add a wireless printer if you need to. You can also use this option to type a path to the printer to locate it manually. See Figure 4-9.

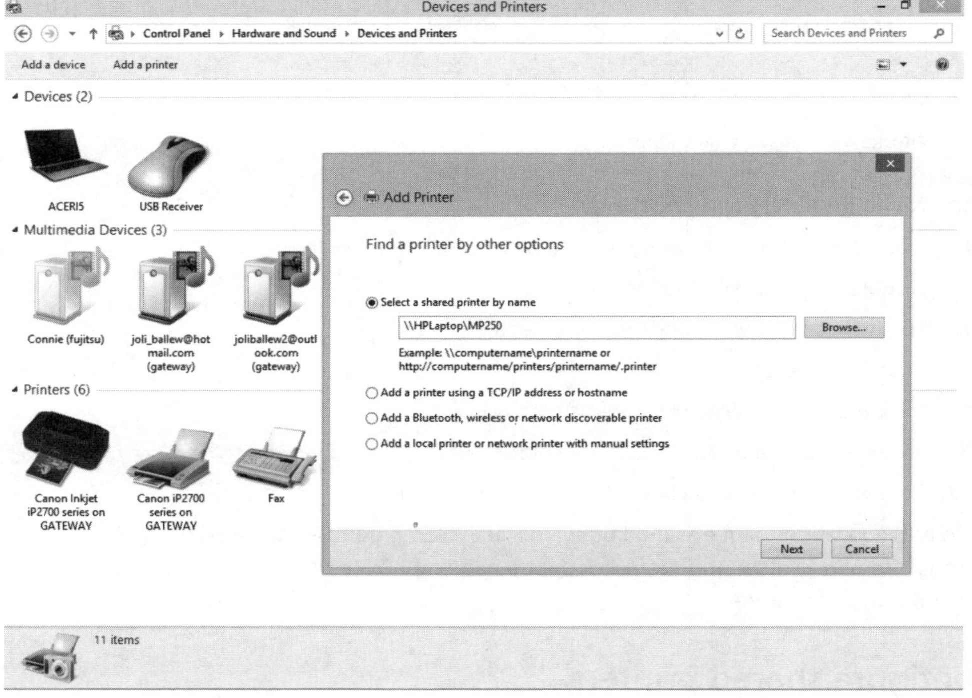

FIGURE 4-9 Add a printer manually.

Table 4-2 shows the basic printer permissions.

TABLE 4-2 Basic printer permissions

Permission	Limitations/capabilities	Default assignment
Print	Connect to a printer; print; control the user's own print jobs	Everyone
Manage this printer	Cancel documents; share and delete printers; change printer properties; change printer permissions	Administrators
Manage documents	Pause, resume, restart, and cancel all documents; control job settings for all documents	Creator Owner

Share and configure a printer manually

To manually share a printer, right-click the device in the Devices And Printers window and then click Printer Properties. From there, use the Sharing tab to share the printer and configure other options. If the computer is a member of an Active Directory domain, you'll see the List In The Directory check box. Select this check box to create a new printer object in the Active Directory database. This will enable domain users to locate the printer by searching in the directory. In this dialog box you can also opt to add drivers, if necessary.

The other tabs offer additional options, including the option to configure when the computer is available and what types of users have access to the Print permissions: Print, Manage This Printer, Manage Documents, and Special Permissions. In Figure 4-10, you can see that the Everyone group has the ability to print. However, if you click Administrators in the Group Or User Names list, you'll see that this group has Print, Manage This Printer, and Manage Documents set to Allow. Table 4-2 explains these options. Make sure you are comfortable with all of these graphical options available in Windows 8.1 before moving on.

> ***NOTE*** **HOW TO ASSIGN PERMISSIONS**
>
> **When assigning permissions in an Active Directory domain, you assign permissions for domain users, groups, and other objects. On a stand-alone computer, you select the local user and group accounts that should receive the permissions.**

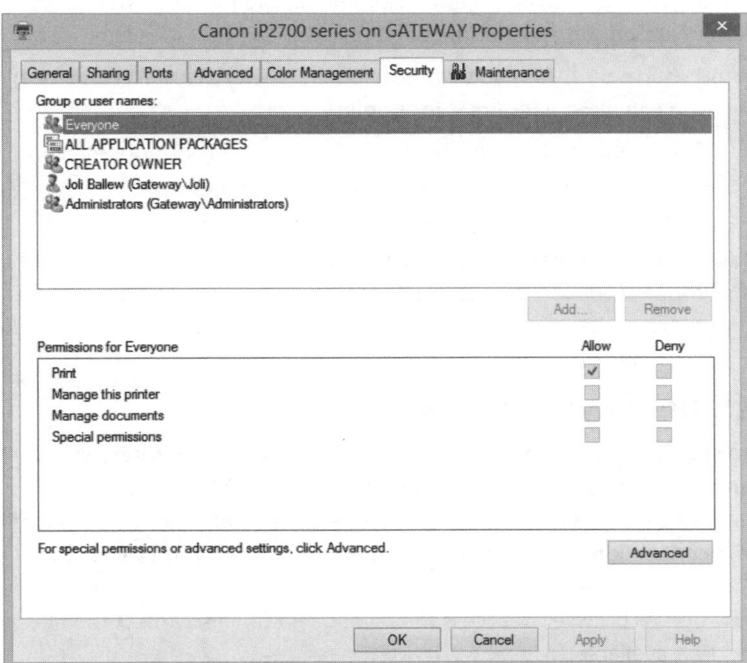

FIGURE 4-10 Use the printer's Properties dialog box to share a printer and configure sharing options.

EXAM TIP

Near Field Communication (NFC) is a radio-based communications technology (based on radio-frequency identification [RFID] standards) that lets users complete tasks with compatible objects, mostly to complete brief transactions without having to physically connect to the device or the network. In the case of printers, NFC allows mobile devices to submit print jobs to printers, provided compatible technologies exist between the two and the proximity between the devices is acceptable.

Know common print terms

Beyond the end-user-friendly options, there are a few terms you need to know about printers and a few features that aren't obvious to most users.

- **Print device** This is the actual hardware, the printer.
- **Printer** This is the software interface through which a computer communicates with the print device. It might be LPT, COM, USB, IEEE, 1394, IrDA, Bluetooth, TCP/IP ports, or others.
- **Print server** This is a computer that receives print jobs and routes them to print devices.
- **Printer control language (PCL)** A printer needs a printer driver to function. The driver takes the commands and converts them to something the printer understands. This is called the PCL. PostScript is an example of a PCL.
- **Password protected sharing** Just as you can configure password protected sharing for files and folders, you can also configure it for printers.
- **Printer priority** This is an option with which you can give users in your organization priority to print before other users, even when print jobs are in the queue.
- **Printer pool** Use this feature to connect multiple print devices so that a print job can be automatically sent to a printer that is not currently busy. You do this in Control Panel, in a printer's Properties dialog box, on the Ports tab, by clicking Enable Printing Pooling.

Set up and configure SkyDrive

SkyDrive enables users to store data in the cloud almost seamlessly from their Windows 8.1 computers. SkyDrive is an app on the Start screen and an option on the File Explorer Navigation tab. When data is stored in SkyDrive, users can access that data from virtually any device that has an Internet connection. Users can also share any part of what they've stored there with others, allowing them to read or read and edit the data. Users need a Microsoft account and the applicable app or browser to access the data. Users can also access the files locally when a connection isn't available.

EXAM TIP

SkyDrive is a storage area that users can access to save data and manage data they've saved there. Be careful when SkyDrive is an answer for any scenario, because it doesn't do much else for users. As an example, you can't share, sync, or access apps from SkyDrive; syncing apps is part of the job of the Microsoft account and has nothing to do with SkyDrive.

Users can access SkyDrive in a number of ways:

- **Using a web browser** Browse to *http://skydrive.com* and log in to access, upload, share, and otherwise manage files and folders. You can also create and edit documents, presentations, notebooks, and so on here.
- **Using the SkyDrive app in Windows** Open the SkyDrive app from the Start screen to access, upload, open, and manage files and to create new folders.
- **Using the SkyDrive app on smartphones** This allows users to view and open files, view recently accessed files, view and access shared files, and upload files. Users can also create new folders and configure a few settings for uploading photos.
- **Through a desktop application** This method allows users to access SkyDrive from an application such as Microsoft Office 2013. See Figure 4-11.

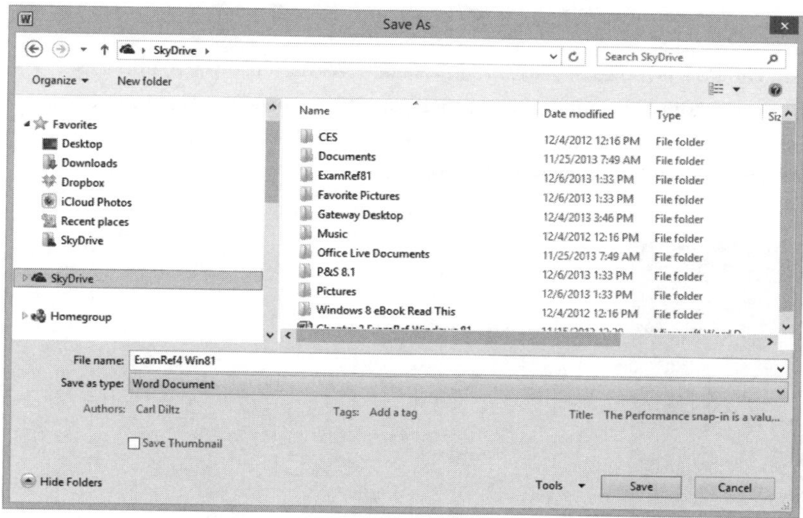

FIGURE 4-11 Save to SkyDrive from a desktop application.

Setting up SkyDrive only involves logging in to the Windows 8.1 computer with a Microsoft account. Windows does the rest. There are some configuration options to look at right away, though. You can configure the option to access all files offline from the Settings charm (click Options) from inside the SkyDrive app. See Figure 4-12. This might be the first thing you'll want to configure if you have the available SkyDrive space.

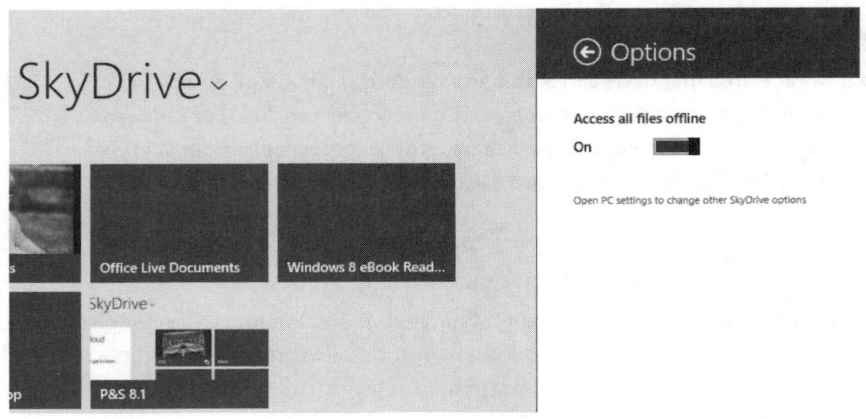

FIGURE 4-12 The SkyDrive app offers the option to access all of your files offline.

Configuration options are available from PC Settings and on the SkyDrive website. Figure 4-13 shows what's available in PC Settings. There are four tabs. On the File Storage tab you can buy more storage and configure your documents to save to SkyDrive by default. You can see that I have an enormous amount of space available on SkyDrive. That's not typical. Make sure you explore all of the settings and options here as time allows.

EXAM TIP

Know what can and can't be saved to SkyDrive. You can save Windows settings, application settings, and some credentials, but you can't save your Xbox music purchases, apps, or even entire folders (such as your Documents or Pictures folders). You must upload files one at a time, although you can upload compressed folders.

FIGURE 4-13 Configure SkyDrive settings from PC Settings in Windows 8.1.

Finally, you can configure SkyDrive settings on the SkyDrive website. Once you log in at *http://skydrive.com* you can click the Tools icon in the top-right corner and click Options. See Figure 4-14. Note the options on the left side:

- **Manage Storage** This allows users to view available storage space and buy more.
- **Upgrade** Use this setting to view storage plans and select one.
- **Office File Formats** This allows users to choose a default format for Office documents: Microsoft Office Open XML Format (.docx, .pptx, .xlsx) or OpenDocumentFormat (.odt, .odp,. ods).
- **People Tagging** Use this option to state how people can tag you on SkyDrive (Your Friends or Just You) and to configure who can add people tags (Your Friends Who Can View Your Photo Album or Don't Allow Anyone To Add People Tags).
- **Device Settings** Use this option to see all of your devices and the date those devices were last backed up.

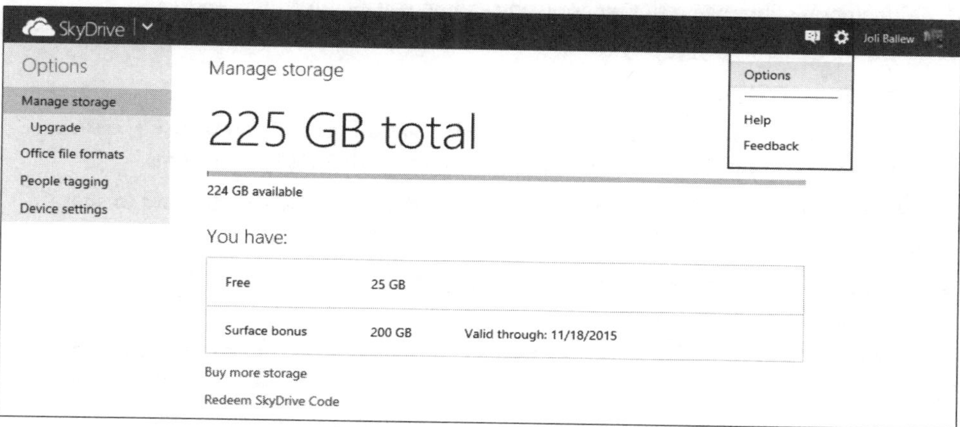

FIGURE 4-14 Configure settings on the SkyDrive website.

MORE INFO **LEARN HOW TO SET UP A MICROSOFT ACCOUNT**

Refer to Objective 4.3 later in this chapter to learn more about setting up a Microsoft account.

Thought experiment

Configure sharing effectively

In this thought experiment, apply what you've learned about this objective. You can find answers to these questions in the "Answers" section at the end of this chapter.

Your client needs to share files and folders with others in his small business workgroup. He wants to set permissions for specific users so they can access sensitive data when they need to, but he wants to make sure that data can't be accessed by anyone who is not specifically named. He has a few folders he's created on his

desktop (Accounts, Invoices, and SalesInformation) and others that are not in any default library (HumanResources, TaxInfo).

1. **What type of sharing would you suggest? Why?**
2. **When assigning permissions to the folders named here, what should you do with the Everyone group that is given read access by default?**
3. **How many simultaneous users can access the data in the shared folder by default?**
4. **If you want users to be able to read and edit what's in a folder but you don't want them to be able to take ownership of the files in the folder or change the file permissions, what share permission should you assign?**

Objective summary

- Share permissions include Read, Change, and Full Control and can be used to secure data in workgroups and on computers configured with FAT32 file systems.
- Homegroups, Public folder sharing, and Any folder sharing are three ways to share data on a private network.
- You can share printers automatically by creating a homegroup or configure them manually with other types of sharing scenarios.
- SkyDrive enables users to save data to the cloud and access it from virtually anywhere.

Objective review

Answer the following questions to test your knowledge of the information in this objective. You can find the answers to these questions and explanations of why each answer choice is correct or incorrect in the "Answers" section at the end of this chapter.

1. Which of the following is true regarding homegroups? (Choose all that apply.)
   - **A.** A wizard is available to set it up, and a homegroup password is automatically generated.
   - **B.** Shares can be configured to allow read or read/write access for all homegroup users, but you cannot configure specific users with specific permissions.
   - **C.** Users can share their default libraries.
   - **D.** Windows XP computers and users can join a homegroup.
   - **E.** Homegroups can be created for public networks.
2. Which sharing option would you choose if you wanted to share files and folders that reside on your desktop and set permissions for select users and exclude others on a computer that was part of a public network?

A. Any folder sharing
B. Public folder sharing
C. Homegroup sharing
D. All of the above

3. You've shared a printer and need users to be able to print and control their own print jobs. How do you need to configure the Share permissions?
   A. Select the Share permission for Manage This Printer.
   B. Select the Share permission for Manage Documents.
   C. Select both Manage This Printer and Manage Documents.
   D. Do nothing; these permissions are already configured by default.
4. With regard to SkyDrive, where do you configure the option to access all of the files you save there offline so they will be available even if the user does not have access to the Internet?
   A. *http://skydrive.com* from Tools, Options
   B. From the SkyDrive app, from the Settings charm under Options
   C. From PC Settings, from Sync Settings
   D. From File Explorer, by right-clicking SkyDrive in the Navigation pane and selecting Properties

Objective 4.2: Configure file and folder access

You learned about Share permissions in Objective 4.1. These permissions are applied when the operating system is configured with FAT or FAT32 or any time you share a folder on a computer. There are only three shared permissions: Read, Change, and Full Control, which are available on the Sharing tab of the resource's Properties dialog box. These sharing options don't offer a lot of control, but they do offer some. Share permissions help you manage access to resources by users over a network, but they offer no security when a user logs on locally.

Because NTFS permissions are so much more robust than Share permissions, when the file system is NTFS, administrators make the most of it. They generally set the Share permissions for Everyone to Full Control and configure the NTFS permissions as desired. You configure NTFS on the Security tab of the resource's Properties dialog box. Remember, the more restrictive of the two types of permissions is applied to the resource when both exist, so it doesn't matter that the Share permissions give everyone unlimited access as long as NTFS is configured, too. NTFS also offers the ability to assign disk quotas, encrypt files and folders, and audit object access. These features are not available on FAT or FAT32 drives.

This objective covers how to:

- Configure NTFS permissions
- Configure disk quotas
- Encrypt files and folders using EFS
- Configure object access auditing

Configure NTFS permissions

There's a lot to learn about NTFS permissions, the Windows permission architecture, the differences between basic and advanced permissions, and how permissions are inherited, among other things, and there just isn't enough room here to discuss all of it. However, we'll try to cover the most important facts you'll need to know for the exam and how to apply NTFS permissions to secure a resource.

EXAM TIP

Make sure you read and study the additional resources listed on the Microsoft certification webpage for this exam so that you are familiar with the test objectives. Navigate to this page and click Show All to obtain that list of additional resources: ***http://www.microsoft.com/learning/en-us/exam-70-687.aspx.***

There are four kinds of permissions. You already know a little about two: Share and NTFS. There are two others: Registry permissions and Active Directory permissions. You might not ever assign these two types, but they do exist. All of these permissions are independent of one another and can be combined if desired.

Permission terminology and rules

Any element or resource that is protected has an access control list (ACL). This is basically just a list of permissions that have been applied to it. The individual permissions applied are access control entries (ACEs). Every ACE has at least one security principal. A security principal is the user, group, or computer given permissions, along with the permissions that have been configured for it (them). This means that permissions are stored with the resource that is being protected. The permissions are not stored with the user, group, or computer that is granted access. This is why you configure permissions on the Security tab of the element's Properties dialog box (see Figure 4-15). If you click Edit in the Test Properties dialog box, you gain access to the Permissions For dialog box shown on the right. There you can add or remove users, groups, and so on and apply the applicable NTFS permissions for those new entries.

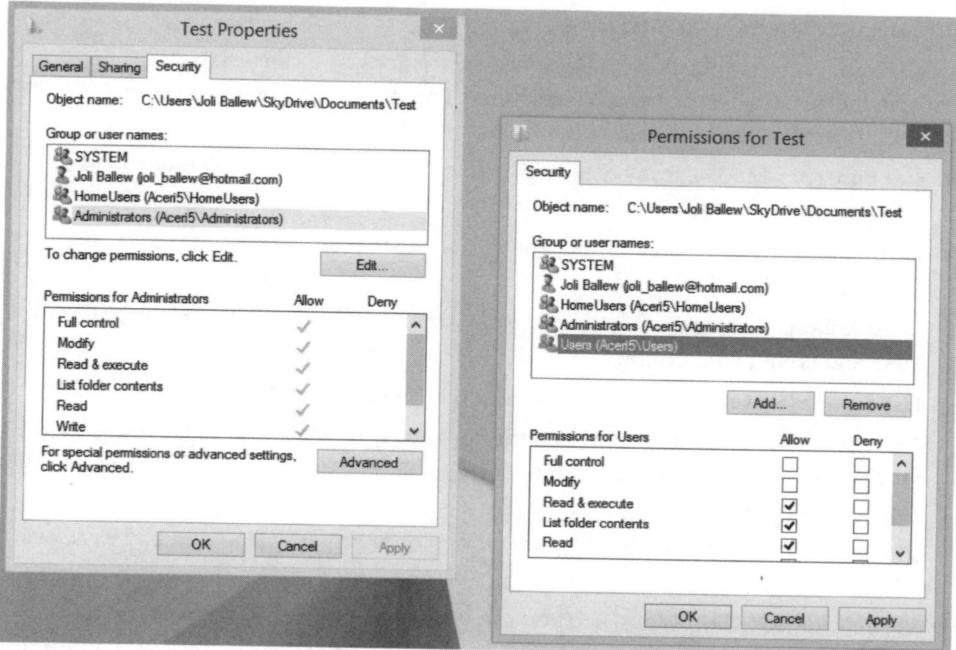

FIGURE 4-15 Configure NTFS permissions from the element's Properties and Permissions For dialog boxes.

You can use the basic permissions shown in Figure 4-15 to create very specific access options to a shared resource. You can grant a single user Full Control to a resource and at the same time grant all of the users in the Users group only Read access. You can configure it so that a specific person or persons can't access the resource at all or so that an entire group, like HomeUsers, can read, write, list folder contents, and read and execute while using the resource, but can't modify or take ownership of it. The scenarios are almost endless.

If a user is configured permissions to a resource from more than one place, the permissions granted are cumulative. As an example, if Bob is a member of the Users group and the Users group has only the NTFS permission Read, but Bob is also a member of the Sales group and the Sales group has the NTFS permission Modify, then Bob has both Read and Modify permissions. Remember, Share permissions are cumulative and NTFS permissions are cumulative, and if both exist, the more restrictive of the results of these are applied. Deny means deny though; if Deny is assigned to a user from anywhere, that user can't access the resource.

EXAM TIP

Allow permissions are cumulative. Deny permissions override Allow permissions. Explicit permissions take precedence over inherited permissions.

Basic and advanced permissions

Basic permissions are combinations of advanced permissions. You can see the basic permissions on the Security tab of any NTFS resource's Properties dialog box, as shown in Figure 4-15 earlier. There are six basic permissions:

- **Full Control** Modify, take ownership, delete items, and perform all other actions listed for the following permissions
- **Modify** Delete the folder, modify the file, delete the file, and perform other actions for Write and Read & Execute
- **Read & Execute** Navigate through folders, run applications, and perform actions for Read and List Folder Contents
- **List Folder Contents** View the names of the files and subfolders in a folder
- **Read** See files and subfolders, read the contents of a file, and view ownership, permissions, and attributes for a file or folder
- **Write** Create new files and subfolders inside a folder, modify folder attributes, view the ownership and permission for a folder or file, modify file attributes, and write over a file

There are 14 advanced permissions, and you can view these by navigating to the Advanced Security Settings For dialog box for any NTFS resource. You should know the names of these advanced permissions, how to find them, and how they protect the element. From this dialog box you can also view the assigned permissions, including Share permissions, and you can view the calculated effective access from the tab with the same name. To open this dialog box and view these settings and options, follow these steps:

1. Right-click any shared folder and click Properties.
2. Click the Security tab.
3. Click Advanced.
4. Click any permission entry (perhaps Administrators) and click View. See Figure 4-16. (Note the Disable Inheritance button. Keep this location in mind when you read the next section.)

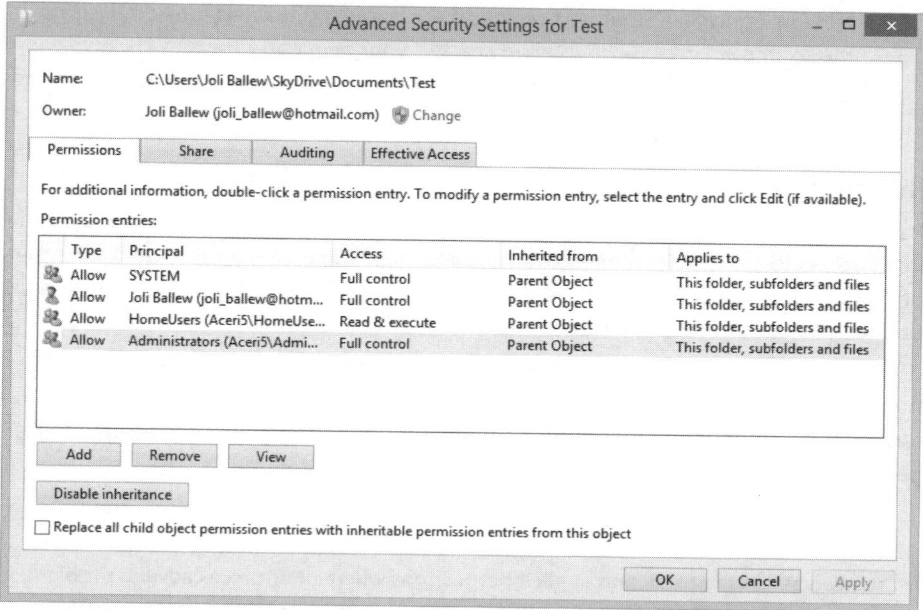

FIGURE 4-16 The Advanced Security Settings dialog box offers a list of security principals and their assigned access.

5. In the resulting Permissions Entry For dialog box you can view the basic permissions that are assigned to this group.
6. Click Show Advanced Properties. The list of assigned advanced permissions is displayed, as shown in Figure 4-17.

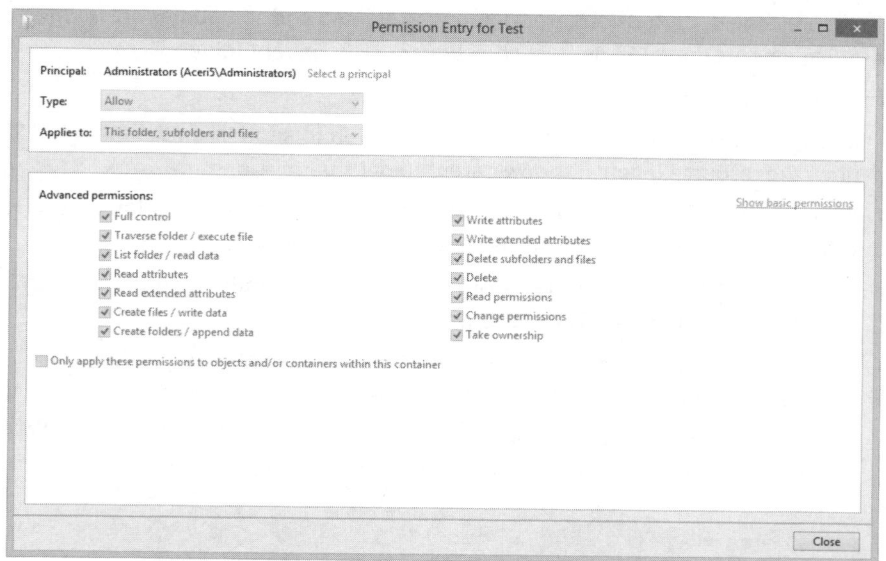

FIGURE 4-17 View Advanced permissions in the Permission Entry dialog box.

Note in Figure 4-17 that you can't edit the permissions listed for Administrators in this example. However, if you had created your own entry (say the Users group, Sales group, and so on) in the Properties dialog box, you would be able to edit the advanced permissions shown here.

Inheritance

Permissions generally run from top to bottom of any folder hierarchy, so if you grant NTFS Read access to a folder for a group of users and then you create a subfolder there, the same permissions are applied to it for the same group of users. If it didn't work this way, assigning permissions would be nearly impossible.

There might be times that you need to turn off inheritance for a folder or other element. As shown in Figure 4-16, Disable Inheritance is an option. If you'd rather not disable inheritance but do need to deny access to a specific person or group, you can assign the Deny permission as applicable.

EXAM TIP

You can assign contradicting explicit permissions when inheritance causes a problem. As an example, if the entire Sales group is denied access to a folder but a single member of the Sales group should have access to it (perhaps the CFO), you can explicitly assign that one user account the Allow permission for Full Control on the resource. Explicit permissions like these override inherited permissions and thus resolve the problem quite easily.

Move, copy, and permission inheritance

Sometimes you need to copy or move an NTFS-protected element. When you do, depending on the circumstances, permissions are sometimes retained and sometimes not. In most cases, the resource inherits the NTFS permission assigned to the parent folder.

Here's how inheritance and move and copy work.

- If you copy NTFS files or folders from one location to another on the same NTFS volume, the resource inherits its new parent folder's permissions.
- If you copy NTFS files or folders from one location to another on a different NTFS volume, the resource inherits its new parent folder's permissions.
- If you move NTFS files or folders from one location to another on the same NTFS volume, the existing permissions move with them.
- If you move NTFS files or folders from one location to another on a different NTFS volume, they inherit permissions from the new parent folder on the new volume.
- If you copy or move NTFS files or folders to a FAT or FAT32 drive, they lose all NTFS permissions because those aren't supported on those file systems.

Icacls.exe

The Icacls.exe command lets you configure basic and advanced permissions from an elevated command line. You can view all of the Icacls.exe parameters on TechNet at *http://technet.microsoft.com/en-us/library/cc753525.aspx*. You should be ready for exam questions based on this, so it's a good idea to review it.

EXAM TIP

If you lock yourself out of an element you can reset the permissions for it from an elevated command prompt. Navigate to the folder and use the command icacls.exe <*file name*> /reset along with additional parameters as desired (perhaps /C to ignore errors).

Succinctly, the Icacls.exe command is used as so: icacls.exe <*file name*> /grant or icacls.exe <*file name*> /deny with various parameters including but not limited to:

- F for full access
- M for modify
- RX for read and execute
- R for read only
- W for write
- MA for maximum allowed
- T to execute the command on all of the files and subfolders inside the <*file name*>
- C to continue even if errors occur

Resource ownership

It's possible to lock everyone out of a resource. The resource is said to be orphaned when this happens. A resource might also be orphaned if the user who originally created it is no longer available to provide access (perhaps to a confidential file or folder). To access the resource, as an administrator you need to take ownership of it. To do this, in the Advanced Security Settings For dialog box, shown earlier in Figure 4-16, click Change. Then you can take ownership of the resource yourself (as an administrator).

Configure disk quotas

Users will keep as much data and use as much server and storage space as you allow. Some users might never delete anything unless you force them to. As a network administrator you must be able to manage this, and you do so by configuring disk quotas.

Once you've enabled disk quotas (which you can do only on NTFS volumes, not on FAT volumes) you can also configure what happens when users meet those limits. You might want to give them a warning, or you might want to force them to delete data before they can save more. You configure NTFS disk quotas as follows:

1. In File Explorer, navigate to the volume to protect with disk quotas.
2. Right-click the volume and click Properties.
3. Click the Quota tab; click Show Quota Settings. See Figure 4-18.
4. Select the Enable Quota Management check box.
5. Configure the options as desired, including:
    A. Deny Disk Space To Users Exceeding Quota Limit
    B. Limit Disk Space To
    C. Log Event When A User Exceeds Their Quota Limit
    D. Log Event When A User Exceeds Their Warning Level
6. Click OK and click OK again to apply.

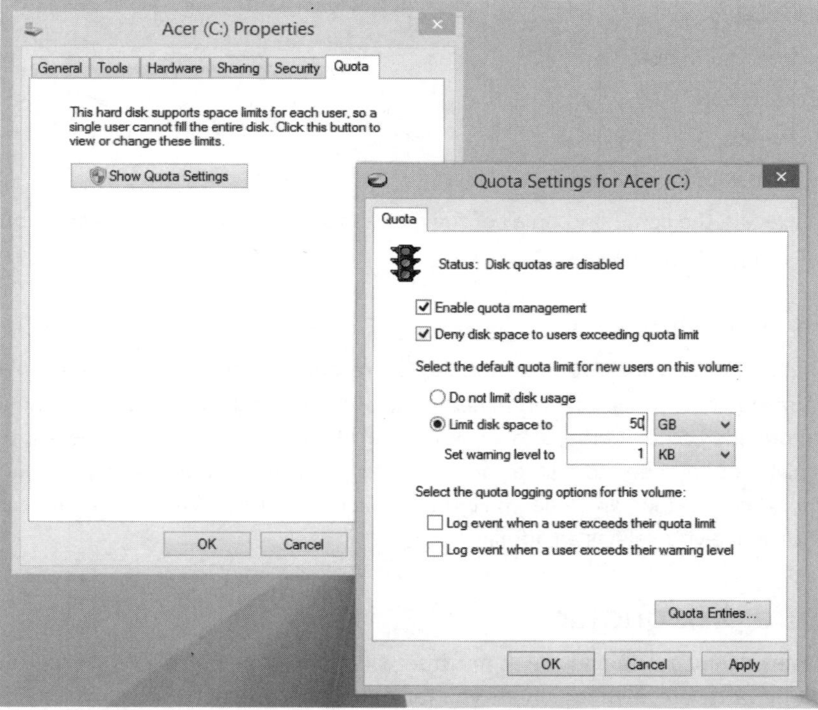

FIGURE 4-18 Set a quota limit and desired action.

EXAM TIP

The command-line tool Fsutil.exe can be used to set quota limits, too. Use the quota and enforce parameters to name the drive to which to apply the quota.

Encrypt files and folders using EFS

Encryption protects data from unauthorized access when other security measures fail. Much of the time failure has to do with someone gaining physical access to a machine and having the knowledge and time to figure out how to access the data on it. There are many ways this type of breach can occur. However, with Encrypting File System (EFS), the public and private keys that are generated during encryption ensure that only the user that encrypted the file can decrypt it. Technically, encrypted data can only be decrypted if the user's *personal encryption certificate* is available, which is generated using the private key. Another user can't access this key, and neither can a person who tries to access data to copy or move it who does not have the proper credentials.

EXAM TIP

The public and private keys that are generated when data is encrypted are the basis of the Windows Public Key Infrastructure (PKI). For more information about PKI, refer to TechNet (search for PKI). Additionally, EFS uses the Advanced Encryption Standard (AES), which uses a 256-bit key algorithm (an industry standard) and can be used to encrypt nonsystem volumes or only selected files and folders.

Here's a little more information about EFS:

- Encryption and decryption performs its duties without any fanfare, and the process is invisible to the user. Encryption occurs when you close files and decryption occurs when you open them.
- EFS can only be used on NTFS volumes and is not available on any form of FAT.
- EFS keys aren't assigned to a computer; instead they are assigned to a specific user. This means if another user logs on to the computer using his own user account, he has no access to another user's private key and can't access another user's data.
- Even if a hacker can sit down at a computer and access an option to copy protected files, she will receive an Access Denied message.
- You can't use EFS and compression together. You must choose one or the other.
- After a file or folder is encrypted, it will appear in green in File Explorer.

To encrypt a folder, right-click the folder to share then click Properties. In the Properties dialog box, on the General tab, click Advanced. Select the Encrypt Contents To Secure Data check box for the folder, as shown in Figure 4-19. You can use this same Advanced Attributes dialog box to remove encryption if you want to later.

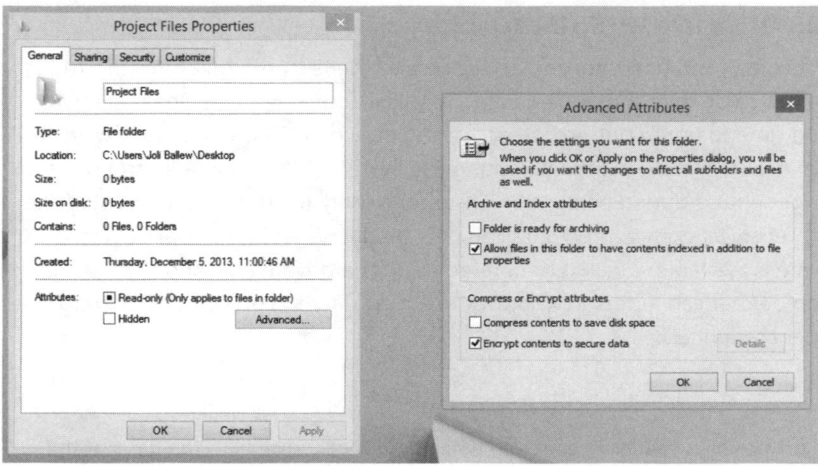

FIGURE 4-19 Enable encryption for a folder in the Advanced Attributes dialog box for the item to encrypt.

After you've performed your first encryption, you'll be prompted to back up your file encryption certificate and key. This helps you avoid permanently losing access to the encrypted files if the original certificate and key (that were generated when you encrypted it) are lost or corrupted. If you miss the prompt, you can follow the steps given next to perform the backup, but it's likely you'll be prompted to back up the key each time you log on anyway. You can back up your personal certificates manually using the Certificate Manager MMC (you should keep the EFS recovery key stored away from the computer in a safe place).

1. Use the Windows key+R to open a Run dialog box.
2. Type **certmgr.msc** and press Enter.
3. In the Certmgr window, expand Personal and click Certificates. See Figure 4-20.
4. Select all of the certificates.
5. Right-click the selected certificates, click All Tasks, and click Export.
6. Work through the Certificate Export Wizard, making sure to select Yes, Export The Private Key when prompted and type a complex password when prompted.

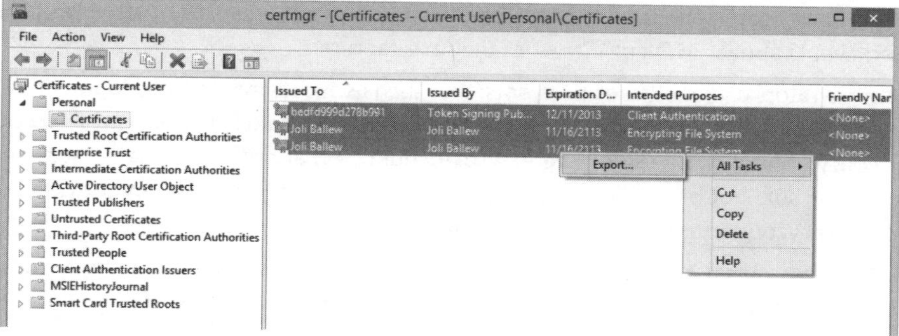

FIGURE 4-20 Opt to export all selected certificates and work through the resulting wizard to complete the process.

You can use CertMgr to recover your EFS encrypted files, too, by importing your EFS certificate backup. As with exporting certificates, this is achieved using a wizard. To get started, select the Personal folder, click Action, and then click All Tasks. From there, select Import. Work through the prompts to import the required data.

You can use the command line to manage encryption, too. You use Cipher.exe to perform encryption and decryption tasks. You might see this command on the exam. For more information about Cipher, refer to this page on TechNet: *http://technet.microsoft.com/en-us/library/cc771346.aspx*. Here are a few of the most common parameters used with Cipher:

- **/d** Use this parameter to decrypt specified files and directories.
- **/s:<Directory>** Use this parameter to perform the specified operation on all subdirectories in the specified directory.
- **/c** Use this parameter to display information about an encrypted file.
- **/u** Use this parameter to find all of the encrypted files on the local drives.
- **/?** Adding this parameter displays help.

> ***MORE INFO*** **BITLOCKER AND BITLOCKER TO GO**
>
> **For information about other types of security, including BitLocker and BitLocker To Go, refer to Chapter 5, "Configure remote access and mobility," and specifically Objective 5.3, "Configure security for mobile devices." BitLocker encrypts the entire disk; this is a different type of protection from EFS.**

Configure object access auditing

Network administrators often audit events to see which have occurred, often for the purpose of maintaining security on a particular object, such as a secure folder. It can also be a file, printer, or almost any other resource available from a computer. It can even be as small as a Registry key. Most of the time this type of object access auditing is done to see how many attempts have been made to access an object and how many times those attempts failed. All audited events appear in Event Viewer as they are captured.

Administrators can audit specific events, too, such as successful or failed logon attempts. This isn't object access auditing, but it deserves a mention because the option is part of the Audit Policy options you'll explore here. Also, it could be that objects are being accessed when they should not be, due to successful logons that aren't performed by the desired users. (See the Real World example for more information on how this can happen.)

In the following set of steps you enable the option to audit successful logon events. You also enable auditing of failures on objects you specify in the second set of steps here.

To enable auditing for successful logons and object auditing, follow these steps:

1. Open a Run box and type **gpedit.msc**. Press Enter.
2. Navigate to Computer Configuration, Windows Settings, Security Settings.
3. Expand Local Policies and click Audit Policy.
4. Double-click any policy to enable auditing for it. Figure 4-21 shows that Audit Account Logon Events is selected.
5. Select the Success or Failure check box and click OK.

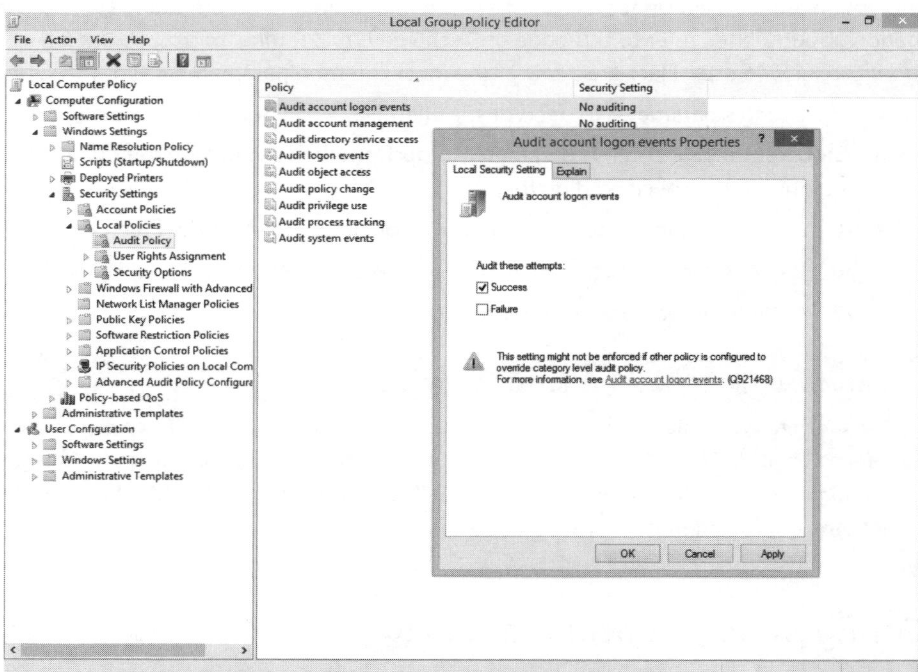

FIGURE 4-21 Audit successful logons for a local computer.

6. Double-click Audit Object Access.

7. In the Audit Object Access Properties dialog box, select the Failure check box.
8. Click OK.

The successful logon attempts will appear in Event Viewer with no other configuration. However, to see events for object access you must specify which objects you want to watch for. You enable auditing on an object in its Properties dialog box, on the Security tab. On the Security tab, click Advanced. This opens the Advanced Security Settings For dialog box you used earlier to disable permission inheritance, view permissions, and learn the effective access when multiple permissions are applied. To enable auditing, click the Auditing tab and click Continue. From there you can add the objects to audit. See Figure 4-22.

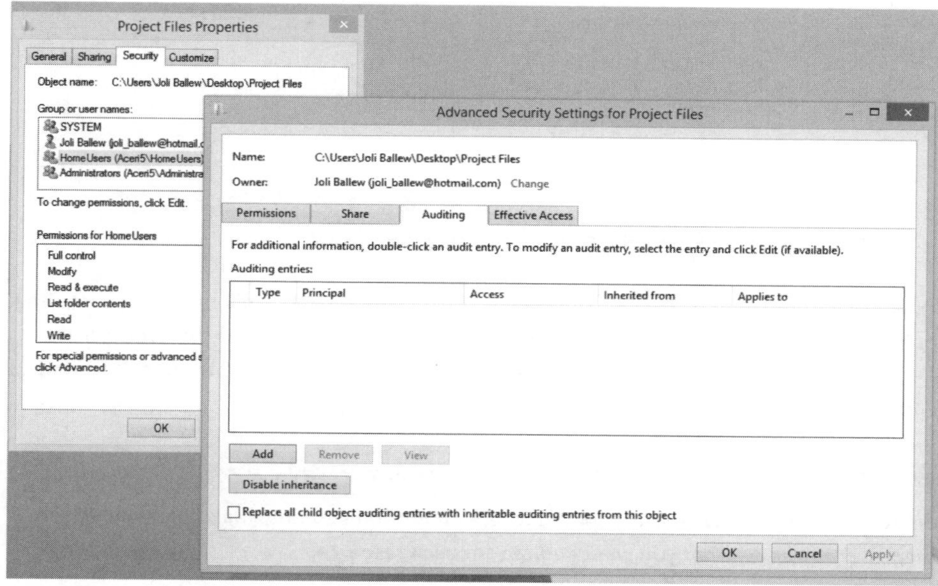

FIGURE 4-22 Configure auditing by adding objects in the Advanced Security Settings For dialog box.

In the Advanced Security Settings For dialog box, click Add. In the resulting window, click Select A Principal and type the name of the users or groups to be audited. (As an example, you might opt for Users.) Select the auditing option, perhaps Success. Finally, choose an option to which the auditing applies (perhaps This Folder Only) and configure the basic permissions. See Figure 4-23. Click OK and close the open dialog boxes.

> ***NOTE*** **BEWARE OF AUDITING SPRAWL**
>
> **You can create thousands upon thousands of events in only a few days if you audit too many folders, subfolders, and other objects. Be careful how many objects you audit!**

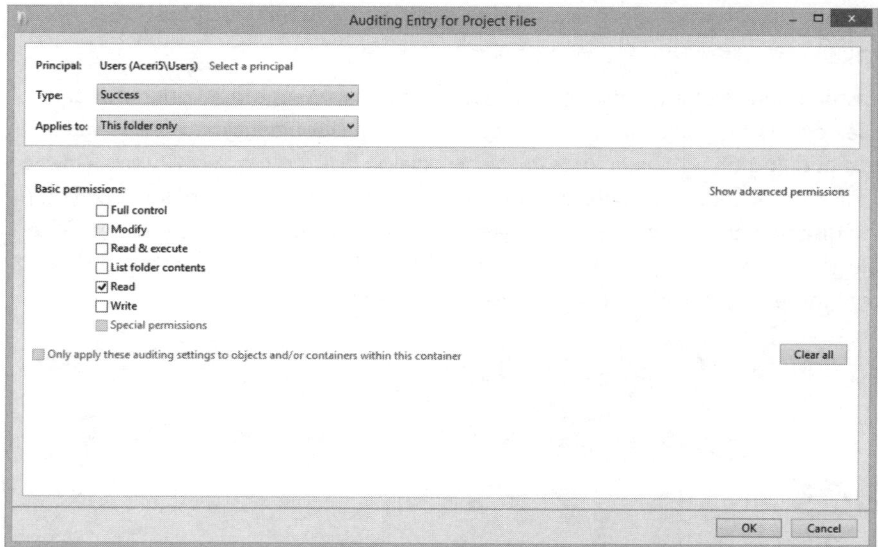

FIGURE 4-23 Configure auditing from the Auditing Entry For dialog box.

To view the audited events, open Event Viewer. Because the events will be entered into the Security logs, navigate to Windows Logs and then Security Logs. You'll see the events listed there. Double-click any event to learn more. See Figure 4-24. (You have to trigger the event to have it appear in the Security log.)

> ***NOTE*** **WHAT TO DO IF YOU DON'T SEE ANY EVENTS IN EVENT VIEWER**
>
> **If you don't see any events in Event Viewer after configuring auditing, make sure you've defined the group and what you want audited for each resource.**

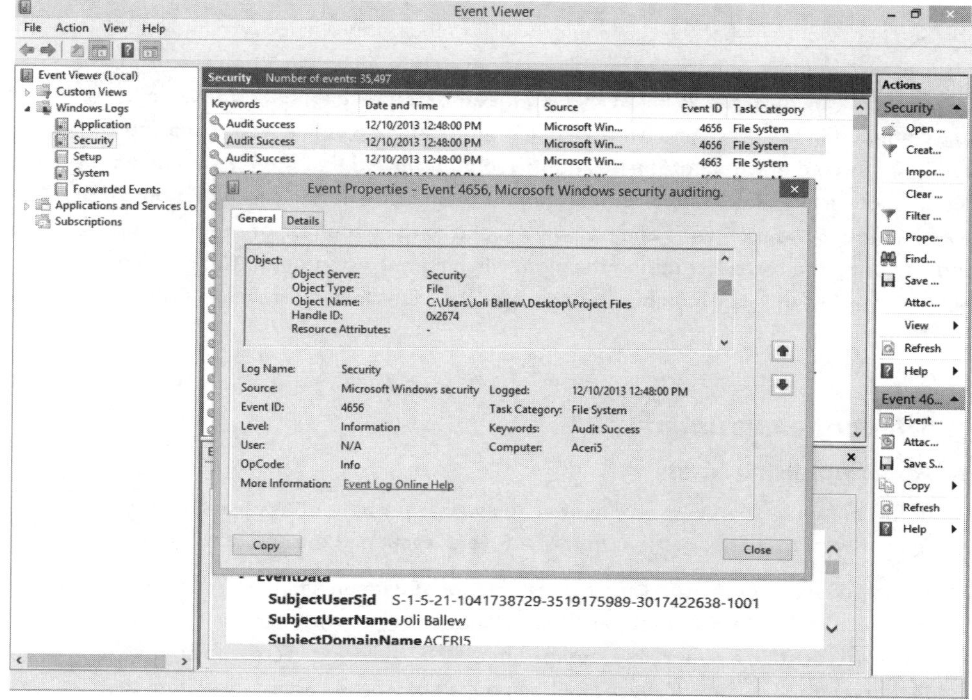

FIGURE 4-24 The Event Properties dialog box details the date and time of the audited event.

EXAM TIP

If you are asked how to set an alert for an audited event, here is the process. In Event Viewer, right-click the event and click Attach Task To This Event. Use the wizard to choose a task and apply an action. You can opt to send an email, start a program, or display a message. Send an email and display a message are deprecated but are still options. (Deprecated means that the feature still works but is no longer considered the desired option and that Microsoft might remove the feature from future updates or newer products or editions.)

REAL WORLD **AUDITING AND THE OVERNIGHT SHIFT**

About five years ago a friend of mine worked for a company that had a cleaning crew come in during the night to clean offices, take out the trash, dust shelves, and vacuum floors. The work was acceptable at first, and the cleaning crew of five seemed quite responsible. As time passed, though, the work got sloppy. She knew the crew was arriving at the proper time and that they were there for the required number of hours because the security guard outside confirmed it.

She began to wonder what the cleaning crew was doing during their overnight shift if they weren't working. She started auditing various events, including logon events for the computers in the main office. She suspected that the staff had figured out how to log on to a computer in the office and were spending time watching online videos, playing games, and so on instead of working. She was right; auditing showed that there were indeed successful logon events for a single computer in the main office during the night hours. The crew had found the user name and password taped to the underside of the keyboard tray and was using the computer during the night when no one was around. The problem was resolved quickly, the staff member was educated, and the cleaning crew was fired.

Thought experiment

Applying disk quotas

In this thought experiment, apply what you've learned about this objective. You can find answers to these questions in the "Answers" section at the end of this chapter.

You have several users who keep a large amount of data on a file server and are monopolizing the available storage there. You want to apply disk quotas to keep those users within a reasonable storage limit. All of the other users who access the file server don't use much space at all, so you're not worried about restricting their use in any way. You want to be sure that the problematic users never use more storage space than they are allowed; you're not interested in sending a warning or managing the issue in any other way. They've been told on several occasions to delete unnecessary files but have yet to do so.

1. Where do you go to enable disk quotas?
2. Besides Enable Quota Management, which other two options should you configure so that users won't ever exceed their quota limit?
3. Will these settings affect other users who store data on the volume for which you've configured disk quotas?

Objective summary

- NTFS permissions are the most secure and flexible way to assign permissions to a resource. By using them, you can lock down any object to control access effectively.
- NTFS inheritance is the backbone of NTFS control and is enabled by default.
- Disk quotas enable you to easily manage how much storage space users can access and what happens when they meet or exceed their limit.

- EFS lets users encrypt files and folders, and the encrypting and decrypting process is seamless to the user. EFS files are displayed in green in File Explorer.
- Audit object access lets you monitor objects by logging successes and failures in a way that you configure.

Objective review

Answer the following questions to test your knowledge of the information in this objective. You can find the answers to these questions and explanations of why each answer choice is correct or incorrect in the "Answers" section at the end of this chapter.

1. A(n) ____________ is the user, group, or computer that is given NTFS permissions and the permissions that have been configured for it (them).
   - **A.** security principal
   - **B.** access control entry
   - **C.** access control list
   - **D.** element, object, or resource
2. Which of the following tasks can you perform in an object's Advanced Security Settings For dialog box? (Choose all that apply.)
   - **A.** Add a new principal, allow or deny access, and set basic permissions
   - **B.** View the Share and NTFS permissions assigned to the object
   - **C.** Enable auditing for the object
   - **D.** View the effective access for a user when multiple permissions are applied
3. Which command-line tool can you use to encrypt files and folders?
   - **A.** Set-Acl
   - **B.** Icacls.exe
   - **C.** Cipher.exe
   - **D.** You can't configure encryption from a command line.
4. What happens if a hacker gains physical access to a machine, compromises the operating system to gain access to encrypted files and folders, and tries to copy those files and folders to a USB drive?
   - **A.** The hacker will be able to copy the files because encryption doesn't protect against copying data to a USB drive.
   - **B.** There is no way that a hacker could get to any data in this manner as long as encryption is enabled and applied.
   - **C.** The hacker can only copy the files after he removes the encryption attribute from each applicable file and folder.
   - **D.** The hacker will receive an Access Denied message.

Objective 4.3: Configure authentication and authorization

Authentication is the process of logging on to a computer, accessing a workgroup or networked computer, or logging on to a domain, which can be achieved using a Microsoft account, local user account, domain account, personal identification number (PIN), password, virtual or physical smart card, or biometrics, among other things. Authorization is what happens after authentication has been achieved; it is what enables authenticated users to access the data and perform the tasks they need to do their job.

In this objective, you learn the various ways users can be authenticated and how to configure user rights, manage credentials, and configure User Account Control (UAC) behavior.

This objective covers how to:

- Set up and configure a Microsoft account
- Configure authentication in workgroups and domains
- Configure virtual smart cards and biometrics
- Configure user rights
- Manage credentials and certificates
- Configure User Account Control behavior

Set up and configure a Microsoft account

The Microsoft account (what used to be called Windows Live ID) is a new way to log on to a computer running Windows 8. This type of account enables users to sync specific settings to the cloud for the purpose of having access to those settings from other computers that they can log on to using that same Microsoft account. With a Microsoft account, users can also access their own cloud space, called SkyDrive. Windows 8.1 comes with a SkyDrive app, and SkyDrive can be accessed from compatible applications, various web browsers, and File Explorer.

Users are prompted to set up a Microsoft account when they first set up their Windows 8 computers. They can opt to do that, or they can decline and create a local account instead. Users might also create a local account if the computer is unable to access the Internet during setup (because they won't be able to create or confirm the Microsoft account if there is no Internet access). Child accounts can also be created. Users generally opt to create a Microsoft account later even when they start with a local account, because many apps are inaccessible if the user is logged in with a local account. Additionally, users cannot get apps from the Store without a Microsoft account.

Once a Microsoft account is created, the user doesn't need to be connected to the Internet to log on in subsequent sessions. The account information is saved locally. If an Internet connection isn't available, the last saved settings will also be applied because they are cached locally as well.

EXAM TIP

Use this setting in Security Policy (local or domain) to block the use of Microsoft accounts: Block Microsoft Accounts. This setting is located here: Security Settings, Local Policies, Security Options.

You can switch from a local account to a Microsoft account from PC Settings. You can also create new users there and let them log on later with their own Microsoft account to finalize account creation. A wizard walks you through the process. To get started, in PC Settings, click Accounts. You switch from a local account to a Microsoft account on the Your Account tab, shown in Figure 4-25. You create additional users with the Other Accounts option by clicking Add An Account, also shown in Figure 4-25. Once the account is created you can return here later to change the account type if desired. (Control Panel is still an option for creating accounts, too.)

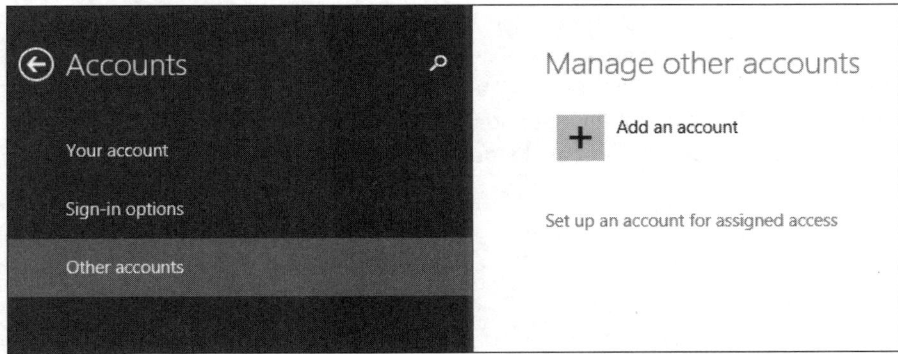

FIGURE 4-25 Add accounts easily in PC Settings.

A Microsoft account can be used in a domain if it isn't restricted through Group Policy. If it's possible at your place of business, once connected you'll see the same desktop background, app settings, browser history, and so on that you see on your main computer at home (or in another office). You make the change through PC Settings, from Users. Once there, click Connect Your Microsoft Account and work through the setup process.

EXAM TIP

There are various ways to log on to a computer running Windows 8 beyond typing a Microsoft account name or local account name and password. You can also create a four-digit PIN or a Picture password. You can set these up from PC Settings, Accounts, and Sign-in Options. Make sure you know how to do this before taking the exam; you'll likely be tested on it. Know that there are three gestures for a Picture password: tap, circle, and line.

Configure authentication in workgroups and domains

The weakest link when protecting computers is most often the password applied to the user account. The password could be nonexistent, too short, too simple, or too predictable. In some cases, the user might simply never change it. Often, users create and use the same password for multiple user IDs, too. This is a secondary weak link. If a hacker finds a password for a user's online bank account, she will try that same password elsewhere, including the user's computer. To protect authentication in both workgroups and domains, administrators can create local and group policies defining how passwords should be created, how often they can or must be changed, and what happens when a user fails to log on after making the attempt a specific number of times.

In this section we look at the password and account policies available in the Local Security Policy for a stand-alone computer or computers in a workgroup, but the same policies exist in Group Policy Management Console for domains as well.

Password policies

Because users likely won't change their password every 30 days or use complex passwords just because you tell them to, administrators can force users to comply with the password policies through group policies. There are six policies that can be configured. To see these policies, open the Local Security Policy MMC. You can do this from a Run dialog box by typing **secpol.msc**. Expand Account Policies and click Password Policy. No policies are configured by default, but you can set them by double-clicking the policy to change. See Figure 4-26.

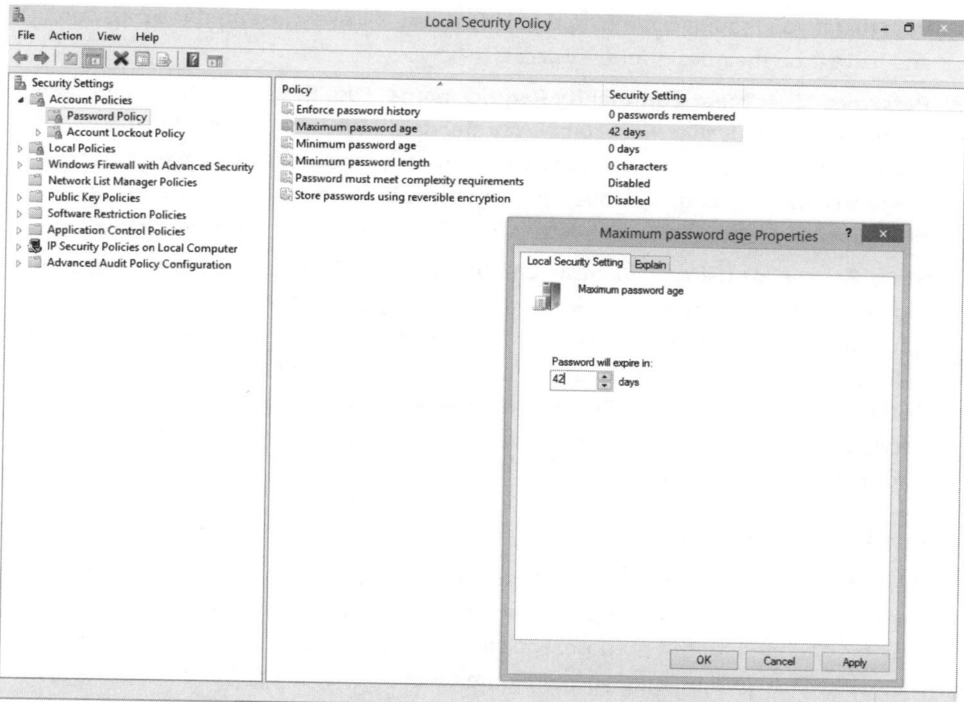

FIGURE 4-26 Create password policies.

If you're unsure what a particular policy does if enabled, click the Explain tab, also shown in Figure 4-26. There you can read a fairly lengthy description of the policy that includes the default settings, available parameters, and best practices, among other things. Briefly, these six policies are defined as follows:

- **Enforce Password History** Configure this when you want to require users to create unique passwords that have not been used before. For example, if you configure the setting to 5, users must create five different and new passwords before they can reuse the one they prefer over all others.
- **Maximum Password Age** Configure this when you want users to change their password after a specific number of days.
- **Minimum Password Age** Configure this when you want users to have to keep their new password for a specific amount of time before they can change it. This is important because if you don't set it, but you do set Enforce Password History, users can just cycle through the required passwords one after another until they can reuse the one they like best.
- **Minimum Password Length** Use this setting to require the password to be a specific length or longer. There's a fine line between security and client happiness and compliance. Although you might think a 14-character password is the most secure option,

note that if you require something that long, users will likely just print the password and leave it on their desks for easy access.

- **Password Must Meet Complexity Requirements** Use this setting to require users to create passwords that meet complexity standards. When this is enabled, passwords must not contain the user's account name or parts of the user's full name, must be at least six characters long, and must contain characters from three of these four categories: uppercase letters, lowercase letters, numbers, and special characters (!, $, #).
- **Store Passwords Using Reversible Encryption** Configure this to have the operating system store the password with reversible encryption. Although it sounds like a good idea, it isn't. When this is enabled, the operating system stores passwords essentially as plaintext versions. You have to select this if you're using Challenge-Handshake Authentication Protocol (CHAP) through remote access or Internet Authentication Services (IAS). It is also required when using Digest Authentication in Internet Information Services (IIS).

Account Lockout policies

If a hacker has enough time and enough information, he might be able to crack a user's password and gain access to the computer. This can be done manually but is often done with programs designed for this purpose. You can configure Account Lockout policies to prevent this. Like Password policies, you configure Local Security Policy for stand-alone and workgroup computers, and you use Group Policy Management Console for Active Directory domain networks. Figure 4-27 shows the Local Security Policy MMC.

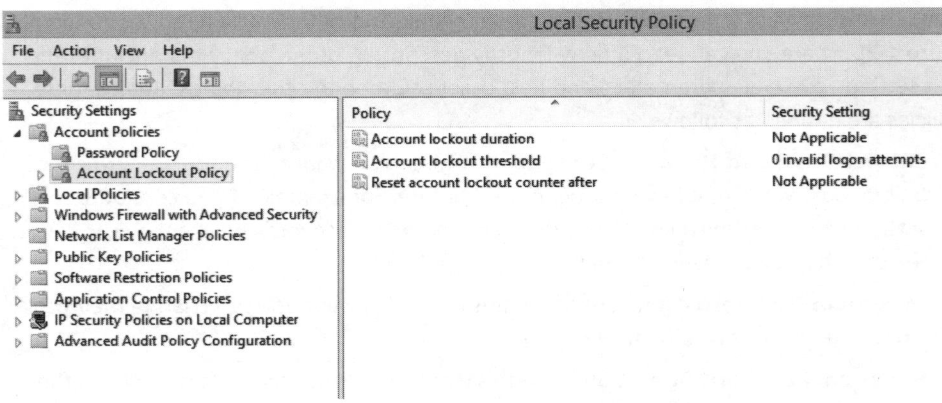

FIGURE 4-27 Configure Account Lockout policies in the Local Security Policy MMC.

There are three Account Lockout policies to consider, and in most instances they must be configured together:

- **Account Lockout Duration** If you've configured an account lockout threshold, and if that threshold is met, this setting defines how long (in minutes) the user will be locked out of her computer. A setting of 5 to 15 minutes is usually fine.

- **Account Lockout Threshold** You must configure this to use the other options. This setting defines how many times users can try to log on to their computer and fail before they are locked out.
- **Reset Account Counter After** This setting defines the number of minutes that must pass after a failed logon attempt before the failed logon attempt counter is reset to zero. If an account lockout threshold is defined, this must be less than or equal to the number of minutes set there.

Configure virtual smart cards and biometrics

User names and passwords are inherently weak ways to protect a computer from unauthorized access. The user is generally the problem, because users can willingly give their password to a person, be tricked into it, or leave their password out on their desks or in a desk drawer. Smart cards can provide better security, especially if used with user names and passwords (or PINs) as part of a multifactor authentication policy (although it's equally likely a user might give a coworker the card and the PIN willingly so that the coworker can access his workstation). Another option is also available: biometrics. This can be a fingerprint, eye scan, and so on.

Smart cards and virtual smart cards

A physical smart card often looks like a credit card, and users are expected to keep it with them. The smart card includes a chip that contains the user's authentication information, which includes a personal certificate. The smart card is inserted into a card reader when the user wants access to the computer (or cash register, kiosk computer, medicine dispensary, and so on). Sometimes users secure their smart card in a wallet or purse, but more often they attach their smart card to a lanyard or smart card holder (which they then attach to a belt loop or article of clothing). Generally, a user knows when a smart card goes missing; in contrast, users don't know when their passwords have been compromised.

EXAM TIP

Windows 8 offers support for the Personal Identity Verification (PIV) standard. This makes it possible for Windows 8.1 to obtain the necessary drivers for PIV smart cards from Windows Update. The operating system also contains its own minidriver if Windows Update is not available.

MORE INFO **THERE ARE POLICIES AVAILABLE TO MANAGE SMART CARDS**

There are settings you can configure in Group Policy Management Console when using physical smart cards in an organization. You can configure these settings to require smart cards and to specify how Windows 8 should respond when the smart card is removed during a computer session. You can see these settings from Computer Configuration, Policies, Windows Settings, Security Settings, Local Policies, Security Options.

Virtual smart cards imitate the functionality of physical smart cards, but they are not physical cards. Instead, they are virtual and use the Trusted Platform Module (TPM) chip available on many newer computers to provide security. This eliminates the need for a card reader. To use virtual smart cards, you must have a personal computer running Windows 8.1 with an installed and fully functional TPM and a network configured to support the use of virtual smart cards.

For a worker in an organization that uses these kinds of virtual smart cards, it's simply a smart card that is always available on the computer. At login, it shows as a user account and below it are options to sign in with the normal password or PIN. If a user needs to use more than one computer, a new virtual smart card must be issued for that computer. If multiple users share a computer, there are multiple virtual smart cards, one for each.

> ***MORE INFO*** **UNDERSTAND VIRTUAL SMART CARD TECHNOLOGY**
>
> **For more information, see Understanding and Evaluating Virtual Smart Cards at *http://www.microsoft.com/en-us/download/details.aspx?displaylang=en&id=29076*.**

At sign in, Windows 8.1 detects whether a smart card reader was installed and if it was used to sign in the last time the computer was used. If a smart card was not installed and the user selects the smart card sign-in icon, the user is prompted to connect a smart card. Additionally, the Smart Card Service runs only when it needs to. The Smart Card Service (scardsvr) automatically starts when the user connects a smart card reader and automatically stops when a user removes a smart card reader and no other smart card reader is connected to the computer.

To configure Windows 8.1 virtual smart cards if you have the required technology and credentials available, follow these steps:

1. Open an elevated command prompt.
2. Type **tpm.msc**.
3. Verify that a compatible TPM can be found and that it is at least a 1.2 or later. If you receive an error but are sure a compatible module is available, enable it in the system BIOS before continuing.
4. Close the TPM management console.
5. At the command prompt, type **TpmVscMgr create /name MyVSC /pin default /adminkey random /generate** and press Enter. To provide a custom PIN value when creating the virtual smart card, use **/pin prompt** instead.

Use biometrics

Windows 8.1 includes a component called Windows Biometric Framework. This makes it possible to use a physical characteristic like a fingerprint to identify a user without having to go to the great lengths required to do so in Windows 7 (and earlier versions). It's important to use this with a secondary authentication method, though, because scanners can fail and it is theoretically possible for the biometric identification method to be compromised. For example, I was able to unlock my smartphone that I configured to use facial recognition using my cat's face instead of mine. That is an issue with the manufacturer and could be an issue for you, too.

You need to make sure the Biometrics Service is running in the Services console to use the service. You also need to install the biometric hardware, generally a scanner of some sort. Device Manager supports these types of devices, as does Windows Update; there are settings available in Group Policy to manage them (see Figure 4-28) and there is a Biometric Devices item in Control Panel that allows users to control the availability of biometric devices and state whether they can be used to log on to a local computer or domain. You can use a biometric device to grant User Account Control elevation, too.

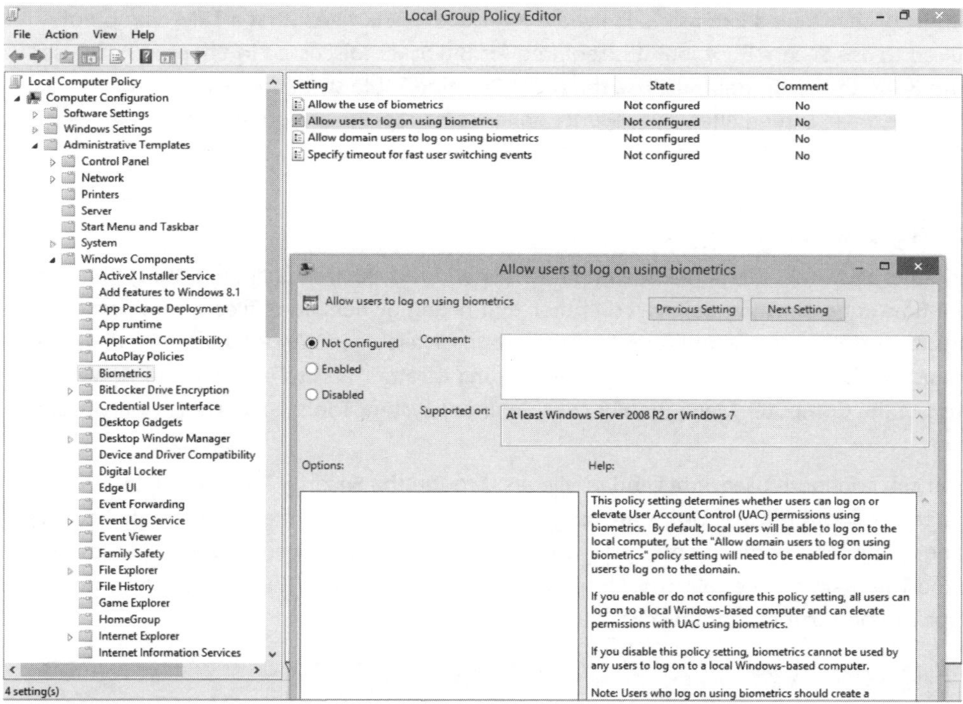

FIGURE 4-28 Configure Group Policy for biometrics.

You can find Group Policy settings related to biometrics in the Group Policy Editor under Computer Configuration, Administrative Templates, Windows Components, Biometrics. There you can select from the following options:

- Allow The Use Of Biometrics
- Allow Users To Log On Using Biometrics
- Allow Domain Users To Log On Using Biometrics
- Specify Timeout For Fast User Switching Events

> ***MORE INFO*** **LEARN MORE ABOUT BIOMETRICS**
>
> For more information about biometrics, refer to this article on TechNet: *http://technet.microsoft.com/en-us/library/dn308564.aspx*.

Local security settings

In the exam for Windows 8, there was an additional entry for Objective 4.2, Local security settings. This was removed for the Windows 8.1 exam update. However, some of the items previously tested are still important to know (and it's possible you might see remnants of them on this exam). Make sure you understand how to configure Local Security Policy (which we've covered in various sections in this book) and how to configure Secure Boot and make the most of the Unified Extensible Firmware Interface (UEFI). Know that a TPM chip is not required to use Secure Boot, but it is required for BitLocker (discussed in Chapter 5). To use Secure Boot, the computer must use the GUID Partition Table structure as well. Also take a look at the SmartScreen filter; this security enhancement protects your computer (and you) from running malicious software unintentionally.

Configure user rights

User rights allow users to perform computer-related tasks, such as changing the system time or the time zone, shutting down a computer, and taking ownership of files, among other things. User rights are preconfigured for the groups available in Windows 8.1, including Users, Administrators, Guests, HomeUsers, Hyper-V Administrators, and so on. (You can view all groups in the Computer Management console under System Tools, Local Users And Groups, Groups.)

You can configure user rights and privileges through the Security Policy console. You can also get a feel for how user rights are assigned already by viewing the entries in the Security Settings pane for a particular policy. Figure 4-29 shows the Local Security Policy console with Change The System Time selected. Note that only the LOCAL SERVICE and Administrators groups can perform this task by default.

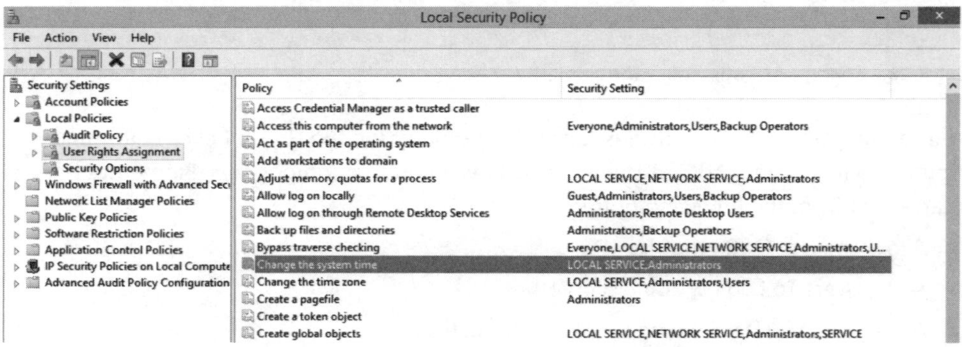

FIGURE 4-29 View defaults from Security Settings\Local Policies\User Rights Assessment.

You can add (or remove) users or groups to any entry in the User Rights Assignment pane. To do so, double-click the entry to change (we'll chose Deny Access To This Computer From The Network), click Add User Or Group, and then use the Select Users Or Groups dialog box to complete the addition. See Figure 4-30. However, before you do this, remember that administrators generally add users to groups first and then go from there. In the case of user rights, administrators traditionally either add the user who should have the rights to the group that already has those rights assigned or assign user rights to groups they create and then add users to those groups when necessary.

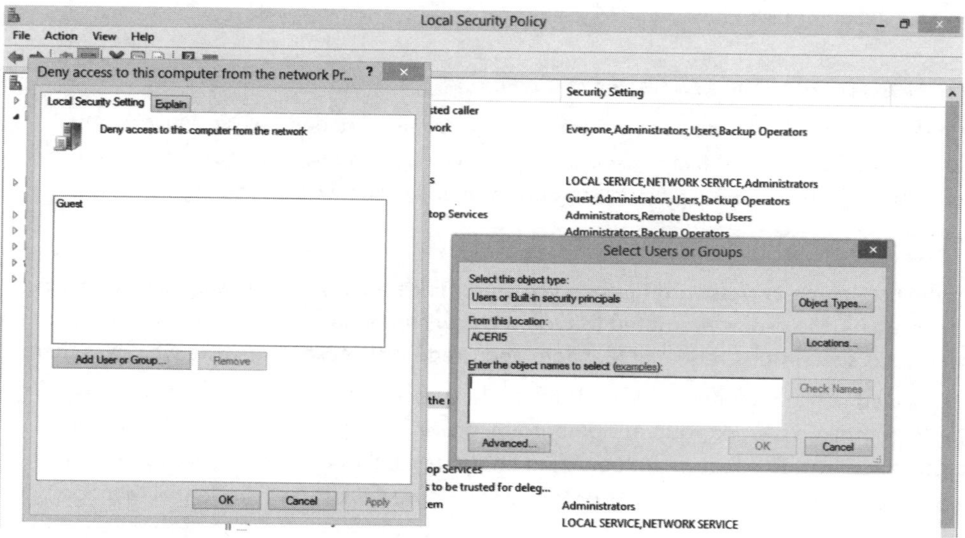

FIGURE 4-30 Configure User Rights Assignment in Local Security Policy.

EXAM TIP

User rights and user permissions are two different things. User rights provide a user the ability to do something. Permissions provide a user the ability to access something. User rights are assigned to users and groups. Permissions are applied to objects like files and folders. User rights can follow a user. Permissions are assigned to users and are generally fixed.

Manage credentials and certificates

Credentials and certificates help secure the computer in different ways. Credentials are user names and passwords; certificates verify the security of a particular thing, like encrypted files or Internet downloads.

Credentials

Credentials are user names and passwords. Windows 8.1 comes with Credential Manager to help manage and maintain them. Credential Manager saves the credentials users enter when they use their own computer to access network servers and resources on local networks (Windows Credentials) and can be used to back up and restore them. The user has to select the Remember My Credentials check box when prompted, though, or else the credential won't be saved. Credential Manager also offers Credential Locker, which saves user names and passwords associated with websites and Windows apps (Web Credentials). It saves all of these in an area called the Windows Vault.

> ***MORE INFO*** **HOW CREDENTIALS ARE SAVED**
>
> **Credentials are saved in encrypted folders on the computer under the user's profile. Applications that support this feature, such as web browsers and Windows 8 apps, can automatically offer up the correct credentials to other computers and websites during the sign-in process.**

If the user name or password has been changed since the last time it was saved and access is unsuccessful, the user is prompted to type the new credentials. When access to the resource or website is successful, Credential Manager and Credential Locker overwrite what was there.

The saved user names and passwords follow the users when they move from one computer to another in a workgroup or homegroup, provided the user logs on with his or her Microsoft account. This feature isn't enabled on domains, though, for security reasons. You can open Credential Manager from Control Panel. Figure 4-31 shows Credential Manager.

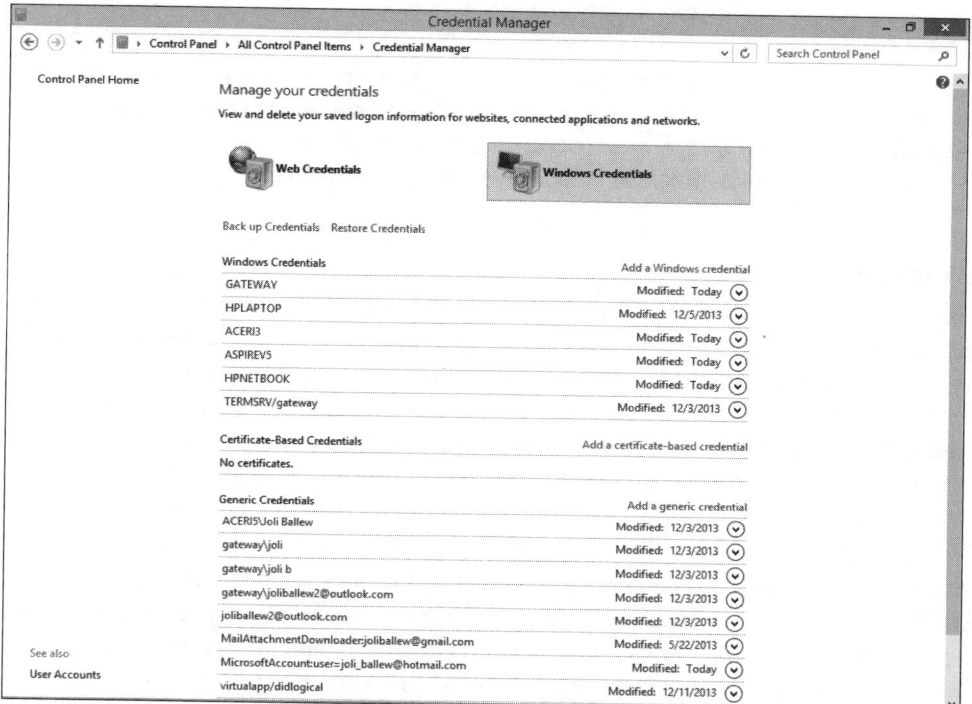

FIGURE 4-31 Open Credential Manager and Windows Credentials.

Here are a few more things to know about Credential Manager:

- Windows Store apps can be programmed to use Credential Locker.
- Credential roaming requires the Microsoft account for synchronization.
- Credential roaming is enabled by default on non-domain-joined computers, and it is disabled on domain-joined computers.
- Credential Locker supports seamless sign in by using Windows Store apps that use Web Authentication Broker and remember passwords for services like Twitter and LinkedIn.

EXAM TIP

To store a credential at a command line, use the command-line tool cmdkey /add.

Note in Figure 4-31 that options exist to back up and restore credentials, but these options are only available when Windows Credentials is selected. When you click Back Up Credentials you are prompted first to browse to a location to which to save the credentials, name the file (it has a .crd extension), and then press Ctrl+Alt+Del to continue the backup process on the Secure Desktop. There you create a password for the file so that only you can access it.

EXAM TIP

It's important to understand that you can't back up credentials you've saved in your web browser from inside Credential Manager. Those credentials are saved as part of your Microsoft account and are synchronized with it. (Those credentials do roam, provided you've logged on with the Microsoft account you used to create them.)

Certificates

Websites use certificates to verify that the site meets specific requirements for security. Executable files you download from the Internet often have certificates, too, to show they have not been tampered with since their creation. These generally come from verified certificate authorities if they are offerings from valid online entities that you can trust. Windows 8 creates its own certificates, including the self-signed certificates used with EFS, discussed earlier in this chapter. Although the use of certificates is invisible to the end user, you might want to manage them, specifically by backing them up. You might want to migrate them, for instance, or just provide one more tool for backup and recovery.

The only place to perform this particular backup task is from the Certificate Manager MMC. You can open it from a Run dialog box or the Start screen by typing **certmgr.msc**. You can see this in Figure 4-32. There are a lot of entries, and each represents a specific kind of certificate. Personal Certificates and Trusted Publishers are two of them. Figure 4-32 shows Trusted Root Certification Authorities expanded and Certificates selected. Look closely and you might recognize some of the names: VeriSign, Go Daddy, Microsoft, and Equifax.

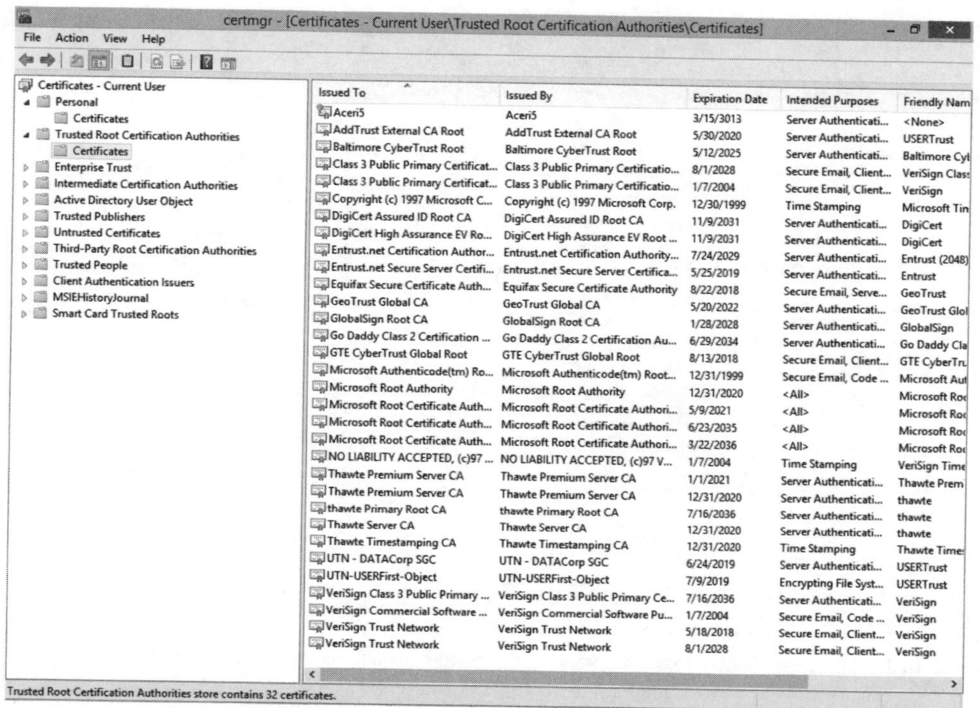

FIGURE 4-32 The Certificate Manager MMC offers a listing of all the certificates available on the computer.

To back up a single certificate, right-click the certificate to back up, click All Tasks, and then click Export. Work through the wizard to select the format to use. This is the only way to back up a certificate and have the options shown in Figure 4-33 available. If you select more than one certificate, you'll have to choose Personal Information Exchange or Microsoft Serialized Certificate Store.

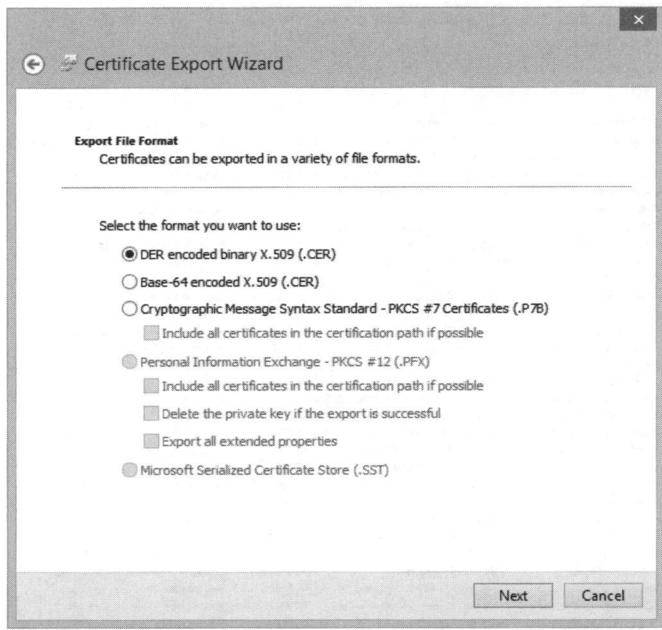

FIGURE 4-33 Select certificates to back up one at a time to have access to the three options shown here.

> ***MORE INFO*** **SUPPORTED FILE FORMATS**
>
> Certificate import and export operations support four file formats:
>
> - Personal Information Exchange (PKCS #12)
>
>   The Personal Information Exchange format (PFX, also called PKCS #12) supports secure storage of certificates, private keys, and all certificates in a certification path. The PKCS #12 format is the only file format that can be used to export a certificate and its private key.
>
> - Cryptographic Message Syntax Standard (PKCS #7)
>
>   The PKCS #7 format supports storage of certificates and all certificates in the certification path.
>
> - DER Encoded Binary X.509
>
>   The Distinguished Encoding Rules (DER) format supports storage of a single certificate. This format does not support storage of the private key or certification path.
>
> - Base-64 Encoded X.509
>
>   The Base-64 format supports storage of a single certificate. This format does not support storage of the private key or certification path.

Configure User Account Control behavior

You are likely familiar with the User Account Control (UAC) prompt that appears when elevated privileges are required to perform a task. When logged on as a Standard user, the user must input both an Administrator user name and password in the UAC dialog box and click Yes before continuing. When logged on as an Administrator, the user must click Yes or No to continue. When these prompts appear, they appear on a Secure Desktop. Nothing can happen until the proper credentials or answer is input or that task attempt is canceled. Secure Desktop keeps anything from happening behind the scenes while the user decides what to do.

> ***NOTE*** **ALL ABOUT TOKENS**
>
> **Although Microsoft recommends that users perform their everyday computing tasks using a Standard account, most don't heed this advice. Because of this, Administrator accounts are given two tokens (one for a Standard user and one for an Administrator user). Tokens define the user's access level at logon. By default, the Standard user token is used most of the time. Administrators are still prompted when particular activities are attempted.**

You might also know how to change the level of UAC in Control Panel using the slider available for that purpose. You can access this from the Action Center by clicking Change User Account Control Settings.

EXAM TIP

If you are questioned about how to configure a computer to require elevated privileges for a specific task to be performed, note that the answer probably has to do with the UAC settings.

There's a lot more to UAC than that, though. One option is to use Local Security Policy to specifically define how UAC is configured. There are too many options to list here, but you can review them in the Local Security Policy window from Local Policies, Security Options. Double-click any User Account Control policy option and click the Explain tab to learn about it. Figure 4-34 shows this, with User Account Control: Behavior Of The Elevation Prompt For Standard Users selected.

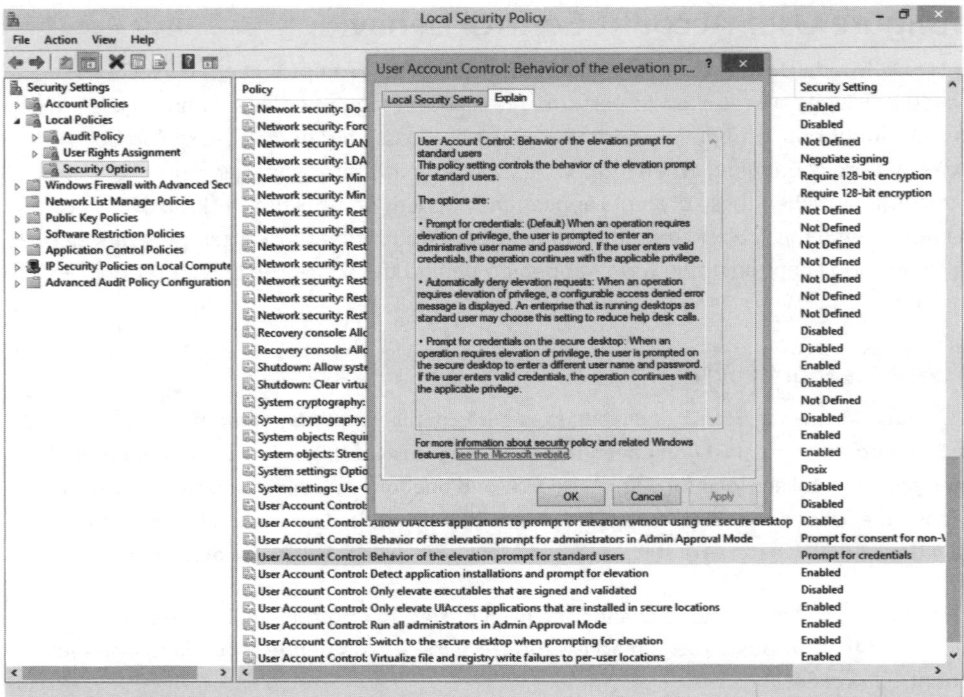

FIGURE 4-34 Change options for the various UAC policies to suit your environment's needs.

Here are a few more things to know about the UAC prompt in Windows 8.1. The elevation prompt color-coding is as follows:

- **Red background with a red shield icon** The application is blocked by Group Policy or is from a publisher that is blocked.
- **Blue background with a blue and gold shield icon** The application is a Windows Server 2012 administrative application, such as a Control Panel item.
- **Blue background with a blue shield icon** The application is signed by using Authenticode and is trusted by the local computer.
- **Yellow background with a yellow shield icon** The application is unsigned or signed but is not yet trusted by the local computer.

MORE INFO **LEARN MORE ABOUT UAC**

Learn more about UAC at *http://technet.microsoft.com/en-us/library/jj574202.aspx.*

Thought experiment

Create a password and Account Lockout policy for a client

In this thought experiment, apply what you've learned about this objective. You can find answers to these questions in the "Answers" section at the end of this chapter.

You need to create a password policy for a company that wants to enforce these parameters: passwords must contain uppercase and lowercase letters, numbers, and special characters. Users can attempt to log on 10 times, but after the tenth time, they are locked out from trying to log on again for 15 minutes. Passwords must also be changed once a month.

1. Which MMC do you use to access these settings?
2. Which two entries do you need to access in the MMC?
3. What four entries do you need to enable and configure?

Objective summary

- The Microsoft account is a new way to log on to a computer running Windows 8 and syncs various settings including web favorites, Start screen settings, and Internet passwords.
- Virtual smart cards can be used to further secure log in, as can biometrics. There are group policies for both.
- User Account Control gives both Standard users and Administrators the option to consider what they (or their computer) is attempting to do and decide whether to allow it. Secure Desktop keeps everything locked down until a decision is made.
- There are many types of authentication, including PINs, Picture passwords, Microsoft accounts, local accounts, and domain accounts.
- Rights enable users to do things like change the system time. Rights are already assigned to the groups available in Windows 8.

Objective review

Answer the following questions to test your knowledge of the information in this objective. You can find the answers to these questions and explanations of why each answer choice is correct or incorrect in the "Answers" section at the end of this chapter.

1. How do you block the use of Microsoft accounts on a stand-alone computer that is shared in the workplace? (Choose all that apply.)
   - **A.** In Local Security Policy from Security Settings, Local Policies, Security Options
   - **B.** In Local Group Policy Editor from Computer Configuration, Windows Settings, Security Settings, Local Policies, Security Options
   - **C.** In Local Security Policy from Security Settings, Local Policies, User Rights Assignment
   - **D.** In Local Security Policy from Security Settings, Account Policies, Password Policy
2. Where do you create a PIN or a Picture password?
   - **A.** Control Panel, in User Accounts and Family Safety
   - **B.** Control Panel, in Credential Manager
   - **C.** In PC Settings, under Accounts and the Your Account tab
   - **D.** In PC Settings, under Sign-in Options
   - **E.** In PC Settings, under Other Accounts
3. Which two Password policies would you configure if you needed to make sure users changed their passwords every 42 days but could not make another password change for at least 21 days? (Choose two.)
   - **A.** Enforce Password History
   - **B.** Minimum Password Age
   - **C.** Maximum Password Age
   - **D.** Minimum Password Length
   - **E.** Maximum Password Length
4. What makes it possible for Windows 8.1 to obtain the necessary drivers for PIV smart cards from Windows Update?
   - **A.** You must enable the related setting from Computer Configuration, Policies, Windows Settings, Security Settings, Local Policies, Security Options.
   - **B.** The Smart Card Service (scardsvr) makes this possible.
   - **C.** At an elevated command prompt, you must type **TpmVscMgr create /name MyVSC /pin default /adminkey random /generate**.
   - **D.** The Personal Identity Verification (PIV) standard makes this possible.
5. Which of the following is a user right?
   - **A.** Allow log on locally
   - **B.** Add workstations to a domain
   - **C.** Change the system time
   - **D.** Create global objects
   - **E.** All of the above

6. Which command opens the MMC required to back up certifications for the purpose of migrating them to another computer?
   - **A.** Gpedit.msc
   - **B.** SecPol.msc
   - **C.** CertMgr.msc
   - **D.** Services.msc

Chapter summary

- There are many ways to share resources and protect those resources on local and domain networks, including but not limited to applying Share and NTFS permissions, using homegroups, configuring EFS, using various types of sharing including Any folder sharing, and more.
- NTFS permissions allow for granular control of shared resources. There are six basic permissions and 14 advanced permissions. When combined with Share permissions, the more restrictive of the cumulative permissions is applied.
- Disk quotas, EFS, and auditing are available on NTFS volumes and help administrators manage and maintain those volumes for multiple users.
- Authentication can be achieved through user names and passwords, PINs, Picture passwords, physical and virtual smart cards, and biometrics, and these can be combined to configure multifactor authentication.
- User rights let users do things; permissions let users access things. Both can be managed through group policies.
- User Account Control helps secure a computer from malware and other threats by making users input the proper credentials or allow the task through a UAC dialog box. UAC settings can be changed in Control Panel and managed through Group Policies.

Answers

This section contains the solutions to the thought experiments and answers to the objective review questions in this chapter.

Objective 4.1: Thought experiment

1. Any folder sharing is best because the client can protect files and folders by specifically configuring access for only those who need it.
2. You must remove the Everyone group from all of the shares you want to configure.
3. 20
4. Read and Change. Do not give Full Control; if you do, the user can do the things listed (change file permissions and take ownership).

Objective 4.1: Review

1. **Correct answers:** A and C
   - **A. Correct:** A wizard does walk you through the process of creating or joining a homegroup, and a password is generated for you.
   - **B. Incorrect:** You can reconfigure shares to include specific permissions for people you select.
   - **C. Correct:** Users can share their default libraries.
   - **D. Incorrect:** Homegroups can only be configured with Windows 7 and Windows 8–based computers.
2. **Correct answer:** A
   - **A. Correct**: Any folder sharing offers these features.
   - **B. Incorrect**: You'd have to move the data from the desktop to the applicable Public folder. Also, you could not have the control needed for this scenario.
   - **C. Incorrect**: You can't configure a homegroup on a public network, only on a private network.
   - **D. Incorrect**: Any folder sharing is the correct answer.
3. **Correct answer:** D
   - **A. Incorrect:** Only the Print permission is required.
   - **B. Incorrect:** Only the Print permission is required.
   - **C. Incorrect:** Only the Print permission is required.
   - **D. Correct:** When you share a printer, the Everyone group has the Print permission so nothing else needs to be done.

4. **Correct answer:** B

   A. **Incorrect:** You must configure this from your Windows 8.1 computer, not from the website.

   B. **Correct:** This is where you configure this setting.

   C. **Incorrect:** Although you can configure many options here, the option in this question isn't one of them.

   D. **Incorrect:** This does not offer the desired option.

Objective 4.2: Thought experiment

1. The Properties dialog box for the storage volume, on the Quota tab
2. Deny Disk Space To Users Exceeding Quota Limit and Limit Disk Space To
3. Probably not. As stated in the scenario, the other users don't use much storage space. The only time this would become an issue is if one of those users suddenly needed more space.

Objective 4.2: Review

1. **Correct answer:** A

   A. **Correct**: A security principal is the user, group, or computer given permissions and the permissions that have been configured for it (them).

   B. **Incorrect**: Any element or resource that is protected has an access control list (ACL). This is basically a list of permissions that have been applied to it.

   C. **Incorrect**: The NTFS permissions in the ACL are access control entries (ACEs). Every ACE has at least one security principal.

   D. **Incorrect**: An element, object, or resource is what is being protected.

2. **Correct answers:** A, B, C, and D

   A. **Correct**: This is a valid task that can be performed here.

   B. **Correct:** This is a valid task that can be performed here.

   C. **Correct**: This is a valid task that can be performed here.

   D. **Correct**: This is a valid task that can be performed here.

3. **Correct answer:** C

   A. **Incorrect:** Set-Acl is a command, but it is used to set the NTFS ACL for a specified resource.

   B. **Incorrect:** Icacls.exe is used to apply permissions at a command line.

   C. **Correct:** Cipher is the proper command-line tool.

   D. **Incorrect:** You can configure encryption from a command line.

4. **Correct answer:** D
   - **A. Incorrect**: Encryption does protect against copy commands.
   - **B. Incorrect:** A hacker can get to data in any number of ways, even if the data is encrypted.
   - **C. Incorrect:** A hacker can't remove the encryption attribute.
   - **D. Correct:** An Access Denied message will appear.

Objective 4.3: Thought experiment

1. You can use Security Policy or Group Policy Management Console consoles.
2. Password policy and Account Lockout policy
3. To do the following:
   - Require users to create complex passwords: Password policy – Password Must Meet Complexity Requirements
   - Limit user to 10 failed logons: Account lockout policy – Account Lockout Threshold (set to 10)
   - Lock out users for 15 minutes after the account lockout threshold has been met: Account lockout threshold – Account Lockout Duration (set to 15)
   - Require users change their password once a month: Password policy – Maximum Password Age (set to 30 or 31)

Objective 4.3: Review

1. **Correct answers:** A and B
   - **A. Correct:** You can access this policy from the Local Security Policy MMC.
   - **B. Correct:** You can access this policy from the Local Group Policy Editor MMC from Local Policies\Security Options.
   - **C. Incorrect:** This is not a valid path to the desired policy. User rights do not offer this option.
   - **D. Incorrect:** This is not a valid path to the desired policy. Password policy can't be set to exclude Microsoft accounts.
2. **Correct answer:** D
   - **A. Incorrect:** You can create accounts, change account types, remove user accounts, set up family safety, and more, but you cannot create a PIN or Picture password here.
   - **B. Incorrect:** You use Credential Manager to manage and maintain Windows and Web credentials.
   - **C. Incorrect:** You cannot make the desired change here.

- **D. Correct:** This is where you create a PIN or Picture password.
- **E. Incorrect:** This is where you create additional accounts or configure them.

3. **Correct answers:** B and C
   - **A. Incorrect:** This keeps users from reusing passwords they've previously created.
   - **B. Correct:** This requires users to keep their password for a certain amount of time; in this instance, 21 days.
   - **C. Correct:** This requires users to change their password after a specific amount of time has passed; in this case, 42 days.
   - **D. Incorrect:** Length has to do with how many characters a password contains and not with a length of time.
   - **E. Incorrect:** Length has to do with how many characters a password contains and not with a length of time.
4. **Correct answer:** D
   - **A. Incorrect:** This is where you configure policies for smart cards, but you do not have to enable any setting for the scenario stated.
   - **B. Incorrect:** The Smart Card Service (scardsvr) automatically starts when the user connects a smart card reader and automatically stops when the user removes a smart card reader and no other smart card reader is connected to the computer.
   - **C. Incorrect:** This is the command to configure a new virtual smart card.
   - **D. Correct:** This standard makes the scenario possible.
5. **Correct answer:** E
   - **A. Incorrect:** All of the items are correct, so E is the correct answer.
   - **B. Incorrect:** All of the items are correct, so E is the correct answer.
   - **C. Incorrect:** All of the items are correct, so E is the correct answer.
   - **D. Incorrect:** All of the items are correct, so E is the correct answer.
   - **E. Correct:** All of the entries are user rights.
6. **Correct answer:** C
   - **A. Incorrect:** This opens the Group Policy Editor.
   - **B. Incorrect:** This opens the Security Policy console.
   - **C. Correct:** This opens the Certificate Manager console.
   - **D. Incorrect:** This opens the Services console.

CHAPTER 5

Configure remote access and mobility

More people are working away from their offices than ever before. They work from home, from hotel rooms, from airplanes, and from company branch sites. Those users need to be able to connect to their own desktop and the company network through secure virtual private networks (VPNs), and they need to be reconnected if the connection is lost. They need to connect using their own broadband connection, too, no matter the carrier or connection type. Finally, they need to work in various ways over the Internet, including from airplanes and via hotel Wi-Fi.

Beyond this, though, their mobile devices need to be protected in case of theft or sabotage. You need to be able to configure BitLocker and BitLocker To Go and configure the appropriate startup and recovery keys to do this. Those users will also need you to set group policies for using offline files and syncing and teach them how to best configure their machines with the most applicable power policies for any situation. There's more, though, including understanding Windows To Go and offering it as an option when applicable.

Objectives in this chapter:

- Objective 5.1: Configure remote connections
- Objective 5.2: Configure mobility options
- Objective 5.3: Configure security for mobile devices

Objective 5.1: Configure remote connections

There are two remote connection options that we have already discussed in this book: Remote Assistance and Remote Desktop. To review those, refer to Chapter 3, "Configure network connectivity," and specifically Objective 3.4. We'll revisit some of that here, but not too heavily. Most of this objective focuses on remote authentication in various scenarios, Remote Desktop technologies, and the types of connections you can use, including VPNs and broadband.

This objective covers how to:

- Configure remote authentication
- Configure Remote Desktop settings
- Configure VPN connections and authentication
- Enable VPN Reconnect
- Configure broadband tethering

Configure remote authentication

You're going to see quite a few questions on the exam that involve understanding what is and is not applicable to a specific type of connection protocol. These protocols are required to configure and complete remote authentication and thus verify that the user who wants to connect is actually the one you want connecting. Before we move forward, make sure you are familiar with the following protocols.

VPN protocols

Windows 8.1 supports lots of protocols, and the ones listed here are used with VPNs (loosely listed from oldest to newest and least secure to most secure):

- **Point-to-Point Protocol (PPP)** When a dial-up connection is used to connect a client to a server, a dedicated link is used and that connection is maintained throughout the session. This link is called Point-to-Point Protocol (PPP) and is a notably secure connection because it is difficult to hack into, being dial-up. PPP can also be used with a VPN over the Internet. This is less secure than a dial-up connection, because it's much easier for a hacker to get to the data transmitted over the Internet. This is not a recommended protocol for these reasons and more, and it should only be used when no other options exist.
- **Point-to-Point Tunneling Protocol (PPTP)** This is the least secure of all of the VPN protocols. PPTP does not require the use of certificates to ensure security. It is a better option than PPP, though, because the packets are encapsulated through tunneling technologies and are better protected during transmission. PPTP only supports the Microsoft Challenge Handshake Authentication Protocol version 1 and version 2 (MS-CHAP v1 and MS-CHAP v2), Extensible Authentication Protocol (EAP), and Protected Extensible Authentication Protocol (PEAP).
- **Layer 2 Tunneling Protocol (L2TP)** This protocol uses the IP Security extension (IPsec) for encryption and encapsulation. It encrypts with Data Encryption Standard (DES) or Triple DES (3DES) with keys obtained from the IPsec Internet Key Exchange (IKE). L2TP/IPsec uses preshared keys or certificates and offers data integrity checks. L2TP/IPsec is supported on Windows XP, Windows Vista, Windows 7, Windows 8, Windows 8.1, Windows Server 2003, and Windows Server 2008.

- **Secure Socket Tunneling Protocol (SSTP)** This protocol encapsulates PPP traffic through the Secure Sockets Layer (SSL) protocol and uses certificates for authentication. Authentication involves Extensible Authentication Protocol-Transport Layer Security (EAP-TLS) and provides integrity checks. SSTP is supported on Windows Vista, Windows 7, Windows 8, Windows 8.1, Windows Server 2008 R2, and Windows Server 2012.
- **Internet Key Exchange, Version 2 (IKEv2)** This protocol supports IPv6 and VPN Reconnect, authentication with EAP, PEAP, EAP-MSCHAPv3, and smart cards. It doesn't support Password Authentication Protocol (PAP) and CHAP as authentication methods. IKEv2 is useful when a user moves from one type of connection to another (wireless to wired, for example) and in many other scenarios. Windows 8.1 clients try to use this protocol first when connecting to remote servers. IKEv2 is supported on Windows 7, Windows 8, Windows 8.1, Windows Server 2008 R2, and Windows Server 2012.

Authentication protocols

Clients must be authenticated before they can access network resources. Here are the most common authentication protocols:

- **PAP** This protocol is the least secure and uses plaintext passwords. It is used as a last resort when other authentication methods can't be negotiated. It's not enabled by default on a Windows 8–based client and is not considered secure.
- **CHAP** The protocol uses a three-way handshake between the client and server using a key for encryption. This is best used for legacy connections and is better than PAP, but other methods are preferred.
- **MS-CHAP v2** This protocol uses a two-way mutual authentication and is stronger than CHAP. Still, better protocols exist, including EAP.
- **EAP-MS-CHAPv2** This protocol authenticates using EAP. EAP offers the strongest and most flexible security option. With it, authentication can be negotiated using something other than passwords, including certificates and smart cards. This is the default selection for new connections on Windows 8–based machines.

You can explore these protocol and authentication options from a VPN connection's Properties dialog box. An example is shown in Figure 5-1.

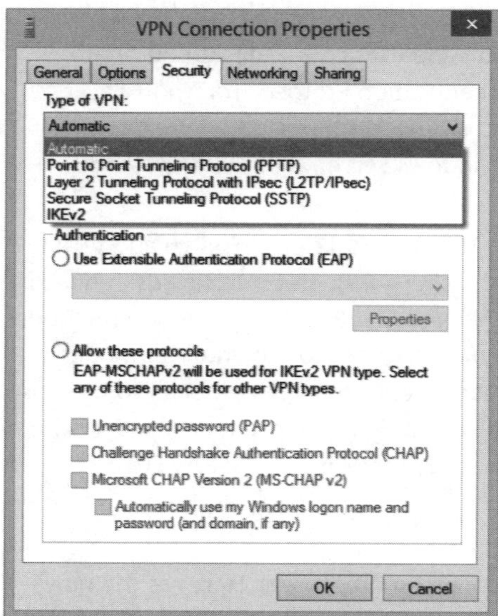

FIGURE 5-1 Explore protocol and authentication options from a VPN connection's Properties dialog box.

MORE INFO **LEARN MORE ABOUT REMOTE ASSISTANCE AND NETSH**

Remote Assistance is covered in Chapter 3. Netsh is also covered there. Refer to Chapter 3 to learn more about these two technologies.

EXAM TIP

IKEv2 supports VPN Reconnect. PPP, PPTP, SSTP, and L2TP do not. EAP supports smart cards. Other authentication protocols do not. If you want to use a preshared key, you have to choose L2TP/IPsec. DES and 3DES and IKE are used with L2TP.

Configure Remote Desktop settings

You learned how to use Remote Desktop in Chapter 3, and you also learned how to make configuration choices in the Remote Desktop Connection dialog box and the available tabs there (General, Display, Programs, Experience, Advanced). Here you'll learn a bit more about the technical aspects of Remote Desktop.

The Remote Desktop Protocol (RDP) is the protocol used to connect workers to their desktops when they are away from them, perhaps when they are at home or in a hotel. Additionally, Remote Desktop is used by network administrators to remotely administer computers and servers, often from another company computer in the same building or in another one close by. Users can connect to a remote desktop from almost any type of computer, including those running Windows XP, Windows Vista, Windows 7, Windows 8, Windows 8.1, or Windows RT. The computer that is the host must be running Windows XP Professional, Windows Vista Enterprise, Windows Vista Ultimate, Windows Vista Business, Windows 7 Ultimate, Windows 7 Enterprise, Windows 7 Professional, Windows 8 Pro, Windows 8.1 Pro, Windows 8 Enterprise, or Windows 8.1 Enterprise.

You can open the Remote Desktop Connection dialog box by typing **mstsc.exe** at a command prompt. You can see both in Figure 5-2.

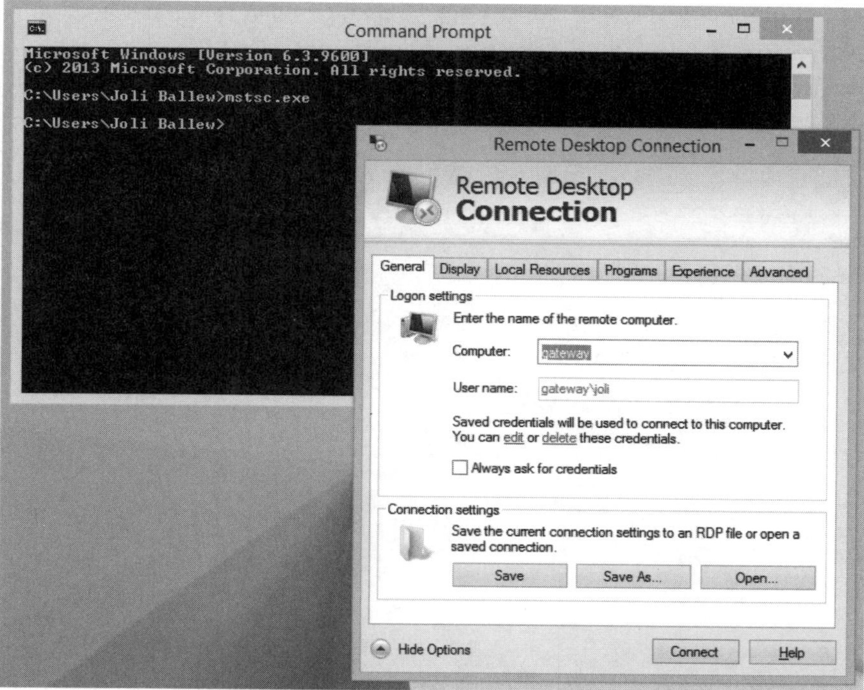

FIGURE 5-2 Use the command-line tool mstsc.exe to open Remote Desktop.

There are parameters you can use with the command mstsc.exe when using Remote Desktop:

- **<connection file>** This parameter specifies the name of an .rdp file for the connection.
- **/edit <connection file>** This parameter opens the specified .rdp file for editing.
- **/v:<Server[:<Port>]** This parameter specifies the remote computer and, optionally, the port number to which you want to connect.
- **/admin** This parameter connects you to a session for administering the server.
- **/f** This parameter starts Remote Desktop Connection in full-screen mode.
- **/w:<Width>** This parameter specifies the width of the Remote Desktop window.
- **/h:<Height>** This parameter specifies the height of the Remote Desktop window.

- **/public** This parameter runs Remote Desktop in public mode. In public mode, passwords and bitmaps are not cached.
- **/span** This parameter matches the Remote Desktop width and height with the local virtual desktop, spanning across multiple monitors if necessary.

Configure VPN connections and authentication

You can create a VPN from the Network And Sharing Center by clicking Set Up A New Connection Or Network. In the resulting dialog box, choose Connect To A Workplace and click Next. Once there, you choose how to create the VPN: Use My Internet Connection (VPN) or Dial Directly. See Figure 5-3.

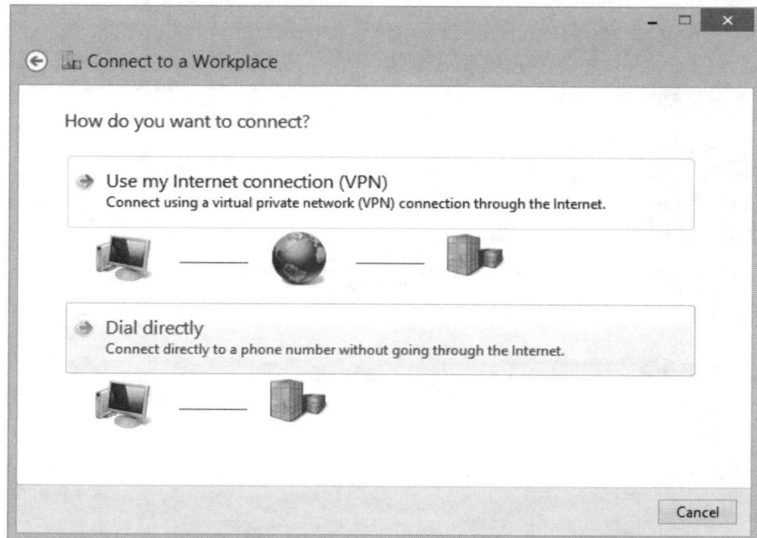

FIGURE 5-3 Create a VPN connection in the Network And Sharing Center.

> ***NOTE*** **HOW VPNS WORK**
>
> **VPNs establish secure connections that use encrypted tunnels to transmit data. Often these connections are used to create a connection from one company site to another or from a worker's home to his office. These are site-to-site and remote access connections, respectively. VPNs can connect via Wi-Fi and broadband, but because of reliability issues with both, it's best to bundle this with VPN Reconnect, discussed in the next section.**

In the resulting dialog box you do the following:

- Type an Internet address name, such as Contoso.com, or an IPv4 or IPv6 address, such as 157.54.0.1 or 3ffe:1234::1111.
- Type a name for the connection (or the destination).

- Opt to:
  - Use a smart card.
  - Remember credentials.
  - Allow other people to use the connection.

You'll see the connection in the Networks pane, shown in Figure 5-4. To activate the connection, click it and input the required credentials. The connection will be made.

FIGURE 5-4 The VPN connection appears in the Networks pane.

Now you can configure the properties for the VPN using its Properties dialog box, available from the Network Connections window in Control Panel. The options enable you to perform tasks including but not limited to the following:

- On the General tab, changing the host name
- On the Options tab, opting to remember your credentials or configuring protocol settings
- On the Security tab, changing the options for type of VPN (automatic, PPTP, L2TP, SSTP, IKEv2); data encryption options (none, options, required, maximum strength); use EAP; allow other protocols
- On the Networking tab, changing or reconfiguring TCP/IP settings and others
- On the Sharing tab, allowing other network users to connect through this computer's Internet connection; select a home networking connection type

Enable VPN Reconnect

When a user connects to a remote site using a VPN and that connection is lost, the user has to reconnect. This is an annoyance for users because it distracts them from their work and takes time. Additionally, with the prevalence of working via broadband and free Wi-Fi on the road, in subways, through tunnels, and on trains, service disruptions can happen frequently. When possible, it's best to use and configure VPN Reconnect for your remote users.

To enable VPN Reconnect—and remember that this feature is only available if IKEv2 is used as the VPN protocol—follow these steps:

1. Open the Network Connections window and locate the VPN connection to configure.
2. Right-click the connection and click Properties.
3. In the Properties dialog box, click the Security tab.
4. Click Advanced Settings.

5. In the Advanced Properties dialog box, click the IKEv2 tab. See Figure 5-5.
6. Configure the Network Outage Time setting and click OK.
7. Click OK again to close the VPN Connection Properties dialog box.

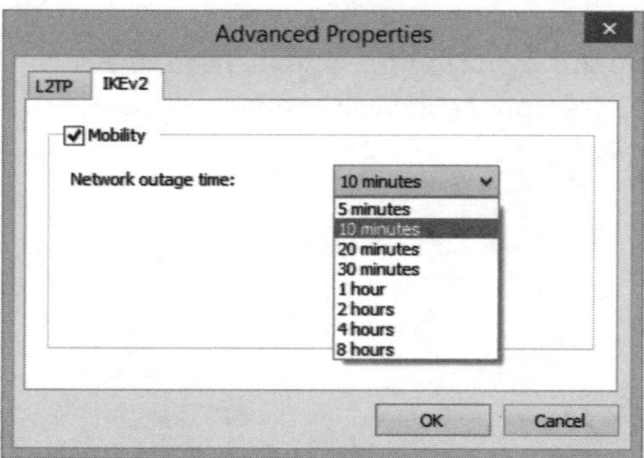

FIGURE 5-5 Configure the Network Outage Time setting for VPN Reconnect.

EXAM TIP

You might see references to other remote technologies and terms on the exam, although the ones listed here are not specifically named as objectives. It's best to cast a wide net when you study, though, so make sure you are at least familiar with the following terms and features:

- **BranchCache** **Distributed and Hosted cache modes reduce network bandwidth usage by caching frequently accessed data between company sites.**
- **Network Access Protection (NAP)** **Helps prevent potentially dangerous local or remote clients from connecting to a network.**
- **DirectAccess** **Enables users to connect to the company network automatically whenever they have Internet access.**

Configure broadband tethering

Some users have mobile devices that let them connect to the Internet when traditional options are unavailable. Traditional options include free and personal Mi-Fi networks, VPNs, workgroup and domain networks, broadband connections from ISPs, and connections to networks via Ethernet. When these options are unavailable, the user can opt for a built-in or personal cellular or metered broadband connection option or for another person's shared Internet connection.

Windows 8.1 comes with built-in support for these newer connectivity models. For instance, any Windows 8.1 user can connect to a shared personal hotspot provided she has the required credentials. The connection is made through the traditional Networks pane used to connect to all other networks. Users can use that pane to disconnect as well. Figure 5-6 shows the Networks pane where the connected network is a shared personal hotspot. Note that the user can also opt to show usage for metered connections (from PC Settings, detailed next).

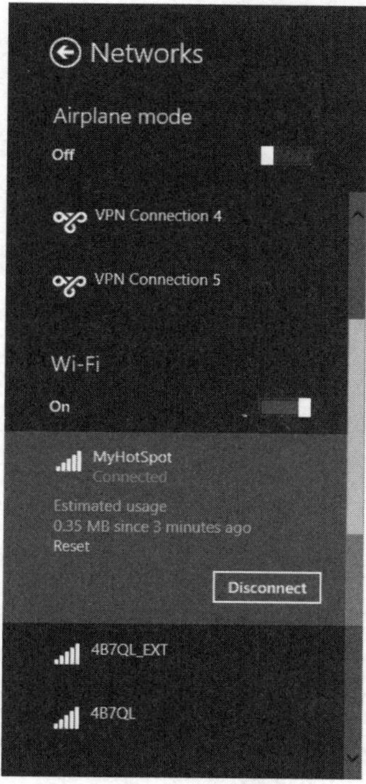

FIGURE 5-6 Use the Networks pane to connect to shared personal hotspots.

To configure the Networks pane to show the estimated usage, navigate to PC Settings, Network, Connections, and select the connection from the list. From there, enable the desired network settings. See Figure 5-7.

Some mobile devices (including those that are Long Term Evolution (LTE)–enabled) come with mobile broadband technology built in. Windows 8.1 supports this, too, and users can share these types of connections with others. This is the same as sharing a connection via a smartphone, but is provided by the mobile tablet. Users connect to the Internet using the connection they have available on their own devices, and then they can opt to share the connection with others. Again, this is done in PC Settings, Network, Connections by clicking the connection to share. Once shared, users can also change the SSID, change the password for the Wi-Fi network, and see how many people are sharing the connection. The person sharing the connection has to have purchased a data plan that supports tethering for this to work.

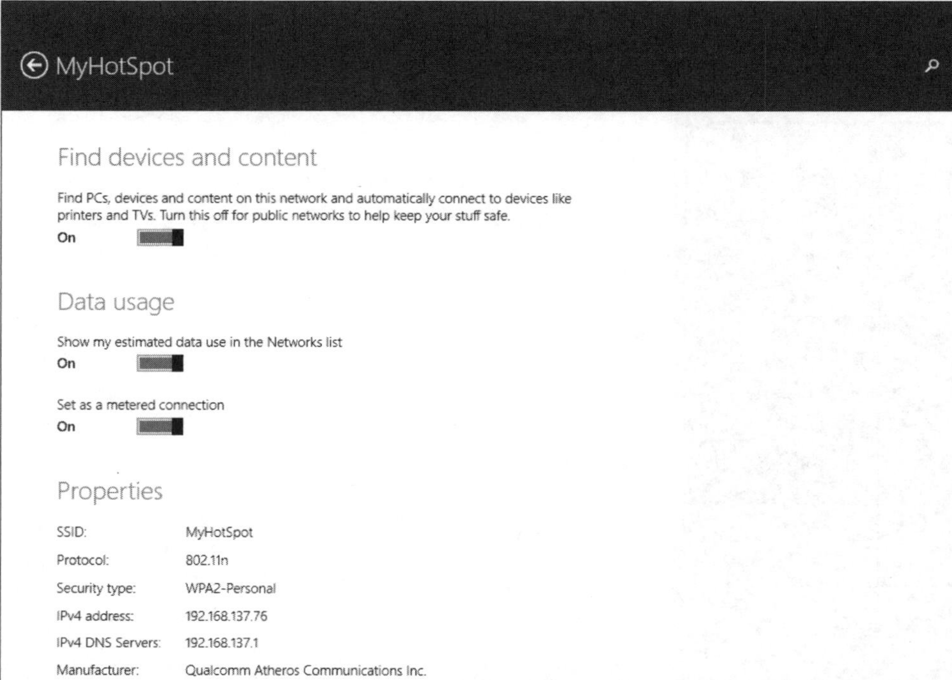

FIGURE 5-7 Configure the settings for a shared broadband connection.

MORE INFO **LEARN MORE ABOUT BROADBAND FEATURES IN WINDOWS 8.1**

Refer to this article for more information about the new features for broadband in Windows 8.1: *http://msdn.microsoft.com/en-us/library/windows/hardware/dn247045.aspx.*

Thought experiment

Choose the ideal VPN protocol

In this thought experiment, apply what you've learned about this objective. You can find answers to these questions in the "Answers" section at the end of this chapter.

You need to choose a VPN protocol for a client whose workstations are all running Windows 7 or later and whose domain controllers are all Windows Server 2012. You do not need to support other authentication methods like PAP and CHAP. You do need to enable users to configure VPN Reconnect.

1. **Which protocol should you select?**
2. **Can the users connect with EAP authentication and smart cards?**
3. **If one of the Windows Server 2012 machines fails and is replaced with an older, currently unused Windows Server 2008 R2 machine, will the protocols and authentication settings have to be changed?**

Objective summary

- Users need to access the workplace remotely in various ways, including through VPNs, broadband, Remote Desktop, personal hotspots, and more.
- There are many types of VPN and authentication protocols, and each offers a different level of features and security. You should use the protocol with the most security for your network infrastructure.
- VPN Reconnect makes it easier for remote users to stay connected by automatically reconnecting when a connection is lost.
- Windows 8.1 supports broadband tethering and Internet sharing to let users get online when traditional methods aren't available.

Objective review

Answer the following questions to test your knowledge of the information in this objective. You can find the answers to these questions and explanations of why each answer choice is correct or incorrect in the "Answers" section at the end of this chapter.

1. Which of the following protocols supports the use of a preshared key for authentication?
   - **A.** PPP
   - **B.** SSTP
   - **C.** L2TP
   - **D.** EAP
   - **E.** RDP
2. Which of the following can host a Remote Desktop session? (Choose all that apply.)
   - **A.** Windows XP Pro
   - **B.** Windows Vista Enterprise
   - **C.** Windows 7 Enterprise
   - **D.** Windows RT
   - **E.** All of the above

3. What command do you use to start a Remote Desktop connection and start the connection in full-screen mode?
   - **A.** rdp.exe /f
   - **B.** mstsc.exe mode=f
   - **C.** rdp.exe /full
   - **D.** mstsc.exe /f
4. A user complains that she keeps getting disconnected while using a broadband connection to connect through a VPN to the company's network server and has to spend a lot of time getting reconnected when this happens. What is the problem with VPN Reconnect?
   - **A.** You can't connect to a VPN via broadband.
   - **B.** VPN Reconnect is disabled by default and you didn't enable it.
   - **C.** The VPN protocol being used isn't IKEv2.
   - **D.** The VPN protocol being used isn't L2TP.
5. A user has a smartphone and has configured it as a personal hotspot, but he isn't prompted to select it and connect to it from his Windows 8.1 computer automatically. What must he do to connect to it?
   - **A.** Windows 8.1 doesn't support connections to personal hotspots.
   - **B.** He must select the connection from the Networks pane.
   - **C.** This feature isn't enabled by default; the user must enable this in Control Panel, Network Connections.
   - **D.** The computer must be running Windows 8.1 Professional to use this feature.

Objective 5.2: Configure mobility options

Once users are connected to the network and authenticated on it (using any protocol or connection method you choose), the tasks required of you, the network administrator, shift. Now you must make sure that users are able to work effectively, both when they are connected to the network and when they aren't. This involves configuring sync folders, work folders, offline file policies, power policies, and more. When users can't or don't want to carry a mobile device with them, you can also opt for Windows To Go. Windows To Go is basically Windows on a USB stick, with some limitations. You'll learn about this and more in this section.

This objective covers how to:

- Configure offline file policies
- Configure power policies
- Configure sync options
- Configure Wi-Fi Direct
- Configure Windows To Go

Configure offline file policies

Users can connect to their desktop computers and network file servers when they are away from the office using many technologies, including connecting through VPNs and cellular connections as detailed in the first part of this chapter. Sometimes, though, no connection can be made, but this doesn't stop the users from needing access to their work files and work folders. You can allow offline access so your users can access their data under these circumstances. You need to start by configuring Offline Files and then creating policies to manage it.

> ***NOTE*** **HOW TO SYNC A FOLDER**
>
> **To synchronize a Windows 8.1 computer with a network folder, you can browse to the folder using File Explorer, right-click the folder name, and select Always Available Offline. Windows 8.1 does the rest and copies the contents of the selected folder to the local hard drive. Along those lines, administrators can prevent users from saving offline copies of files. Administrators use the Advanced Sharing dialog box and click Caching to open the Offline Settings dialog box. There they can configure specific settings.**

When Offline Files are enabled and configured, when the user works online files can be accessed from the network server. When the user must work offline, files are retrieved from the Offline Files folder available from the computer. A computer switches to Offline Mode when:

- The new *Always Offline* mode has been enabled. This feature provides faster access to files and uses less bandwidth by letting the user always work offline, even when a connection is available.
- Cost-Aware Synchronization is configured and enabled. This helps users avoid high data usage costs from synchronization while using metered connections that have usage limits or while roaming on another provider's network.
- The server is unavailable due to a network outage or server malfunction.
- The network connection is slower than a threshold you've configured, and thus working offline would be more efficient for the user.
- The user manually switches to Offline Mode (perhaps to optimize bandwidth usage on a metered connection) by using the Work Offline button in File Explorer.

> ***NOTE*** **USE ALWAYS OFFLINE MODE**
>
> **To use the new Always Offline mode, clients must use Windows 8 or later and the Active Directory domain server must be Windows Server 2012 or later.**

Administrators create policies that define the use of Offline Files, either in a domain or on the local machine. Those policies can be located in the applicable Group Policy Editor. Two policies are discussed here—enabling Always Offline mode and enabling file synchronization on costed networks—but you should become familiar with all of the Group Policy options for working with Offline Files.

To enable the Always Offline mode, use Group Policy to enable the Configure Slow-Link Mode policy setting and set the latency to 1 (millisecond). Doing so causes client computers running Windows 8, Windows 8.1, or Windows Server 2012 to automatically use the Always Offline mode. Follow these steps:

1. Open Group Policy Management Console.
2. Right-click the Group Policy Object (GPO) you want to use and click Edit.
3. Navigate to Computer Configuration, Policies, Administrative Templates, Network. Expand Offline Files.
4. Right-click Configure Slow-Link Mode and click Edit.
5. Click Enabled.
6. In the Options box, click Show (you might have to scroll).
7. In the Value Name text box, specify the file share for which you want to enable Always Offline mode or type ***.** to enable this for all file shares. See Figure 5-8.

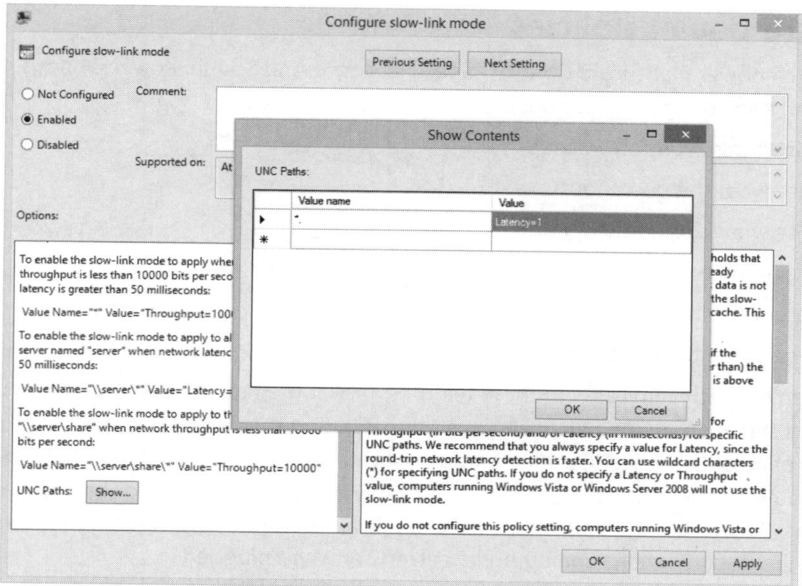

FIGURE 5-8 Configure Group Policy for Offline Files.

8. In the Value box, type **Latency=1** and then click OK.
9. Click OK again.

To enable background file synchronization of Offline Files for a group of users while using metered connections, use Group Policy to enable the Enable File Synchronization On Costed Networks policy setting for the appropriate GPO by following this procedure:

1. Open Group Policy Management Console.
2. Right-click the GPO you want to use and click Edit.
3. Navigate to Computer Configuration, Policies, Administrative Templates, Network. Expand Offline Files.
4. Right-click Enable File Synchronization On Costed Networks and click Edit.
5. Click Enabled.
6. Click OK and click OK again.

EXAM TIP

Explore each entry available from the Offline Files options in Group Policy including but not limited to Configure Slow Link Speed, Synchronize All Offline Files Before Logging Off, Synchronize All Offline Files When Logging On, and Enable Transparent Caching.

Configure power policies

You can switch power plans from Control Panel, Hardware And Sound, Power Options. From there you can also configure these options:

- Require a password on wakeup
- Choose what the power buttons do
- Choose what closing the lid does
- Create a power plan
- Choose when to turn off the display
- Change when the computer sleeps

If you aren't already familiar with these features, take some time now to explore them. Make sure to create your own personal power plan by using the Create A Power Plan option in the Tasks pane of the Power Options window, as you might see something about that on the exam. You might also be asked to state how many minutes must pass for each of the three default plans (Balanced, High Performance, Power Saver) before the computer goes to sleep or turns off the display, when running on its battery, or when plugged in.

Additionally, and you can explore this on your own, you'll have to know how to monitor battery usage (from the Notification area of the Taskbar and from Mobility Center) and how to use Mobility Center to change common mobility settings such as the power plan type, display brightness, and so on. Control Panel, the link to Power Options, and the Mobility Center are shown in Figure 5-9.

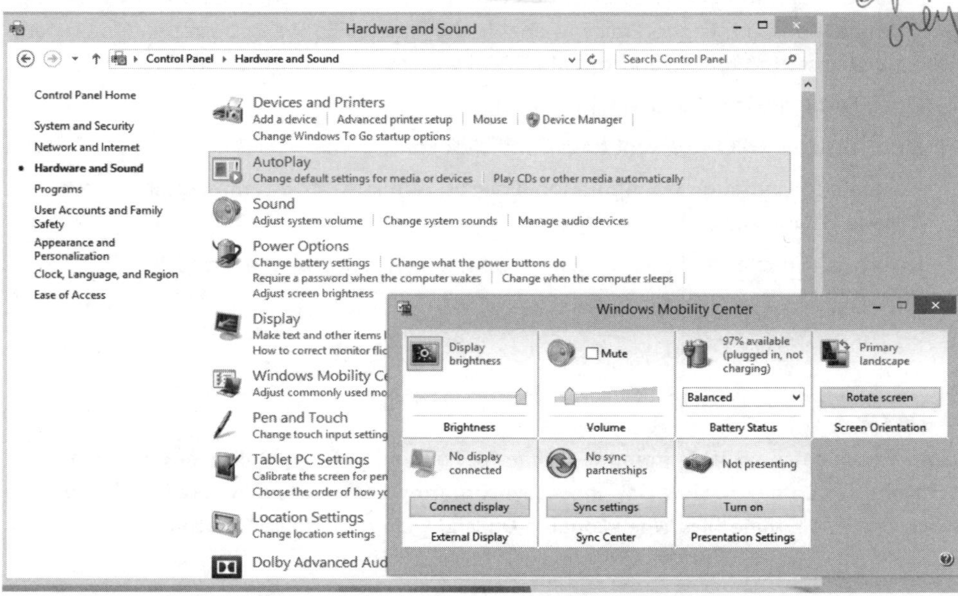

FIGURE 5-9 Review everything related to the Power Options from Control Panel.

Beyond these end-user tools for managing power, there are other power-related items on which you'll be tested, including how to use the command-line tool Powercfg.exe to view and export power plans and configure power policies using Group Policy. Because these are less common and likely less familiar, we'll use these pages to cover these concepts.

Use powercfg.exe

Powercfg.exe is a command-line tool you can use to configure settings that aren't available from Control Panel or Group Policy. One of the things you can do here is to export a power management plan to a file and then import it to another computer. To get a list of the available power plans using this command, type **powercfg.exe –list** at a command prompt. If you haven't yet created any custom plans, you'll only see the three default plans that come with Windows 8.1, as shown in Figure 5-10. Choose the plan to export and note the GUID value. To export the policy, type **powercfg.exe –export power.pow GUID** (where this is the GUID value for the plan to export).

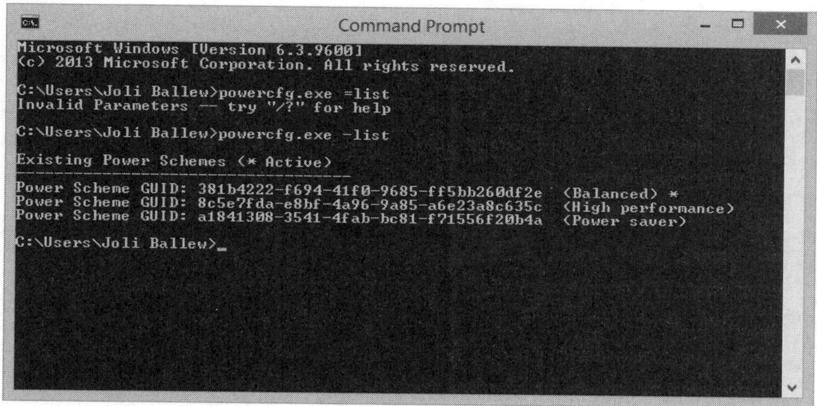

FIGURE 5-10 View power policies from the command line.

There are some other parameters you can use with Powercfg.exe, and they are listed here: *http://technet.microsoft.com/en-us/library/cc748940(v=WS.10).aspx*. You should review these so that you are familiar with everything that's offered. Here are a few you might want to try now, just to get a feel for the command:

- –changename
- –delete
- –setactive
- –deviceenablewake and –devicedisablewake

Create power policies

As with practically everything else, you can use Group Policy to set policies related to the available power plans. Use the Group Policy Management Editor to navigate to Computer Configuration, Policies, Administrative Templates, System, Power Management. When you expand Power Management in the left pane you can see the additional containers: Button Settings, Hard Disk Settings, Notification Settings, Sleep Settings, and Video And Display Settings. In the right pane you can see two options: Specify A Custom Active Power Plan and Select An Active Power Plan. The available options from Windows 8.1 using the Local Group Policy Editor are shown in Figure 5-11. As with any other Group Policy, you double-click the policy to access the options to configure it.

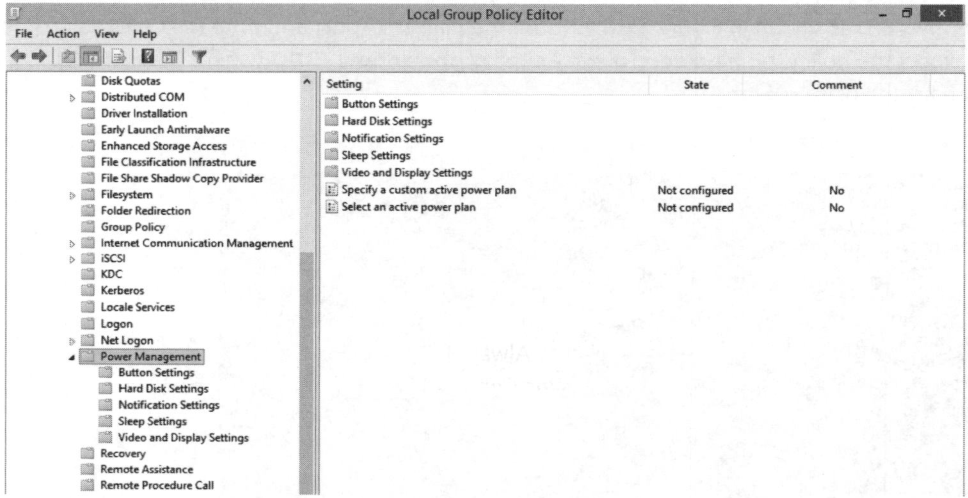

FIGURE 5-11 Group policies can be configured for Power Management.

When you click one of the five nodes under Power Management, more options appear. You can control every aspect of the power options here. For instance, in the Sleep Settings node you can configure, enable, and disable the following (and more):

- Specify the system sleep timeout (plugged in)
- Specify the system sleep timeout (on battery)
- Require a password when the computer wakes (plugged in)
- Require a password when the computer wakes (on battery)
- Allow standby states (S1–S3) when sleeping (plugged in)
- Allow standby states (S1–S3) when sleeping (on battery)

Make sure to explore all of the policies in every node before continuing.

Configure sync options

This objective focuses on configuring sync options, not on creating sync partnerships. However, you should know how to create a sync partnership anyway, so we briefly cover that here. With that done, you'll learn how to configure sync options in Sync Center, including scheduling when syncing should happen and under what circumstances.

You can also configure Sync Settings from PC Settings, but this doesn't have anything to do with syncing offline files. However, because it does have to do with syncing in general, we mention it for good measure. This kind of syncing is what occurs when the user logs on to multiple computers with her Microsoft account and what settings sync when she does.

You'll also learn about a new feature in Windows 8.1, Work Folders. There are several steps to designing a Work Folder implementation in a domain, including installing Work Folders on the Active Directory Domain file server, creating security groups for those Work Folders, and creating sync shares for user data. Although that's beyond the scope of this book, we introduce the concept here, and Work Folders is an option for end users in the Windows 8.1 Control Panel. There, users can opt to set up Work Folders (if you have set it up and configured it on the company network), if desired.

Sync Center and configuring Sync Options

To practice with Sync Center and configure options you must first create a sync partnership on a computer running Windows 8.1. To do this, navigate to a share on a different computer or file server, right-click that share, and click Always Available Offline. After that is done, on that same Windows 8.1 computer, open Sync Center. You can type **Sync Center** on the Start screen, if desired. You should see what's shown in Figure 5-12. Make a note of the options on the left side before moving forward here; you can use these once syncing is configured to manage syncing. One option, Manage Offline Files, lets you view the Offline Files dialog box, where you can disable offline files, view offline files, check disk usage, encrypt your files, and more.

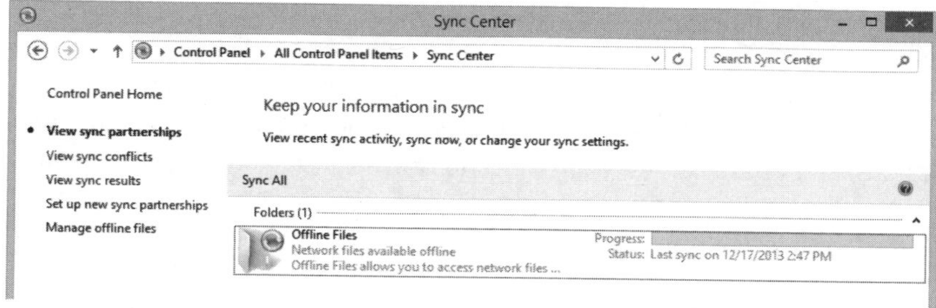

FIGURE 5-12 Open Sync Center to view and manage sync partnerships.

In Sync Center, once a sync partnership is available, you can opt to sync everything (Sync All is shown in Figure 5-12) or you can select the Offline Files folder, click Schedule (not shown), and work through the wizard provided to configure sync settings. There are two options:

- At A Schedule Time; for example, every Monday at 11 A.M. or every day at 2 A.M.
- When An Event Occurs; for example, every time you log on to your computer

Depending on your choice you can opt for more scheduling options, such as only syncing when the computer has been idle for a specific amount of time or if the computer is running on external power (and not on its battery). Figure 5-13 shows the options to schedule a time for syncing and the optional scheduling options.

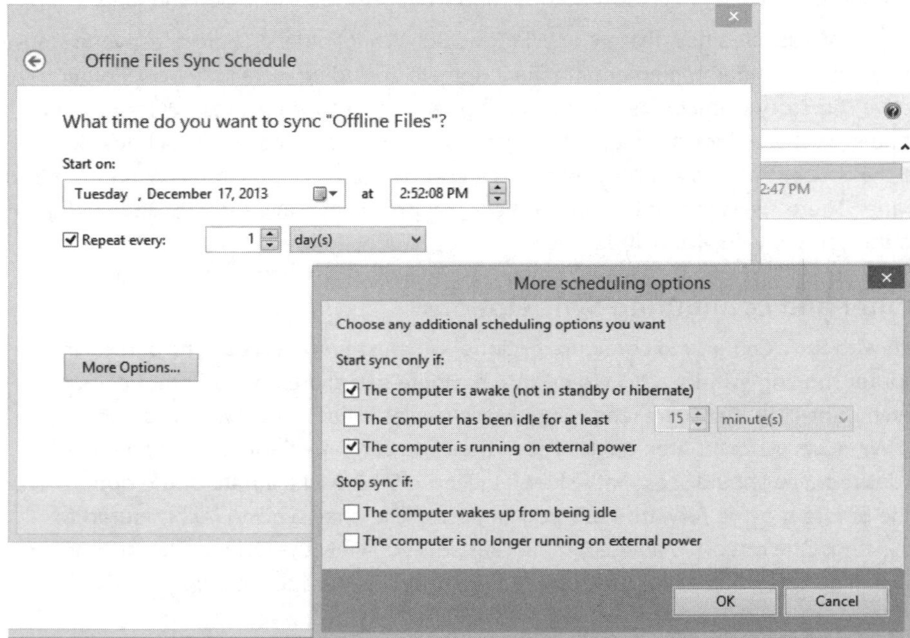

FIGURE 5-13 You can be very specific about how and when to sync files.

Figure 5-14 shows the options that appear when you opt to trigger synchronization to coincide with a specific event. Again, there are additional scheduling options to configure (if you click More Options) and various events from which to choose, including When I Log On To My Computer.

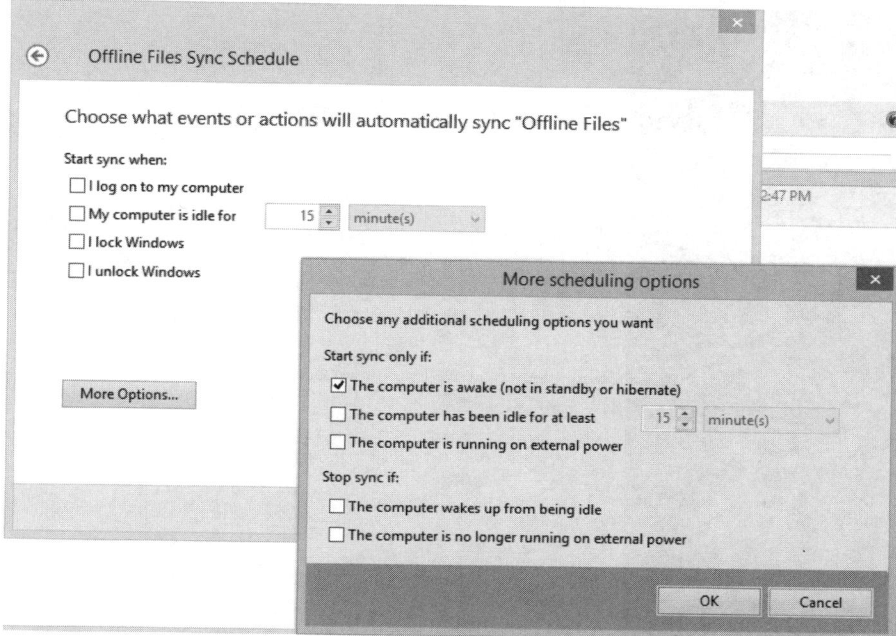

FIGURE 5-14 Configure syncing to occur when trigger criteria are met.

EXAM TIP

Users can force a sync from Windows Mobility Center by clicking Sync in the Sync Center box anytime they like.

Configure sync options in PC Settings

When you create and sign in with a Microsoft account, you are able to sync settings related to your Start screen, desktop, web browser, some passwords, language preferences, and so on, to servers in the cloud. Whatever you opt to sync will be applied to any computer you log on to later using that account. You configure what to sync in PC Settings, from SkyDrive and Sync Settings. These options are shown in Figure 5-15. Make sure you are familiar with what can be synced here; you might be tested on it.

NOTE

The name SkyDrive is changing to OneDrive and at some point the exam will also make the terminology change.

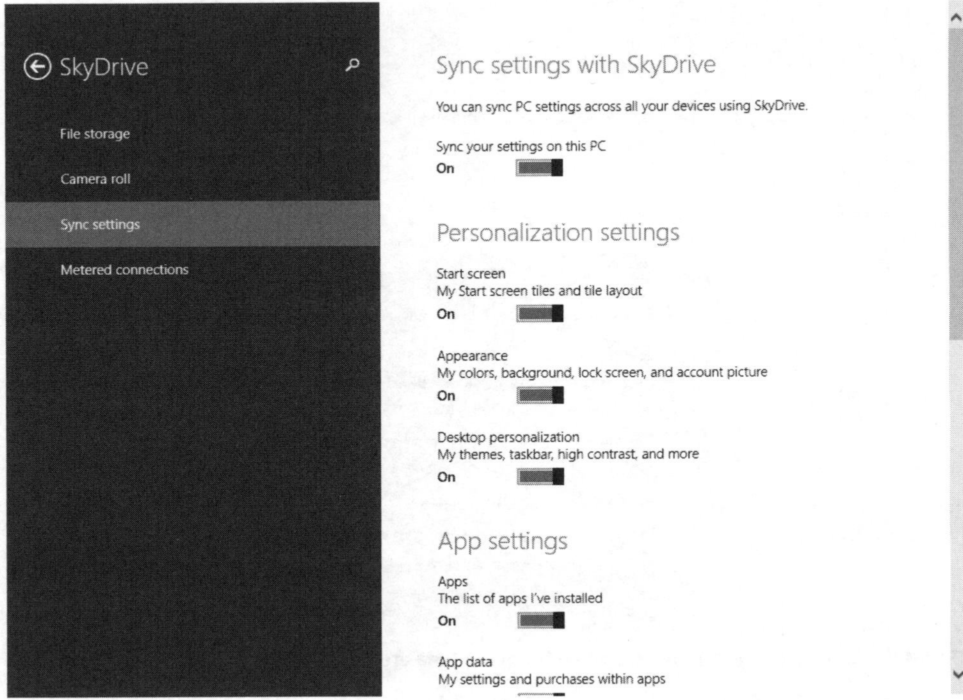

FIGURE 5-15 Use PC Settings to configure what settings to sync on the computers you log on to with your Microsoft account.

Work Folders

Work Folders is a new feature in Windows 8.1. Work Folders allows users to sync data from their user folder, located in their company's domain or data center, to their device and back again. This is done automatically and is part of the file system. Before this feature was introduced, users had to be joined to the domain or were at least required to input domain credentials before syncing could occur. Now, users can retain local copies of their work files on their devices, with automatic synchronization back to the company file servers occurring behind the scenes.

There are Group Policies available for Work Folders that you as an administrator should be aware of. There are two to consider:

- From User Configuration, Policies, Administrative Templates, Windows Components, WorkFolders, you can specify Work Folders settings.
- From Computer Configuration, Policies, Administrative Templates, Windows Components, WorkFolders, you can force automatic setup of Work Folders for all users.

There is also an option end users can configure on their Windows 8.1 computers from Control Panel, Work Folders. To get to this option, open Control Panel, switch views to either

Large Icons or Small Icons, and then click Work Folders. The Work Folders window appears with Set Up Work Folders available for configuring. See Figure 5-16.

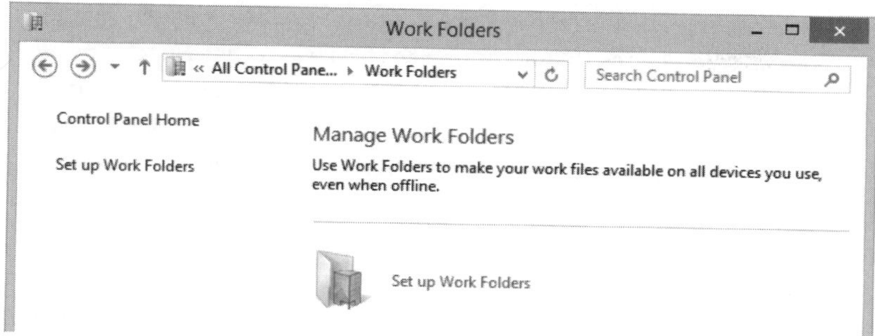

FIGURE 5-16 Users can set up their own Work Folders from Control Panel.

For users to set up their own work folders, you have to have set up the Work Folders infrastructure required for them to have access to perform the setup tasks. A great walkthrough of the process is available at *http://blogs.technet.com/b/canitpro/archive/2013/11/13/step-by-step-creating-a-work-folders-test-lab-deployment-in-windows-server-2012-r2.aspx.*

Once the infrastructure is ready, when users opt to set up Work Folders they must work through the following setup tasks:

1. They must input their company email address.
2. They must wait while the wizard searches the network for their Work Folders.
3. Once the folders are found, the users must accept (or change) where the files will be saved on their computer.
4. The users must read the security policy and then accept those policies.
5. Once that is done, Work Folders appears, as a folder, in File Explorer when This PC is selected in the Navigation pane.
6. Users can now access the documents under the Work Folders location from any device, and the documents will be kept in sync by Work Folders automatically.

> ***NOTE*** **WORK FOLDERS REQUIREMENTS**
>
> **When using Work Folders, the client and server must be running the same milestone release for Work Folders to function properly. For example, if the server is running this milestone release of Windows Server 2012 R2, the client must be running the same milestone release of Windows 8.1.**

> ***MORE INFO*** **LEARN MORE ABOUT WORK FOLDERS**
>
> **To learn more about Work Folders, refer to this article on TechNet: *http://technet.microsoft.com/en-us/library/dn265974.aspx.***

Configure Wi-Fi Direct

Windows 8–based computers can now directly connect to compatible devices one on one, using Wi-Fi Direct, without requiring an intermediary like a router or network access point. Users might use these types of connections to quickly transfer files with other workers using a computer-to-computer connection, or they might even transfer media or perform media streaming to other devices as they become compatible. Those devices might include smartphones and music players, as examples. Wi-Fi Direct might even replace Bluetooth eventually.

For now, you'll need to use the Netsh command you learned about in Chapter 3 to pair the two devices (only one of which has to support Wi-Fi Direct). There aren't any apps or GUIs built into Windows 8.1 for this feature yet. Once connected, the connected device will appear in PC Settings in the same way other devices do when they are connected (like smartphones).

> ***MORE INFO*** **LEARN MORE ABOUT HOSTED NETWORKS**
>
> **For more information about hosted networks, refer to this MSDN article: *http://msdn.microsoft.com/en-us/library/windows/desktop/dd815243(v=vs.85).aspx*. For more information about Wi-Fi Direct, search for the term on TechNet. There wasn't very much written about it at the time this book was published.**

You'll combine Netsh with wlan and the desired parameters to connect with Wi-Fi Direct. Here are some of the available parameters you can use with Netsh wlan at an elevated command prompt:

- **Connect** This parameter connects to a wireless network. You'll have to use connect name= to input the profile name and SSID= to input the SSID.
- **Export hostednetworkprofile** This parameter saves wireless local area network (WLAN) profiles to Extensible Markup Language (XML) files.
- **Refresh hostednetwork** This parameter refreshes hosted network settings.
- **Set** This parameter sets configuration information. You'll have to add tags such as the SSID, name of the profile, and so on.
- **Show all** This parameter displays information for all networks that are currently visible. Figure 5-17 shows the partial results of running this command.
- **Start hostednetwork** This parameter starts the hosted network.
- **Stop hostednetwork** This parameter stops the hosted network.

```
Administrator: Command Prompt
Interface name : Wi-Fi
There are 10 networks currently visible.

SSID 1 : KF85J
    Network type            : Infrastructure
    Authentication          : Open
    Encryption              : WEP
    BSSID 1                 : 00:24:d2:4d:e7:bf
         Signal             : 62%
         Radio type         : 802.11g
         Channel            : 1
         Basic rates (Mbps) : 1 2 5.5 11
         Other rates (Mbps) : 6 9 12 18 24 36 48 54

SSID 2 : 5YSV2
    Network type            : Infrastructure
    Authentication          : Open
    Encryption              : WEP
    BSSID 1                 : 00:18:01:f0:18:ee
         Signal             : 72%
         Radio type         : 802.11g
         Channel            : 1
         Basic rates (Mbps) : 1 2 5.5 11
         Other rates (Mbps) : 6 9 12 18 24 36 48 54

SSID 3 : ZEZ83
    Network type            : Infrastructure
    Authentication          : Open
    Encryption              : WEP
    BSSID 1                 : 00:18:01:f2:27:d1
         Signal             : 34%
         Radio type         : 802.11g
         Channel            : 1
         Basic rates (Mbps) : 1 2 5.5 11
         Other rates (Mbps) : 6 9 12 18 24 36 48 54

SSID 4 : 4B7QL_EXT
    Network type            : Infrastructure
    Authentication          : WPA2-Personal
    Encryption              : CCMP
    BSSID 1                 : 20:e5:2a:21:7d:6a
         Signal             : 88%
         Radio type         : 802.11n
         Channel            : 11
         Basic rates (Mbps) : 1 2
         Other rates (Mbps) : 5.5 6 9 11 12 18 24 36 48 54

SSID 5 : DIRECT-roku-697
    Network type            : Infrastructure
    Authentication          : WPA2-Personal
    Encryption              : CCMP
    BSSID 1                 : b8:3e:59:85:37:85
         Signal             : 78%
         Radio type         : 802.11n
         Channel            : 11
         Basic rates (Mbps) : 6 12 24
         Other rates (Mbps) : 9 18 36 48 54

SSID 6 : 4B7QL
    Network type            : Infrastructure
```

FIGURE 5-17 Use the Netsh wlan command and the appropriate parameters to configure Wi-Fi Direct.

> ***MORE INFO*** **SEARCH FOR WI-FI DIRECT APPS**
>
> Because Wi-Fi Direct is still in its infancy, there isn't much information about how to use it. However, new apps are becoming available that can do the heavy lifting for you. Perform a search in the Store for Wi-Fi Direct to see what's available.

Configure Windows To Go

Windows To Go is a new feature that lets users run Windows 8.1 from a USB stick. They can use this on any computer that can be booted to a USB drive. It's like having a virtual PC in your pocket. However, it does have limitations and specific requirements.

> ***EXAM TIP***
>
> **A new feature in Windows 8.1, a Windows To Go image running Windows 8.1 is capable of booting from a drive that contains a built-in smart card. These kinds of drives are composite drives and have both a mass storage drive and smart card together in one device.**

- The host PC must meet the Windows 7 Certification requirements, but it can run any operating system. Those requirements are available here: *http://msdn.microsoft.com/en-us/library/windows/hardware/dn423132*. They include but are not limited to USB boot compatibility, 1 gigahertz (GHz) or faster processor, 2 GB or more RAM, DirectX 9 graphics device with Windows Display Driver Model (WDDM) 1.2 or greater driver, and an available USB 2.0 port or greater.
- Windows To Go is not intended to replace desktops, laptops, or mobile devices such as tablets. It is meant to support short-term, alternative workplace scenarios.
- Windows To Go is only available for Enterprise customers who are part of the Microsoft Software Assurance program.
- Internal disks are offline to ensure data isn't accessed from the Windows To Go device. Likewise, if a Windows To Go drive is inserted into a running system, the Windows To Go drive will not be listed in File Explorer by default.
- Trusted Platform Module (TPM) can't be used because TPM is tied to a specific computer and Windows To Go drives are associated with multiple computers.
- Hibernate is disabled by default in Windows To Go, although this can be changed in Group Policy settings.
- Windows Recovery Environment isn't available, and neither is refreshing or resetting. If there is a problem with Windows To Go, the drive should be reimaged.
- In addition to the USB boot support in the BIOS, the Windows 8.1 image on the Windows To Go drive must be compatible with the processor architecture and firmware type (32-bit Windows To Go for 32-bit hosts, 64-bit Windows To Go on 64-bit hosts for Unified Extensible Firmware Interface [UEFI] BIOS, and 32-bit Windows To Go on 64-bit Legacy BIOS).

Windows To Go also has these features:

- Store apps can roam between multiple PCs on a Windows To Go drive.
- Windows To Go will detect all hardware on the host computer and install necessary drivers. When the Windows To Go workspace is used again on that same computer it will recognize it's already been used and load the correct set of drivers automatically.
- Administrators can create Windows To Go drives using the same deployment tools they use to deploy Windows in an enterprise, namely DiskPart and the Deployment Image Servicing and Management (DISM) tool. When creating an image, make sure to include everything you'll need, such as device drivers, sync tools, and remote connectivity options if used outside the company network.
- Windows To Go is best configured on certified Windows To Go USB drives. The drives must be USB 3.0, although they can be used in USB 2.0 ports on a host computer.

EXAM TIP

Make sure that the applications that you want to use from Windows To Go support roaming. Some applications bind to the computer hardware and thus can't be used on multiple host computers.

There are also a few Group Policy settings for Windows To Go. You can find those settings in Computer Configuration, Administrative Templates, Windows Components, Portable Operating System. Figure 5-18 shows this in the Local Group Policy Editor. You can enable or disable these to manage hibernation options and sleep states and to set default startup options. To learn more about these settings, double-click an option to review and read the relevant information in the Help window. The Help information for Allow Hibernate (S4) When Starting From A Windows To Go Workspace offers this: Specifies whether the PC can use the hibernation sleep state (S4) when started from a Windows To Go workspace. It goes on to explain that if enabled, the PC can hibernate; if disabled, the PC can't hibernate.

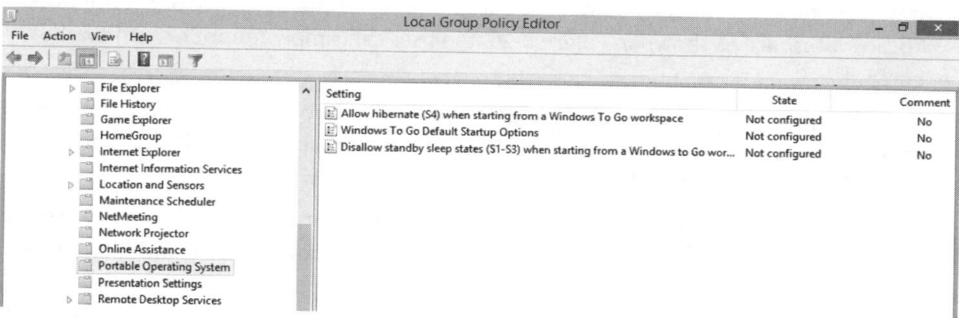

FIGURE 5-18 Windows To Go settings are listed under Portable Operating System in Group Policy.

On the host side, users can search for **Windows To Go** from the Start screen and click Change Windows To Go Startup Options. From there they can enable the host to boot from a Windows To Go workspace. Note this and the Windows To Go requirements in the dialog box shown in Figure 5-19.

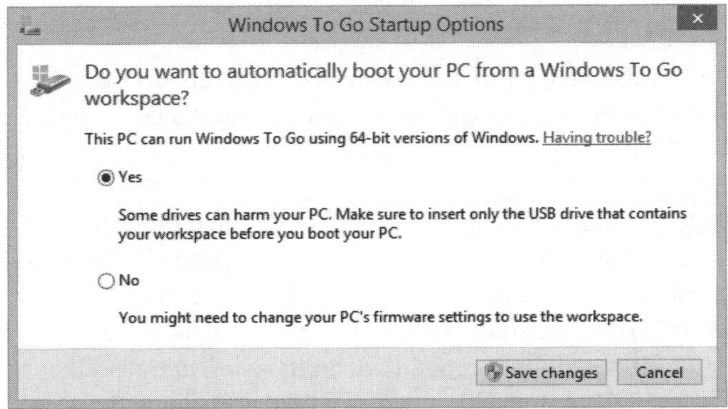

FIGURE 5-19 Configure the host to boot to a Windows To Go workspace.

To boot to the Windows To Go workspace, insert the USB drive and do one of the following:

- If the computer has already been configured to boot to the USB drive and a Windows To Go workspace as shown in Figure 5-19, the user can simply reboot or turn on the computer.
- If the computer is not USB boot enabled, the user can reboot the computer, press the required key combination to access the boot menu (perhaps F12 or F2), and choose the USB Drive from the list.
- If the computer is turned on and the operating system is available, the user can use the PC Settings Advanced Startup options to reboot using a device. You'll find that under PC Settings, Update And Recovery, Recovery, shown in Figure 5-20.

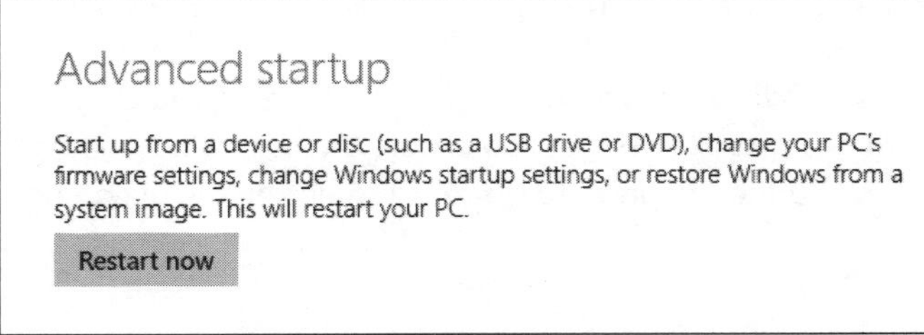

FIGURE 5-20 Advanced Startup options in PC Settings lets users boot to a USB drive if the computer is turned on and available to them.

> ***MORE INFO*** **LEARN MORE ABOUT WINDOWS TO GO**
>
> **To learn more about Windows To Go, including the differences between a Windows installation and Windows To Go, how roaming works with Windows To Go, how to prepare for a Windows To Go deployment, and hardware considerations, refer to this article on TechNet: *http://technet.microsoft.com/en-us/library/hh831833.aspx#BKMK_newblue*. To learn about best practices regarding Windows To Go, refer to the article here: *http://technet.microsoft.com/en-us/library/jj592681.aspx*.**

Create a workspace with the Create a Windows To Go Workspace Wizard

To create a Windows To Go workspace on a USB drive, you must work through the Create A Windows To Go Workspace Wizard. There's a video on TechNet that shows you all of the steps for doing so (although it is on a Windows 8 machine and not on Windows 8.1) at *http://technet.microsoft.com/en-us/windows/dn127075.aspx*. The basic steps are outlined here.

1. Mount the Windows 8.1 installation file or image on the Windows 8.1 Enterprise computer.
2. Insert the certified Windows To Go 3.0 USB drive into an available USB port and start the Create A Windows To Go Workspace Wizard.
3. Work through the wizard to do the following:
   - **A.** Select the USB flash drive to use
   - **B.** Select the image to use
   - **C.** Opt whether to protect and encrypt the drive with BitLocker and a password, which is a good idea because USB drives can be lost or stolen easily
   - **D.** Opt whether to boot to the new Windows To Go workspace now

Create a workspace with Windows PowerShell

You can use Windows PowerShell to create a Windows To Go workspace. Although the wizard is easier to use, you'll need to use Windows PowerShell if you want to automate or customize the process or if you want to create multiple workspaces simultaneously. The script required to perform these tasks is quite complex and includes preparing the flash drive with a system partition and a Windows partition and assigning drive letters. You'll have to apply the image using the available DISM tools. You can use the Bcdboot command to install the applicable boot files for both UEFI and BIOS. There are quite a few steps involved, but in an enterprise it's worth the effort. You can view a sample Windows PowerShell script here: *http://technet.microsoft.com/en-us/library/jj721578.aspx*.

Thought experiment

How to best configure Offline Files

In this thought experiment, apply what you've learned about this objective. You can find answers to these questions in the "Answers" section at the end of this chapter.

You have users who need access to the files stored in your company's file servers no matter where they are. You have configured Offline Files to allow this. It's working well except that when the users are on metered connections or are roaming with a cellular connection, the costs are high. You want to reduce—or better yet, eliminate—these costs. All users are running Windows 8.1.

1. **What feature available with Offline Files should you enable in Group Policy to help users avoid high data usage costs from synchronization while using metered connections that have usage limits or while roaming on another provider's network?**
2. **What feature available with Offline Files should you enable in Group Policy to provide fast access to files while also limiting the bandwidth used by having the users work offline even if a connection is available?**
3. **You also want users to work offline when they aren't on metered networks if the connection is very slow. You've configured a threshold for this in Group Policy. Does the user have to do anything when this threshold is met?**
4. **Can you configure Offline Files and these settings if your servers are running Windows Server 2008 R2?**

Objective summary

- Offline Files and Work Folders enable users to work with their personal files even when they aren't connected to the network. Administrators can control behavior through group policies.
- Power plans help users manage battery life. Administrators can manage their plans using Powercfg.exe and Group Policy.
- Wi-Fi Direct lets users share files without an intermediary network device. For now, you can only create connections using the Netsh wlan command.
- Windows To Go enables users to use Windows 8.1 from other computers using a USB stick that contains the operating system.

Objective review

Answer the following questions to test your knowledge of the information in this objective. You can find the answers to these questions and explanations of why each answer choice is correct or incorrect in the "Answers" section at the end of this chapter.

1. How do you enable Always Offline mode?
   - **A.** Use Group Policy to enable the Configure Slow-Link Mode policy setting and set Enable Transparent Caching to Enabled.
   - **B.** Use Group Policy to enable the Configure Slow-Link Mode policy setting and set the latency to 1 (millisecond).
   - **C.** Use Group Policy to enable the Configure Slow-Link Mode policy setting and set the latency to 0 (millisecond).
   - **D.** Open Sync Center and click Offline Files. Click Schedule and configure the schedule to only sync manually.

2. You need to export a power plan you've created in the Power Options window. What two commands do you use to achieve this? (Choose all that apply.)
   - **A.** powercfg.exe –list
   - **B.** powercfg.exe –export power.pow GUID (where this is the GUID value for the plan to export)
   - **C.** powercrg.exe –show all
   - **D.** powercfg.exe –export GUID (where this is the GUID value for the plan to export)
3. What is the first thing end users need to do before they configure sync options in Sync Center?
   - **A.** In Sync Center, click Offline Files and then click Schedule to configure when to sync files.
   - **B.** In Sync Center, click Set Up New Sync Partnerships and in the right pane, click Set Up New Sync Partnerships.
   - **C.** In Sync Center, click Manage Offline Files and on the General tab, click Enable Offline Files.
   - **D.** Navigate to a share on a different computer or file server, right-click that share, and click Always Available Offline.
4. Where does an administrator configure the option to force users to set up Work Folders?
   - **A.** Computer Configuration, Policies, Administrative Templates, Windows Components, Work Folders
   - **B.** User Configuration, Policies, Administrative Templates, Windows Components, Workplace Join
   - **C.** User Configuration, Policies, Software Settings, Windows Components, Work Folders
   - **D.** User Configuration, Policies, Administrative Templates, Shared Folders
5. Which of the following is a limitation of Windows To Go?
   - **A.** Windows To Go is only available for Enterprise customers who are part of the Microsoft Software Assurance program.
   - **B.** TPM can't be used because it is tied to a specific computer and Windows To Go drives are used on multiple computers.
   - **C.** Windows Recovery Environment isn't available, and neither is refreshing or resetting. If there is a problem with Windows To Go, it should be reimaged.
   - **D.** All of the above.

Objective 5.3: Configure security for mobile devices

You can prevent data from being accessed when mobile devices (or hard drives) are lost or stolen. You can use the same technologies to protect against boot attacks, too, like rootkits. There are other ways to secure devices, though, by using group policies, preventing apps from obtaining a user's location, encrypting data, using VPNs, and more. Here, you'll learn only about BitLocker and BitLocker To Go and how to manage startup keys.

This objective covers how to:

- Configure BitLocker
- Configure BitLocker To Go
- Configure startup key storage

Configure BitLocker

BitLocker Drive Encryption lets you encrypt entire hard disks and disk volumes, which include the Windows operating system drive, user files, and system files. This is not EFS. EFS encrypts user files; BitLocker Drive Encryption protects the entire disk. You can use BitLocker to protect 32-bit and 64-bit computers running Windows 8.1 Professional, Windows 8.1 Enterprise, and Windows Server 2012. On computers that have a TPM version 1.2 or 2.0, BitLocker can also ensure that data is accessible only if the computer's boot components haven't been compromised (altered) and if the disk is still installed in the original computer.

EXAM TIP

You can enable BitLocker before you deploy the operating system. When you do, you can opt to encrypt used disk space only or encrypt the entire drive.

When using BitLocker, you can require users to enter a password to unlock the drive when they want to use it. However, you can require multifactor authentication, too—perhaps by adding a smart card or a USB drive with a startup key on it—on computers with a compatible TPM. BitLocker can also be managed through Group Policy. For instance, you can require that BitLocker be enabled before the computer can be used to store data.

EXAM TIP

Two partitions are required to run BitLocker because prestartup authentication and system integrity confirmation have to occur on a separate partition from the drive that is encrypted.

You'll need to read all you can about BitLocker on TechNet, because there isn't enough room here to discuss everything. Here, only the most basic information is listed. Refer to *http://technet.microsoft.com/en-us/library/hh831507.aspx#BKMK_Overview* to learn more about the following:

- **The requirements for hardware and software** This includes TPM versions, BIOS configuration, firmware requirements, drive size, and so on.
- **How to tell if your computer has a TPM** An administrator might opt to type **TPM .msc** and press Enter in a Run dialog box. An end user might opt to access Control Panel, All Items, open BitLocker Drive Encryption and see if he can turn on BitLocker. If a TPM isn't found, you'll have to set the required Group Policy, Require Additional Authentication At Startup, which is located in Computer Configuration, Administrative Templates, Windows Components, BitLocker Drive Encryption, Operating System Drives. You must enable this and then select the Allow BitLocker Without A Compatible TPM check box. See Figure 5-21.

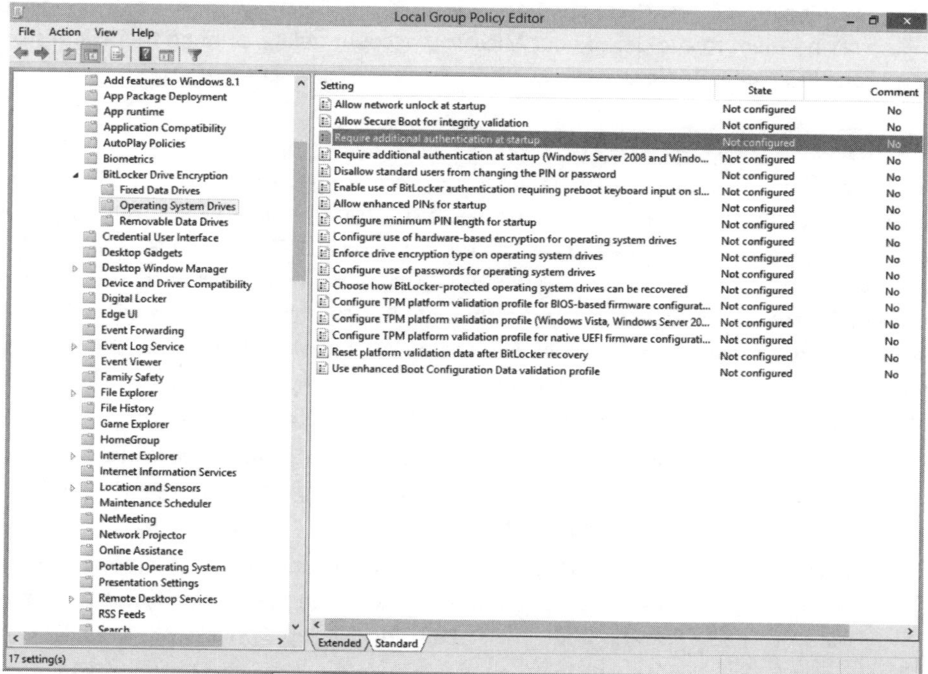

FIGURE 5-21 If the computer doesn't have a compatible TPM, opt to require additional authentication in Group Policy.

EXAM TIP

You can only enable BitLocker on an operating system drive without a compatible TPM if the BIOS or UEFI firmware has the ability to read from a USB flash drive in the boot environment. This is because BitLocker requires a startup key. If you do this, though, you won't be able to take advantage of the prestartup system integrity verification or multifactor authentication.

- **What credentials are required to configure BitLocker** Only Administrators can manage fixed data drives, but Standard users can manage removable data drives (the latter can be disabled in Group Policy). Standard users can also change the PIN or password on operating system drives to which they have access via BitLocker.
- **How to automate BitLocker deployment in an enterprise** One way is to use the command-line tool Manage-bde.exe. Manage-bde command-line tools you might use in your own work are detailed later in this section. There are other ways, including using Windows Management Instrumentation (WMI) and Windows PowerShell scripts.
- **The reasons why BitLocker might start in recovery mode** Reasons include disabling the TPM, making changes to the TPM firmware, making changes to the master boot record, and so on.
- **How to manage recovery keys** Recovery keys let you access a computer if BitLocker won't allow access. There are many ways to store these keys for fixed drives including saving them to a folder or your Microsoft account online, printing them, and storing the keys on multiple USB drives.

Configure BitLocker from Control Panel

Before you configure BitLocker, there are a few more things to know. The first time you enable BitLocker you'll be prompted to create a startup key. This is what's used to encrypt and decrypt the drive. The startup key can be stored on a USB drive or the TPM chip. If you opt for USB, you'll have to insert that USB drive every time you want to access the computer, and you'll also have to enter the key. If a compatible TPM chip is used, the key retrieval is automatic. You can also opt for a PIN. This can be created only after BitLocker is enabled. If you lose the startup key, you'll have to unlock the drive using a recovery key. This is a 48-digit number that can be stored in numerous ways, including on a USB drive.

There are five authentication methods for protecting encrypted data using BitLocker, consisting of various combinations of TPM, startup PIN, and startup keys; just a TPM; or just a startup key. Here is a brief summary of these options:

- **TPM + startup PIN + startup key** This is the most secure, but it requires three authentication tasks. The encryption key is stored on the TPM chip, but an administrator must type a PIN and insert the startup key (available on a USB drive).
- **TPM + startup key** The encryption key is stored on the TPM chip, and an administrator must insert a USB flash drive that contains a startup key.
- **TPM + startup PIN** The encryption key is stored on the TPM chip, and an administrator must enter a PIN.
- **Startup key only** An administrator must insert a USB flash drive with the startup key on it. The computer does not have to have a TPM chip. The BIOS must support access to the USB flash drive prior to the operating system loading.
- **TPM only** The encryption key is stored on the TPM chip, and no administrator login is required. TPM requires that the boot environment has not been modified or compromised.

In addition, the drive that contains the operating system must have two partitions, the system partition and the operating system partition, both of which must be formatted with NTFS.

To configure BitLocker and encrypt the operating system drive on a Windows 8.1 computer, follow these steps:

1. Open Control Panel, change the view to Small Icons or Large Icons, and click BitLocker Drive Encryption.
2. Click Turn On BitLocker. (If you receive an error that no TPM chip is available, enable the required Group Policy setting. See Figure 5-20 earlier.)
3. Choose how to unlock your drive at startup; we'll choose Enter A Password in this example. See Figure 5-22.

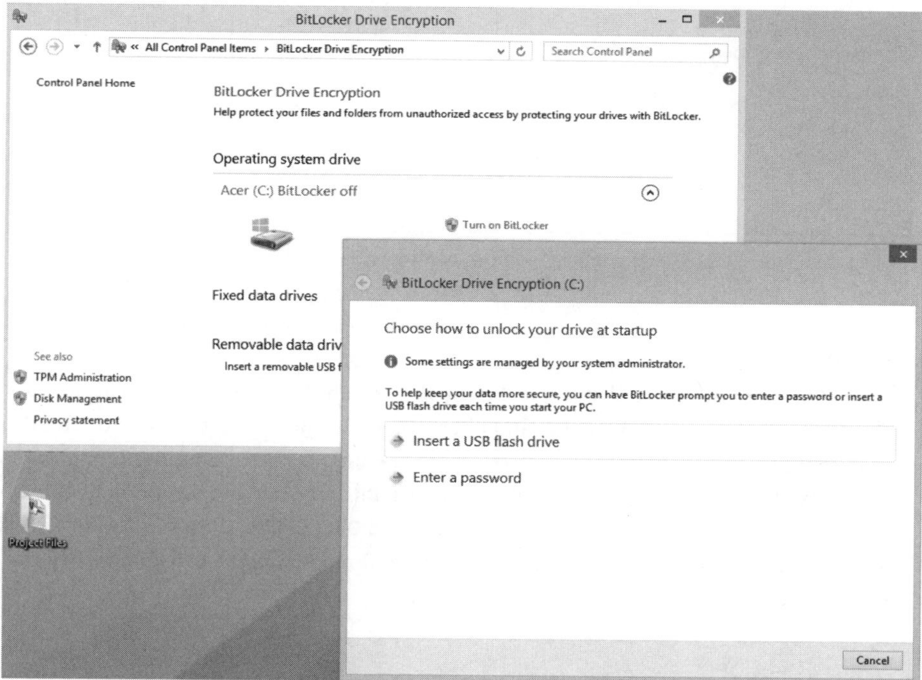

FIGURE 5-22 Enable BitLocker on a fixed drive.

4. Enter the password, reenter to confirm, then click Next.
5. Make a choice to save the password; we'll choose Save To Your Microsoft Account. Click Next. (In this instance, you can perform this step again to perform a secondary backup before moving on.)
6. Choose to encrypt either the used disk space or the entire drive. Click Next.
7. Leave Run BitLocker System Check selected and click Continue.

8. Click Restart Now. If prompted, perform any final tasks, such as removing CDs or DVDs from drive bays, and then click Restart Now again if necessary.
9. On boot up, type or provide the startup key.
10. Note the pop-up notification in the Desktop taskbar that encryption is in progress. It will take some time to complete.

Return to Control Panel and review the BitLocker window. Note that from there you can perform additional tasks, including backing up your recovery key, changing your password, removing the passwords, and turning off BitLocker. You can see which actions require administrator approval by the icon next to the options. See Figure 5-23.

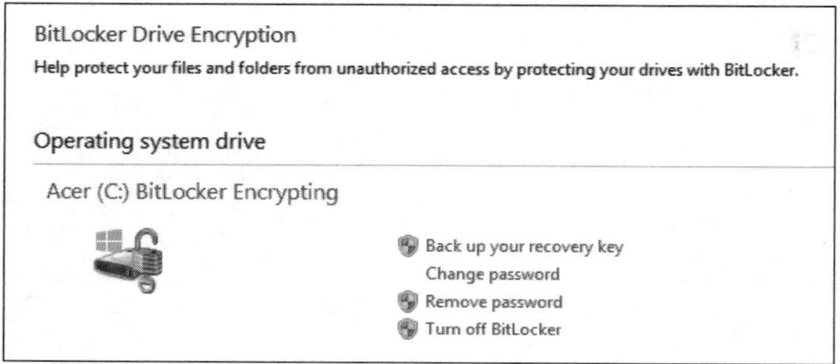

FIGURE 5-23 Once BitLocker is enabled, you can configure it.

EXAM TIP

We're not sure how many, if any, questions you'll see on the exam about the available Group Policy settings for BitLocker and BitLocker To Go. However, it's better to be safe than sorry. Make sure to at least scan the available options here: Computer Configuration, Administrative Templates, Windows Components, BitLocker Drive Encryption from a Group Policy Editor console. There are three folders (Fixed Data Drives, Operating System Drives, and Removable Data Drives), along with a few stand-alone options you'll find when the BitLocker Drive Encryption container is selected.

Configure BitLocker using Manage-BDE

You don't have to use Control Panel to manage BitLocker Drive Encryption. You can work from a command line. A few of the commands you can use will turn on or turn off BitLocker, specify unlock mechanisms, update recovery methods, and unlock BitLocker-protected data drives. Many of these commands are used in large enterprises and are not applicable to this objective; however, there are several parameters you might use with the Manage-BDE command, including but not limited to the following:

- **–status** Use this parameter to provide information about the attached drives including their BitLocker status, size, BitLocker version, key protector, lock status, and more.

- **–on** This parameter encrypts the drive and turns on BitLocker, used with a drive letter such as C that follows the *–on* parameter.
- **–off** This parameter decrypts and then turns off BitLocker, used with a drive letter such as C that follows the *–off* parameter.
- **–pause and –resume** Use *–pause* with a drive letter to pause encryption; use *–resume* and a drive letter to resume encryption.
- **–lock and –unlock** Use these parameters to lock and unlock the drive, used with a drive letter.
- **–changepin** This parameter changes the PIN for the BitLocker-protected drive.
- **–recoverypassword** Use this parameter to add a numerical password protector.
- **–recoverykey** This parameter adds an external key protector for recovery.
- **–password** Use this parameter to add a password key protector.

EXAM TIP

Refer to this article on TechNet to see all of the available parameters: *http://technet.microsoft.com/en-us/library/dd875513(v=WS.10).aspx*. You can also type manage-bde /? at a command prompt to see a list on your own computer.

Configure BitLocker To Go

BitLocker To Go lets you protect removable USB devices with BitLocker Drive Encryption. These devices can be flash drives, Secure Digital (SD) cards, or removable hard disks formatted with NTFS, FAT16, FAT32, or exFat file systems. Just like BitLocker, users must input a password or a smart card with a PIN to unlock the drive. It can be automatically unlocked as well, with administrator approval. TPM isn't required because there's no boot device like there is with a laptop, tablet, or desktop computer.

The process used to create a BitLocker To Go drive is similar to the process used to encrypt a fixed disk using BitLocker. Just insert the USB drive, open Control Panel, and access the BitLocker window. Under Removable Data Drives – BitLocker To Go (see Figure 5-24), work through the setup process.

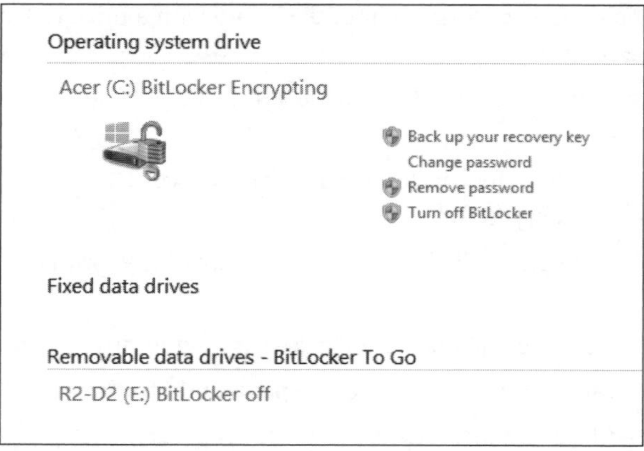

FIGURE 5-24 Configure BitLocker To Go from Control Panel's BitLocker Drive Encryption window.

As noted in an Exam Tip earlier, you should familiarize yourself with the available BitLocker and BitLocker To Go Group Policy settings. You can locate them in a Group Policy Editor in Computer Configuration, Administrative Templates, Windows Components, BitLocker Drive Encryption. The BitLocker To Go options are available in the Removable Data Drives container. The eight items listed are summarized briefly here.

- **Control Use Of BitLocker On Removable Drives** This option defines whether users can add or remove BitLocker encryption from removable drives.
- **Configure Use Of Smart Cards On Removable Drives** This option defines whether users must use a smart card to access an encrypted drive.
- **Deny Write Access To Removable Drives Not Protected By BitLocker** This setting prevents users from writing to removable drives that aren't encrypted.
- **Configure Use Of Hardware-Based Encryption For Removable Data Drives** This option defines whether BitLocker software encryption can be used instead of hardware encryption on computers that do not support the latter.
- **Enforce Drive Encryption Type Of Removable Data Drives** This option defines a specific encryption type that must be used with removable drives: Full encryption or Used Space Only encryption. (This option was added in Windows 8.1, so look for it on the exam.)
- **Allow Access To BitLocker-Protected Removable Data Drives From Earlier Versions Of Windows** This setting defines whether FAT-formatted removable BitLocker drives are accessible from earlier versions of Windows.
- **Configure Use Of Passwords For Removable Data Drives** This setting defines whether removable drives must be password-protected.
- **Choose How BitLocker-Protected Removable Drives Can Be Recovered** This option defines whether Data Recovery Agents (DRAs) can be used to access the data

on removable BitLocker Drives. The DRA is a user account that an administrator has authorized to recover BitLocker drives in an organization. By default, domain administrators are DRAs.

Configure startup key storage

This objective covers how to configure startup key storage. However, to understand what a startup key is, you must first understand what it isn't. There are several key management terms to contend with:

- **TPM owner password** You must initialize the TPM before you can use it with BitLocker Drive Encryption. When you do, you create a TPM owner password that is associated only with the TPM. You supply the TPM owner password when you need to enable or disable the TPM or reset the TPM lockout.
- **Recovery password and recovery key** The first time you set up BitLocker, you are prompted to configure how to access BitLocker-protected drives if access is denied. This involves creating a recovery key. You will need the recovery key if the TPM cannot validate the boot components, but the majority of the time a failure to access a BitLocker drive occurs because the end user has forgotten the PIN or password.
- **Password** A password can be used to protect fixed, removable, and operating system drives. It can also be used with operating system drives that do not have a TPM. The password can consist of 8 to 255 characters as specified by the Configure Use Of Passwords For Operating System Drives, Configure Use Of Passwords For Removable Data Drives, and Configure Use Of Passwords For Fixed Data Drives Group Policy settings.
- **PIN and enhanced PIN** If you use a TPM, you can configure BitLocker with a PIN that the user has to type to gain access to the computer. The PIN can consist of 4 to 20 digits as specified by the Configure Minimum PIN Length For Startup Group Policy setting. Enhanced PINs use the full keyboard character set in addition to the numeric set to allow for more possible PIN combinations. You must enable the Allow Enhanced PINs For Startup Group Policy setting before adding the PIN to the drive.
- **Startup key** You use a startup key, which is stored on a USB flash drive, with or without a TPM. The USB flash drive must be inserted every time the computer starts. The USB flash drive must be formatted by using the NTFS, FAT, or FAT32 file system.

Now that you know what a startup key is, you can save your computer's startup key on a USB flash drive. Right-click the BitLocker-protected drive to get started and then follow the prompts.

EXAM TIP

BitLocker Network Unlock makes it easier to manage BitLocker-enabled TPM + PIN workstations and servers in a domain. Network Unlock allows the PIN entry prompt to be bypassed when a domain-connected computer reboots. The computer is automatically unlocked using a trusted key that is provided by the Windows Deployment Services server as its secondary authentication method.

Thought experiment

Choose a BitLocker option

In this thought experiment, apply what you've learned about this objective. You can find answers to these questions in the "Answers" section at the end of this chapter.

A client wants to enable BitLocker on her laptop and has called you to set it up. She wants to protect the data on the computer if the computer is stolen or if the hard drive is removed. You need to find out if a compatible TPM chip is available, and if not, configure the computer so that BitLocker can be used effectively.

1. **What can you type in a Run box to find out if a compatible TPM is available on the computer?**
2. **If a TPM is not found, what policy do you need to change in Local Group Policy on the computer?**
3. **If a TPM is not found, what must be true regarding the BIOS or UEFI firmware?**
4. **If a TPM is found, what is the most secure authentication option to apply during startup?**

Objective summary

- BitLocker and BitLocker To Go can be used to protect mobile devices and mobile drives from theft, loss, or attacks by hackers.
- You need to carefully manage startup keys, recovery keys, and other items related to BitLocker Drive Encryption so that you can get back into the drive if it is compromised or if the user forgets the PIN or password.
- The command-line tool Manage-bde along with applicable parameters lets you manage BitLocker from a command line.

Objective review

Answer the following questions to test your knowledge of the information in this objective. You can find the answers to these questions and explanations of why each answer choice is correct or incorrect in the "Answers" section at the end of this chapter.

1. You opted to store your startup key on a USB flash drive when you set up BitLocker. Which of the following is true? (Choose all that apply.)
   - **A.** You now have to insert that drive every time you want to access the computer and enter the key.
   - **B.** If you lose the startup key, you'll have to unlock the drive using a recovery key. This is a 48-digit number that can be stored in numerous ways, including on a USB drive.
   - **C.** The computer must have a compatible TPM chip.
   - **D.** All of the above.
2. When using Bit Locker To Go in an enterprise, how can you prevent users from copying data to USB drives that aren't encrypted with BitLocker To Go?
   - **A.** You should enable the Group Policy Control Use Of BitLocker on removable drives.
   - **B.** You should enable the Group Policy Deny Write Access To Removable Drives Not Protected By BitLocker.
   - **C.** You should enable the Group Policy Enforce Drive Encryption Type Of Removable Data Drives.
   - **D.** A and B.
3. Which command shows how to enable encryption and thus BitLocker on a drive D on a Windows 8.1 computer and add numerical and external key protectors?
   - **A.** Manage-bde –on D: -ForceRecovery –RecoveryKey f:\
   - **B.** Manage-bde –on D: -unlock –RecoveryKey f:\
   - **C.** Manage-bde –on D: -enable –RecoveryKey f:\
   - **D.** Manage-bde –on D: -RecoveryPassword –RecoveryKey f:\
4. Which of the following is true of BitLocker To Go? (Choose all that apply.)
   - **A.** BitLocker To Go lets you protect removable USB devices with BitLocker Encryption.
   - **B.** A BitLocker To Go device can be a USB flash drive.
   - **C.** A BitLocker To Go device can be a Secure Digital (SD) card.
   - **D.** A BitLocker To Go device can be a removable hard disk.
   - **E.** BitLocker To Go drives can be formatted with NTFS, FAT16, FAT32, or exFat file systems.
   - **F.** All of the above.

Chapter summary

- Users must be able to connect to your organization remotely and securely. There are many options you can consider including VPNs, broadband, cellular, and so on.
- You must choose the best VPN authentication method for your network infrastructure and client support. IKEv2 is currently the best option for Windows 8.1 users on Windows Server 2012 domain networks.
- VPN Reconnect lets users automatically reconnect to the network through a VPN when the connection is lost.
- Windows 8.1 supports tethering and can connect to shared, personal hotspots created by others.
- Sync Center, Offline Files, and Work Folders allow users to work away from the office and sync data between their computers and network servers when it is appropriate or configured by Group Policy.
- Windows To Go is Windows 8.1 on a USB flash drive. This offers workers additional options when working away from the office.
- Wi-Fi Direct lets users share files without a network intermediary like a router or access point and is currently enabled and managed with third-party apps and the command-line tool Netsh.
- BitLocker, BitLocker To Go, and the various authentication options (with and without a TPM) help keep mobile computers and the data on them safe even if those devices are lost, stolen, or hacked.

Answers

This section contains the solutions to the thought experiments and answers to the objective review questions in this chapter.

Objective 5.1: Thought experiment

1. IKEv2 supports VPN Reconnect and can be used on Windows 7, Windows 8, and Windows Server 2012 computers.
2. Yes, IKEv2 supports smart cards and EAP authentication.
3. No. IKEv2 and EAP support Windows Server 2008 R2.

Objective 5.1: Review

1. **Correct Answer:** C
   - **A. Incorrect**: This protocol does not support the use of a preshared key.
   - **B. Incorrect**: This protocol does not support the use of a preshared key.
   - **C. Correct**: This is the only protocol listed that supports the use of a preshared key.
   - **D. Incorrect**: This protocol does not support the use of a preshared key.
   - **E. Incorrect**: This is Remote Desktop Protocol and is not correct.
2. **Correct Answers:** A, B, and C
   - **A. Correct**: The host must be running Windows XP Professional, Windows Vista Enterprise, Windows Vista Ultimate, Windows Vista Business, Windows 7 Ultimate, Windows 7 Enterprise, Windows 7 Professional, Windows 8 Pro, or Windows 8 Enterprise.
   - **B. Correct**: The host must be running Windows XP Professional, Windows Vista Enterprise, Windows Vista Ultimate, Windows Vista Business, Windows 7 Ultimate, Windows 7 Enterprise, Windows 7 Professional, Windows 8 Pro, or Windows 8 Enterprise.
   - **C. Correct**: The host must be running Windows XP Professional, Windows Vista Enterprise, Windows Vista Ultimate, Windows Vista Business, Windows 7 Ultimate, Windows 7 Enterprise, Windows 7 Professional, Windows 8 Pro, or Windows 8 Enterprise.
   - **D. Incorrect**: The host cannot be running Windows RT, although Windows RT can be used to connect to a Remote Desktop host.
   - **E. Incorrect**: The host must be running Windows XP Professional, Windows Vista Enterprise, Windows Vista Ultimate, Windows Vista Business, Windows 7 Ultimate, Windows 7 Enterprise, Windows 7 Professional, Windows 8 Pro, or Windows 8 Enterprise.

3. **Correct Answer:** D

   A. **Incorrect**: mstsc.exe /f is the correct answer.

   B. **Incorrect**: mstsc.exe /f is the correct answer.

   C. **Incorrect**: mstsc.exe /f is the correct answer.

   D. **Correct**: This is the proper syntax and /f is the correct parameter.

4. **Correct Answer:** C

   A. **Incorrect**: You can connect to a VPN via broadband.

   B. **Incorrect**: VPN Reconnect is enabled and is set to 30 minutes.

   C. **Correct**: The VPN protocol must be IKEv2.

   D. **Incorrect**: The VPN protocol can't be L2TP, it must be IKEv2.

5. **Correct Answer:** B

   A. **Incorrect**: Windows 8.1 does support connections to personal hotspots.

   B. **Correct**: They must select the connection from the Networks pane.

   C. **Incorrect**: This feature is enabled by default.

   D. **Incorrect**: The computer can be running any edition of Windows 8 or Windows 8.1 to use this feature.

Objective 5.2: Thought experiment

1. Cost-Aware Synchronization
2. Always Offline mode
3. No, the computer will go offline when the threshold is met.
4. No. Always Offline and Cost-Aware Synchronization are only available for clients and servers running the latest operating systems, currently Windows 8 and Windows Server 2012.

Objective 5.2: Review

1. **Correct Answer:** B

   A. **Incorrect**: You must configure the Slow-Link Mode setting to 1 millisecond to achieve your goal.

   B. **Correct**: This is the proper way to make the configuration change.

   C. **Incorrect**: You must configure the Slow-Link Mode setting to 1 millisecond to achieve your goal.

   D. **Incorrect**: Always Offline mode is a setting in Group Policy, not in Sync Center.

2. **Correct Answers:** A and B

   A. **Correct**: First, you must list the power plans to obtain the GUID for the one to export.

B. **Correct**: Second, you must export the power plan using this command.

C. **Incorrect**: The parameter *–show all* is used with the Netsh command and is not used here to list the available power plans.

D. **Incorrect**: You must include a name for the file, such as power.pow, in the command.

3. **Correct Answer:** D

A. **Incorrect**: In Sync Center, you can click Offline Files and then click Schedule to configure when to sync files, but you must first have set up a sync partnership for which to schedule syncing.

B. **Incorrect**: In Sync Center, Set Up New Sync Partnerships is an option, but you are only prompted to configure the sync partnerships manually. There is no option there to click to set up new sync partnerships.

C. **Incorrect**: In Sync Center, you can click Manage Offline Files, and there is a General tab. However, the first step to configuring Offline Files is to set up a sync partnership.

D. **Correct**: You must navigate to a share on a different computer or file server, right-click that share, and click Always Available Offline to get started.

4. **Correct Answer:** A

A. **Correct**: Computer Configuration, Policies, Administrative Templates, Windows Components, Work Folders.

B. **Incorrect**. Workplace Join is not related to Work Folders and is not the proper place to configure the desired option.

C. **Incorrect**: User Configuration, Policies, Administrative Templates, Windows Components, Work Folders is where you specify Work Folders settings. You do not configure this in Software Settings.

D. **Incorrect**. User Configuration, Policies, Administrative Templates, Shared Folders is a valid path, but it is not where you configure Work Folders.

5. **Correct Answer:** D

A. **Incorrect**: All answers are correct.

B. **Incorrect**: All answers are correct.

C. **Incorrect**: All answers are correct.

D. **Correct**: All of the above are correct.

Objective 5.3: Thought experiment

1. TPM.msc.
2. You'll have to set the required Group Policy Require Additional Authentication At Setup, which is located in Computer Configuration, Administrative Templates, Windows

Components, BitLocker Drive Encryption, Operating System Drives. You must enable this and then select the Allow BitLocker Without A Compatible TPM check box.

3. The BIOS or UEFI firmware must have the ability to read from a USB flash drive in the boot environment.
4. TPM + startup PIN + startup key

Objective 5.3: Review

1. **Correct Answers:** A and B
   - **A. Correct:** This is true.
   - **B. Correct:** This is true.
   - **C. Incorrect:** The computer does not need a compatible TPM chip. It can have one, but it doesn't have to.
   - **D. Incorrect:** Because C is incorrect, this is incorrect also.
2. **Correct Answer:** B
   - **A. Incorrect:** Control Use Of BitLocker On Removable Drives defines whether users can add or remove encryption from removable drives.
   - **B. Correct:** You should enable the Group Policy Deny Write Access To Removable Drives Not Protected By BitLocker.
   - **C. Incorrect:** Enforce Drive Encryption Type Of Removable Data Drives relates to how much of the drive should be encrypted with BitLocker.
   - **D. Incorrect:** Because A is not correct, this is not correct.
3. **Correct Answer:** D
   - **A. Incorrect**: *–forcerecovery* is not a key-related parameter.
   - **B. Incorrect:** *–unlock* is used to allow access to BitLocker-encrypted data.
   - **C. Incorrect:** *–enable* is used to enable automatic unlocking of a drive.
   - **D. Correct:** This is the proper syntax. *–recoverypassword* and *–recoverykey* are both key protectors.
4. **Correct Answer:** F
   - **A. Incorrect:** Because all answers are correct, F is the correct answer.
   - **B. Incorrect:** Because all answers are correct, F is the correct answer.
   - **C. Incorrect:** Because all answers are correct, F is the correct answer.
   - **D. Incorrect:** Because all answers are correct, F is the correct answer.
   - **E. Incorrect:** Because all answers are correct, F is the correct answer.
   - **F. Correct:** All of the above are true of BitLocker To Go drives.

CHAPTER 6

Monitor and maintain Windows clients

There are many tasks involved in keeping Windows clients secure and performing at their best. Microsoft helps in that regard by offering the tools you need to manage and maintain them. You can use Windows Update to protect computers from hackers and known security holes. If by chance an update causes problems, you can remove it easily. You can also use Disk Management to manage disk volumes and use tools like Disk Defragmenter, Disk Cleanup, and Check Disk to keep your drives healthy and running efficiently. Finally, you can use myriad tools to monitor performance, including but not limited to Task Manager, Performance Monitor, and Event Viewer.

Objectives in this chapter:

- Objective 6.1: Configure and manage updates
- Objective 6.2: Manage local storage
- Objective 6.3: Monitor system performance

Objective 6.1: Configure and manage updates

Windows Updates are provided by Microsoft and have been part of the ongoing attempt to keep Microsoft operating systems safe and secure week after week, year after year, for decades. These updates often offer new features or functionality, but for the most part they are pushed out to fix security issues, address new security threats, and provide new device drivers. This is a necessary part of any company's maintenance plan, because there will always be those who will try to hack into systems, unleash viruses, hide malware, and so on. You need to be protected. Thus, you have to install these updates and it's best if you create a policy for doing so.

In small organizations that do not make use of an Active Directory infrastructure and instead are small peer-to-peer networks, most client computers are configured to automatically install updates. There's often no policy and no one to oversee the process. In larger organizations, even those that are configured as workgroups (and not Active Directory domains), administrators often prefer to set policies for updates through Local Group Policy. In Active Directory domains, there's commonly an isolated lab where updates are tested before they are rolled out, and sometimes there's even a specialized server that caches those updates first to lessen the bandwidth that would be required should each client get updates directly from Microsoft. With this approach, updates can be tested before releasing them to clients, too. Of course, there are Group Policies for Windows Update in domains to help administrators manage them as well.

This objective covers how to:

- Update Windows Store apps
- Configure update settings
- Manage update history
- Roll back updates
- Configure Windows Update policies

Update Windows Store apps

Windows Store apps update themselves automatically unless you change the default configuration or apply Group Policies. These updates are generally safe to install, because all apps and app updates go through Microsoft first and are offered through the Microsoft Store only after thorough testing. However, in some instances you might want or need to disable these automatic updates.

> ***NOTE*** **DEFAULT APPS**
>
> **The first time you log on to a new Windows 8.1 installation, the default apps will be updated.**

On a single workstation, you can disable automatic app updates by following these steps:

1. On the Start screen, click Store.
2. Press Windows key+I to open the Settings charm.
3. Click App Updates.
4. Move the Automatically Update My Apps slider from Yes to No.

If you opt to disable automatic updates, you'll have to update them manually. Watch for updates from the Store in the upper-right corner.

Before moving on, here are a few more things you should know about Windows Store and app updates:

- There are four settings in Group Policy that relate to the Store in Computer Configuration, Administrative Templates, Windows Components, Store. See Figure 6-1. They are:
  - Turn Off Automatic Download Of Updates On Win8 Machines
  - Turn Off Automatic Download And Install Of Updates

    - Turn Off The Offer To Update To The Latest Version Of Windows
    - Turn Off The Store Application
- There are two settings in Group Policy that relate to the Store in User Computer Configuration, Administrative Templates, Windows Components, Store. They are:
    - Turn Off The Offer To Update To The Latest Version Of Windows
    - Turn Off The Store Application
- Network administrators can control how updates are installed from the Windows Store in an Active Directory domain using AppLocker. For more information about AppLocker, refer to the TechNet article at *http://technet.microsoft.com/en-us/library/ee424367.aspx*.

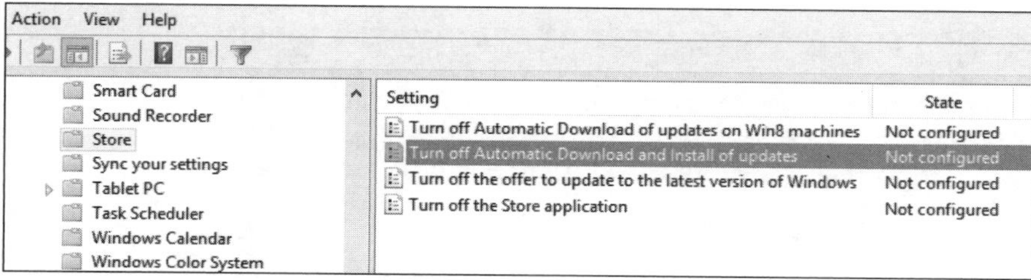

FIGURE 6-1 Group Policy settings can be configured for the Windows Store.

MORE INFO **SIDELOADING**

Organizations can create their own apps through a process called *sideloading*. Sideloading enables companies to create their own apps and forgo Microsoft's inspection process. Apps must be digitally signed and the computers to which you want to offer the apps must be configured to allow the installation (use Group Policy to enable Allow Trusted App To Install).

You might see something about sideloading on the exam, so make sure you're familiar with these Windows PowerShell commands:

- **Add-AppxPackage** Adds a signed app package (.appx) to a user account
- **Get-AppxPackage** Gets a list of the app packages (.appx) that are installed in a user profile
- **Remove-AppxPackage** Removes an app package (.appx) from a user account

Also, at an elevated command prompt you can use these commands:

- **Slmgr /ipk <sideloading product key>** Adds a sideloading key
- **slmgr /ato (followed by the key)** Activates the sideloading key

The following is a sample command:

```
add-appxpackage C:\companyapp8.appx -DependencyPath C:\winjs.appx.
```

Configure update settings

Unless you are specifically asked about Store updates or something very specific such as firmware updates, any references to updates on the exam refer to Windows Updates. These are the updates you're familiar with from Control Panel; these are the updates you've been working with for years.

The settings you need to access are available in the Windows Update window, from Control Panel, in System And Security, from Windows Update. Here you'll find the options Check For Updates, Change Settings, View Update History, Restore Hidden Updates, Installed Updates, and Add Features To Windows 8.1. You'll also see any available updates that are scheduled to install, optional updates, and information about when you received updates. Figure 6-2 shows this window.

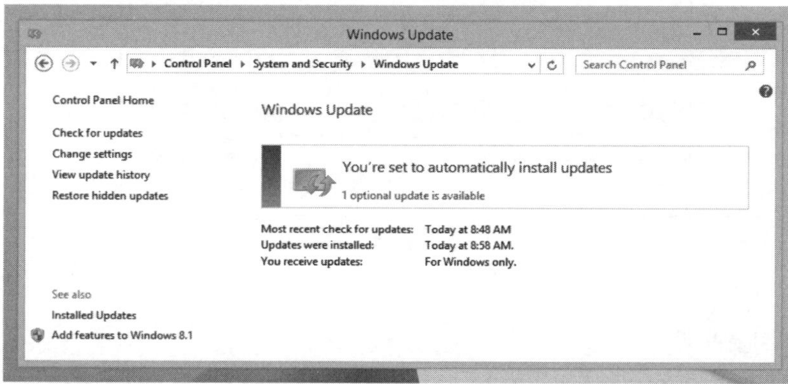

FIGURE 6-2 You configure Windows Update settings in Control Panel.

> ***NOTE* WHERE TO SET WINDOWS UPDATE**
>
> **You can use PC Settings, Update And Recovery to quickly see if a client machine is configured to receive updates. You can also view the update history and choose how updates get installed. However, most network administrators still prefer the Windows Update window, available from Control Panel, because all options are available there, not just the ones that end users would likely access.**

To configure update settings from Control Panel, follow these steps:

1. Click System And Security and click Windows Update.
2. In the Windows Update window shown in Figure 6-2, click Change Settings.
3. Make your preferred choices using the options available in the Important Updates drop-down list. See Figure 6-3.

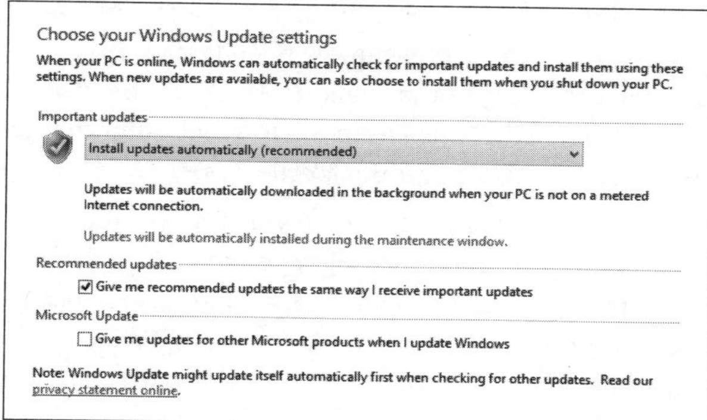

FIGURE 6-3 There are four options for obtaining and installing Windows Updates.

4. Click the scheduling option shown. The default entry is Updates Will Be Automatically Installed During The Maintenance Window. See Figure 6-3.
5. If desired, use the Run Maintenance Tasks Daily At drop-down list to choose a different time. The default is 3 A.M.
6. If desired, select the Allow Scheduled Maintenance To Wake Up My Computer At The Scheduled Time check box.
7. Click OK.
8. Click OK.
9. Make sure you are knowledgeable about the four options from step 3:
   - Install Updates Automatically (Recommended)
   - Download Updates But Let Me Choose Whether To Install Them
   - Check For Updates But Let Me Choose Whether To Download Or Install Them
   - Never Check For Updates (Not Recommended)

EXAM TIPS

- **When a new device is connected to a computer, Windows 8.1 searches for a driver on the computer. If it doesn't find one, it looks to Windows Update.**
- **Standard users can install drivers that have been downloaded from Windows Update without a User Account Control (UAC) prompt.**
- **Optional updates might be available in the Windows Update window that weren't installed automatically, so occasionally check to see if any are available.**

Windows Server Update Services

Windows Update, configured as detailed in this section, is a good solution for small workgroups and organizations (50 or fewer users is a general rule of thumb). If your organization is larger, you should install and configure a Windows Server Update Services (WSUS) server.

With WSUS, updates are downloaded to the WSUS server and then the administrator can make them available when they are ready, perhaps after they've been tested. They can even pass on the updates to other WSUS servers in large organizations. This saves bandwidth, too, because the updates only need to be downloaded once from the Internet. After that they can be pushed out or downloaded from server to client over the local network.

To use WSUS, Windows clients must be configured to use the WSUS server through Group Policies. You can't make that change in Control Panel. The policy you're looking for is Specify Intranet Microsoft Update Service Location. It's located in the applicable Group Policy editor: Computer Configuration, Administrative Templates, Windows Components, Windows Update. This is only one of many policies available in the Windows Update node. You'll learn about these later in this section.

Manage update history

In Figure 6-2 you saw the View Update History option in the task pane of the Windows Update window. You click that option to view all of the updates that have been installed on the computer. They are organized by the date installed by default, but you can click any tab on the tab bar to sort them in other ways. You can sort by Importance, which organizes the updates by their type. If you look closely at Figure 6-4, you'll notice there are lots of updates marked Important and only a handful marked Recommended.

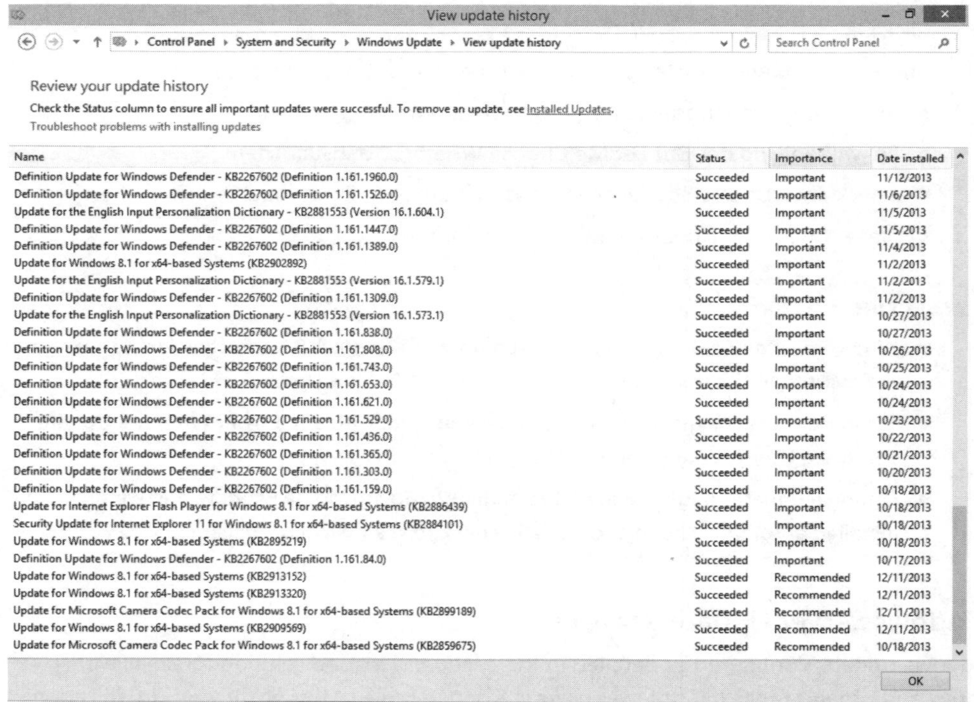

FIGURE 6-4 Review your update history to see what kinds of updates have been installed.

EXAM TIP

Make sure you're familiar with the various types of updates, what they offer, and why they are used: Important, Recommended, Optional, Security, Critical, and Service Packs.

You can also sort updates by name. When you do, you can more easily see what is being updated. You'll likely see a lot of Definition updates for Windows Defender, updates for the Windows 8.1 operating system, updates for the Windows Malicious Software Removal Tool, updates for the dictionary, and more. You'll also see Cumulative Security Updates for various items including Internet Explorer 11. To learn more about any update, including any related Knowledge Base articles, double-click it, as shown in Figure 6-5. (You can also right-click to copy it.)

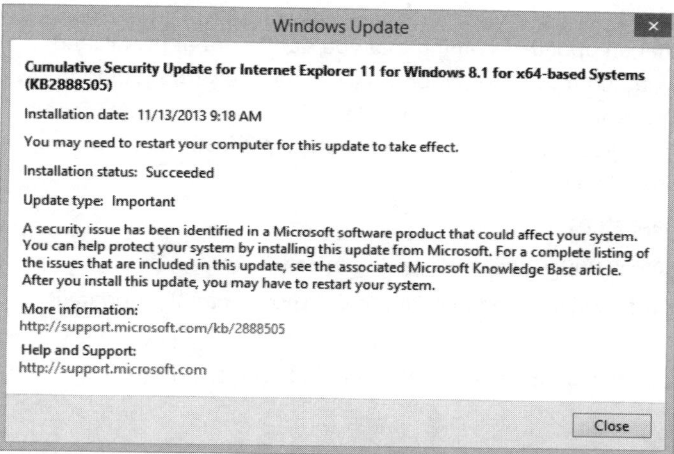

FIGURE 6-5 Learn more about any update by double-clicking it.

Roll back updates

When you roll back an update, you uninstall it. Logically then, it must have been installed first. To access an installed update, you need to open the Windows Update window and click Installed Updates in the upper-left corner. Once you've found the update to uninstall, click it and then click Uninstall. See Figure 6-6.

Uninstall an update

To uninstall an update, select it from the list and then click Uninstall or Chang

Organize ▾ Uninstall

Name	Program
KB2565063	Microsoft Visual C+...
Microsoft Windows (33)	
Update for Microsoft Windows (KB2903939)	Microsoft Windows
Update for Microsoft Windows (KB2911134)	Microsoft Windows
Security Update for Microsoft Windows (KB2898785)	Microsoft Windows
Security Update for Microsoft Windows (KB2893984)	Microsoft Windows
Security Update for Microsoft Windows (KB2893294)	Microsoft Windows

FIGURE 6-6 Uninstall problematic updates.

If you know ahead of time that an update is coming that you don't want to install (and you don't use a WSUS server), you might want to temporarily change the settings in Windows Update so that you are prompted when updates are available while retaining control regarding what to install and when. Then, you can hide the update before it is installed automatically and forgo the need to uninstall it later.

To hide an update, follow these steps:

1. Open the Windows Update window.
2. Click the notification for the available updates. Figure 6-7 shows that one update is available.
3. Locate the update in the Select Updates To Install pane that appears, right-click it, and click Hide Update.

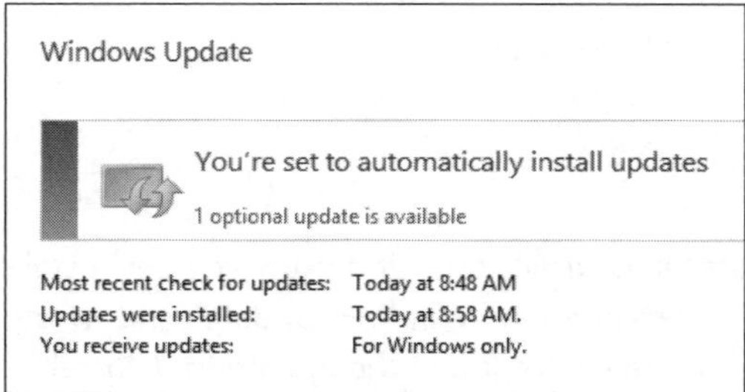
Windows Update
You're set to automatically install updates
1 optional update is available
Most recent check for updates: Today at 8:48 AM
Updates were installed: Today at 8:58 AM.
You receive updates: For Windows only.

FIGURE 6-7 Locate the update before it's installed to hide it and keep it from installing.

If you decide later to install the update, from the Windows Update window, click Restore Hidden Updates. Select the desired updates and click Restore.

Configure Windows Update policies

When you need more control over how Windows Updates are applied to client machines, you can set local and domain Group Policies. You'll find the settings in the Group Policy Editor from Computer Configuration, Administrative Templates, Windows Components, Windows

Update. There are quite a few to review, and because they aren't always self-explanatory, we'll cover them in more depth than previous Group Policy settings.

Remember, when you enable a specific Group Policy setting, you are configuring the policy to do exactly what it says it will do. So, if the policy setting starts with the words "Do not display...," then when you enable the setting whatever it is will not be displayed. If the policy starts with the words "Turn on...," then when you enable the policy the thing will be turned on. Unless otherwise stated, when you disable a policy the result is the same as not configuring it at all. So, unless there is a specific issue with a setting, we'll only discuss what happens when you enable it here. The settings are shown in Figure 6-8.

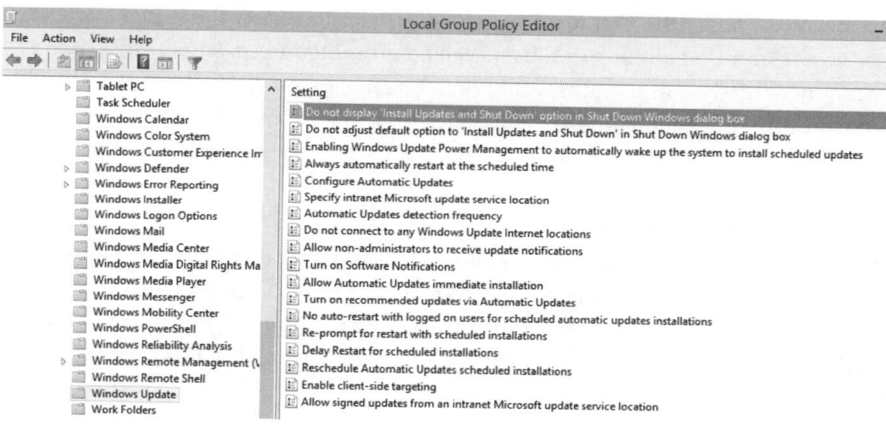

FIGURE 6-8 Windows Update policies in the Local Group Policy Editor.

Do Not Display "Install Updates And Shut Down" Option In Shut Down Windows

When enabled, Install Updates And Shut Down will not appear as a choice in the Shut Down Windows dialog box, even if the updates are available for installation when the user selects the Shut Down option.

Do Not Adjust Default Option To "Install Updates And Shut Down" In Shut Down Windows

When enabled, the user's last shut down choice is the default option in the Shut Down Windows dialog box, no matter if the Install Updates And Shut Down option is available in the What Do You Want The Computer To Do? list.

Enabling Windows Update Power Management To Automatically Wake Up The System To Install Scheduled Updates

When enabled, Windows Update wakes up a system that is hibernating (using the Windows Power Management feature) to install the updates. If Windows Update wakes the system but discovers it is running on battery power, it goes back into hibernation in two minutes and does not install any updates.

Always Automatically Restart At The Scheduled Time

When enabled, a restart timer will begin immediately after Windows Update installs important updates. It will not notify the user in advance of any plans to restart the system. You will then set your own restart timer in minutes. Users will be prompted to save their work, but a restart will occur no matter what the user would rather have happen. (If the No Auto-Restart With Logged On Users For Scheduled Automatic Updates Installations policy is enabled, this policy has no effect. This is another instance of Deny always overriding other settings.

Configure Automatic Updates

This sets a Group Policy for how Automatic Updates are configured. If enabled, you choose the auto download and installation settings, and if you select Auto Download And Schedule The Install, then you can also opt to make those installs during automatic maintenance periods. You can also configure how often to schedule the installation and the install time. See Figure 6-9.

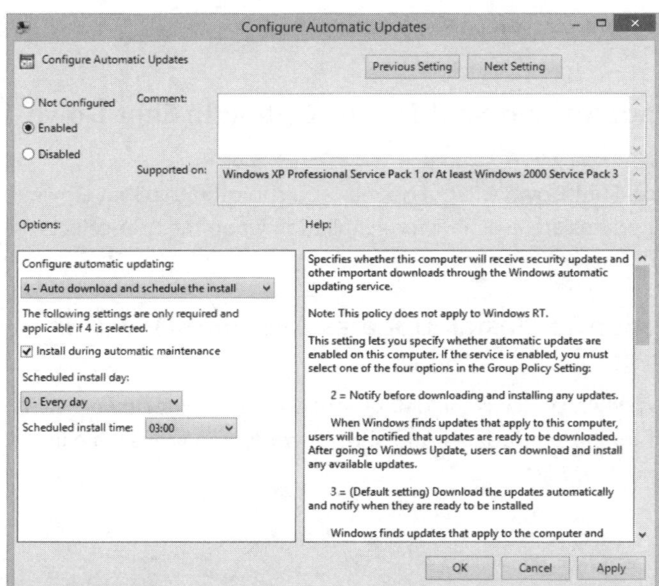

FIGURE 6-9 Configure Automatic Updates has more choices than most policies do.

Specify Intranet Microsoft Update Service Location

When enabled, you specify a server on your network that will hold Windows Updates. Clients will get the updates from this server. It's likely a WSUS server, as noted earlier in this chapter. Larger networks will use a System Center Configuration Manager (SCCM) server instead. You need to type two fully qualified domain names (FQDNs) when you enable this policy:

- Set The Intranet Update Service For Detecting Updates
- Set The Intranet Statistics Server

Automatic Updates Detection Frequency

When enabled, you specify the hours that Windows will use to determine how long to wait before checking for available updates. When you set an interval, say every 20 hours, the interval is actually calculated to 80 percent of this number to give a window. For 20 hours, the window becomes between 16 and 20 hours. Windows will check for updates during this interval.

Do Not Connect To Any Windows Update Internet Locations

When enabled, the client will not try to obtain any updates, even from the public Windows Update service or the Windows Store. Note that because this policy disables this, it might cause the Windows Store to stop working.

Allow Non-Administrators To Receive Update Notifications

When enabled, non-administrators will receive update notifications. Users can install the updates for which a notification was received. There is a lot more information offered about this setting in the Policy Settings window. Make sure to review this as time allows. See Figure 6-10.

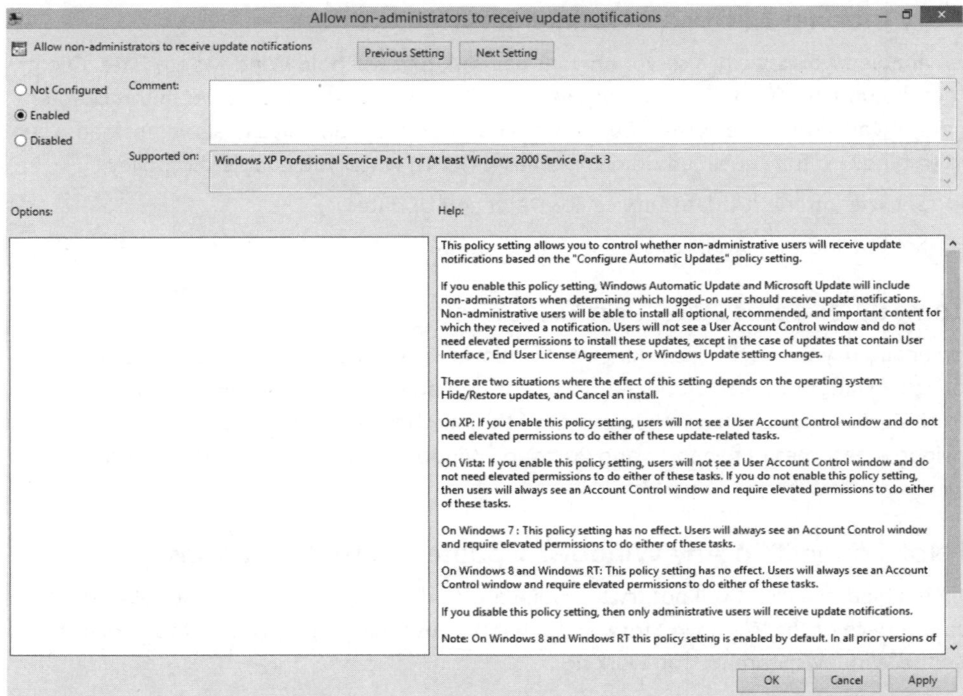

FIGURE 6-10 Review the settings for Allow Non-Administrators To Receive Update Notifications.

Turn On Software Notifications

When enabled, a notification message will appear on the user's computer when featured software updates are available. The featured software notifications come from the Microsoft update service. This feature should only be used in loosely managed environments.

Allow Automatic Updates Immediate Installation

When enabled, Automatic Updates will immediately install once they are downloaded and ready. If the Configure Automatic Updates policy is disabled, this policy has no effect.

Turn On Recommended Updates Via Automatic Updates

When enabled, Automatic Updates will install recommended updates and important updates.

No Auto-Restart With Logged On Users For Scheduled Automatic Updates Installations

When enabled, Automatic Updates will not restart a computer automatically during a scheduled installation if a user is logged in. Instead, the user will be prompted to restart the computer. If disabled or not configured, the computer will notify the user and then restart after five minutes to complete the installation. If the Configure Automatic Updates policy is disabled, this setting has no effect.

Re-Prompt For Restart With Scheduled Installations

When enabled, a scheduled restart will occur the specified number of minutes after the previous prompt for a restart was postponed. If this is not set or disabled, the default interval is 10 minutes. If the Configure Automatic Updates policy is disabled, this policy has no effect. It has no effect on Windows RT, either.

Delay Restart For Scheduled Installations

When enabled, a scheduled restart will occur the specified number of minutes after the installation is finished. If disabled or not configured, the default is 15 minutes. If the Configure Automatic Updates policy is disabled, this policy has no effect.

Reschedule Automatic Updates Scheduled Installations

When enabled, a scheduled installation that did not take place earlier will occur the specific number of minutes after the computer is next started. When disabled, a missed scheduled installation will occur with the next scheduled installation. If this is not configured, a missed scheduled installation will occur one minute after the computer is next started. If the Configure Automatic Updates policy is disabled, this policy has no effect.

Enable Client-Side Targeting

When enabled, the specified target group you name will be sent to the intranet Microsoft update server. This server can be configured to deploy updates as desired to the specified group. You might configure a setting for all laptop users, say, so that you can specify when and how updates are sent or downloaded.

Allow Signed Updates From An Intranet Microsoft Update Service Location

When enabled, Automatic Updates from non-Microsoft companies that are received through the Microsoft update server will be accepted if they are signed with a certificate from within the Trusted Publishers certificate store. Updates signed by Microsoft will also be installed. When this is disabled or not configured, only those signed by Microsoft will be installed.

> ***Thought experiment***
>
> **How to manage Windows Update in larger companies**
>
> In this thought experiment, apply what you've learned about this objective. You can find answers to these questions in the "Answers" section at the end of this chapter.
>
> You work for an organization that has grown a lot over the past three years. You used to manage Windows Updates using Local Group Policy, but you only had two dozen client computers to manage then. Now you have to manage 65 client computers and the task is taking much too long. You want to work smarter and manage the updates more effectively. Also, you'd like to be able to test the updates on a group of similarly configured test machines before you let your clients install them on their own.
>
> 1. What type of server can you put into place to help you manage the Windows Updates in your larger organization?
> 2. What is the name of the Group Policy you must enable to point client computers to this new server for obtaining updates?
> 3. Where can you find this policy?

Objective summary

- It's important to keep the Windows 8.1 operating system as up to date as possible with Windows Store updates and Windows Updates.
- After Windows Updates are applied, you can access the updates from the Windows Update window and roll them back if they cause problems.
- You can configure Group Policies to manage how and when computers in an organization are updated.

Objective review

Answer the following questions to test your knowledge of the information in this objective. You can find the answers to these questions and explanations of why each answer choice is correct or incorrect in the "Answers" section at the end of this chapter.

1. Is it possible to remove the option from the Windows Store that lets users upgrade their Windows 8 machines to Windows 8.1? If so, how?
   - **A.** No, it is not possible to remove the prompt to upgrade to Windows 8.1 in the Windows Store.
   - **B.** Yes. From the Store, click the Settings charm, click App Updates, and clear the option to update to Windows 8.1.
   - **C.** Yes. You must set a Group Policy here: Computer Configuration, Administrative Templates, Windows Components, Store.

D. Yes, but you must use AppLocker and the computers must be part of an Active Directory domain.

2. Which of the following statements is false regarding Windows Updates?

   A. Windows Updates can include device drivers.

   B. Standard users can't install drivers that have been downloaded from Windows Update without a UAC prompt.

   C. Not all updates are installed even if you choose Install Updates Automatically (Recommended) from the Windows Update, Change Settings options.

   D. You can use PC Settings, Update And Recovery to quickly see if a client machine is configured to receive updates.

3. You need to uninstall a Windows Update that has caused problems with a few specific client computers. You open Windows Update in Control Panel. What do you click in the task pane to locate the offending update and uninstall it?

   A. Change Settings

   B. View Update History

   C. Installed Updates

   D. Both View Update History and Installed Updates will work.

4. What happens when you enable the Group Policy setting Enabling Windows Update Power Management To Automatically Wake Up The System To Install Scheduled Updates?

   A. When enabled, Windows Update will wake up a system to install the updates. If Windows Update wakes the system but discovers it is running on battery power, it will go back into hibernation in two minutes and will not install any updates.

   B. When enabled, Windows Update will wake up a system to install the updates. If Windows Update wakes the system but discovers it is running on battery power, it will install the updates and then put the computer back into hibernation mode.

   C. When enabled, Windows Update will wake up a system to install the updates. It will not wake the computer if it is running on battery power.

   D. When enabled, Windows Update will not wake up a system to install the updates.

Objective 6.2: Manage local storage

Although it might seem—especially with the integration of SkyDrive (which is being renamed OneDrive) and all the talk about domains and file servers—that no one stores anything locally anymore, they do. Even users who depend on cloud or on- or off-site storage might still use the local machine or attached drives for backups if for no other reason. Thus, it's still important you understand how to manage local storage. In this objective, you'll explore disk volumes, learn about file system fragmentation, and learn about a new feature, Storage Spaces.

This objective covers how to:

- Manage disk volumes
- Manage file system fragmentation
- Manage Storage Spaces

Manage disk volumes

This objective addresses how to manage existing hard disks. It likely does not ask questions about how to prepare a raw disk for use. However, you should know a little about this, if only to be comfortable with some of the terms you'll see both on the job and on the exam. So, before we dive in to managing disk volumes, we'll review (or introduce you to) some common disk-related terms.

Terms you need to know

When you install Windows 8.1, the installation program configures the hard disks for you. This includes but is not limited to selecting a partition style, selecting a disk type, creating the required volumes or partitions, and formatting the volumes with the desired file system. Once this is done and the operating system is up and running, you can make changes to the options you chose during installation or the options applied automatically.

To fully understand how the installation is achieved and what can be done using the various disk management tools, you need to be familiar with the following terms:

- **Partition style** Master Boot Record (MBR) and GUID Partition Table (GPT). MBR is the default partition style for x86- and x64-based computers. GPT can be used on x86- and x64-based Windows 8 computers and was first introduced with Windows Vista. Before then, only MBR was available.

EXAM TIP

MBR uses a table to point to locations on a disk. It supports partitions up to 2 TB; up to either four primary partitions or three primary and one extended. A hidden partition holds important data that is critical to computer operations. GPT with Windows 8.1 supports up to 128 primary partitions and volumes up to 18 exabytes, and data that is critical is saved on a partition that is not hidden. To use GPT, the computer must support Extensible Firmware Interface (EFI) boot partitioning. GPT offers redundancy for improved security and reliability.

- **Partition types** Primary and extended. These are used with basic disks. Primary partition types function as a separate disk, can be marked as the active partition, can host an operating system, and have their own drive letter. Extended partitions cannot host an operating system, cannot be marked as active, and can contain an unlimited number of logical partitions.

EXAM TIP

When creating an extended partition, the logical drives inside it are formatted, not the extended partition itself. Drive letters can be assigned to the logical drives.

- **Volume types** Volumes (in contrast to partitions) are used with dynamic disks. They can be simple, spanned, striped, mirrored, or Redundant Array of Independent Disks-5 (RAID-5). Windows 8.1 doesn't support RAID-5, though. You can't use dynamic disks or any option here on a multiboot system. If you have basic disks you want to configure this way, the disks must be converted to dynamic. The system can do this for you.
  - **Simple** A single disk that can be extended to create a spanned or striped volume. If a disk fails, the data on the disk is lost.
  - **Spanned** From 2 to 32 dynamic disks that are created to combine disk space from those disks. Windows fills the first disk and then writes to the next and the next until all disks are full.
  - **Striped** From 2 to to 32 dynamic disks. Data is written in stripes to each disk, increasing the write time. Data is written to one disk while the other(s) get ready to accept data. If one disk fails, the data on that disk is lost.
  - **Mirrored** Two dynamic disks that are exactly the same size. Data is written to both simultaneously to provide fault tolerance. If a disk fails, the other disk contains mirrored data and thus data is not lost.
- **File systems** FAT, FAT32, exFat, NTFS. A file system defines how the drive is structured; NTFS is preferred.

EXAM TIP

If any of the terms here are new to you (dynamic, basic, partition, volume, MBR, GPT), make sure to do your own research to become familiar with them. For more information about these terms, refer to the MSDN article at *http://msdn.microsoft.com/en-us/library/windows/desktop/aa363785(v=vs.85).aspx.*

Use Disk Management

You learned about the Disk Management Microsoft Management Console (MMC) and related snap-in in Chapter 1, "Install and upgrade to Windows 8.1," where you learned how to use it to create a virtual hard disk (VHD). Here you'll explore this console further and discover options for managing existing disks, including viewing a disk list and disk properties and creating, managing, shrinking, and extending disk volumes, among other things.

One way to open the Disk Management tool is to type **compmgmt.msc** in a Run dialog box. You can also right-click the Start button and click Computer Management to gain access. In the Navigation pane, click Disk Management (under Storage). See Figure 6-11. Here you can see a list of disks, their status, volume letters, file system types, and so on.

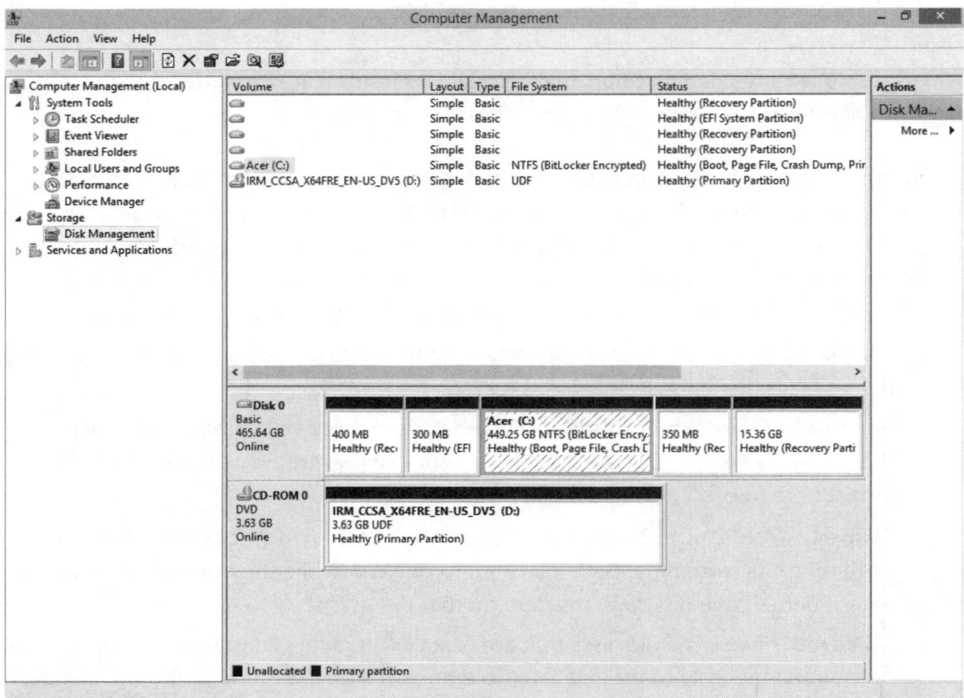

FIGURE 6-11 The Disk Management console lets you review and make changes to disk properties.

To view the options for any disk partition or volume, right-click it. You'll see different options for different entries. For instance, if you right-click the Recovery partition, you'll only see one option, Help. If you right-click the primary partition, you'll see other options, including but not limited to Change Drive Letter And Paths, Extend Volume, Shrink Volume, Delete Volume, Properties, and so on, as shown in Figure 6-12. If you right-click the volume and click Properties, you'll see a familiar Properties dialog box that includes access to various tools including Disk Cleanup, Check Disk, Disk Defragmenter, and even the option to set disk quotas and log events when quota limits are set. Finally, if you right-click the disk box (in Figure 6-11 this is labeled Disk 0 Basic 465.64 GB Online), you'll see the option to convert to Dynamic Disk and Convert to MBR Disk.

There are limitations to what you can do here, though. For example, you can't extend a partition if there is no free space to extend to. You can shrink an existing volume (see Figure 6-12) and use the space you've created to perform additional tasks, however. You can't add a mirror if a second disk isn't available. You can't delete a volume if it's the primary volume, and so on. For the most part, though, if you opt to perform a task, you work through a wizard to complete it. You can do a lot of things, including adding disks.

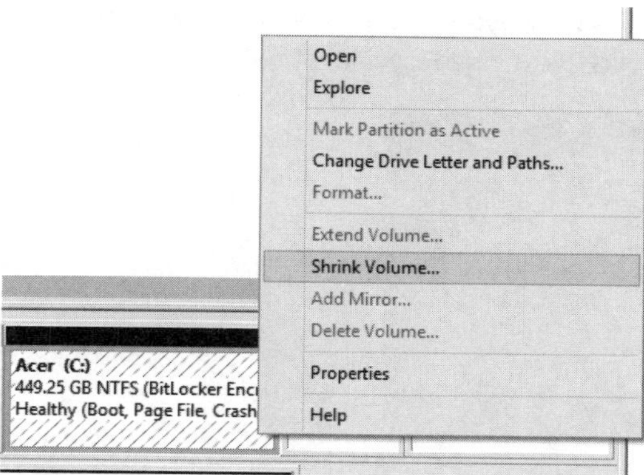

FIGURE 6-12 Right-click an active partition to view options such as Shrink Volume.

To introduce you to a few of these tasks, in this section you'll shrink a partition and create a new, simple volume by following these steps:

1. Open Disk Management.
2. Select a disk that has extra storage space that you can shrink.
3. Right-click the disk and click Shrink Volume.
4. In the Shrink dialog box, enter the amount of space to shrink in MB. You might want to accept the default for this exercise.
5. Click Shrink.
6. Note the newly created space and note that it is unallocated. Right-click it and click New Simple Volume. See Figure 6-13.

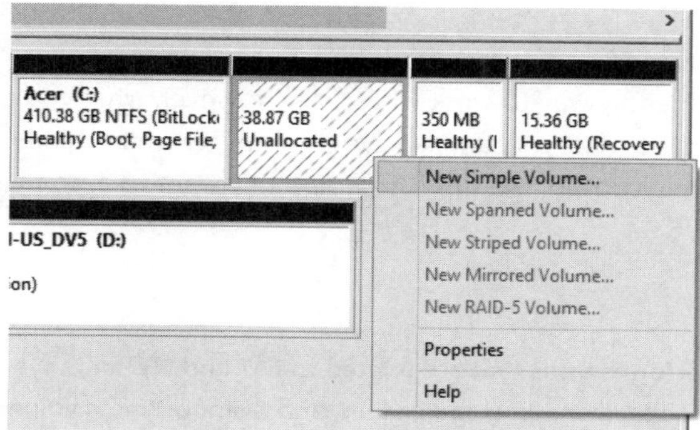

FIGURE 6-13 You can create new volumes from unallocated space on a hard disk.

7. Click Next to start the New Simple Volume Wizard. Click Next again to accept the defaults for the volume size (you could enter your own size here).
8. Click Next to accept the assigned drive letter or choose a new letter as desired.

9. Choose how to format the volume. NTFS is best. Type a new name for the volume (New Volume is the default name) and click Next. See Figure 6-14.

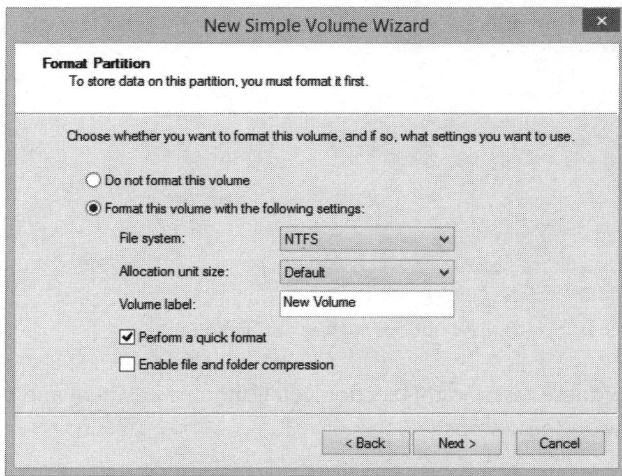

FIGURE 6-14 Set the file system and volume label.

10. Click Finish.
11. Note the new disk entry in the disk list. Then, open File Explorer, click This PC, and view your new simple volume there.

To explore further, in Disk Management, right-click the new volume. Note that Delete Volume is now available, as is Format. You can also save data to this new volume, as you would do if this were a USB drive or external backup device.

Use Diskpart

The Disk Management console is a friendly way to work with disks. However, what you can do there is limited, at least compared to what you can achieve through command-line tools, including Diskpart.exe. Network administrators use this tool when they want to automate disk tasks with scripts and batch files.

EXAM TIP

The command-line utility Fsutil performs tasks that are related to FAT and NTFS file systems, such as managing reparse points, managing sparse files, and dismounting a volume. If it is used without parameters, Fsutil displays a list of supported subcommands. This command is sometimes associated with tasks that can also involve Diskpart and might be included as a red herring on an exam question.

> ***MORE INFO*** **ALTERNATIVELY, YOU CAN USE WINDOWS POWERSHELL COMMANDS**
>
> **Diskpart is a command-line tool, but there are Windows PowerShell commands you can use, too. Make sure to review at least a few of these, including Format-Volume, New-Partition, Set-Disk, and Set-Partition.**

There are a lot of Diskpart command parameters, including some with which you might already be familiar if you've ever created a bootable USB drive. If you have, you'll likely recognize the commands Create Partition, Select Partition, Active, Format, and so on. You can view all of the command options by typing **Diskpart** at an elevated command prompt and pressing Enter on the keyboard. When you see the DISKPART> prompt, type **Help** and press Enter. See Figure 6-15.

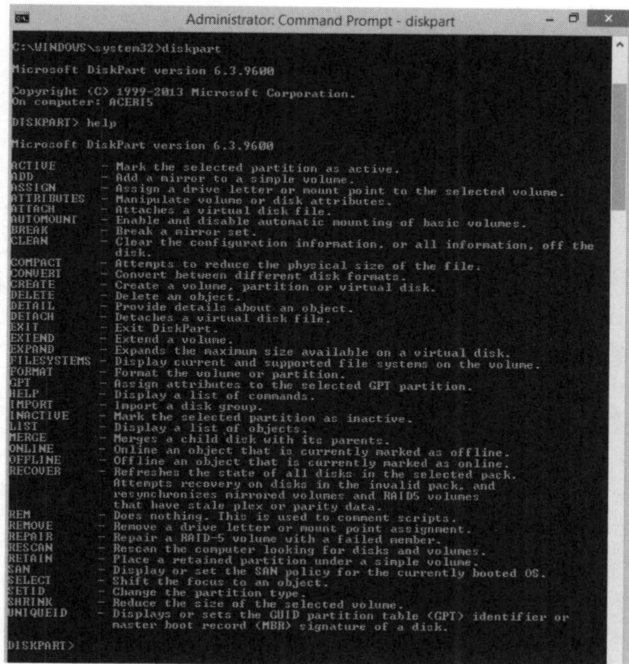

FIGURE 6-15 Review the Diskpart command-line parameters.

Although you'll need to familiarize yourself with all of the Diskpart parameters, here are a few you should pay special attention to:

- **Active** To mark the selected partition as active.
- **Add** To add a mirror to a simple volume.
- **Assign** To assign a drive letter to a selected volume.
- **Convert** To convert between basic and dynamic disks. (Basic to dynamic can be done without data loss; the opposite is not true.)

- **Create** To create a volume, partition, or virtual disk.
- **Exit** To exit Diskpart.
- **Extend** To extend a volume.
- **Format** To format the volume or partition. (You can convert a FAT partition to NTFS using something like FORMAT FS=NTFS LABEL="New Volume" QUICK COMPRESS.)
- **Shrink** To reduce the size of a volume.

MORE INFO **DISKPART PARAMETERS**

To review all of the Diskpart command-line parameters, refer to the article at *http://technet.microsoft.com/en-us/library/cc766465(v=WS.10).aspx*.

EXAM TIP

It might or might not be on the exam, but every network administrator should be familiar with how to create a bootable USB flash drive using the Windows ADK, Windows PE, and various Diskpart commands. Review this article to learn how: *http://technet.microsoft.com/en-us/library/hh825109.aspx*.

Check Disk and Disk Cleanup

Two tools, Check Disk and Disk Cleanup, help you manage disks in two distinct ways. Check Disk will scan the physical disks, look for errors, and fix them automatically (most of the time). Specifically, Check Disk looks for bad storage blocks. You opt to scan the drive, and if errors are found you'll be prompted to reboot the machine to let Windows fix them. The run line command is **Chkdsk**. You can also access this tool from the drive's Properties dialog box on the Tools tab.

Disk Cleanup is also a disk management tool, and with it you can clean the drive by removing temporary files, emptying the Recycle Bin, deleting downloaded program files, and more. Disk Cleanup can be accessed from a drive's Properties dialog box on the General tab. See Figure 6-16.

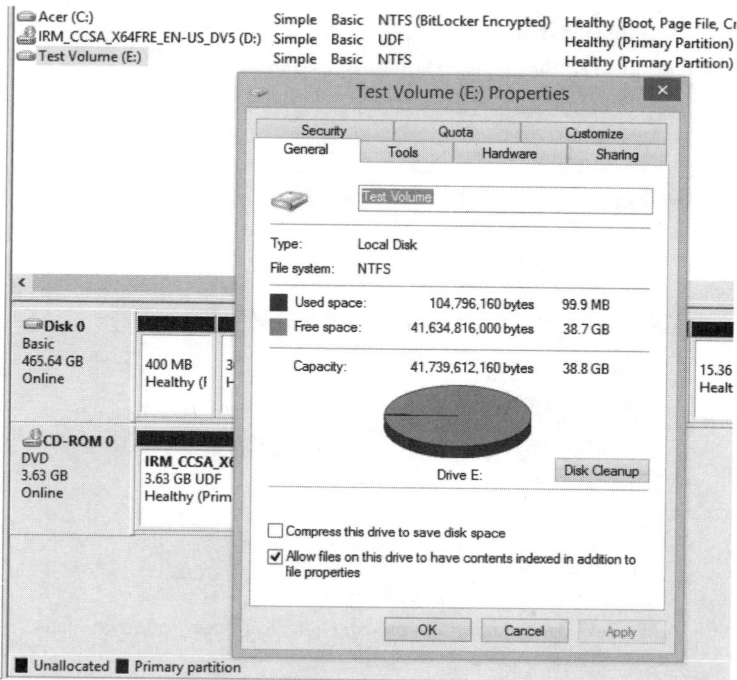

FIGURE 6-16 Disk management tools are available in the disk's Properties dialog box.

Manage file system fragmentation

Data is written to physical, spinning disks sequentially, from outside to inside, in clusters. When a disk is new, the data is written contiguously, but as data is added and then deleted, areas become open. Data is written to these open areas, too, and eventually data becomes fragmented (stored in noncontiguous segments or clusters). When the disk has to look in multiple places to pull data and offer it to the user, it takes longer than if the data was stored together. Thus, it's optimal to keep a disk defragmented.

The Disk Defragmenter tool runs automatically and in the background to keep your drives defragmented, but you can run it manually at any time (make sure to do a complete backup first, though). Like Disk Cleanup and Check Disk, you can access Disk Defragmenter from a drive's Properties dialog box on the Tools tab. When you click Optimize, you'll see what's shown in Figure 6-17. From there you can analyze any drive or click Optimize to run Disk Defragmenter. You can also click Change Settings to choose how and when Disk Defragmenter runs on its own.

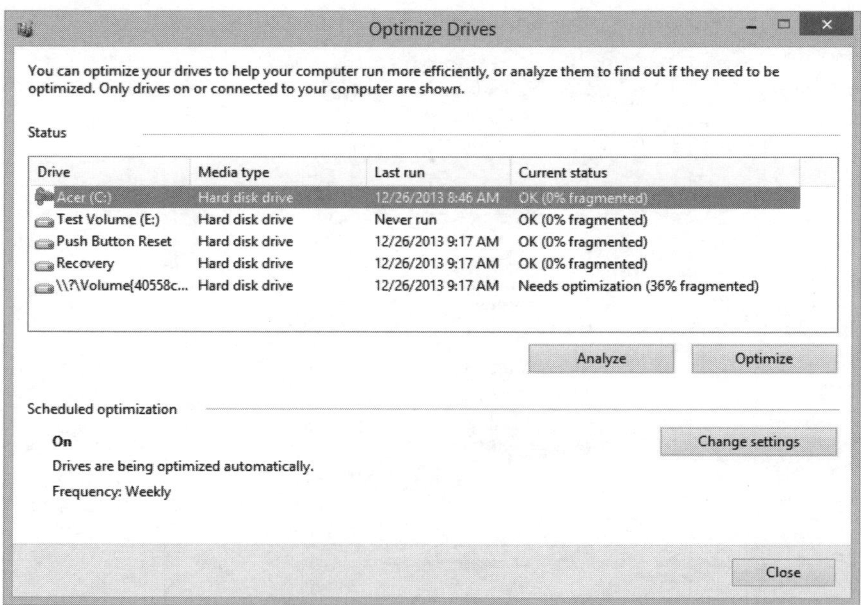

FIGURE 6-17 Disk Defragmenter runs weekly by default, but you can analyze and run your own scans anytime you want.

Manage Storage Spaces

Storage Spaces is new to computers running Windows 8 and lets you combine free space from multiple disks to create a new type of virtual disk for storing data. It does this by using the unallocated space on those disks to create a storage pool. This makes it easy to expand the storage space just by adding disks. You can create a maximum storage limit before you add the disks as well (a limit that exceeds the disk capacity currently connected), and as you near the limit of the currently installed disks, you'll be prompted to add more.

Here are a few things to know before you get started:

- You cannot use the disk that contains the operating system as part of the storage space.
- Serial ATA (SATA) or Serial Attached SCSI (SAS) connected disks are acceptable.
- RAID adapters, if used, must have all RAID functionality disabled.
- USB flash drives can be used, but USB 3.0 drives are recommended for best performance.
- When using USB 2.0 drives, plug them directly into different USB controllers on your computer; do not use USB hubs.
- There are various kinds of storage spaces, including simple (no fault tolerance), mirror, and parity. A two-way mirror mirrors data on two drives; a three-way mirror mirrors

data on three. Parity enables two drives to hold data and a third to hold parity information, for fault tolerance. You can create a storage space from one disk, but there is no fault tolerance when you do.

- You can use Windows PowerShell to manage Storage Spaces. Review common Windows PowerShell commands including Set –PhysicalDisk, Repair –VirtualDisk, and Remove –PhysicalDisk.
- You can use Storage Spaces in place of more expensive storage area network (SAN) devices under the right circumstances.
- If you move a storage pool, you must keep the pool together.
- If you remove and then try to reuse a disk used in a storage pool, you have to format it first.

MORE INFO **STORAGE SPACES**

Refer to this TechNet article to learn more about Storage Spaces: *http://technet.microsoft.com/en-us/library/hh831739.*

To use this feature, you must first create a storage pool by following these steps:

1. Connect the disks to use. Format them prior to setup (or make sure you're willing to let Windows do it during setup).
2. Open Control Panel, click System And Security, and click Storage Spaces.
3. Click Create A New Pool And Storage Space.
4. Select the check boxes for the drives to use and click Create Pool.
5. In the Create A Storage Space window, make additional configurations such as the name of the pool, resilience type, capacity, and so on. Click Create Storage Space.

EXAM TIP

When creating a storage space, create a capacity larger than the installed drives to use a feature known as thin provisioning. When you do, you'll be prompted when more space is required.

Thought experiment

Choose a fault tolerance disk configuration

In this thought experiment, apply what you've learned about this objective. You can find answers to these questions in the "Answers" section at the end of this chapter.

Your client has a Windows 8.1 computer with two physical disks installed. They are configured as basic disks. He wants to use these disks to protect his data. It is most important that the solution work to provide fault tolerance, but it is also important

to keep costs down and make recovery as quick and easy as possible. He's not worried about read and write performance, because the computer is well equipped with RAM and CPU resources.

1. **Of simple, striped, spanned, mirrored, or RAID-5 disks, which would you suggest the client use?**
2. **Will the user have to install additional disks or otherwise spend any money on the solution?**
3. **To implement the solution you selected in Question 1, what must be true of the two hard disks with regard to their size?**
4. **What is going to happen to the basic disks when you implement your plan?**

Objective summary

- Diskpart enables you to manage disks from a command line. You can use the tool to automate tasks and perform tasks not available in the Disk Management snap-in.
- Disk Cleanup, Check Disk, and Disk Defragmenter help you maintain your disks by removing unwanted data, repairing bad disk sectors, and keeping files from being fragmented.
- Storage Spaces enables you to create a storage pool using various kinds of external disks, including SATA drives and USB flash drives, among others.

Objective review

Answer the following questions to test your knowledge of the information in this objective. You can find the answers to these questions and explanations of why each answer choice is correct or incorrect in the "Answers" section at the end of this chapter.

1. You have a Windows 8.1 computer with a single, solid-state 512 GB drive. You also have two external drives that are 4 TB each. How can you configure Storage Spaces for these two additional drives?
   - **A.** Create an 8 TB three-way mirror.
   - **B.** Create a 4 TB three-way mirror.
   - **C.** Create an 8 TB three-way parity.
   - **D.** Create a 4 TB two-way mirror.
   - **E.** None of the above.
2. You have several USB flash drives that contain data you need to remove. You also want to remove the partition table to completely wipe the drive. What command-line utility should you use?
   - **A.** Diskpart
   - **B.** Fsutil

   C. Format
   D. Diskpart or Format
3. You suspect there's something wrong with the hard disk in a computer and you want to scan the disk, locate errors, and fix them. What tool do you use?
   A. Fsutil
   B. Chkdsk
   C. Disk Cleanup
   D. Disk Defragmenter
   E. Diskpart
   F. Disk Management snap-in
4. You need to improve the performance of a computer by increasing how quickly data can be written to it. You've added four hard disks. How should you configure these to improve write time?
   A. As dynamic disks configured as spanned volumes
   B. As dynamic disks configured as striped volumes
   C. As basic disks configured as mirrored volumes
   D. As basic disks configured as primary volumes
   E. As dynamic disks configured as mirrored volumes

Objective 6.3: Monitor system performance

Once computer systems are configured and protected, you'll need to monitor system performance to make sure those systems are functioning effectively and efficiently. There are many tools available to help you with this. In this objective, you'll learn about some of these tools, specifically those that will be covered on the exam, including Task Manager and Performance Monitor.

This objective covers how to:
- Configure Task Manager
- Monitor system resources
- Configure indexing options
- Configure and analyze event logs
- Configure event subscriptions
- Optimize networking performance

Configure Task Manager

Task Manager is one of the most useful tools available in Windows 8.1. Task Manager enables you to manage processes (discrete tasks) that use system resources and see how those resources are affected by those active processes. Because of its simplicity, end users can use it to end problematic processes, disable apps that don't need to run at startup, view logged-on users, and more. Because it is such a powerful and feature-rich tool, the savviest network administrator can use it to monitor, diagnose, and improve computer performance quickly.

Because running processes are so important to system performance, Task Manager has been redesigned so you can see the *process tree*, which groups related processes together. The entire interface is much more user-friendly, too. Task Manager has seven tabs. You need to know how you can use each of these to improve performance, and you need to be well versed in what each offers before you take the exam. There are several ways to open Task Monitor, but the simplest is to use the Ctrl+Shift+Esc key combination. Open Task Manager on your own computer now and explore the tabs as you read the rest of this section.

Processes tab

The Processes tab shows all running processes, grouped together as process trees. Processes with trees have a right-facing arrow beside them. You click the arrow to see the related processes. Click a single process or a process tree name and click End Task when you want to close a process that is problematic.

You can sort the processes based on resource usage. As shown in Figure 6-18, the Store is using 53.5 MB of memory. If you believe the Store app is causing problems, you can click End Task to end and close it. Also note in Figure 6-18 that underneath the Store, Internet Explorer is using 47.8 MB of memory and has a right-facing arrow beside it, showing it includes a process tree.

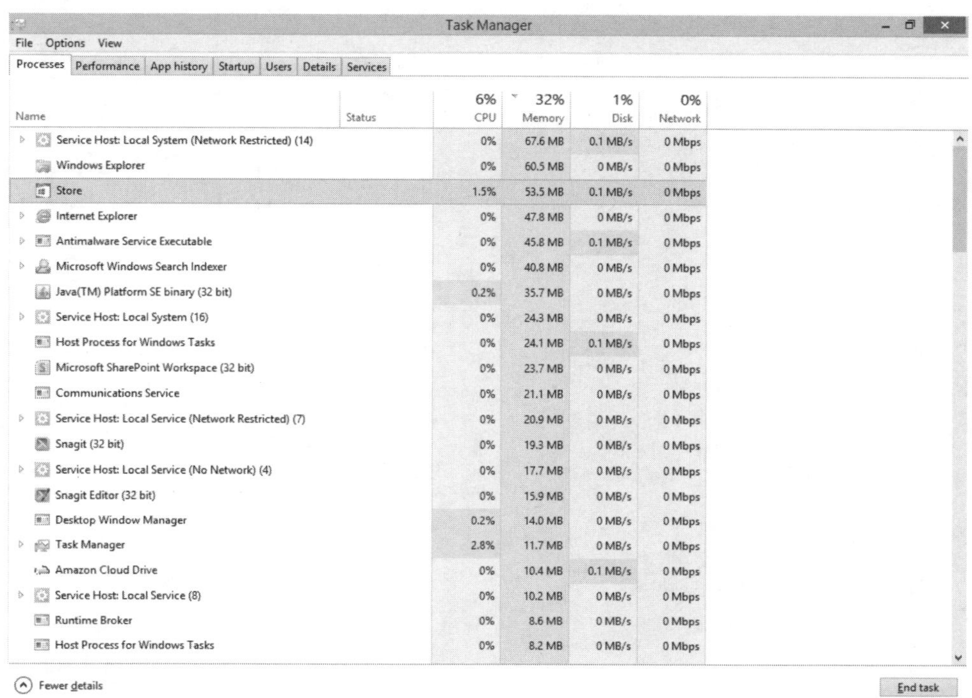

Task Manager
File Options View
Processes Performance App history Startup Users Details Services
Name
Status
6% CPU
32% Memory
1% Disk
0% Network
Service Host: Local System (Network Restricted) (14) 0% 67.6 MB 0.1 MB/s 0 Mbps
Windows Explorer 0% 60.5 MB 0 MB/s 0 Mbps
Store 1.5% 53.5 MB 0.1 MB/s 0 Mbps
Internet Explorer 0% 47.8 MB 0 MB/s 0 Mbps
Antimalware Service Executable 0% 45.8 MB 0.1 MB/s 0 Mbps
Microsoft Windows Search Indexer 0% 40.8 MB 0 MB/s 0 Mbps
Java(TM) Platform SE binary (32 bit) 0.2% 35.7 MB 0 MB/s 0 Mbps
Service Host: Local System (16) 0% 24.3 MB 0 MB/s 0 Mbps
Host Process for Windows Tasks 0% 24.1 MB 0.1 MB/s 0 Mbps
Microsoft SharePoint Workspace (32 bit) 0% 23.7 MB 0 MB/s 0 Mbps
Communications Service 0% 21.1 MB 0 MB/s 0 Mbps
Service Host: Local Service (Network Restricted) (7) 0% 20.9 MB 0 MB/s 0 Mbps
Snagit (32 bit) 0% 19.3 MB 0 MB/s 0 Mbps
Service Host: Local Service (No Network) (4) 0% 17.7 MB 0 MB/s 0 Mbps
Snagit Editor (32 bit) 0% 15.9 MB 0 MB/s 0 Mbps
Desktop Window Manager 0.2% 14.0 MB 0 MB/s 0 Mbps
Task Manager 2.8% 11.7 MB 0 MB/s 0 Mbps
Amazon Cloud Drive 0% 10.4 MB 0.1 MB/s 0 Mbps
Service Host: Local Service (8) 0% 10.2 MB 0 MB/s 0 Mbps
Runtime Broker 0% 8.6 MB 0 MB/s 0 Mbps
Host Process for Windows Tasks 0% 8.2 MB 0 MB/s 0 Mbps
Fewer details
End task

FIGURE 6-18 Use the Processes tab to select and end problematic processes.

Performance tab

The Performance tab shows real-time statistics for CPU, Memory, Disk, Ethernet, Bluetooth, and Wi-Fi usage. Figure 6-19 shows this tab with Wi-Fi selected. Under the graph you can see the adapter name, Service Set Identifier (SSID), Domain Name Service (DNS) name, connection type, IPv4 and IPv6 addresses, and signal strength. Right-click any entry on the left and click Summary View to minimize the window and show only the left pane. Doing this lets you keep an eye on the usage without using up much of your desktop area.

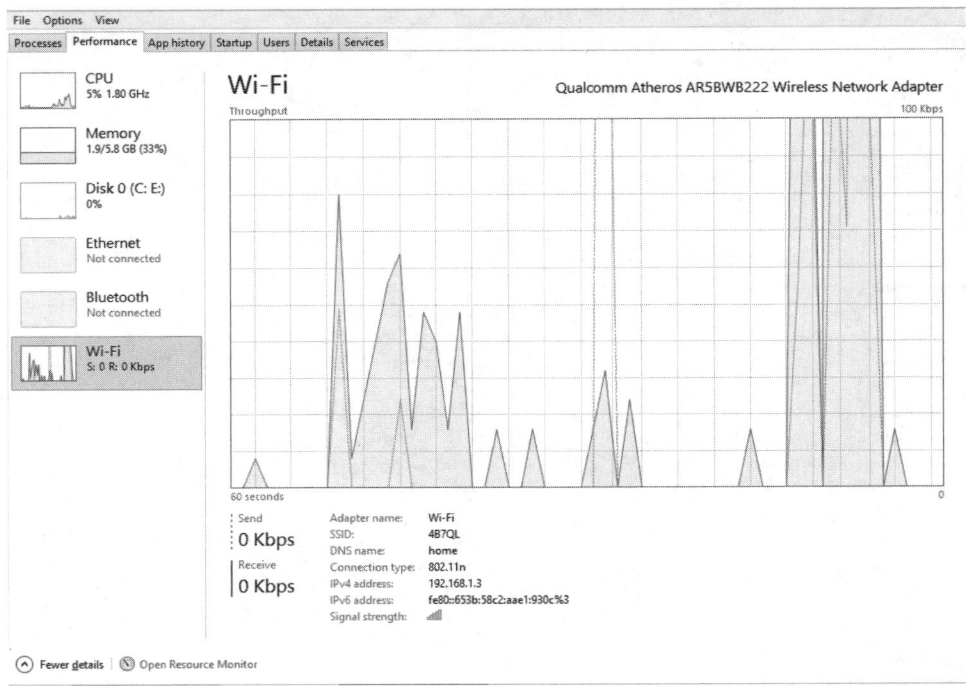

FIGURE 6-19 View real-time usage statistics on the Performance tab.

App History tab

The App History tab shows usage associated with apps (not desktop apps). All apps are represented here, even if they are not currently in use. You can use this tab to determine the load placed on the system from these apps. Columns here include CPU Time, Network, Metered Network, and Tile Updates. Like the Processes tab, you might see related trees. For instance, the Mail, Calendar, and People app has a right-facing arrow beside it. You can double-click any entry here to open the app or switch to it.

Startup tab

The Startup tab shows what applications start when the computer boots. You can select any application listed here and disable it to keep it from starting when Windows does. Once disabled, you can return to this tab to enable it. You can also view the startup impact caused by the application, which can be marked None, Low, Medium, or High; its status (Enabled or Disabled); and more. You can also right-click any entry to open the file location for it.

EXAM TIP

In previous operating system editions, you could type msconfig.exe in the Run dialog box to open the System Configuration dialog box (which you can still do), and from there you could click the Startup tab to configure what applications started when Windows did. If

you do that now, on the Startup tab of the System Configuration dialog box, you'll only see one option: Open Task Manager.

Users tab

The Users tab shows all of the users logged on to the computer, including those logged on remotely. You can expand the tree associated with any user (click the right-facing arrow) to view the processes open for that user. You can select any of these processes and end them by clicking End Task at the bottom of the window, and you can disconnect a user by clicking that user's name and clicking Disconnect. The active user will be prompted regarding the disconnect command when you use it.

Details tab

The Details tab shows what the Processes tab showed in previous versions of Task Manager. You can right-click any process to end the task, end the process tree, set a priority, set affinity, create a dump file, and more. Like other tabs, you can click any category name to sort the lists appropriately. See Figure 6-20.

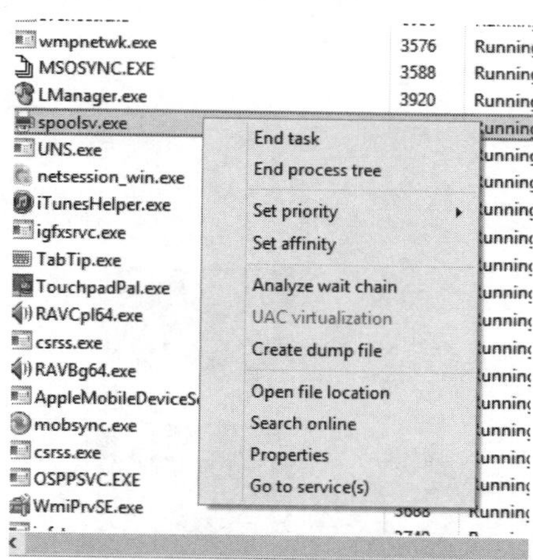

FIGURE 6-20 End tasks and processes on the Details tab by using a right-click.

Services tab

The Services tab displays all of the enabled services. Like other tabs, you can right-click a service to perform a task. The options include Start, Stop, Restart, Open Services, Search Online, and Go To Details.

EXAM TIP

Explore the bottom of each tab of Task Manager. Know that on the Performance tab there's an option to Open Resource Monitor and on the Services tab there's an option to Open Services.

Monitor system resources

Resource Monitor is a powerful tool you can use to see even more statistics regarding real-time resources than Task Manager offers. You can open Resource Monitor on the Performance tab of Task Manager or in myriad other ways including searching for it from the Start screen. You can also launch it directly by typing **resmon.exe** in a Run dialog box. Once it is open, you'll need to spend some time reviewing each tab.

Figure 6-21 shows Resource Monitor, the Overview tab, the graphs available (which are available from any tab), and what happens when you right-click a process that has been suspended. Suspended processes can cause problems, so if you see them, take note.

For the most part, you use Resource Monitor to troubleshoot problems that you were unable to uncover and resolve using Task Manager and other tools. For instance, on the Memory tab, you can sort processes by how much memory is committed to them. You might find that a single process is using a lot of memory and is problematic. You might not even need to run the application. From there you can right-click to end the process and then return to the Task Manager Startup tab to stop it from starting when Windows does to keep the problem from occurring in the future. This also reduces the load on memory, which will improve computer performance. As you can see in Figure 6-21, there are four graphs: CPU, Disk, Network, and Memory. These also show real-time information.

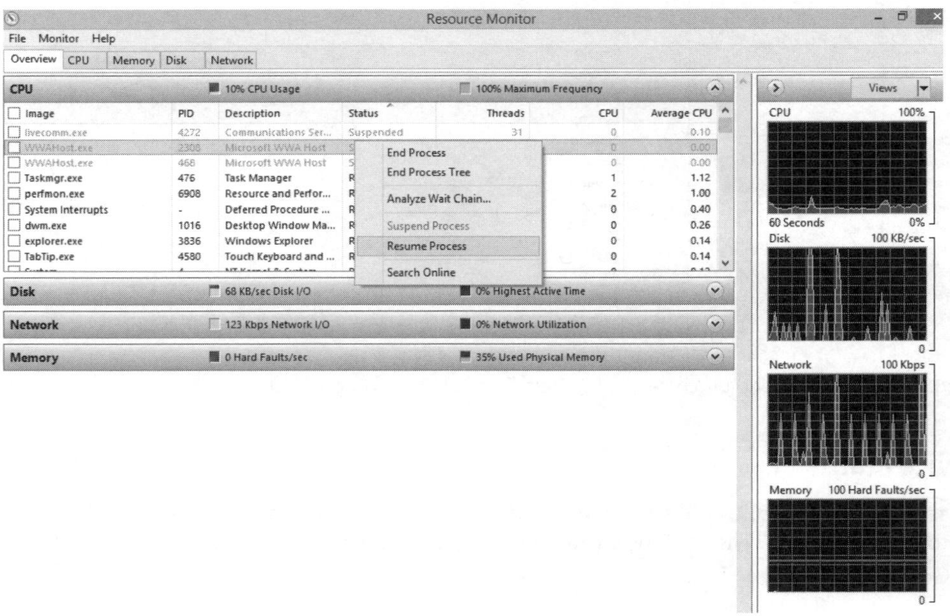

FIGURE 6-21 Resource Monitor lets you view real-time graphs for hardware components.

MORE INFO RESOURCE MONITOR TERMS YOU SHOULD KNOW

As you explore each tab, you'll see a lot of terms you'll need to know with regard to Resource Monitor, including PID (the Process ID of the application) and Commit (the amount of memory committed by an application). There's not enough space here to discuss all of these terms, so you'll have to take on that task yourself. You can learn about Resource Monitor from the TechNet article at *http://technet.microsoft.com/en-us/library/dd883276(WS.10).aspx*.

Configure indexing options

Windows 8.1 indexes the files, folders, documents, and other data on your computer so that the data can be found quickly when it's needed. By default, specific areas are indexed, including the data associated with users and application data you access often, such as Microsoft Office Outlook or Windows Sticky Notes. You can control what is indexed from the Indexing Options dialog box and add or remove locations to suit your needs. You'll need to do this if you store files on the hard drive where indexing doesn't occur by default or if areas are being indexed that don't require it. You can also reconfigure advanced settings from the Indexing Options dialog box to gain even more control. Type **Index** on the Start screen and click Indexing Options to see the Indexing Options dialog box shown in Figure 6-22.

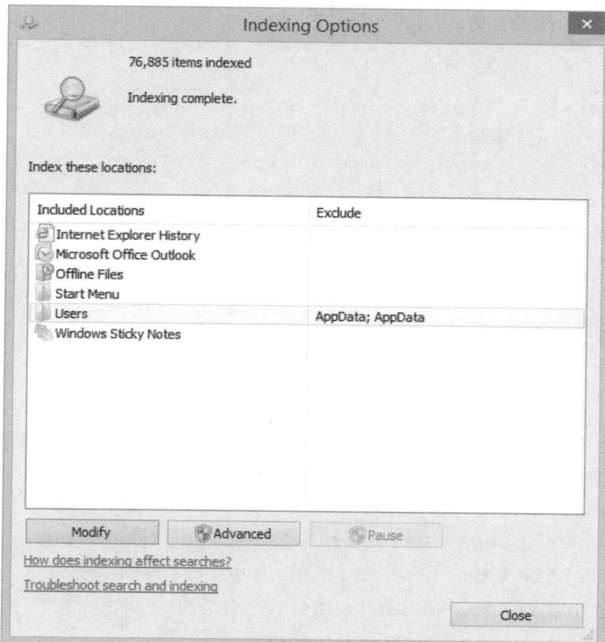

FIGURE 6-22 Data is indexed to decrease the amount of time it takes to retrieve data.

> ***NOTE*** **DON'T INDEX EVERYTHING**
>
> **Although you might think that indexing your entire hard disk would improve performance, it won't. The size of the index, which would then include things like program and application files, would hinder searches.**

When you click Modify in Figure 6-22, you can see exactly what's being indexed and you can click Show All Locations to see any locations that are hidden by default. From there you can clear the check boxes for items you feel don't require indexing. You can also click any right-facing arrow to see the subfolders available from the parent folder and from there you can add areas to index. Figure 6-23 shows this.

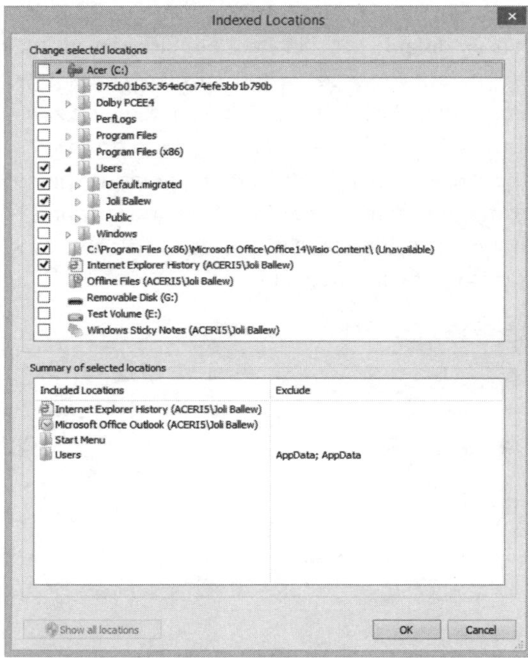

FIGURE 6-23 You can select what to index.

Finally, in the Indexing Options dialog box you can click Advanced. The Advanced Options dialog box has two tabs: Index Settings and File Types. The Index Settings tab lets you add or exclude encrypted files, treat similar words as different words, delete and rebuild the index (if it becomes corrupt), and change the index location. The File Types tab lets you exclude any type of file you want, and hundreds might be listed there. You can opt not to index files of a specific type or you can add file types that Windows doesn't currently list. Some programs create proprietary file formats that you'll need to add manually to index.

Configure and analyze event logs

Another way you can manage and maintain computer performance is to use Event Viewer to analyze Windows logs. These include Application, Security, Setup, System, and Forwarded Events. These logs can help you uncover problems that are difficult if not impossible to diagnose elsewhere.

You can launch Event Viewer in many ways, including searching for it from the Start screen, adding it as a snap-in to an MMC, and opening it from the Administrative Tools window or from the Computer Management console. You learned how to configure object access auditing in Chapter 4, "Configure access to resources," set alerts for the events when they occur, and more. Thus, you already know quite a bit about Event Viewer if you read this book from start to finish.

Each log you'll explore here offers information about events that occur and their importance. While reviewing logs, you'll see these levels of events:

- **Information** Events labeled as Information are normal events, but they have been logged to provide information about a change related to a component or process.
- **Error** These events warn that a problem has occurred, but the problem probably won't affect the performance of the component being called out. It might affect the performance of other components, though.
- **Warning** These events warn of problems that you might need to deal with (unless noted otherwise in the log entry). If they are not resolved, problems will likely ensue.
- **Critical** These events warn of catastrophic failure or loss of function of a component. These events must be addressed quickly.
- **Verbose** These events only provide information related to progress or successes and do not imply any problem has or might occur.

Like other lists you've seen so far, including the lists you viewed earlier in Task Manager, you can sort any log's entries by clicking any category title at the top of the log (such as Date And Time, Source, Level, and so on). Figure 6-24 shows the Application log.

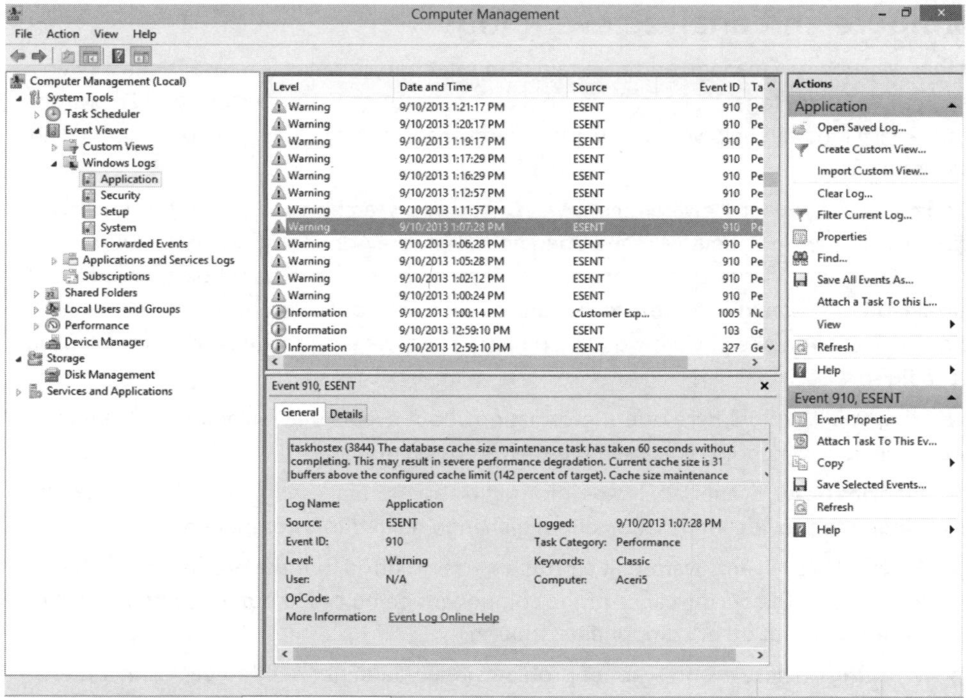

FIGURE 6-24 Event logs offer information about events, including what level event has occurred.

Make sure you are familiar with the default logs:

- **Application** This log contains entries related to applications installed on the computer.
- **Security** This log contains entries related to security events, including successes and failures due to audited events. The events that are recorded are configured through audit policies in local computer policies and Group Policy.
- **Setup** This log contains entries that apply to system installation and setup history.
- **System** This log contains entries that have to do with the operating system. Entries might have to do with the failure of a service or a device driver that doesn't start when it should.
- **Forwarded Events** This log contains events you create yourself using subscriptions. You'll learn how to create a subscription later in this section.

You'll want to explore Event Viewer and make sure you understand what is available from the interface, how to configure different views, how to create custom views, how to add and remove columns using those views, and so on. The Actions pane also offers tools with which you need to be familiar, including but not limited to saving a log, clearing a log, opening a saved log, and attaching a task to an event. Like other areas of this book, there is simply too much to cover here, and thus it's up to you to learn what's available on your own. However, for the sake of completeness, here are the steps required to create a custom view that shows only Critical events created in the System log.

To create a custom view in Event Viewer, follow these steps:

1. Open Event Viewer.
2. Click the Action menu and click Create Custom View.
3. On the Filter tab, for Event Level, select Critical (you could select additional entries).
4. From the By Log option, in the Event Logs window, click the down arrow, expand Windows Logs, and select the System check box (you could select additional entries as well).
5. Click outside the drop-down list to hide it.
6. Optionally, include entries for Keywords, User, or Computer(s); click OK. See Figure 6-25.

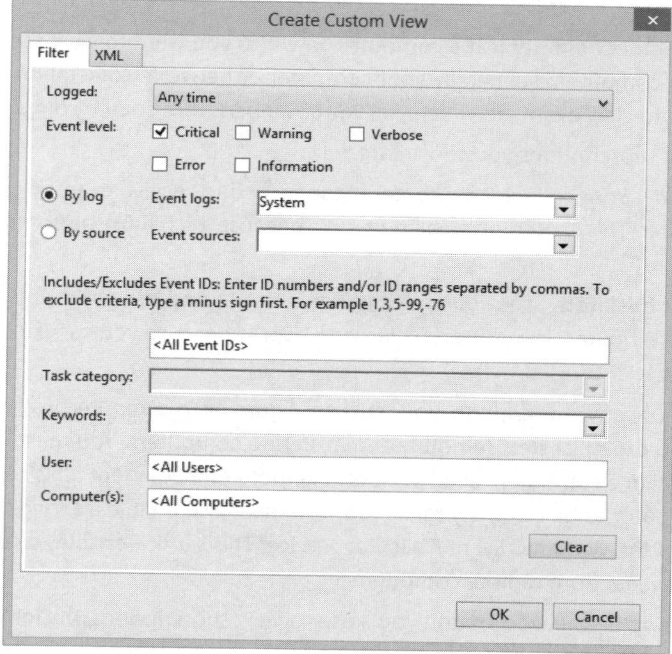

FIGURE 6-25 Create a custom log.

7. Type a name for the log (perhaps Critical System) and click OK.
8. Note any entries.

Configure event subscriptions

You can use Event Viewer for more than sorting already-logged events on a local computer or creating custom views. When you add the Event Viewer snap-in to an MMC, you can also opt to view other computers' event logs. As you've likely experienced, though, these logs (whether they are local or on remote computers) are cumbersome because they contain so many entries. When you only want to receive information about specific events from other computers, you create event subscriptions. There are a few terms to know first, though:

- **Subscription** A subscription is a group of events you configure that meet specific criteria you name. You configure subscriptions so you can receive events from other computers called sources.
- **Source** A source computer is the computer from which you want to obtain events. A source computer is generally a workstation on your network that you need to manage remotely. You name the remote computer when you configure the Event Viewer snap-in.
- **Collector** A collector computer is the computer on which you want to view the events. A collector computer is generally your computer or network workstation—the one where you go to view events to which you've subscribed from source computers.

There are two kinds of subscriptions you can create:

- **Collector initiated** Your collector computer is configured to receive events from the source computer. This is used on small networks because each must be configured manually.
- **Source computer initiated** The source computer is configured to send events from it to the collector computer. This is used on large networks because you can use Group Policy to configure it.

Before you can configure any subscription, you must configure both computers to run the required services. You can't just start remotely administering computers. You must first enable a service on the source computer called Windows Remote Management. This service enables the remote computer to be remotely managed. You must also enable a service on the collector computer called the Windows Event Collector service. This service enables a collector computer to collect events from remote computers.

On your collector computer, the workstation you'll use to view subscriptions, perform the following steps:

1. Open an elevated command prompt.
2. Type **wecutil qc** and press Enter.
3. Type **Y** and press Enter when prompted to start the service.

   Note the entry: Windows Event Collector service was configured successfully.
4. Close the command prompt window.

On the source computer, the workstation from which you'll collect events, follow these steps:

1. Open an elevated command prompt.
2. Type **winrm quickconfig** and press Enter.
3. Type **Y** and press Enter when prompted; repeat when prompted.

   Note the entry: WinRM firewall exception enabled.
4. Close the command prompt window.

EXAM TIP

For event log subscriptions to be successfully configured, the firewalls on both must be configured to allow traffic on TCP port 80 for HTTP or on TCP port 443 for HTTPS.

Recall that you can create two kinds of subscriptions: collector initiated and source computer initiated. Follow these steps to create a source computer–initiated subscription:

1. Open Event Viewer.
2. Right-click the Subscriptions node and click Create Subscription.
3. Type a name for the subscription.
4. Select Source Computer-Initiated and click Select Computer Groups. See Figure 6-26.

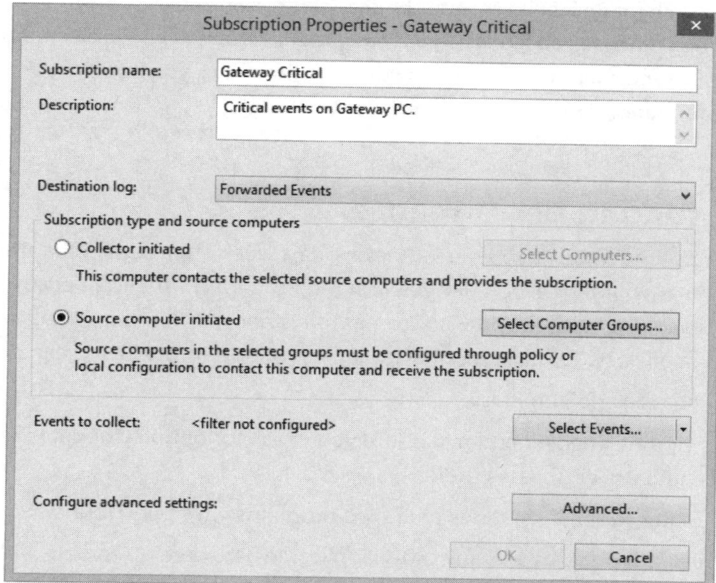

FIGURE 6-26 Create a source computer–initiated subscription.

5. Click either Add Domain Computers or Add Non-Domain Computers as applicable.

6. Enter a computer name and click OK. What you must do here depends on your choice in step 5.
7. If prompted, perform additional steps, such as adding a certificate, entering credentials, and so on.
8. Click Select Events (shown in Figure 6-26).
9. Select Critical in Event Level, choose the desired logs to monitor, add keywords, and so on, as detailed earlier during the creation of Custom Logs.
10. Click OK and click OK again.

After you complete the process to create a source computer–initiated subscription, you must then enable the source computers to forward their events. The setting is in Group Policy, from Computer Configuration, Policies, Administrative Templates, Windows Components, Event Forwarding. You'll enable the Configure Target Subscription Manager and input the applicable information there.

EXAM TIP

There are a lot more tools than those detailed in this chapter for managing computer performance. You should review all of the available tools before taking the exam. One way to access some of them is to open Administrative Tools. From there, explore Resource Monitor and Performance Monitor in depth, as well as System Configuration and System Information. Also, search for Reliability Monitor on the Start screen and click View Reliability History. This is where you'll review your computer's reliability and problem history. Finally, make sure you check out the Windows Experience Index; you can find this in the Performance Information And Tools window in Control Panel.

Optimize networking performance

Users expect network uptime to be at 100 percent, every day, week after week, year after year. This might be one of your biggest challenges with regard to performance, because when the network is down, everyone notices and work comes to a standstill. You must maintain network components at all costs to make sure network performance is the best it can be.

There are a few things to keep in mind:

- Keep Windows Update enabled and make sure you check for optional updates regularly. You might find driver updates there.
- Check Action Center to see if solutions to known problems have been found.
- Keep the routers and modems and any other applicable hardware up to date with firmware and read-only memory (ROM) updates.
- If Ethernet is used, make sure cables are in good condition and away from the users' chairs, desks, and other places where they might get damaged.

- For Wi-Fi, check the positioning of access points occasionally to make sure they are placed optimally.
- Keep network hardware away from anything that can interfere with its signals, which includes other electronics that give off radio signals, walls, and energy sources.
- Update hardware when substantially better devices become available (routers, modems, cabling, network cards, and so on).
- Know what tools are available to troubleshoot network problems and rank them from the simplest to the most complex. During troubleshooting sessions, start with the easiest solutions and work your way through your list.

In addition, before trying any troubleshooting that involves wizards or tools, check for these common issues:

- A broken, loose, or otherwise damaged cable
- A nonfunctioning network card
- A nonfunctioning power supply or power outlet
- A virus
- A new device driver that failed or a bad device driver
- Improperly configured firewall, security, Group Policy, and other settings
- Unexpected (or expected) data traffic surges, such as when all users log on to their workstations at 8 A.M.
- Outages with the Internet service provider (ISP)

Basic troubleshooting tools

You are likely familiar with the most basic troubleshooting tools available in Windows. There is an icon on the taskbar that will show when a network is unavailable. You can right-click the network icon in the taskbar to access the troubleshooting wizards (click Troubleshoot Problems) or to open the Network And Sharing Center. When you choose the former, the Windows Network Diagnostics Wizard opens and lets you state what type of problem you're having if Windows doesn't detect it automatically (Figure 6-27). The latter opens the Network And Sharing Center where you can review the most basic configurations, including whether the computer is connected to the Internet, part of a homegroup, part of a public or private network, and so on.

If the Windows Network Diagnostics Wizard doesn't solve your problem, there are still a few options you can try before you turn to the more advanced tools. Return to Chapter 3, "Configure network connectivity," and review the options that enable you to reconfigure IP settings, networking settings, or change the network location; configure name resolution; and use command-line tools such as Ping, IPconfig, Netsh, and others to troubleshoot problems.

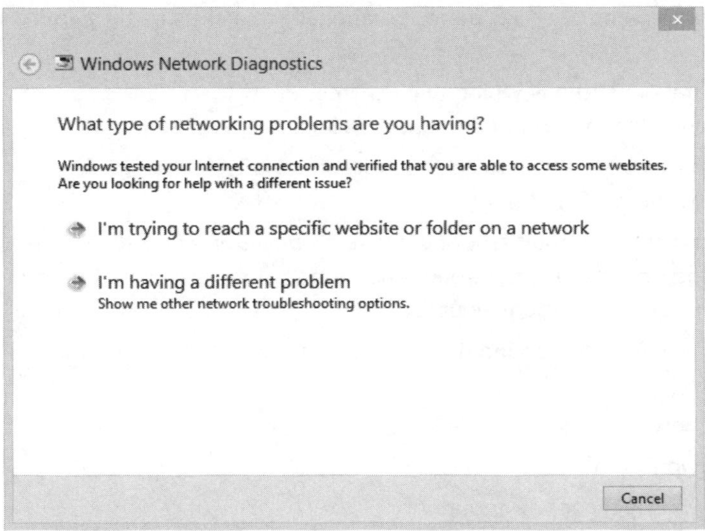

FIGURE 6-27 The Windows Network Diagnostics Wizard lets you state the type of problem you're having.

Performance Monitor

Performance Monitor (Perfmon.exe) lets you view your computer's current performance. What you see is a snapshot, but you can use the information to uncover otherwise difficult-to-diagnose networking problems. For instance, you can monitor very specific performance data related to both the network adapter and the network interface. You can also monitor statistics related to the physical network interface card activity. You can monitor TCP/IP performance diagnostics, too, among other things. You create your own personal console views by adding counters for only the statistics you want to watch.

To understand what counters are available to add, open Performance Monitor and browse what's available by following these steps:

1. In a Run dialog box, type **perfmon.exe** and press Enter.
2. In the left pane, click Performance Monitor. Note the single counter already configured: %ProcessorTime.
3. Right-click inside the graph and click Add Counters. See Figure 6-28.

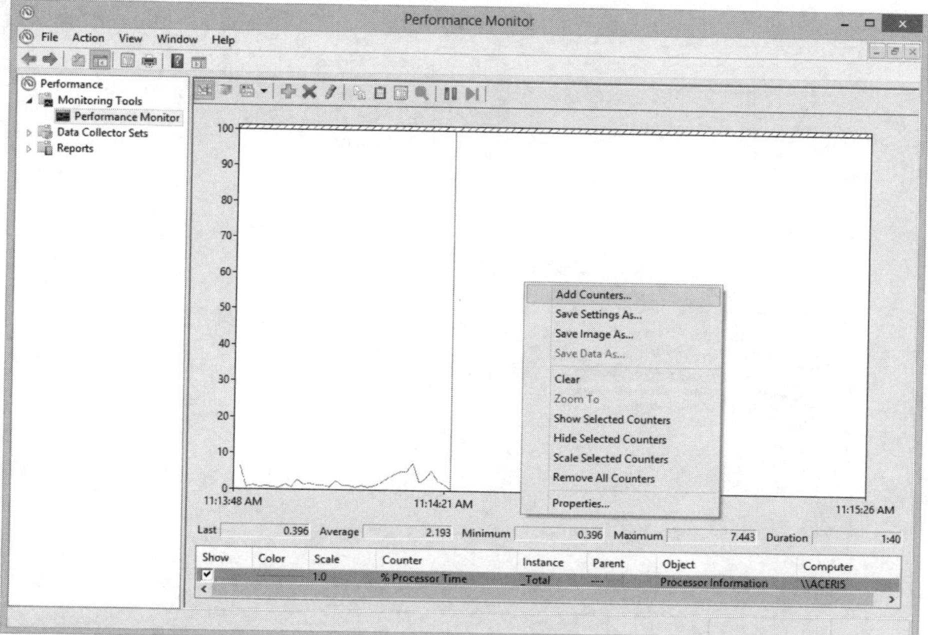

FIGURE 6-28 Add counters to choose what statistics to monitor.

4. Although you could browse to a different computer, verify Local Computer is selected in the Select Counters From Computer window.
5. In the window under Local Computer, click the arrow beside Network Interface.
6. Click Bytes Total/sec. See Figure 6-29.
7. Click Add.
8. If desired, select an option under Instances Of Selected Objects.
9. Repeat to add any other counters you'd like to review.
10. Click OK when finished.

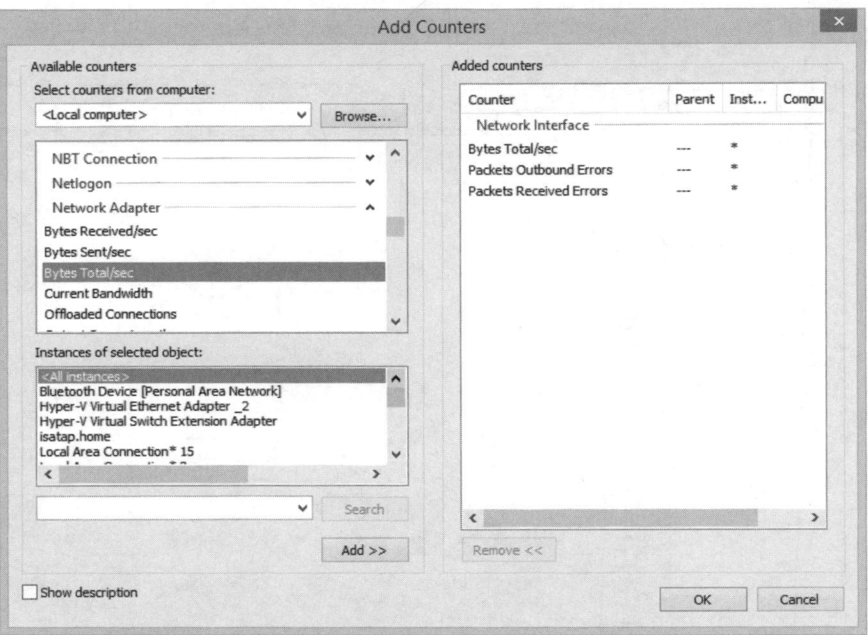

FIGURE 6-29 Add counters to choose what statistics to monitor.

11. Inside the graph, click any line to see what it represents; in the list underneath the graph, click any line to see its representation on the graph.
12. Deselect any counter instance to hide it on the graph.
13. Right-click inside the graph to configure properties, save the image, remove all counters, and more.

> ***MORE INFO*** **COUNTERS IN PERFORMANCE MONITOR**
>
> **For more information about the available counters in Performance Monitor, review this TechNet article: *http://technet.microsoft.com/en-us/library/cc749249.aspx*.**

There's a lot more you can learn about Performance Monitor, including how to create Data Collector Sets. A Data Collector Set can be used to monitor multiple data collections that can be incorporated into logs. You can configure the data collected so that Performance Monitor will generate alerts when thresholds are reached. To learn more about Data Collector Sets, refer to this TechNet article: *http://technet.microsoft.com/en-us/library/cc749337.aspx*. Beyond that you can create user-defined reports and view system reports. You can review Event Trace Sessions. *Event trace data* is collected from trace providers, which are components of the operating system or of individual applications that report actions or events. Output from multiple trace providers can be combined into a *trace session*.

As you can see, there's quite a bit to Performance Monitor, and too much to discuss here. However, there are many resources available on the Internet, specifically from TechNet and MSDN. Make sure you familiarize yourself with this tool and the terms related to it before taking the exam.

Thought experiment

Monitor computers remotely

In this thought experiment, apply what you've learned about this objective. You can find answers to these questions in the "Answers" section at the end of this chapter.

You notice that a computer on your small business network is having performance problems. You suspect that this has to do with a desktop application you've recently installed. You want to monitor the computer remotely, specifically looking for errors that occur because of this application. Answer the following questions to state how you'd do this.

1. **What snap-in will you need to add to an MMC to access these kinds of errors on a remote computer?**
2. **What kind of subscription would you create to best obtain the data on your small business network?**
3. **What command must you enter on the source computer to enable Windows Remote Management?**
4. **What command must you enter on the collector computer to enable the Windows Event Collector service?**
5. **If you have problems with this event subscription, what ports must be enabled in the firewall to allow TCP, HTTP, and/or HTTPS traffic?**

Objective summary

- There are many ways to improve and troubleshoot performance using tools such as Task Manager, Reliability Manager, Resource Monitor, and Performance Monitor, among others.
- You can manage computers remotely using the Event Viewer snap-in and enabling the applicable services on all affected computers.
- Files are indexed so that they are easier to locate; you can configure how indexing works and add or delete file types and folders as desired.

Objective review

Answer the following questions to test your knowledge of the information in this objective. You can find the answers to these questions and explanations of why each answer choice is correct or incorrect in the "Answers" section at the end of this chapter.

1. Which tab of Task Manager would be most helpful in determining an overloaded CPU?
   - **A.** App History
   - **B.** Performance
   - **C.** Startup
   - **D.** Users
   - **E.** Services
2. You use an application that saves files in a proprietary file format in a file folder it created on the root drive. You want to index these files. How do you do this?
   - **A.** There is no need to do this. All file types are indexed by default. You can exclude files if desired, though.
   - **B.** In the Indexing Options dialog box, click Modify. Then, click the File Types tab. Add the file type to index there.
   - **C.** In the Indexing Options dialog box, right-click inside the Index These Locations window. Add the root drive as a location.
   - **D.** In the Indexing Options dialog box, click Advanced. From there, click the File Types tab. Add the file type to index there.
3. Which of the following Windows logs in Event Viewer do not have anything in them by default? (Choose all that apply.)
   - **A.** Application
   - **B.** Security
   - **C.** Setup
   - **D.** System
   - **E.** Forwarded Events
4. In Performance Monitor, what counter is always available in the Performance Monitor graph before any counters are added?
   - **A.** No counters are added by default.
   - **B.** Bytes Total/Sec
   - **C.** % Processor Time
   - **D.** Current Bandwidth

Chapter summary

- You must strive to keep your computers up to date with Windows Updates. In doing so you have additional tools at your disposal, including the ability to apply Group Policies, roll back problematic updates, configure update settings, and so on.
- You can use Disk Management to manage hard disks, disk volumes, and file systems. When you need more options than Disk Management offers, you can use Diskpart, a command-line utility for configuring and managing disks.
- Check Disk, Disk Defragmenter, Action Center, Disk Cleanup, and other tools help you maintain disks once they are configured and healthy.
- Task Manager is a powerful tool for end users and network administrators and enables you to end processes, view performance summaries, view app history and usage history, configure applications to start or not when Windows does, view logged-on users and the computer resources they are using, and so on.
- Other tools, including Performance Monitor, can help you troubleshoot network problems when traditional and more common solutions can't be found.
- Storage Spaces enables you to create a storage pool using various kinds of external disks including SATA drives and USB flash drives, among others.

Answers

This section contains the solutions to the thought experiments and answers to the objective review questions in this chapter.

Objective 6.1: Thought experiment

1. A WSUS server
2. Specify Intranet Microsoft Update Service Location
3. Computer Configuration, Administrative Templates, Windows Components, Windows Update

Objective 6.1: Review

1. **Correct Answer**: C
   - **A. Incorrect**: It is possible to remove the prompt to upgrade to Windows 8.1 in the Windows Store.
   - **B. Incorrect**: You can configure whether apps are updated automatically from the Settings charm while in the Store, but this is not a place where you can remove specific app updates from the Store.
   - **C. Correct**: You must set a Group Policy to remove that option here: Computer Configuration, Administrative Templates, Windows Components, Store.
   - **D. Incorrect**: You can control the Store using AppLocker in an Active Directory domain, but you don't have to do so in this instance.
2. **Correct Answer**: B
   - **A. Incorrect**: Windows Updates can include device drivers.
   - **B. Correct**: Standard users can install drivers that have been downloaded from Windows Update without a UAC prompt.
   - **C. Incorrect**: This is true: not all updates are installed even if you choose Install Updates Automatically (Recommended) from the Windows Update, Change Settings options.
   - **D. Incorrect**: This is true: you can use PC Settings, Update and Recovery to quickly see if a client machine is configured to receive updates.
3. **Correct Answer**: C
   - **A. Incorrect**: Change Settings lets you change how and when updates are downloaded and installed.
   - **B. Incorrect**: View Update History lets you view and sort updates by type, name, date, and other options, but offers no way to uninstall an update.

C. **Correct**: Installed Updates is where you can uninstall a specific update.

D. **Incorrect**: View Update History can't be used to uninstall unwanted updates.

4. **Correct Answer**: A

   A. **Correct**: When enabled, Windows Update will wake up a system to install the updates. If Windows Update wakes the system but discovers it is running on battery power, it will go back into hibernation in two minutes and will not install any updates.

   B. **Incorrect**:. When enabled, Windows Update will wake up a system to install the updates. If Windows Update wakes the system but discovers it is running on battery power, it will not install the updates; instead, it will go back into hibernation mode.

   C. **Incorrect**: When enabled, Windows Update will wake up a system to install the updates even if it is running on battery power.

   D. **Incorrect**: When enabled, Windows Update will wake up a system to install the updates.

Objective 6.2: Thought experiment

1. Mirrored. Simple does not support any fault tolerance, nor do striped or spanned disks. RAID-5 isn't supported in Windows 8.1. That leaves mirrored, which will write the data two times, once to each disk. Although this will cause a performance hit, the client is not worried about this.
2. No.
3. They must be the same size.
4. The basic disks will be converted to dynamic disks.

Objective 6.2: Review

1. **Correct Answer:** D

   A. **Incorrect**: You cannot create an 8 TB three-way mirror because you can't use the disk with the operating system on it as part of the storage space. Thus, you only have two disks to work with.

   B. **Incorrect**: You cannot create a three-way mirror because you can't use the disk with the operating system on it as part of the storage space.

   C. **Incorrect**: You cannot create a three-way parity because you can't use the disk with the operating system on it as part of the storage space.

   D. **Correct**: You can create a 4 TB two-way mirror.

   E. **Incorrect**: You can create a two-way mirror that is larger than the capacity of the connected drives.

2. **Correct Answer**: A
   - **A. Correct**: Diskpart with the appropriate parameters can completely wipe the drive and partition table.
   - **B. Incorrect**: Fsutil can't be used to remove the files from the drive.
   - **C. Incorrect**: Format lets you remove the data but does nothing with regard to the disk volumes and related partition tables.
   - **D. Incorrect**: Format is not a valid option. Format lets you remove the data but does nothing with regard to the disk volumes and related partition tables.
3. **Correct Answer**: B
   - **A. Incorrect**: Fsutil is used to manage reparse points and dismount volumes.
   - **B. Correct**: Chkdsk (Check Disk) scans for hard disk errors including bad storage blocks and attempts to repair them automatically.
   - **C. Incorrect**: Disk Cleanup lets users safely delete temporary files, downloaded program installation files, and more to maintain a hard drive.
   - **D. Incorrect**: Disk Defragmenter runs automatically in the background and is used to move fragmented files closer together so they are stored on contiguous hard drive sectors.
   - **E. Incorrect**: Diskpart is used to create bootable USB drives, to create boot partitions, to manage drives, and to wipe files from drives, among other things.
   - **F. Incorrect**: The Disk Management snap-in is used to manage installed drives and can be used to extend and shrink volumes, among other things.
4. **Correct Answer**: B
   - **A. Incorrect**: Dynamic disks configured as spanned volumes is a type of solution, but data is written sequentially onto the disks, which does nothing to improve the write time.
   - **B. Correct**: Dynamic disks configured as striped volumes will write data in stripes to each disk (one disk at a time), increasing the write time.
   - **C. Incorrect**: Only dynamic disks can be configured as mirrored volumes. However, mirrored volumes actually slow down the write time because data is written twice, once to each disk.
   - **D. Incorrect**: Basic disks configured as primary volumes are just normal disks. This does not improve write time.
   - **E. Incorrect**: Although dynamic disks can be configured as mirrored volumes, this does nothing to improve write time. In fact, data must be written two times, once to each disk, slowing write time.

Objective 6.3: Thought experiment

1. Event Viewer
2. Collector initiated
3. Winrm quickconfig
4. Wecutil qc
5. For event log subscriptions to be successfully configured, the firewalls on both must be configured to allow traffic on TCP port 80 for HTTP or on TCP port 443 for HTTPS.

Objective 6.3: Review

1. **Correct Answer:** B
   - **A. Incorrect:** The App History tab lists the available apps and information about data usage. Although it does have a tab for CPU, because it only offers information about apps and not all aspects of the system, it is not the proper choice.
   - **B. Correct:** The Performance tab offers an overview of CPU, Memory, Disk, Ethernet, Bluetooth, and Wi-Fi in the form of a graph. You can easily tell here if the CPU is overworked.
   - **C. Incorrect:** The Startup tab lists the applications configured to start when Windows does. It does not offer a CPU tab.
   - **D. Incorrect:** The Users tab shows who is logged on and what apps, services, and applications are running. Although it offers a CPU tab, what is shown there only relates to the selected user, not the entire system.
   - **E. Incorrect:** The Services tab lists services and does not offer a CPU tab.
2. **Correct Answer:** D
   - **A. Incorrect:** All file types are not indexed by default, only those that Windows recognizes.
   - **B. Incorrect:** You must click the Advanced option to add file types to the indexing list.
   - **C. Incorrect:** This is not how you add areas of the hard drive to index. Additionally, it would be a bad idea to index the entire root drive.
   - **D. Correct:** In the Indexing Options dialog box, click Advanced. From there, click the File Types tab. Add the file type to index there.
3. **Correct Answer:** E
   - **A. Incorrect:** Application does contain events.
   - **B. Incorrect:** Security does contain events.
   - **C. Incorrect:** Setup does contain events.

- **D. Incorrect:** System does contain events.
- **E. Correct:** Forwarded Events does not have any entries by default. You must choose the events you want to appear here by creating subscriptions.

4. **Correct Answer:** C
   - **A. Incorrect:** One counter is added by default: % Processor Time.
   - **B. Incorrect:** Bytes Total/Sec is not shown by default and must be added from Network Adapter or Network Interface.
   - **C. Correct:** % Processor Time is added by default.
   - **D. Incorrect:** Current Bandwidth is not shown by default and must be added from Network Adapter or Network Interface.

CHAPTER 7

Configure system and data options

In this chapter, you'll learn about system and data recovery options as they relate to the exam. Most of these tasks are performed by using wizards, and thus won't require too much instruction. They are covered on the exam, though, so you'll need to work through all of the wizards when instructed to do so here. You might already be familiar with many of the objectives, including but not limited to performing a device driver rollback, configuring System Restore, and recovering files from SkyDrive (which is being renamed OneDrive).

Objectives in this chapter:

- Objective 7.1: Configure system recovery
- Objective 7.2: Configure file recovery

Objective 7.1: Configure system recovery

System recovery involves, as you might guess, recovering from system failures. System failures can be caused by unstable device drivers and failed hard drives or by buggy or compromised third-party software, among other things. Sometimes resolving these problems is as simple as rolling back a device driver or using System Restore to return to a more stable date. When that doesn't work, you can let Windows apply automatic repairs. As you'll learn here, there are other recovery features available, including safe mode and boot logging, along with other familiar recovery options. You can also use a recovery drive you've created to resolve startup problems.

This objective covers how to:

- Perform a driver rollback
- Configure a recovery drive
- Configure System Restore and create a restore point
- Perform a refresh or recycle

Perform a driver rollback

The option to perform a device driver rollback is available in Device Manager only after you install a newer device driver for a piece of hardware. The option is not available if the device has only had one driver and it was never updated. You will need to use this feature when a newly installed or upgraded device driver causes problems. Device driver rollback can only roll back to the driver installed before it and cannot be used to roll back to a driver that was installed previous to the last one or any before it.

To find the option to roll back a driver, open Device Manager, double-click the problematic device, click the Driver tab, and click Roll Back Driver, as shown in Figure 7-1, to perform the task.

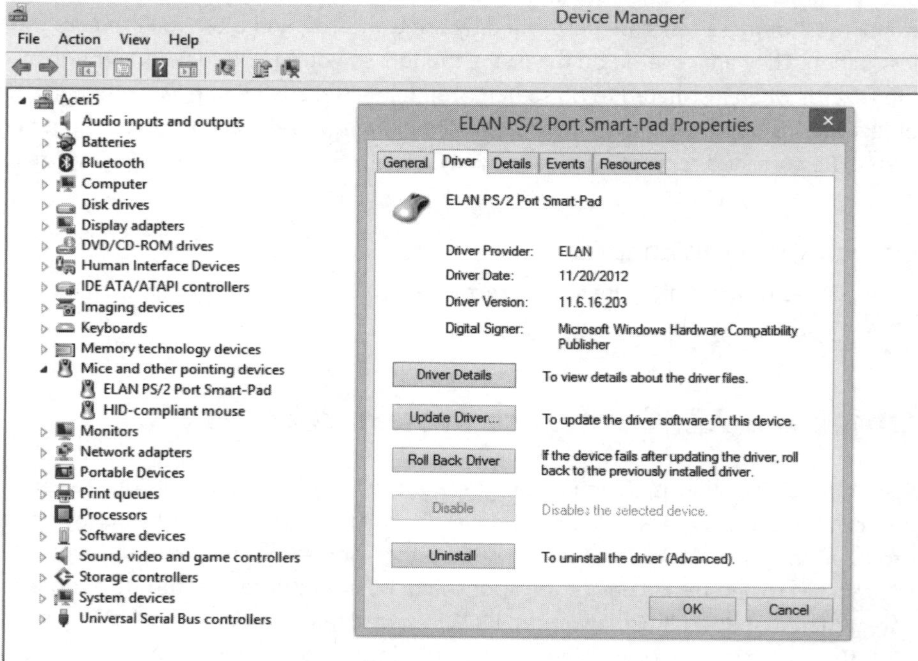

FIGURE 7-1 Use Device Manager to roll back a driver to the previous one.

Configure a recovery drive

A recovery drive can help you troubleshoot problems with your computer and recover from them even if it can't start. You create a recovery drive using a wizard available for that purpose. If your computer also has a recovery partition, you can copy that as well so that you can use it to refresh or restore your computer should the need arise. To get started, type **Recovery Drive** on the Start screen and click Create A Recovery Drive in the results.

EXAM TIP

If your computer does not have a recovery partition, the option to copy the recovery partition will be unavailable when creating a recovery drive. When this happens, the recovery drive will only include the recovery tools and a bootable image, not a recovery image you can use to refresh or reset the computer.

As you work through the Recovery Drive Wizard, you'll be prompted to include any available recovery partitions created by the manufacturer, if desired. You'll also be prompted to choose a drive to save the information to. On a physical machine (in contrast to a virtual one), you must choose a USB drive that can hold at least 512 MB of data, but you can also use a CD or DVD. Whatever you choose, it must be available to format (because anything on the drive will be erased when you configure it for the recovery drive). The wizard will get the drive ready, format the drive, and copy utilities.

EXAM TIP

If your computer came with Windows 8 and you upgraded to Windows 8.1, any recovery drive you created while it was Windows 8 will have Windows 8 on it. Make sure to create a new recovery drive when you upgrade. 

Use Windows RE

Windows Recovery Environment (RE) can help you repair an operating system that won't boot. Windows RE is based on the Windows Preinstallation Environment (Windows PE) and offers troubleshooting and diagnostic tools. These include automatic repair options, push-button reset (detailed later), and system image recovery. By default, Windows RE is preloaded onto machines running Windows 8.1 and Windows Server 2012 R2.

You can access the Windows RE tools from the Boot Options menu, which you can launch in various ways including booting the computer using recovery media. You can also use the Update And Recovery tab of PC Settings, specifically the Recovery tab, where you'll find options to restart the computer (under Advanced Startup, click Restart Now). See Figure 7-2. Additionally, Windows RE will open automatically if the computer encounters any of the following:

- A BitLocker error on touch-only devices
- Two sequential failed attempts to start Windows
- Two unexpected shutdowns that occur within two minutes of boot completion and are consecutive
- A Secure Boot error (except for issues related to Bootmgr.efi)

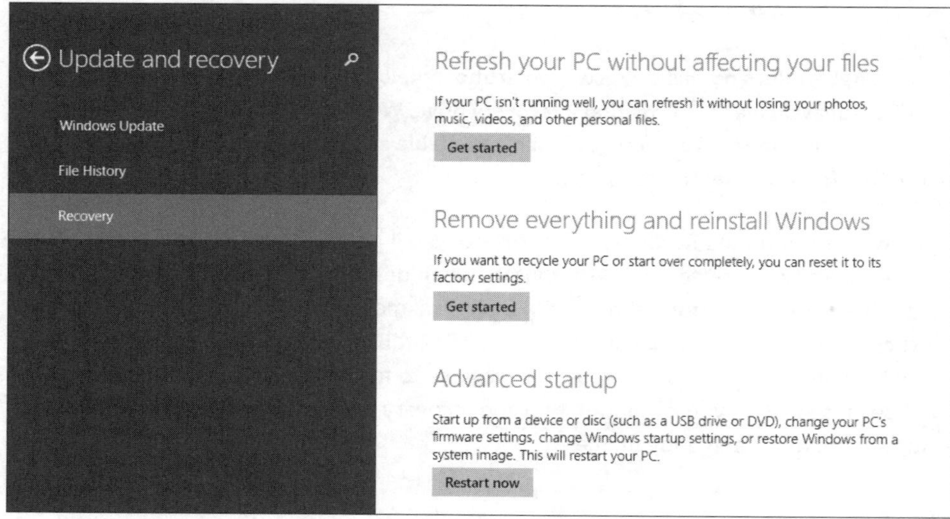

FIGURE 7-2 Click Restart Now under Advanced Startup to reboot the computer to have access to Windows RE options.

EXAM TIP

Last Known Good Configuration (LKGC) is no longer available in Windows 8.1 (however, LKGC can be accessed in Windows Server 2012 by pressing the F8 key during startup).

Use additional recovery tools

You can use Msconfig.exe and its Boot tab to opt to boot into safe mode when the computer restarts. Other options exist, including but not limited to No GUI Boot and Boot Log. Make sure you know how to use the System Configuration tool to disable services, change the startup type, configure boot options, and so on. System Configuration is shown in Figure 7-3. (Remember, if you click the Startup tab you don't see options that enable you to choose what applications boot with Windows; you only see the option to go to Task Manager to perform that task.)

MORE INFO **LEARN MORE ABOUT THE WINDOWS RE ENVIRONMENT**

Make sure you understand the options available in Windows RE and how to access them. Learn more here: *http://technet.microsoft.com/en-us/library/hh825173.aspx*. To learn how to perform tasks, including how to add a custom tool to the Windows RE Boot Options menu and how to deploy Windows RE, refer to this article: *http://technet.microsoft.com/en-us/library/hh824896.aspx*.

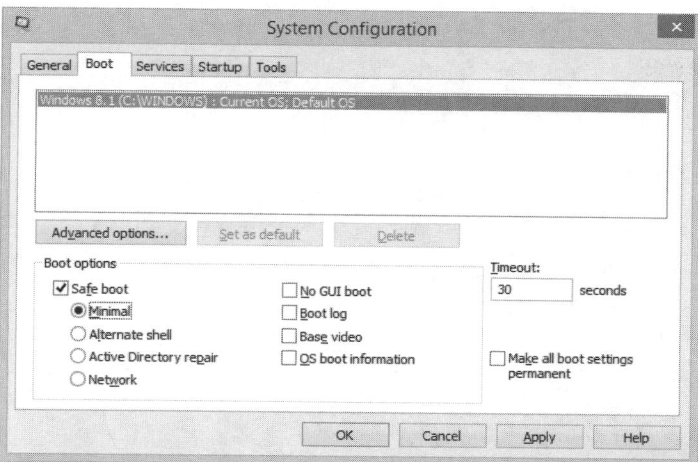

FIGURE 7-3 Choose Restart Now under Advanced Startup to reboot the computer to have access to choose from Windows RE options.

Configure System Restore and create a restore point

You can use System Restore to restore a computer to a previous time when it was stable. System Restore keeps restore points, and they are created automatically if the feature is enabled. You should try System Restore before you try solutions that are more destructive, such as restoring a computer to its factory settings. You can access System Restore by typing **Create a Restore Point** on the Start screen and clicking it in the results. In the System Properties dialog box, click Create to create a new restore point. Click Configure to see the configuration options. System Restore will be unavailable on drives that are not NTFS.

EXAM TIP

There are some Windows PowerShell cmdlets you can use to manage System Restore, and they often include "ComputerRestore" in the cmdlet itself. Review cmdlets such as Enable-ComputerRestore, Disable-ComputerRestore, Get-ComputerRestorePoint, and so on before you take the exam. You can find these and others here: *http://technet.microsoft.com/en-us/library/hh849785.aspx*. Additionally, you might see questions that ask about command-line utilities for controlling System Restore. Make sure to review Vssadmin, where VSS stands for Volume Shadow Copy, which is used to manage restore points.

As you can see in Figure 7-4, you can opt to turn on or off system protection (System Restore) and change how much disk space you want to use to keep restore points. You can also create your own restore points manually when you are considering doing something you feel might compromise the machine, such as installing an untested device driver. When you use System Restore, available from the boot options, you choose the desired restore point.

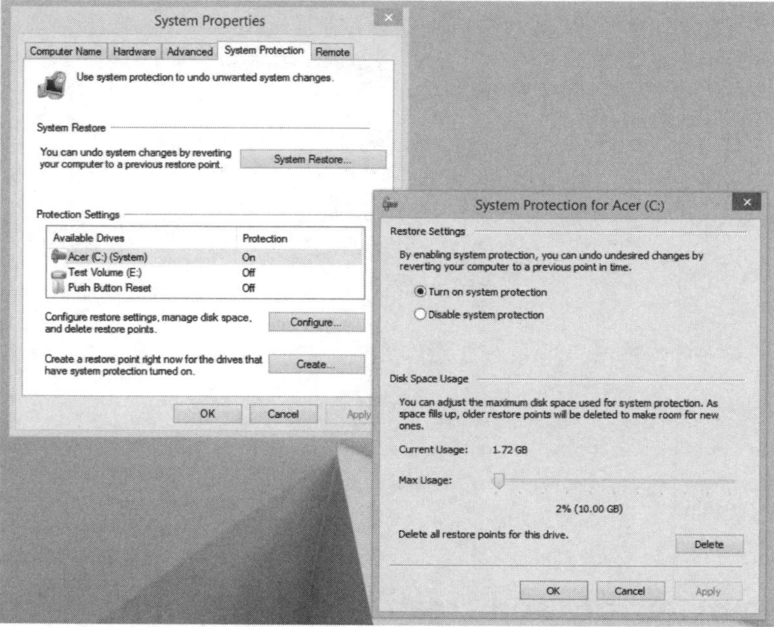

FIGURE 7-4 Configure System Restore properties in the System Properties dialog box.

EXAM TIP

Make sure you know how to create a system image backup. This is an option in the File History window under Control Panel, All Control Panel Items. A system image is a copy of the drives required for Windows to run and can include additional drives if you desire. You can use this system image to restore your computer if your hard drive fails. With an image, though, you can't pick and choose files to restore. It's all or nothing.

Perform a refresh or recycle

When the computer is so damaged that System Restore doesn't resolve the problem, rolling back disruptive device drivers isn't effective or warranted, and you've tried other options available in Windows RE including attempting automatic repairs, booting into safe mode, and so on, you will likely need to refresh (push-button refresh) or recycle your computer. (Recycle is the new word for a reset, although the interface options still refer to the process as resetting your PC.) Of course, in an Active Directory directory service domain you will likely just push out a system image using domain-related tools, but in the case of stand-alone workstations and small organizations, refresh and recycle generally get the job done.

EXAM TIP

If you want to keep your settings and traditional applications during a refresh, you need to use a utility called Recimg.exe to capture an image of your computer after you've installed applications and made customizations. Then if you ever need to perform a refresh later, that image is used and your settings and applications are retained.

You'll find these two tools in PC Settings, under Update And Recovery. Both tools and the option to boot into Advanced Startup mode are available, as well as the option to use Advanced Startup. These options were shown earlier in Figure 7-2. The three options are defined here:

- **Refresh Your PC Without Affecting Your Files** Choose this option to remove third-party programs, Internet Explorer add-ons, printer and scanner software, and so on. You won't lose any personal files. This resolves most problems.
- **Remove Everything And Reinstall Windows** Choose this option when you want to recycle your PC or to start over completely. This resets the computer to factory settings and removes all personal data.
- **Advanced Startup** This option is neither a refresh nor a recycle; instead, it restarts the computer into the Windows RE environment where you can start your computer from a device or disk, change firmware settings, change Windows startup settings, or restore Windows from a system image.

EXAM TIP

Make sure you know what happens when you reboot the PC using Advanced Startup under PC Settings, Update And Recovery, on the Recovery tab. There are many options, some of which are outlined here from Microsoft: *http://windows.microsoft.com/en-us/windows-8/windows-startup-settings-including-safe-mode*. A more thorough description of Windows RE troubleshooting features is available here: *http://technet.microsoft.com/en-us/library/hh824837.aspx*. You'll be expected to know these features.

Thought experiment

Troubleshooting startup issues

In this thought experiment, apply what you've learned about this objective. You can find answers to these questions in the "Answers" section at the end of this chapter.

You support a small business with eight computers. You get a call that one of the computers won't boot. The user has a lot of installed programs and quite a bit of data. The data is backed up to an external drive and is well organized, so data recovery isn't an issue. The user has a recovery disk. Answer the following questions with regard to how you'd resolve the problem.

1. **Would you opt for a push-button reset to resolve the problem before trying other options? Why or why not?**
2. **Would you insert and boot using the recovery disk? Why or why not?**
3. **Would you opt to use the recycle option in PC Settings to restore the computer to factory settings? Why or why not?**

Objective summary

- If you suspect a newly installed or updated device driver is causing problems, you can roll back to the previous device driver in Device Manager.
- You can create and then use a recovery drive to recover from startup problems. Windows RE offers many options for recovery, including but not limited to automatic repair, System Restore, and restore and recycle, among others.
- When you restore a computer, no personal files are affected, but third-party applications and Internet Explorer add-ons are removed. When you recycle a computer, you restore it to factory settings.

Objective review

Answer the following questions to test your knowledge of the information in this objective. You can find the answers to these questions and explanations of why each answer choice is correct or incorrect in the "Answers" section at the end of this chapter.

1. You are having problems with a hardware device installed inside your computer. You try to roll back the driver, but the option to do this is unavailable in the device's Properties dialog box in Device Manager. What is the problem?
   - **A.** You cannot install or roll back drivers for internal hardware.
   - **B.** The driver was updated but is configured by its creator in such a way that it cannot be rolled back.
   - **C.** The driver was not updated, and the problem is due to something else.
   - **D.** If the option to roll back the driver is not available, you need to opt to uninstall it.
2. You are creating a recovery drive. Which of the following is true with regard to the USB drive you select for storing the data?
   - **A.** The USB drive must be at least 1 GB in size.
   - **B.** If the USB drive has data on it, that data is safe.
   - **C.** Any USB drive must be formatted before you start the Recovery Drive Wizard.
   - **D.** None of the above.

3. You restart a computer, and it immediately has an unexpected error and reboots. On reboot, this happens again. What will happen the third time?
   - **A.** The Windows RE environment will open.
   - **B.** Windows will begin automatic repairs.
   - **C.** The computer will boot into safe mode.
   - **D.** The computer will shut down.
   - **E.** The computer will boot to LKGC.
   - **F.** The computer will boot into System Restore mode.
4. You perform a push-button reset from PC Settings by selecting Restart Now under Refresh Your PC Without Affecting Your Files. Which of the following folders are not disturbed on C, the local drive? (Choose all that apply.)
   - **A.** C:\Users*<your user name>*
   - **B.** C:\Program Files
   - **C.** C:\Windows
   - **D.** C:\PerfLogs
   - **E.** C:\MyPersonalDiary (a folder you created on the C drive)

Objective 7.2: Configure file recovery

Users must be able to recover files and folders when they become unavailable due to corruption, data loss, computer loss, and so on. There are many ways to achieve this. Home users might opt to run a simple backup program that stores data on an external drive; large corporations likely have users store their data on data servers and have an employee who is responsible for backing up and securing that data. Somewhere in the middle are a couple of other options: using SkyDrive and File History. These are the two backup options covered on the exam.

This objective covers how to:

- Recover files from SkyDrive (soon to be renamed OneDrive)
- Configure File History
- Restore previous versions of files and folders

NOTE

The name SkyDrive is changing to OneDrive and at some point the exam will also make the terminology change.

Recover files from SkyDrive

SkyDrive is an online repository for saving files. You can retrieve files stored there from just about any computer or device that has an Internet connection. There are a couple of ways you can recover files from SkyDrive that have gone missing. You can recover files from the Recycle Bin, and you can recover previous versions of existing files if they exist.

For now, you can only access the Recycle Bin from SkyDrive in a web browser, not from the SkyDrive Start screen app. As shown in Figure 7-5, the Restore All Items and Empty Recycle Bin options are available at the top. If you don't want to restore everything, which is what will happen by default if nothing is selected when you click Restore All Items or Empty Recycle Bin, you can select the check box next to each item you'd like to manage. We've sorted the data in the Recycle Bin by the date each was deleted, but there are other options.

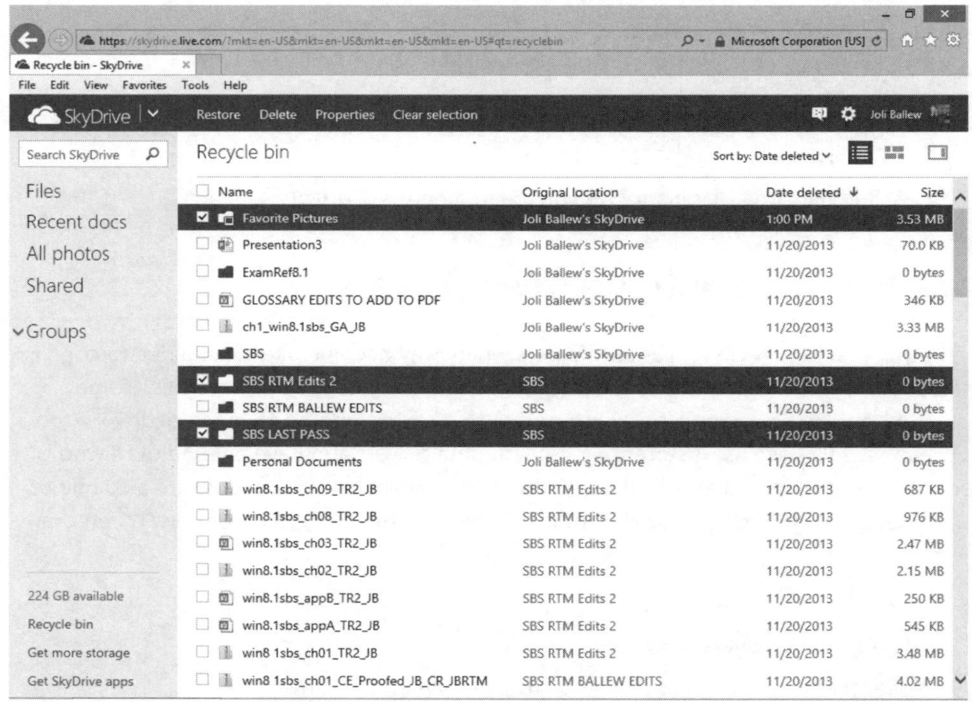

FIGURE 7-5 SkyDrive in a web browser offers access to the Recycle Bin.

You can also access previous versions of files in the SkyDrive window. Just right-click the file to recover and click Version History; this is shown in Figure 7-6. In the resulting window, you'll see a list of versions. To select one, just click it in the list.

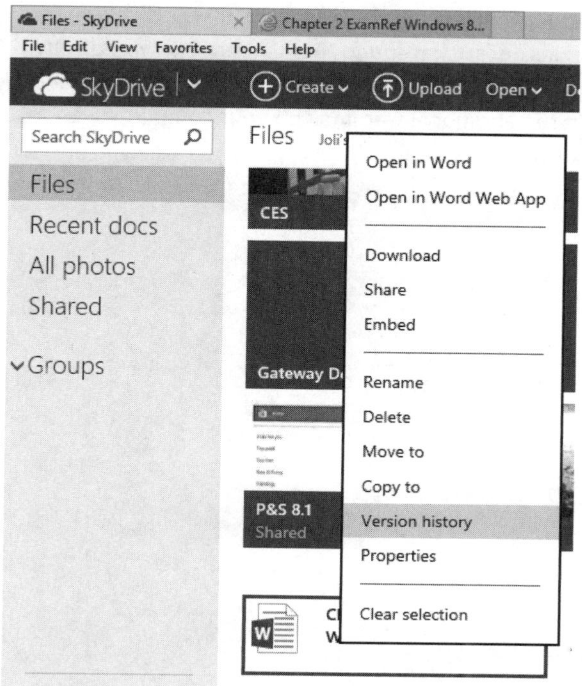

FIGURE 7-6 SkyDrive keeps previous versions of files that you can access.

> ***MORE INFO*** **LEARN MORE ABOUT SKYDRIVE**
>
> **You can learn more about SkyDrive on TechNet:** ***http://blogs.msdn.com/b/b8/archive/2012/04/23/the-next-chapter-for-skydrive-personal-cloud-storage-for-windows-available-anywhere.aspx*****. Make sure to search for SkyDrive Recycle Bin and SkyDrive Previous Versions to stay on top of new features as they become available.**

Configure File History

File History is the primary feature available in Windows 8.1 for backing up data. The alternative, Windows 7 File Recovery, is no longer an option (it was in Windows 8). Windows Backup And Restore isn't available either. Therefore, it's important to know about File History, including how to set it up and use it to restore files. It should not be your only backup method, though; make sure you have a complete backup system in place, which might include a system image, the use of SkyDrive, manual backups to external drives, or third-party backup software that runs on a schedule. In fact, it's best to use a combination of these.

You open File History by searching for it on the Start screen or in Control Panel. If you opt to show All Control Panel Items, File History is an icon there. In the File History window, you'll see several configuration options and perhaps a few warnings. Figure 7-7 shows this.

The first warning states that this particular PC is protected by BitLocker Drive Encryption, but File History is not; the second states that File History has found files that are encrypted with Encrypting File System (EFS), on a network location, or on a drive that doesn't use NTFS, and these files won't be backed up. You might see additional warnings on your computer. File History won't back up what's stored in SkyDrive, just as an FYI.

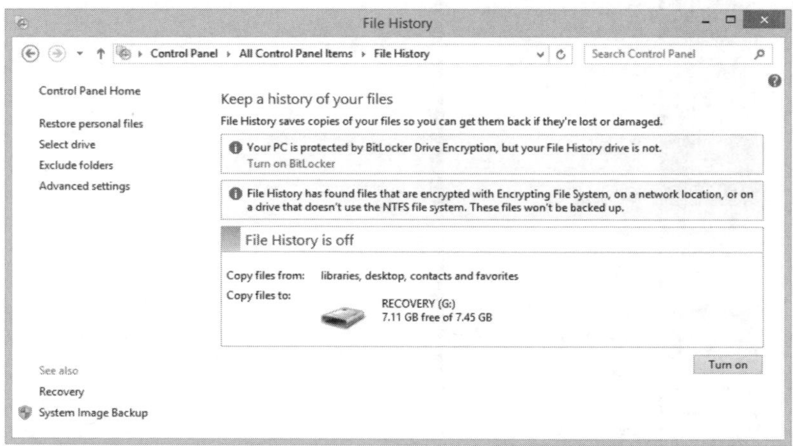

FIGURE 7-7 File History is the primary means of backup in Windows 8.1.

The left pane offers the following options:

- **Restore Personal Files** Use this option to recover files when necessary. You can select which files to restore, and you can choose the versions of them you want.
- **Select Drive** Use this option to select a drive or enter a network location for saving your File History data. File History can only be enabled if it detects an external drive to which to save data.
- **Exclude Folders** Use this option to view or add folders you do not want to include in File History.
- **Advanced Settings**
  - Some of the advanced settings options allow you to configure how long to save copies of files, the size of the offline cache, and how long to keep saved files. Know that if you opt to save files once a day instead of every hour, which is the default, you might find yourself in a position in which you can't restore the file you want to restore because it was not yet backed up. Make sure you review other defaults for the size of the offline cache (5 percent of disk space) and how long to keep saved versions (Forever).
  - You can opt to clean up versions saved in File History. You can choose the default, which is to delete files older than one year, or another option, such as older than one month, three months, and so on.

  - You can recommend the drive you've selected to use with File History data to homegroup users.
  - Using advanced settings, you can open File History event logs in Event Viewer to troubleshoot File History. If you see a question on the exam about these logs, note they are named FileHistory-Engine and FileHistory-Core. You might never need to do this; you'll be prompted by the Action Center when problems occur with File History, including disconnected or full drives and the inability of File History to run.
- **Recovery** Use this option to access advanced recovery tools, including creating a recovery drive, using System Restore, configuring System Restore, and to access restore options in PC Settings.
- **System Image Backup** Use this option to create a system image backup. This is an image of your computer, a copy of the drives that Windows uses to run. You should create a system image so that you can restore your computer if your hard drive or computer fails. This is an image, and it cannot be used to select specific files or folders.

EXAM TIP

There is one Group Policy you can configure for File History, which is to turn it off. You can find it under Computer Configuration, Administrative Templates, Windows Components, File History.

EXAM TIP

You can use the command-line utility FhManagew.exe to manage and clean up File History backups.

Although we could walk you through each of these options, the process is fairly self-explanatory. You will be prompted when you turn on File History (see Turn On as an option in the lower-right corner of the File History window shown in Figure 7-8) to select a drive and request the selected drive to other homegroup users before the process starts. You can then opt to add folders you don't want to back up. You can use Advanced Settings to change default settings for File History, including the Keep Saved Versions option. The default is Forever. This will cause a drive to fill up—perhaps rather quickly—if you have a lot of data and a small drive, so it might be best to change that setting to something else, perhaps six months or one year.

MORE INFO **BACK UP FROM A COMMAND PROMPT**

You can use the command-line tool Wbadmin to back up and restore your operating system, volumes, files, folders, and applications from an elevated command prompt. You'll need to be an Administrator or Backup Operator to use this tool. Make sure you are at least familiar with this command and its available parameters, as detailed here: *http://technet.microsoft.com/en-us/library/cc754015.aspx*.

Restore previous versions of files and folders

After File History has completed its first backup, you can click Restore Personal Files in the File History window to restore files. Figure 7-8 shows a sample restore window. Look closely here and you'll see that the selected window is 397 of 399 and was created on January 17, 2014. However, File History has been running on this computer for a long time, and files can be restored here as far back as 1 of 399, which in this case is about three months.

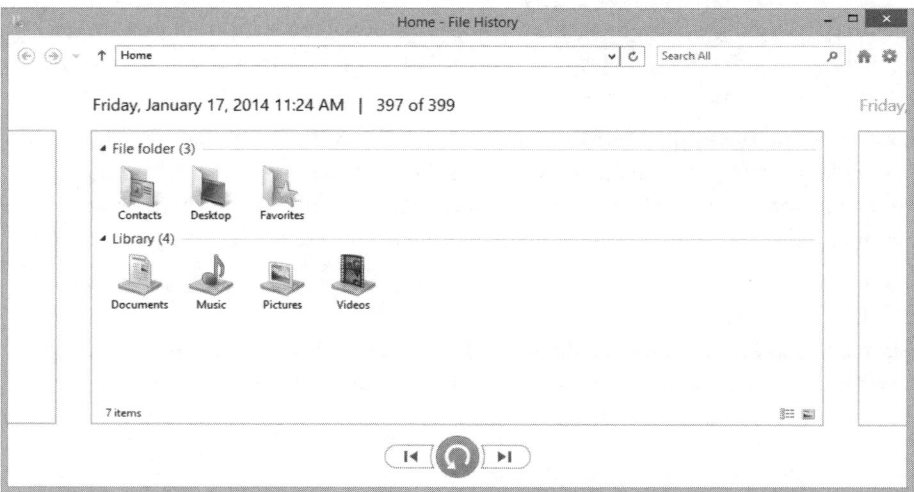

FIGURE 7-8 Use the File History window to restore personal files.

Once you've found what you want to restore (use the back and forward arrows to move around in the window), select them and then right-click and select Restore (to the original location) or Restore To (a specific place).

Thought experiment

Create a backup strategy

In this thought experiment, apply what you've learned about this objective. You can find answers to these questions in the "Answers" section at the end of this chapter.

You have been asked to create a backup strategy for 50 computers in a small but growing organization. Forty of those computers are desktop computers running Windows 8; 10 are tablet computers running Windows 8.1. Users need to be able to access older versions of files, file backups must be protected from loss or theft and available when needed, and backups should be completed daily.

1. **What type of backup strategy would you suggest and why?**
2. **Where should you store the backups?**
3. **Should you also create a system image backup?**

Objective summary

- You can use SkyDrive's Recycle Bin to recover files you've deleted from SkyDrive folders.
- SkyDrive offers Previous Versions, a tool you can use to access previous versions of working files.
- File History is a backup option in Windows 8.1 that can be used to perform automatic backups of files, and you have complete control over what's backed up and what you restore, when necessary.

Objective review

Answer the following questions to test your knowledge of the information in this objective. You can find the answers to these questions and explanations of why each answer choice is correct or incorrect in the "Answers" section at the end of this chapter.

1. Which of the following is true regarding files and file backup and restore using SkyDrive? (Choose all that apply.)
   - **A.** You can use the Recycle Bin from SkyDrive in Internet Explorer to recover recently deleted files.
   - **B.** You can use the Recycle Bin from the SkyDrive app in Windows 8 to recover recently deleted files.
   - **C.** You can recover deleted SkyDrive files using File History.
   - **D.** You can recover previous versions of files in SkyDrive in Internet Explorer.
2. Regarding File History, which of the following is true? (Choose all that apply.)
   - **A.** You can use a USB flash drive or a network drive to save File History data.
   - **B.** The default setting for when to save copies of files is every two hours.
   - **C.** The default setting for the size of the offline cache is 5 percent.
   - **D.** The default length of time to keep saved versions is six months.
3. What command-line utility can be used to clean up File History versions?
   - **A.** Vssadmin
   - **B.** FhManagew
   - **C.** Enable-ComputerRestore
   - **D.** Wbadmin
4. What is the most likely problem you'll have if you accept all of the defaults associated with File History when you set it up?
   - **A.** You won't have access to all of the files you work on in a day because they won't be backed up often enough.
   - **B.** The size of the offline cache configured for files is too small, and you'll run out of cache space too quickly.

C. The drive you use to save File History data will eventually become full, and you'll have to manage the problem that arises because of this at a later date.

D. Event logs created by File History will eventually cause the computer's hard drive to fill, and you'll be required to delete old logs.

Chapter summary

- The Windows Recovery Environment offers many options for recovery, including restore, recycle, safe mode, command prompt, Automatic Startup Repair, System Restore, and more.
- You can create a recovery drive to help you recover from any future startup issue.
- Device Driver Rollback, MSConfig, WBAdmin, VSSAdmin, FhManageW, Enable-ComputerRestore, Recimg, and others are tools administrators can use to troubleshoot computers and manage restore options.
- Refresh and recycle are two ways end users can quickly restore their PCs to stability. Refresh keeps personal files but removes third-party applications and add-ons, and recycle (or reset) returns the computer to factory standards.
- SkyDrive and File History can both be used as backup options, as can creating a system image backup. The best way to protect yourself is to use a combination of options.

Answers

This section contains the solutions to the thought experiments and answers to the objective review questions in this chapter.

Objective 7.1: Thought experiment

1. It would be better to try other options first. The user has a lot of applications installed, and if you do a push-button reset you'll have to reinstall all of them. Additionally, the problem might be with the boot configuration data and have nothing to do with the installed applications.
2. You would. You can use the Recovery Disk to boot the computer and access the options to recover startup. One option is to choose Startup Repair to let Windows fix problems that are likely keeping the computer from starting.
3. Recycling restores the computer to its factory settings, so this would be a bad idea given the circumstances.

Objective 7.1: Review

1. **Correct answer:** C
   - **A. Incorrect:** You can install or roll back drivers for internal hardware.
   - **B. Incorrect:** It is not possible to configure a device driver so that it cannot be rolled back.
   - **C. Correct:** If the driver were updated, the option to roll it back would be available. Thus, the driver was not updated and the problem is due to something else.
   - **D. Incorrect:** If rolling back the driver is not an option, then uninstalling it won't resolve the problem. The driver will likely be reinstalled by Windows, and the problem will still exist.
2. **Correct answer:** D
   - **A. Incorrect:** A USB drive must be at least 512 MB in size, not 1 GB.
   - **B. Incorrect:** A USB drive can have data on it prior to starting the wizard, but that data will be erased because the drive will be formatted.
   - **C. Incorrect:** A USB drive does not have to be formatted before you start the Recovery Drive Wizard; the wizard can format the drive for you.
   - **D. Correct:** None of the answers above are correct, thus None of the above is the correct answer.
3. **Correct answer:** A
   - **A. Correct:** The Windows RE environment will open.
   - **B. Incorrect:** Windows will not begin automatic repairs.

C. **Incorrect:** The computer will not boot into safe mode.

D. **Incorrect:** The computer will not shut down; it will reboot into the Windows RE environment.

E. **Incorrect:** The computer will not boot to LKGC. LKGC no longer exists in Windows 8.

F. **Incorrect:** The computer will not boot into System Restore mode; however, you can choose that from Windows RE.

4. **Correct answers:** A and E

   A. **Correct:** Personal files are not disturbed.

   B. **Incorrect:** C:\Program Files will be overwritten.

   C. **Incorrect:** C:\Windows will be overwritten.

   D. **Incorrect:** C:\PerfLogs will be overwritten.

   E. **Correct:** Any personal files you create, no matter where they are on the local drive, are not disturbed.

Objective 7.2: Thought experiment

1. File History would meet all of the needs of all users and is available in Windows 8 and Windows 8.1. Windows 7 File Recovery is not available for the Windows 8.1 users. File History keeps older versions of files and can be configured to run daily. This is better than saving data to an external drive, too, because you can store the data on corporate servers to protect and make the data available when needed.
2. You should store the backups on a network drive that is backed up regularly.
3. Because it's better to be safe than sorry, when you can, you should create a system image backup.

Objective 7.2: Review

1. **Correct answers:** A and D

   A. **Correct:** It is possible to recover files using the Recycle Bin from SkyDrive in Internet Explorer.

   B. **Incorrect:** You cannot use the Recycle Bin from the SkyDrive app in Windows 8 to recover recently deleted files.

   C. **Incorrect:** You cannot recover deleted SkyDrive files using File History. File History does not back up files saved to SkyDrive.

   D. **Correct:** You can recover previous versions of files in SkyDrive in Internet Explorer.

2. **Correct answers:** A and C

   A. **Correct:** You can use a USB flash drive or a network drive to save File History data.

   B. **Incorrect:** The default setting for when to save copies of files is once per hour.

- **C. Correct:** The default setting for the size of the offline cache is 5 percent.
- **D. Incorrect:** The default length of time to keep saved versions is Forever.

3. **Correct answer:** B
   - **A. Incorrect:** Vssadmin is used to manage System Restore points.
   - **B. Correct:** FhManagew is used to manage File History at a command prompt.
   - **C. Incorrect:** Enable-ComputerRestore is a Windows PowerShell cmdlet you use to enable System Restore.
   - **D. Incorrect:** Wbadmin is used to back up and restore your operating system, volumes, files, folders, and applications from an elevated command prompt.
4. **Correct answer:** C
   - **A. Incorrect:** Because files are backed up every hour, it's unlikely you'll lose too much data in a single day that you can't recover quickly.
   - **B. Incorrect:** The size of the offline cache is 5 percent, which is big enough for most users and won't cause cache problems.
   - **C. Correct:** The drive you use to save File History data to will eventually become full because the default setting for Keep Saved Versions is Forever.
   - **D. Incorrect:** Event logs created by File History should never be large enough to cause any problems. Although you might see warnings and errors, you'll be notified through the Action Center and should resolve those quickly.

Index

Numbers and Symbols

A

B

C

D

G

H

I

J

K

L

M

N

O

P

R

S

T

U

V

W

X

Z

About the author

JOLI BALLEW is an award-winning, best-selling author of over 50 books, including *Windows 8.1 Step By Step* and *Windows 8.1 Plain and Simple*, both with Microsoft Press. Joli is a Microsoft MVP (10 years) and holds many Microsoft certifications starting with the original MCSE for Windows Server 2000. Joli is a Microsoft Certified Trainer and a professor at Brookhaven Community College, and also serves as their Microsoft Academy Coordinator. Joli teaches certification classes, including the class related to this exam, Configuring Windows 8.1 (70-687) and the one that follows, Managing and Maintaining Windows 8.1 (70-688).